Rites and Passages

M000105813

Rites and Passages

The Beginnings of Modern Jewish Culture in France, 1650–1860

JAY R. BERKOVITZ

PENN

University of Pennsylvania Press

Philadelphia

Publication of this volume was assisted by a grant from the Lucius N. Littauer Foundation.

10 9 8 7 6 5 4 3 2 1

First paperback edition 2007

Published by
University of Pennsylvania Press
Philadelphia, Pennsylvania 19104-4112

Library of Congress Cataloging-in-Publication Data
Berkovitz, Jay R., 1951–
    Rites and passages : the beginnings of modern Jewish culture in France, 1650–1860 / Jay R. Berkovitz.
        p. cm. — (Jewish culture and contexts)
    Includes bibliographical references and index.
    ISBN-13: 978-0-8122-2008-7 (pbk. : alk. paper)
    ISBN-10: 0-8122-2008-0 (pbk. : alk. paper)
    1. Jews—France—History—17th century. 2. Jews—France—History—18th century.
3. Jews—France—History—19th century. 4. Jews—France—Liturgy—History. 5. Jews—
France—Identity. 6. Jews—Cultural assimilation—France. 7. Jews—France—Social life and
customs. 8. Religion and culture—France. I. Title. II. Series.

DS135.F82B47 2004
944'.004924—dc22   2004049472

For Sharon, Song of Songs 2:1–2

Contents

viii   Contents

Introduction

This book delves deeply into the dynamics of Jewish society and culture in an era when, according to most accounts, the most interesting events and developments were taking place outside the Jewish community. Accordingly, the history of European Jewry has focused mainly on the process leading to the attainment of citizenship, on what was expected of Jews in order to gain acceptance in their host countries, on the resistance they frequently encountered, and on the ease or difficulty they experienced in their efforts to integrate into the society around them. Selected aspects of this extremely complex social, political, and cultural process have been taken to epitomize the modern Jewish experience *in toto*, insofar as they seem to confirm the durability of antisemitism and assimilation or explain the emergence of Jewish nationalism—to mention a few of the most powerful forces affecting Jewish life today. The Jewish fascination with general culture has, likewise, attracted the unending attention and considerable talents of historians, philosophers, and students of literature. Each of the foregoing subjects is as contemporary as it is historical.

Although I do not ignore the importance of representation and symbolic meanings, in the present study I am interested principally in the social significance of culture, that is, how the internal cultural dynamic shapes the social ethos and communal policy. My main interest is the inner life of the Jews and the manifold ways they have struggled to make sense of their unique historical predicament. These concerns fall under the general rubric of "cultural history," an enterprise aiming to clarify the history of meaning and feelings. It seeks to explain how generations have labored to reconcile the heritage of the past with the unprecedented demands of the present and future. In each of these respects, Jewish history exemplifies cultural patterns characteristic of humanity at large; indeed, no less than others, the Jews have wrestled with *la condition humaine*. At the same time, it is abundantly clear that the Jews' historical experiences over the course of centuries, and the weight of the social and religious teachings of Judaism, have thoroughly informed their perceptions of the world around them and have influenced virtually all of the choices they make as individuals. Historically and in the present day, to be Jewish has meant, inexorably, to live in tension between the universal and the peculiarly "Jewish" aspects of their identity.

An overwhelming emphasis on the status and image of the Jew in general society has been the dominant concern of most historical accounts. Invariably, this has come at the expense of the scholarly attention that Jewish culture deserves. In the pages that follow, I intend to examine aspects of the Jews' social, intellectual, and cultural history by investigating the central role of religion in traditional and modern societies. I have become convinced that patterns of religious thought and behavior represent invaluable indices of the transition to modernity. I am hopeful that this study will illumine the age-old tensions between faith and reason, and will advance our understanding of the erosive impact of secularization, the staying power of traditional values, and the manner in which minorities struggle to preserve their identities against the homogenizing tide of modernization. These are, first and foremost, human struggles, and the protagonists must not be studied as faceless members of a corporate group. To gain a clearer understanding of the role that religion has played in modern culture, I decided to make ritual this book's primary focus.

In order to appreciate the shifting role of religion in the modern history of European Jewry, I have employed a broad conceptual and chronological framework of analysis that includes the latter stages of the *ancien régime* in addition to the era of Jewish emancipation. "Emancipation" in the narrowest sense refers to the attainment of civic equality, which the Jews of France first achieved in 1790 and 1791; more broadly, it is used to signify the extended processes of acculturation and social integration that unfolded over the course of nearly a century. Historians have hardly been able to contain their enthusiasm concerning its effects, seeing that it enabled western and central European Jews to enter the mainstream of modern culture and society. In this book I challenge the conventional view that emancipation was the defining experience in modern Jewish history. Emancipation has served, routinely, as the major organizing principle and analytic model for the study of the Jewish encounter with modernity. However, research on England, France, Italy, and the Habsburg Empire has more recently exposed the inadequacy of the German-Jewish paradigm of emancipation-assimilation-reform by giving attention to emancipation's wide range of legal, social, and political expressions, and its variegated effects on urban and rural populations, class, and gender.[1] The transformative power of emancipation can hardly be denied, but its standing as the preeminent framework for exploring what modernity meant for the Jews ought to undergo careful reconsideration. Emancipation is widely commended for having reversed the civic and political disabilities of the medieval period, thus enabling Jews to participate fully in the political and cultural life of the modern state. But this view has contributed inexorably to a pervasive failure to take account of dominant social and cultural trends in the *ancien régime* when considering the course of modern Jewish history.

France offers an instructive case study of what modernity meant to the generations preceding and following the Revolution of 1789. Though small in comparison to communities elsewhere in central and eastern Europe, the Jewish community in France offers an excellent opportunity to examine the *mentalités* of this transitional era, including adjustments in outlook and behavior inspired by the onset of modernity and the attainment of citizenship. As its title suggests, this book examines the modernization of the Jews through the lens of ritual and in light of the various passages they experienced in the century preceding and following the French Revolution. Focusing on the transitions accompanying European Jewry's "passage to modernity," this book calls attention to the changing function of ritual, its differentiation in the private and public realms, its relationship to class and gender, and its role in generational tensions. It will also highlight the passages of Jews to and from other countries, the cultural interplay of eastern and western European traditions, and the efforts of rabbinic and lay elites to remake the Jewish tradition in light of social and political changes. These transitions—whether within the context of individual lives, or as a measure of geographical shifts or intellectual vivacity—promise to illumine the dynamics of cultural change and stability in an era of wide-ranging political and social transformation.

Impassivity toward the pre-revolutionary era has, historically, rested on the assumption that the cultural and religious traditions of the *ancien régime* were rendered obsolete by the powerful forces unleashed in 1789.[2] This dominant thread in the narrative of modern Jewish history has not only limited the kinds of questions raised with respect to the *ancien régime*. No less importantly, it has compromised the study of the nineteenth century. In the case of France, especially, historical studies have routinely focused on the arduous struggle for civic equality and on the structural and political effects of the revolutionary upheaval. However, very little is known of the religious rites and liturgical traditions that predominated in early modern and post-revolutionary France. The voluminous rabbinic scholarship of the region, including manuscripts and published works, has been largely ignored; even less is known of the reinterpretation, rejection, or reassertion of Jewish religious and cultural traditions on French soil. Regrettably, the powerful impact of the Revolution has tended to blind the modern historian to the more opaque—though potentially most revealing—aspects of French Jewish history, including popular and rabbinic culture.

In its appraisal of pre-revolutionary Jewish culture, Franco-Jewish historiography has, to a remarkable degree, mirrored the dominant perspective of emancipated French Jewry. For those Jews who first bore the title *citoyens* and for the generations that followed, interest in the rich communal history of the *ancien régime* faded precipitously amid the exuberance and future-oriented mentality of the revolutionary era.[3] Their growing detachment from the cultural universe of previous centuries went hand in hand with the belief that to remain committed to the social mores and rituals of

Alsace-Lorraine was to be anti-modern, even anti-French.[4] History, wrote François Furet, began with the French Revolution, or more precisely for the Jews, on 27 September 1791, when the National Assembly voted to admit their ancestors to citizenship. Generations would recall this momentous event as a turning point of uncommon magnitude and would view themselves as conclusive evidence of its transformative power. Memories of the Revolution were draped in the triumphant imagery of the Sinaitic revelation and were reconceived in messianic-redemptive terms, while the numerous setbacks suffered by the generation of 1789 received inordinately short shrift. These recollections were rooted in an abiding sense of optimism—if not a certain naïveté—that credited the Revolution with having put an end to centuries of degradation, discrimination, and social exclusion. For later generations, the surrender of the special privileges of communal autonomy and rabbinic jurisdiction in civil affairs appeared to have been a small price to pay for the many blessings that citizenship bestowed.[5] Against this view, this study asserts the significance of the lives of Jews who lived in a world still defined by the terms of religious tradition.

Scholarly investigation into the history of eighteenth-century French Jewry has been further complicated by a host of technical difficulties and conceptual challenges. Due to the unfortunate dispersal of archival documents and the destruction of numerous community records during the ravages of World War II, and some before,[6] historical documentation is often woefully incomplete. Many of the surviving records of Jewish communal life are widely scattered in archives in France, Israel, and the United States, yielding, at best, a deficient picture of Jewish life in the *ancien régime*. Moreover, with several notable exceptions, such as the work of Simon Schwarzfuchs and Arthur Hertzberg, as well as the project headed by the late Bernhard Blumenkranz, research on the pre-revolutionary period has concentrated mainly on individual communities. Inspired by sentiments of local pride, the writing of communal history became popular in early twentieth-century Europe. After World War II the trend continued, prompted by a renewed concern for Jewish survival and continuity, and expressed in the dual effort to preserve what had remained and to memorialize what was lost. One may also note the appearance of a moderate number of monographs that have systematically researched the full range of social, economic, and political forces at work in individual communities. Precisely because knowledge of communal life in the *ancien régime* is so highly fragmented, scholars have refrained from drawing general conclusions about the Jewish communities dispersed in hundreds of localities in France.[7] All in all, the Revolution of 1789 has remained the firm dividing line in most historical accounts.

If the historical portrait of French Jewry is in some measure deficient, the reason is only partly related to the fragmentary documentation and the general failure to take notice of rabbinic sources. I intend to make a broader claim: No serious treatment of modernity, certainly not Jewish emancipation, can afford to ignore the cultural history of the *ancien régime*, especially as reflected in religious rites and communal ethos. It hardly needs to be stated that any discussion of ruptures, modifications, and continuities in the cultural history of emancipated Jewry depends on a clear understanding of where things stood before the onset of the emancipation process. Moreover, by taking the long view, one is alerted to several important paradigms that emerged in the late seventeenth and eighteenth centuries and left a lasting imprint on the process of modernization as it unfolded in the century following 1789. These included the formation of a lay leadership, the creation of divergent social contexts for religious and cultural change, tensions between popular and elite religion, and the sociocultural interaction between Jews and non-Jews.

The study of ritual offers entrée into intricacies of meaning that are frequently overlooked or are considered too elusive to be of much use to historians. Pioneering studies in the field of cultural anthropology, starting with the research of Arnold van Gennep and other students of popular culture, have illustrated how traditional communities devised systems to explain the world based on rites of passage and collective mentalities.[8] It is the signs and symbols of rituals that reveal underlying structures of thought.[9] Serving as a crucial repository of memories and values that were specific to a community or region, religious customs (*minhagim*) were a matter of communal pride and identity. They also represented a mode of continuity with past generations, which was of particular importance at a time of rampant social, cultural, and political transformation. For these reasons, *minhagim* demanded vigorous efforts to ensure precision. Debates about the authenticity of such rituals also revolved, increasingly, around the question of the centrality of textual traditions.

Those rituals practiced by French Jews during the *ancien régime* reflected modes of thinking about their historical origins, their relationship to the surrounding culture and society, and their identification with certain Jewish cultural traditions. In Alsace-Lorraine, Jews commonly shared with their non-Jewish neighbors a perception of the world as a dangerous place where demons wreaked havoc. Rituals lent order to their lives while shielding them from the ruinous effects of evil spirits. They were designed to meet a variety of needs relating to life passages: the need of the individual for public acknowledgment; the need for the community to join in marking the passages of each member; the need to forge bonds among individuals; and the need to reenact the great stories and messages of the tradition. Rituals provide security in times of transition and/or loss.

Following the Revolution, the Jewish self-image was powerfully transformed by the promise of full civic equality and the concomitant demand of *régénération*. Nineteenth-century ritual reflected changes in the identity of emancipated Jewry, especially in its new relationship to the state, French society, and culture (in Chapters 4–8). Pre-revolutionary rituals explained, however imperfectly, the meaning of life; they were formative elements of people's worldviews. From the beginning of the revolutionary era and throughout the nineteenth century, ritual assumed more of a performative function that was designed to dramatize, in a concrete manner, the epoch-making changes of the day. Though undeniably expressive of how Jews defined their identity, especially in the public space of the French city, the newer rituals were mainly reflections of the life that was shaped so completely by the powerful forces of revolution. The changing function of ritual will be of far greater importance for explaining the development of Jewish culture in France than the focus on whether traditional mores, learning, and piety were deteriorating with emancipation and the advance of modernity. Although these are important concerns, they must not dominate the discourse of Jewish history.

The modern history of French Jewry begins in the mid-sixteenth century when *converso émigrés* from the Iberian Peninsula were invited to settle in Bordeaux and Bayonne as *nouveaux Chrétiens*. In roughly the same years, the foundations of the Metz *kehillah* (community) and, later, numerous communities in Alsace and Lorraine were established. The coincidence of these two processes, though independent of one another, invites a comparison of the systems of self-government that prevailed in the Sephardic and Ashkenazic communities. With our lens focused on the changing structures of communal life, three main areas will be treated: the scope of communal authority and jurisdiction; the composition of leadership; and the enactment of legislation to regulate religious, social, and moral behavior. My intent is to discover where and how modernity made itself felt in the last stages of the *ancien régime* and to assess communal responses to these new challenges.

Social and religious controls evince two additional dimensions of the transition to modernity that are shared, in varying degrees, by Jewish communities elsewhere. First, they contain evidence of the unique challenges facing a minority seeking to maintain its cultural distinctiveness while continuing to be part of the larger social and economic matrix. For the Jews of central and western Europe, these tensions reveal a greater degree of contact and involvement with the surrounding Christian society than may be commonly assumed. In varying degrees, the Ashkenazic Jews of France adopted elements of non-Jewish culture, often incorporating them into the ritual system of Judaism. Often unconscious, this strategy made it possible to participate in a culture that would normally be viewed as a serious threat to Jewish survival.[10] Second, efforts of lay communal leaders to regulate public and private behavior, especially in the realm of consumption, call attention to the process by which central elements of a religious tradition undergo secularization. Although virtually every one of the criticisms di-

rected against Jewish religious and social behavior had been heard in previous centuries, in the seventeenth and eighteenth centuries their moral
underpinnings were subordinated to a new, overarching concern about the
ordering of society.

The cultural history of the Jews of Alsace-Lorraine prior to the Revolution is informed by a struggle between two competing claims, namely, that
the region belonged to the larger cultural universe of Ashkenaz versus the
view that there was an indigenous Alsatian Jewish culture that was native to
the region. By investigating trends in Talmud study, rabbinic appointments, halakhic rulings, religious customs, and liturgy, I will show when
and where the cultural identity of the Jews either reflected an affinity to
western Ashkenaz or evinced a regional consciousness that was already
emerging several decades before the Revolution. The tension between the
two would continue to manifest itself well into the nineteenth century and
may be observed in the discourse on the role of religion in communal life.

Throughout this volume I use the term *emancipation* to signify the extended processes of acculturation and social integration that unfolded over
the course of nearly a century, rather than to refer to a single event in the
aftermath of the French Revolution. Emancipation varied significantly
from state to state, even from community to community within the same region. Recent studies have debunked the older view that emancipation led
inexorably to rampant assimilation and the rupture of tradition. In the case
of the Jews of rural Alsace and Lorraine, occupational patterns, family life,
and religious observance were resistant to change because social and economic conditions in the region remained relatively stable for much of the
nineteenth century. The conservatism of the rural population is evident in
the persistence of folk customs, the use of Yiddish, fertility patterns, opposition to religious reform, use of Jewish names, sentiments of ethnic solidarity, and in the slow pace of assimilation to bourgeois standards of
behavior. Urban centers, by contrast, facilitated economic transformation,
acculturation to bourgeois lifestyle, and accommodation to the norms of
non-Jewish society; in larger cities such as Paris, Berlin, Prague, and Vienna
traditional loyalties and affiliations waned more rapidly. Economic and intellectual urban elites active in communal institutions typically labored to
"regenerate" the lower classes in accordance with ideals expounded by the
Haskalah, and their efforts found expression both in the creation of philanthropic schools for the Jewish urban poor and in broader activities directed at the transformation of Jews in rural areas.

The pronounced rural-urban split calls attention to clear links between
social and religious history in modern Judaism. Patterns of emigration of
Jews within Europe in the nineteenth century added to the complex mix.
Numerous Russian and Polish Jews moved west, interacting with more assimilated coreligionists in places like Berlin, and even internal migration,
as from Alsace to Paris, affected religious outlook and relations with the

wider society. Divergences based on social class also emerged within the Jewish community. Many Jews took advantage of opportunities in higher education, and their religious perspective therefore tended to diverge from that of other social groups within the Jewish community.

Barriers to social integration were at the forefront of internal Jewish discussions concerning adaptation to modern society. Concerns about the compatibility of Jewish ritual with the demands of social integration and patriotic loyalty were aggravated by the growing awareness that emancipation had shattered the traditional theological underpinnings of Exile, the return to the Land of Israel, and the ethos of social separation from non-Jews. The full realization of citizenship—or its elusive character in the case of Germany—was frequently invoked as an argument for the removal of ostensibly problematic elements of the Jewish religion. Proponents of modernization, including a sizable number of the delegates to the Napoleonic Sanhedrin, repudiated the social and political dimensions of traditional Judaism. Other factors, including growing indifference to religious observance and the assimilation of bourgeois values, led some to conclude that moderate ritual reform was absolutely necessary if Judaism was to survive the difficult challenges posed by modernity. Typically, efforts to enhance the aesthetic appeal of the synagogue included recitation of prayers in the vernacular, the regularization of the modern sermon, the use of the organ, and the insistence on greater decorum. In Germany, disappointment with the slow progress of legal emancipation, the decline in Jewish observance, the increasing wave of conversion to Christianity, and rising antisemitism appear to have induced more radical efforts. In France, as in England and Italy, proponents of ritual reform refused to consider seriously the removal of references to the Land of Israel and the Messiah from the prayer book, and rejected the eradication of the dietary laws, traditional Sabbath observance, the prohibition of intermarriage, and circumcision.

The moderate character of ritual reform in France, as I have suggested elsewhere, is clearly related to the successful achievement of civic equality and to the religious pluralism typical of communal institutions under the aegis of the Consistoire. However, the crucial—but heretofore underrated—issue of timing offers an important perspective on the pace of cultural transformation. Developments over the course of the nineteenth century suggest that while Jewish life was dramatically transformed in the social and political realms, the Revolution appears, ironically, to have hindered the modernization process. Although changes in the nature of community leadership and rabbinic culture were already evident before the Revolution, the general patterns of social, economic, and religious life tended to be more unyielding. Compared to developments in neighboring Germany where cultural transformation was relatively swift, modernization in France lagged behind. This may also be explained by the devastation of Jewish communal institutions caused by the Revolution and the Reign of

Terror. Without an essential communal framework for administering and implementing regenerative programs, many communities in France, especially in Alsace and Lorraine, failed to advance along the modernization path. We should nonetheless be careful not to draw the wrong conclusion. The effects of the delay in the modernization process were nothing short of imposing and ought to be understood as belonging indisputably to the Revolution's legacy as well. Perhaps most crucially, the majority of France's Jews first encountered the trauma of emancipation several decades *after* the bestowal of civil equality—a fact whose significance was not lost on at least some Jewish proponents of regeneration. In their view, the timing of emancipation relative to the state of socioeconomic and cultural modernization was a critical factor; in the case of the Jews of rural Alsace-Lorraine, the early bestowal of citizenship may have inhibited the progress of cultural and religious regeneration.[11]

Where the impact of the Revolution is most visible is in the construction of a Franco-Jewish identity and in the development of strategies designed to meet the demands of the new civic status. My objective is to alert the reader to the distinctiveness of French Jewry's efforts to meet the challenges of modernity, without losing sight of those aspects of the struggle that it shared with other Jewish communities. This will entail examining the impact of the Revolution over a period of several generations, with special attention to the evolution of French Jewry's "ideology of emancipation" through its principal stages, including transformations in Jewish self-understanding in the areas of rabbinic and modern scholarship, as well as religious innovation. Comparisons with Jewish communities beyond the borders of France will assist in distinguishing between the changes produced by the general transformation of European society beginning in the late eighteenth century and those that can be traced specifically to the attainment of civic equality.

In order to gauge the cultural impact of the revolutionary upheaval, I will call attention to the transformation of religious values within the Ashkenazic population in Alsace-Lorraine and Paris.[12] This will involve, principally, an analysis of the efforts of rabbis and Jewish intellectuals who reexamined the texts and reassessed the knowledge formerly restricted to traditionalist interpretation. Rabbinic and non-rabbinic writings of numerous genres, drawn from the eighteenth and nineteenth centuries, offer abundant evidence of new thinking about the nature of Jewish tradition in the period from the *ancien régime* until the Second Republic. In the case of Rabbi Aaron Worms of Metz, a major figure whose life spanned the *ancien régime* and the revolutionary era, his rigorous criticism of trends in halakhic decision making in the two centuries preceding the Revolution served as a bridge between normative-traditional perspectives and reformist views.

However, my objective is not simply to assess shifts in behavior and thought that reflected a dissatisfaction with or, conversely, a reaffirmation of the traditional religious worldview. Rather, it is to determine how they served as the basis for a new consciousness, a reconstructed identity. In charting the evolution of the new Franco-Jewish self-image, the point of reference to which we shall return periodically in the second half of this volume, is the role of the Revolution as an *idea*—a legacy—that lent itself to an ongoing hermeneutic.[13] Its themes—cultural and social integration, etc.—remain issues still to be resolved, but they are approached differently with the passage of time. Precisely how did Franco-Jewish leaders understand the meaning of the changes that had begun to be felt in their communities, and how did they integrate the significance of the Revolution into their conception of Jewish culture and tradition? Moreover, what role did traditional Jewish religious culture play in the construction of modern Jewish identity?[14]

The overarching goal of this book is to examine the vitality and resilience of religious traditions during periods of social and political turbulence. Related to this is a concern with the struggles of religious minorities to maintain their cultural distinctiveness and identity while remaining part of the larger social and economic matrix. Finally, and no less important, I have sought to clarify the changing role of ritual and authority in the nineteenth century and, ultimately, how the religious and social implications of civic equality came to be viewed by various sectors of the French-Jewish community. With its lens focused on the evolution of a new Franco-Jewish self-image, this book offers what I hope is a fresh perspective on the dynamic relationship between tradition and modernity.

Part I
Leadership, Community, and Ritual in the *Ancien Régime*

Chapter 1

Communal Authority and Leadership

The wealth of theories seeking to establish when the modern era began reflects a wide range of historical methodologies and considerable disagreement on the essence of modernity itself. In view of the panoply of political, cultural, social, and economic conditions affecting Jewish life in Europe, historians have understandably found it difficult to concur on the types of sources and data they consider reliable or on the interpretative models they employ. For cultural historians, the roots of modernity—whether humanism, rationalism, or the decline of rabbinic hegemony—are located in either the sixteenth or the seventeenth centuries. Others have stressed the determinative role of social and political forces, pointing to *raison d'état*, mercantilism, and the French Revolution as having paved the way for the major transformations of the nineteenth century.[1] Despite these widely differing views on precisely what launched the modernization process, there is broad agreement that until the late eighteenth century the main features of medieval life—ghetto segregation, legal disabilities, the threat of expulsion, and the primacy of Halakhah—remained resistant to the forces that had begun to transform European society and culture at large. Ultimately, according to this conception, it was not until the demise of communal autonomy that the erosive impact of modernity may first be discerned.[2] Until then, the *kehillah* continued to be the primary venue for the cultivation of Jewish social and religious ideals and the framework for their realization in daily life. As long as the *kehillah* remained intact, the perils of modernity could presumably be kept at a distance.[3]

As the data collected in this and the following two chapters suggest, this view of the *ancien régime* is overly static and can no longer be sustained. Evolving patterns of communal authority and leadership in the century preceding the Revolution illustrate how the governing bodies in northeastern France already showed signs of transformation. This is evident in the emergence of a powerful urban laity in Metz that began to assert its authority over the rabbinate. Lay control over the rabbinate was not at all unique to Metz or, for that matter, to France; indeed, this was the rule across most of Europe. In Alsace and Lorraine, as in Metz, it is discernible in the gradual consolidation of rabbinic duties, the widening differentiation in the roles of rabbi and communal leader, and the growing independence of the rabbinate from commercial dealings. In the particular case of Metz, however, the enactment of communal legislation went further, aiming to regulate religious, social, and moral behavior. These efforts not only confirm the progressive secularization of the leadership structure; they also provide substantial evidence of dynamic cultural change with respect to age, gender, and family in the late seventeenth and eighteenth centuries. Paradoxically, these modernizing trends were more salient than in Sephardic communities, even though religious traditionalism in the regions of Alsace and Lorraine was noticeably more robust.

The aim of the detailed portrait of communal government that follows is to illuminate the cultural history of modern French Jewry by examining the dynamics of social change in the century preceding the Revolution. The focus in this chapter on the relationship between the lay and religious spheres, and on the issues surrounding the appointment of rabbis, punctuates a larger theme that stands at the center of the present study: How did the communities of Alsace-Lorraine relate to the general legacy of Ashkenazic history and culture? Until the Revolution, at least, the region of northeastern France was still an integral part of the cultural orbit of central and eastern Europe. However, in the last decades before 1789, the Jews of the region exhibited the first signs of cultural self-reliance. In this respect, and in regard to communal governance, ritual practice, and the pace of modernization, important differences between rural Alsace and urban Metz were already discernible in the late seventeenth century. This contrast is perhaps most apparent in the Metz community's regulation of consumption and the general effort to freeze the existing social hierarchy (Chapter 2). Following an examination of the dynamics of religious culture in the *ancien régime*, Chapter 3 concludes with a portrayal of Alsace and Metz as two distinct frameworks—rural and urban—that would continue to shape the multitextured process of modernization through the next century. Under the impact of the Revolution, the Terror, and the Napoleonic regime, the durability of these forces would be tested by a powerful trend to break with the religious and cultural traditions of the east and to create an autochthonous Franco-Jewish identity.

The Transition to the Modern Era

By the end of the Middle Ages, the presence of Jews in western Europe came to be viewed as a hindrance to the cultural and religious hegemony of Catholicism. Despite important local variations, the Jews of England, France, and Spain were expelled over the course of two centuries, beginning in 1290 and ending in 1492. The French monarchy had flirted frequently with the idea of expulsion but had failed to implement the policy definitively until the late fourteenth century. The final order of expulsion in 1394 put an end to six centuries of Jewish life in France, excluding a small number of communities and synagogues that remained in Alsace. Despite the immediate and decisive effects of this policy, signs of change were not far off. Economic expansion, *raison d'état*, and tolerance account for shifting settlement patterns in the sixteenth and seventeenth centuries leading, eventually, to the renewal of Jewish communal life in western and central Europe.

Less than a century after the expulsion, in 1474, Louis XI endeavored to attract foreigners to Bordeaux by promising them exemption from the *droit d'aubaine* (the right of the government to assume the estate of a deceased foreigner) and extensive commercial privileges. Among the newcomers to Bordeaux and Bayonne were *conversos* who had left the Iberian peninsula to escape the strong arm of the Inquisition. Henri II officially recognized them as *nouveaux Chrétiens* in the *lettres patentes* issued in 1550. The basic conditions under which they were permitted to remain in Bordeaux and pursue their livelihood depended on the often conflicting interests of the monarchy, the Bordeaux *parlement*, and the local merchant guilds. Aiming to stimulate the economy, the kings extended protection to the Portuguese merchants for their contribution to the growth of maritime commerce. There were occasions, however, when the monarchy reversed itself, as in 1615 when Louis XIII demanded that all Jews, converted or not, leave France. This edict was issued in deference to the concerns of local Bordelais merchants who objected to the competition posed by the *nouveaux Chrétiens*. Consistently supportive of the Portuguese population, the *parlement* fought the royal edict and prevented its ratification. Later in the century, in 1684, Louis XIV considered expelling Jews and *conversos*, along with the Protestants, but the order was never executed. The devastating economic downturn resulting from the revocation of the Edict of Nantes (1685) doubtless induced Louis XV to pursue a more favorable policy toward the Jews. This is most evident in the *lettres patentes* of 1723, which, for the first time, recognized the *nouveaux Chrétiens* as Jews.[4]

In precisely the period when the Portuguese émigrés were first accorded official recognition and protection in Bordeaux, the eastern border of France expanded to encompass a small but growing Jewish population. From the 1560s until the Peace of Westphalia in 1648, the territories of Alsace and Lorraine gradually came under French jurisdiction, and the number of Jews in these areas grew steadily. The Jewish population in Alsace increased from a few dozen families at the end of the sixteenth century to about 2,000 individuals by 1650. In the period from 1689 to 1716, the population rose from 522 families to 1,269 families (ca. 6,500 individuals). Filling the ranks of the rapidly increasing Jewish population were immigrants from Poland, Bohemia, and Moravia. By 1784 there were 3,910 families in Alsace (nearly 19,624 individuals) and as many as 5,000 individuals in the duchy of Lorraine, according to the census. France took dominion over Metz in 1552, and after a few years several Jewish families from Germany and Poland were permitted to settle there in order to provide credit to the city residents and to the military garrison. The ordinance of 1567 formalized their status and introduced several provisions regulating admission, entrance duty, taxes, residence restrictions, moneylending, and the requirement to listen to a sermon in church each month. By the end of the century the Jews of Metz constituted an official community whose privileges were confirmed by the *lettres patentes* of 1603. Its steady growth in the seventeenth century—from a handful of households to nearly 3,000 individuals, representing approximately 7 percent of the total population of the city—was a clear sign of the protection extended by the monarchy in recognition of the Jews' usefulness as provisioners of horses for the cavalry.[5] The subordination of religious concerns to the economic and political interests of the state permitted the French monarchy to break, however cautiously, with the medieval policy of expulsion and subjugation. By the end of the seventeenth century, the concerted efforts of Colbert and Colbert de Croissy steered Louis XIV away from parochial Christian interests so that France could continue to benefit from the manifold contributions of its Jewish population.[6]

Nevertheless, such efforts met with periodic resistance—most often inspired by the commercial jealousy of local merchants opposed to Jewish competition and fueled by the long legacy of Christian anti-Judaism. The view of St. Augustine—that the misery of the Jews was proof of the truth and superiority of Christianity—was still popular among seventeenth-century French theologians such as Blaise Pascal and Jacques Bossuet. Pascal stressed the Jews' spiritual and carnal blindness, while Bossuet characterized them as a monstrous people, animated by Satan, who are universally mocked and hated. Even Jacques Basnage, author of a generally sympathetic history of the Jews, wrote that their miserable condition was proof of God's anger with them.[7] Pierre Bayle, a severe critic of biblical history and morality, anticipated much of the denunciation advanced by English Deists and French *philosophes*. Voltaire's attitude toward the Jews was rooted in his negative assessment of biblical Judaism. He disapproved of its tribalism, of its insistence on social and cultural separatism, and of its general failure to meet the standards of utilitarianism, humanism, toleration, and morality accepted by all civilized societies. Anti-Jewish hostility, he reasoned, was a natural response to the fact that the core values of Jewish culture were exclusivist, hostile toward other religions, and, generally, misanthropic. "They maintain all their customs which are exactly the opposite of sociable; they were therefore justifiably treated as a nation opposed to all the others; serving them from avarice, detesting them from fanaticism, and making of usury a sacred duty." He was especially critical of Moses for establishing laws to separate the Hebrews from other peoples, whereas Rousseau praised him for his role in transforming the Israelites into a free people. Voltaire had little regard for ritual but was prepared to accept unlimited cultural diversity, provided it did not disrupt civil order and was relegated to the private sphere.[8]

Popular hatred of the Jews stemmed from the convergence of religious hostility and economic tension. For most believing Christians of the medieval period, the Jews were Christ-killers and possibly cohorts of the devil, viewed routinely as immoral and seditious. Charges of ritual murder and host desecration remained credible, even in the early modern period, as is apparent from the case of Raphael Lévy, who was executed in 1670 for the alleged murder of a Christian child. To the end of the *ancien régime* and even well into the nineteenth century, the Catholic clergy was overwhelmingly critical of the Jews, as is evident in the *cahiers* of 1789. In the words of Abbé Perrin des Chavanettes, a contemporary of Voltaire, "[T]heir exile represents the final seal on all the prophecies which foretold that they would be punished for their deicide," and they would forever be objects of unceasing hatred. Others, such as Abbé Charles Louis Richard, who viewed the Jews as sworn enemies of all Christians, denounced the Jews' superstitions, especially those found in the Talmud. It was doubtless in order to curb their potentially harmful influence on the Christian population that the Jews in Metz were required to attend church each month and listen dutifully to the pastor's sermon.[9]

As in the medieval period, tensions between Christians and Jews found expression not only in the theological and intellectual realms but also in daily life. In the northeastern provinces Jews were repeatedly accused of unscrupulous commercial practices. Economic complaints against the Jews by local Christian tradesmen in mid-seventeenth-century Metz made use of assumptions concerning the Jews' religious inferiority and the justice of selective commercial restrictions. Until the end of the *ancien régime*, the Jews in Alsace and Lorraine were limited to those economic pursuits that had been permitted them by imperial decrees of the fifteenth and sixteenth centuries, that is, trade in old clothes, cattle, and moneylending. With the exception of Bordeaux and Bayonne, where Jews enjoyed substantial commercial freedom, vigorous resistance to Jewish membership in the guilds prevailed most everywhere. In addition to suffering numerous legal disabilities, French Jews found that older restrictions, such as the requirement to wear yellow hats in the city of Metz, were randomly reimposed. The question whether the Jews of France enjoyed the status of *régnicoles* (natives) or were subject to the *droit d'aubaine* was debated throughout much of the eighteenth century. Repeated efforts to apply the *droit d'aubaine* to the Sephardic Jews of Bordeaux ceased only by order of the Bordeaux parliament in 1758, though in the case of the Jews of the northeast such efforts were virtually unknown.[10] Disabilities specific to Alsatian Jewry, most notably the humiliating *péage corporel* (body tax), remained in force throughout the *ancien régime* until they were abolished by the king's edict in 1784. Even with the persistence of anti-Jewish sentiment, the Jews in Alsace and

Lorraine were becoming increasingly integrated into the general economy and had succeeded, to some degree, in forming alliances among the towns-people.[11]

The notion of economic *utilité*, whether of the Sephardic or Ashkenazic variety, was one factor that accounts for the changing status of the Jews of the *ancien régime*. One can also detect far less anti-Jewish rancor among those who idealized the life of the Old Testament. The fact that no mention of Jewish culpability for ritual murder or deicide is present in the writings of Dom Augustin Calmet, a leading Catholic scholar and favorite foil of Voltaire, may be taken as one indication of a more positive attitude toward the Jews. Protestant writers, in particular, assumed a major role in defending the religion of the Old Testament against Voltaire's attacks. Basing themselves on the work of Abbé Claude Fleury, *Les Moeurs des Israélites*, they associated Old Testament Judaism with the life of nature and reason, whereas the Talmud was viewed disparagingly. This distinction between biblical and rabbinic Judaism would be used by both supporters of Jewish civic equality and opponents. The vision of the end of days set forth by Jansenists and millenarians took this a step further: for Christianity to become redeemed it was necessary to convert the Jews, but until this ultimate goal could be realized, it was necessary to treat them with kindness.[12]

Over the course of the seventeenth and eighteenth centuries, as communities of Ashkenazic Jews in Alsace-Lorraine and Sephardic Jews in southwestern France grew in size, they developed the full range of institutions characteristic of communities across the continent. In addition, communities formed in Paris and in the papal province of Avignon and Comtat Venaissin in the southeast; smaller communities were located in Lyon, Marseilles, and Nîmes as well.[13] The vastly different political history of each community, as well as conditions peculiar to each region, shaped the character of Jewish communal organization and the system of self-government in its various settings. Regional variations in the governing style of the *kehillah* were influenced by the degree of integration into the surrounding non-Jewish society,[14] the range of authority granted by the state, and the social impact of ethnic-cultural traditions. Focusing on the changing structures of communal life, we shall compare the systems of self-government in the Sephardic and Ashkenazic communities in three main areas: (1) the scope of communal authority and jurisdiction; (2) the composition of leadership; and (3) the appointment of rabbis.[15]

The Scope of Communal Authority and Jurisdiction

Detailed statutes for the exercise of self-government in the communities of Bordeaux and Bayonne were formulated over the course of the eighteenth century and were included in their respective *pinkasim* (communal registers). The Bayonne *takkanot* (regulations) date from 1752, and the Bordeaux *takkanot* were approved by the king and were entered into the communal *Registre* on 25 December 1760.[16] Although no significant differences either in the theoretical underpinnings of communal authority or in the general structure of the governing body can be observed in the Ashkenazic and Sephardic models of self-government, there were crucial variations in the areas of civil jurisdiction and social control. This may be attributed to the fact that as a rule, Sephardic communities were less constrained by talmudic and halakhic literature and were able to draw freely upon external sources, including Christian writings.[17] The Sephardic communities of Bordeaux and Bayonne never acquired exclusive jurisdiction over civil cases involving Jews. Initially formed as communal charitable funds, known as the *Ḥebera* in Bayonne and the *Sedaca* in Bordeaux, these self-governing bodies bore lasting traces of their crypto-Jewish origins.[18] Owing to the secrecy in which Judaism was practiced and to the considerable integration of Jews in public life, the Sephardic communities did not maintain their own civil courts and could not prevent members from resolving their differences in the French courts.[19] Only from 1710, the year when the Bordeaux communal *Registre* opens,[20] and undoubtedly more so after 1723 when members of the Nation (the term preferred by Jews of Spanish and Portuguese descent) were first accorded official recognition as Jews, were there signs that Jewish communal life was conducted in an open and organized fashion. Bordeaux's *beit din* (rabbinic court) almost certainly started to function in the 1740s, although the first direct evidence in the *pinkas* can be found only in 1755. Questions concerning marriage, divorce, and certification of *shoḥatim* (ritual slaughterers) were typical of the cases brought before the *beit din*, in contrast with the general practice of Ashkenazic communities to convene an ad hoc rabbinic tribunal to deal with problems as they arose. As a rule, a litigant would bring his complaint to communal leaders, who would then decide whether the case deserved to be heard by the court.[21] While divorce cases were under the exclusive authority of the *beit din*, civil and criminal disputes were settled by arbitration before the *parnassim* (syndics), who, unlike the rabbis, enjoyed the right to serve in this capacity. Arbitration, it should be stressed, depended on the willingness of the parties to come before the court and to accept its judgment as binding. In the absence of governmental authorization to enforce their jurisdiction in civil affairs, Sephardic communities resorted to various forms of social pressure and moral suasion to maintain local control over civil disputes.[22]

Modes of self-government in the region of Alsace-Lorraine and Metz followed the general pattern of Ashkenazic *kehillot* in central and eastern Europe. Political, economic, and legal conditions varied from region to region, affecting not only the status of the Jews but also their internal affairs. Thanks to its role in support of the Metz military garrison, the Metz *kehillah* became the largest Jewish community in France and a model of self-

government for Alsatian Jewry.[23] In 1595, three years after the territory of
the bishoprics—formerly part of the Rhenish Imperial District—came
under French control, Henri IV laid the foundation for the Metz community of 120 members by issuing privileges guaranteeing the public practice
of Judaism. From 1603, the small Jewish population was clustered in the
Saint Ferroy quarter, where it erected a synagogue (in 1619) and set up various communal agencies. At the administrative helm sat an elected council, headed by a rabbi, which executed its decisions in accordance with
traditional Jewish law and with recourse to the full range of punitive powers available. These included fines, the public announcement of wrong-
doings at the synagogue, and the deprivation of religious honors; for more
serious offences such as fraud, slander, or violations of sexual morality, the
punishment was the communal ban, known as the *ḥerem*. Reconfirmed
throughout the seventeenth century, the right to self-government "in religion and in their inner concerns" was generally taken to include jurisdiction in the civil ands ritual spheres. However, not long after the death of
R. Gershon Ashkenazi, head of the Metz *beit din*, in 1693, a Jewish resident
of the community approached the French authorities with a request to
conduct his legal battles in the royal courts. The Metz *kehillah* responded
aggressively by sending a delegation to Paris and, with the support of the
Metz *parlement*, ultimately prevailed.[24]

The authority of the community to judge in civil matters was challenged
repeatedly from within and without,[25] forcing the community council to
seek confirmation from the *parlement*, as it did in 1706, that cases involving
Jewish litigants were not to be tried in the *Cour de Parlement* but only in rabbinic tribunals. In 1709 Jacob Schwab threatened to take a dispute concerning family inheritance to the civil courts of Metz because he was
dissatisfied with the decision rendered by the *beit din* of the community.
Rabbi Abraham Broda responded by pronouncing the *ḥerem* against
Schwab who, in turn, sought to bring civil suit against the community. In
the end, the exclusive authority of rabbis and communal leaders to judge
in civil cases was upheld by new *lettres patentes* of 1715, but this victory was
short-lived.[26] Well before mid-century, the Metz *parlement* endeavored to
put an end to the community's civil jurisdiction by prohibiting the use of
the *ḥerem* as well as the right to impose disciplinary measures in resolving
internal rifts. In 1734 the Metz *parlement* ruled that members of the Jewish
community could not be forced to bring their civil disputes to the rabbinic
court, thus limiting its authority to cases where the parties agreed voluntarily to submit to arbitration. Moreover, the *parlement* subsequently demanded that the rabbis and *parnassim* furnish an abridged translation of
Ḥoshen Mishpat, the code of Jewish civil law, so that cases between Jews
could be properly adjudicated in the French court.[27]

In Alsace, civil jurisdiction in cases involving Jews only was more firmly
established than in Metz, although recourse to general courts would sur-

face there as well in the last decades of the *ancien régime*. Its strength may be traced to the expansion of Jewish settlement in communities along the Upper and Lower Rhine valley from the mid-seventeenth century onward. Alsatian Jewry owed its resurgence to the growth of Jewish commercial activity during the Thirty Years War. Jews played a crucial role as provisioners for the French military garrisons and as cattle and horse dealers—a role that became more extensive with the steady conquest of Alsace. Garrisons in Breisach and Philippsburg depended heavily on Jewish suppliers, whose involvement was considered so vital to military operations that French generals refused to accede to the protests of local Christian burghers. The emergence of new Jewish communities east of the Rhine was accompanied by a readiness on the part of the Alsatian authorities not only to permit communal autonomy for the Jewish population but also to support it; in Lorraine it was actively affirmed. From the government's standpoint, autonomy was essential for tax-collecting purposes. Accordingly, the monarchy remained committed to autonomy and the primacy of rabbinical law, as each king from Henri III to Louis XVI issued *lettres patentes* confirming the council's authority in all local matters and reiterated the unqualified authority of the rabbis to judge in civil disputes.[28]

The range and authority of civil jurisdiction in Alsace corresponded directly to the prominence of the rabbinate within the governing body. Following the Thirty Years War, governmental authorities enacted a series of regulations concerning Jewish communal organization in the bishopric of Strasbourg, including the *règlement* of 1658 that placed all that concerned cultural life under Jewish jurisdiction. Another decree, of 1669, defined the limits of rabbinic authority.[29] The official appointment of a rabbi in Upper and Lower Alsace to direct communal affairs dates from 1681, when Aaron Worms was named as the sole civil and religious authority, and although there were rabbis there who preceded him, he was the first to be nominated by the king (Louis XIV) and to be required to report directly to the Intendant.[30] Furthermore, owing to the small size of each of the numerous Jewish communities in rural Alsace, it is likely that the authority of rabbinic leadership and of the rabbinic courts was more keenly felt than in the larger urban communities of Metz and Bordeaux.

Rabbis and *Parnassim*

Differences in the composition of the *kehillah* leadership, the procedures by which leaders were appointed to their positions, the functions they filled, and the relationships among them reflect the impact of specific historical forces and ethnic traditions in the northeast and southwest. Initially, in the first years following the formal establishment of the Bordeaux community, all members of the Nation who had contributed to the *rôle* of the poor were eligible to attend the general assemblies and vote in the elections. Beginning in 1716, however, participation in the elections of community officers, as in the decision-making process, became more restricted; the electoral body was subsequently limited to those members of the community who had already served as *gabbai* (trustee). This limited group of electors chose the officers of the Nation by majority vote. As a rule, the newly elected officers numbered three: a syndic and two adjuncts, also called *parnassim*, directed the affairs of the community. The first adjunct, also known as "*parnas* president," was generally the outgoing syndic; his colleague was called "second *parnas*." From 1728 the governing council was known by the same term used in the Portuguese communities of London and Amsterdam, the *Mahamad*, although in Bordeaux the electors, the *anciens* or *ansianos* (elders), were vested with greater powers. The number of electors (in 1780) was composed of the syndic, the two adjuncts, and eighteen *anciens*.[31] Until 1760, only the elders could be tax assessors; from that point, the Nation decided that the syndics and his deputies should be included in the number of assessors.

The concentration of power in a small group of rich merchants and bankers was consistent with the aristocratic tradition of the Iberian peninsula. In Bordeaux and Bayonne, the wealthiest families were all interrelated by bonds of marriage.[32] But the autocratic regime of the Nation also had its roots in the specific circumstances surrounding the establishment of the community. Because many of the first immigrant families were poor, the wealthier among them acted as their patrons, extending assistance and paying taxes on their behalf. This small group of wealthy Jews emerged as the Nation's legal representatives, and even as the economic condition of most members of the community improved enough to share the tax burden, power remained in the hands of nine families. Beginning in the 1730s, the communal leadership faced growing opposition to its autocratic style. In response to the protesters' refusal to pay taxes, the syndics enacted, with the assent of the king in 1760, new by-laws that arbitrarily reinforced their authority. This precipitated a second cycle of dissent, a tax strike, and a new set of by-laws approved by the king in 1763. In expressing their desire for more representation in the leadership body, the fifty-two dissident members of the community demanded that the title *ancien* be applied not only to former syndics but to all taxpayers and that four representatives duly elected by all taxpayers be permitted to attend meetings on taxation. They also demanded an end to the system of life appointments. Supportive of the established leadership, the king upheld the validity of the by-laws of 1760 and 1763, conceding only that two non-elders, appointed by the elders themselves, could attend all tax-related meetings. Moreover, the composition of the body of elders, which was limited to former syndics, was preserved. Similar disputes in Saint-Esprit-lès-Bayonne would continue to disrupt communal affairs through the end of the century. As in Bordeaux, the royal authority generally stood behind the official administration of the Nation.[33]

Though unquestionably disruptive, the aforementioned demands for increased representation did not seriously challenge the authority of lay leaders in Bordeaux and Bayonne. Their position remained largely uncontested, least of all by the rabbis. In contrast to the communities in Alsace-Lorraine where rabbis were, from the start, entrenched in leadership positions, the rabbinate as a communal institution in Bordeaux dates only from 1738 when Jacob Hayim Attias was appointed rabbi. Denied a role in the determination of public policy, rabbis generally filled functions as officiants, inspectors, and teachers. Strict limitations on the rabbi's authority subordinated him to the syndics in every area beyond the narrowly defined ritual sphere, and even in this latter regard his independence was severely restricted. According to the 1752 Bayonne communal statutes, the rabbi was not to take part in the communal affairs of the Nation and was to restrict himself to purely ritual functions. By the time the rabbinate finally emerged as a recognized communal institution, the leadership of the community had already become the clear and undisputed domain of wealthy laymen. The responsa published by R. Raphael Meldola, *av beit din* (head of the rabbinic court) of Bayonne, reveal that an effort had been made in the 1730s to exercise greater rabbinic authority in communal affairs, but this was of short duration and proved ultimately unsuccessful.[34]

Communal governance in northeastern France diverged from the Sephardic paradigm in two important areas, first with respect to the role of rabbis in the governing body, and second in relation to the democratic foundations of the community. For most of the *ancien régime*, the Alsatian rabbinate enjoyed considerable authority in local community affairs, and until the beginning of the eighteenth century, numerous rabbis were included within the ranks of communal leadership in Metz as well.[35] Patterns of leadership in Alsace and Metz contrasted sharply with those of communities in Poland and Germany where rabbis were generally excluded from the governing body, as was the case in Bordeaux and Bayonne.[36] Only about half the communities in the entire Alsace region were led by a *parnas*, and even in those instances rabbinic authority was largely uncontested. At Brisach, for example, the duties of the three elected *parnassim* were limited to directing the budget and carrying out the decisions of the rabbis. At the end of the seventeenth century there was one *parnas* per community in the bishopric of Strasbourg, whether a community consisted of one or several villages. In Saverne the *parnassim* were named by the episcopal authority and had a part in the interior policing and *répartition* of taxes. In Haguenau the *parnassim* bought their charges, which were subsequently confirmed by the Intendant and Magistrat. Elie Schwab, rabbi of the Prefecture, sought to control the appointment of local *parnassim* in his jurisdiction by opposing several of the nominations, and on at least one occasion attempted to nominate a family relative.[37] As a rule, the local *parnassim* were either named by the seigneur (as in Strasbourg), elected (as in Neuf-Brisach or in Haguenau), or in some instances chosen by the rabbi. For all practical purposes, those appointed by the seigneur acted as representatives of the feudal authority, while those who were elected to their position performed a variety of communal functions, from policing to forming lists for taxation.

Throughout the eighteenth century, the Alsatian rabbinate itself was engaged in a vigorous struggle to maintain its authority in communal affairs. In 1741, R. Samuel Weyl of Haute-Alsace sought government approval for a set of proposed changes in the election and appointment of communal officials, and called for the direct involvement of the government to supervise these procedures. According to the plan, local *parnassim* were to be elected democratically and installed by the rabbis and the regional *parnassim*. Weyl's legislative initiative was approved as an *ordonnance* and had the force of law in Haute-Alsace, the lands of Klinglin, the abbey of Murbach, the county of Ribeaupierre, the county of la Noblesse-Immédiate, and the bishopric of Strasbourg. It offers evidence of the incipient centralization that had begun to reinforce rabbinic authority in local communal affairs and of the common interests of the grand rabbinate, the regional leadership, and governmental authorities.[38] Consistent with this trend, rabbinic duties typically pertained to most areas of family and community law, including marriage, divorce, hearing witnesses, certifying *shoḥatim*, alimony, guardianship, and the conferral of rabbinic titles. The rabbi alone was considered qualified "to judge, to teach religion, to contract marriages, to pronounce divorces," and he was also obliged to oversee "the conduct of all the Jews in the entire Haute-Alsace." As a rule, the *parnassim* were required to support the rabbi in each of these areas.[39]

In Metz, the prominence of rabbis within the communal governing body had begun to decline even before the turn of the eighteenth century;[40] by mid-century the offices of *parnassim* were dominated by a small number of families that acquired their wealth in commerce, cattle dealing, and financing.[41] As in Poland, Lithuania, and Moravia a century earlier, evidence of tensions between the spheres of religious and lay leadership surfaced in rabbinic writings of eighteenth-century Metz. But in contrast to the strong condemnation issued by R. Jacob Sasportas, R. Judah Loew b. Beẓalel, and R. Joel Sirkes, for example, R. Jacob Reischer's 1711 responsum on the creation of a standing *beit din* in Metz reflected a shift in the balance of communal power and an acquiescence, though no doubt reluctant, to the new reality. Unhappy with the routine appointment of *dayyanim* (judges) who failed to meet the basic religious and professional qualifications set forth in Jewish law, Reischer nonetheless upheld the practice of establishing lay courts alongside rabbinic tribunals. Likewise, he acknowledged the jurisdiction of non-ordained (lay) judges in matters of personal property and damage, and upheld granting to them extrajudicial authority when the situation demanded it.[42] A sermon pronounced by R. Jonathan Eibeschütz confirms that by 1745 the two realms had become separate and that the functions of *dayyan* and *parnas* were already quite distinct. In his view, authoritative tasks were unevenly divided in favor of lay leaders. A decade later, according to the *takkanot* of 1753 and 1756, the functions of *dayyan* and *parnas* were officially deemed incompatible: if a *dayyan* were elected *parnas* he would have to temporarily relinquish his judicial duties. This legislation thus served to distinguish the offices more clearly and undoubtedly discouraged the involvement of rabbis in communal leadership.[43]

Important changes in the duties and in the authority of the office of the Metz grand rabbi at mid-century suggest that the separation between the lay and religious domains had already begun even earlier. Initially, during the half-century following the reestablishment of the Jewish community in 1595, the *kehillah* failed to delineate the range of rabbinic duties carefully. Local rabbis assumed various teaching and judicial functions that would later be included among those performed by the grand rabbi.[44] Beginning with the rabbinate of Moses Cohen Narol in 1649, the duties of the grand rabbi were consolidated. From this point, the grand rabbinate of Metz bore overall responsibility for religious and judicial affairs in the Metz *kehillah* and in the surrounding countryside. However, by the end of the seventeenth century, as the prestige of the Metz community grew larger and as rabbinic authority reached its apogee, rabbinic duties were more carefully circumscribed by the lay *parnassim*. The contract issued in 1708 to R. Abraham Broda reveals that he had been given free reign "to compel the people with punishments . . . but . . . not [to] issue the *ḥerem* [ban] without the permission of the *parnassim*."[45] Although Broda may have enjoyed a measure of authority that exceeded what rabbis elsewhere had been granted, such authority unequivocally derived from the lay-dominated community council; it was this same body that would ultimately restrict rabbinic authority when it overstepped the limits set by communal leaders.[46] Such powers had already been anticipated by the thirteenth-century synod in Mayence, which had authorized the community to issue the *ḥerem* without the consent of the *av beit din*, and in the sixteenth century the *Va'ad Arba Arazot* (Council of the Four Lands) and the community of Friedberg acknowledged the same authority of the *parnassim* in exceptional circumstances.[47] In the duchy of Lorraine, by contrast, the *av beit din* exercised greater independence from the *parnassim*. Nehemiah Reischer, the first rabbi appointed to the position (1737), had the authority to summon litigants to appear before the *beit din* and to enforce his own judgments or those of another court, "and to take any action in order to publicize, prohibit, fine, and pronounce the communal ban, all in accordance with his view."[48]

The embrace of democratic ideals, though undeniably not without certain limitations, represents a second characteristic that clearly distinguished self-government in Ashkenazic communities. Accordingly, the system of election of communal leaders in Alsace-Lorraine tended to be more broadly based than in Bordeaux and Bayonne,[49] as indicated by a detailed description of electoral and administrative procedures contained in a fragment of the Metz *pinkas* from 1699 to 1702: an electoral college of forty members was elected by the contributors of the community, and of the forty, an electoral body of eleven members was charged with the task of naming the *Va'ad* (administrative council) of the community for a period of three years. This administrative body was composed of twelve members, consisting of five administrators and seven assistants. In 1702 this number was reduced to nine; from then on, no more than four *parnassim* and five *tovim* (assistants) were named. Communal legislation was entrusted exclusively to the college of forty. It alone could establish new statutes, while a special commission of nine members was charged with overseeing the legislative process. A committee of five was to ensure the implementation of the statutes, and was also charged at the same time with overseeing the fiscal accounts of the community. The two colleges had full powers to execute their decisions, and the *Va'ad* was obliged to endorse them without restriction.[50] In contrast to Metz, most communities in Alsace elected the *parnas* by universal suffrage, though in some instances he was appointed by the seigneur on whose territory the Jews resided. The election or appointment of *parnassim* in Alsace was doubtless a reflection of the relatively small size of the communities that dotted the Upper and Lower Rhine regions. Whichever process was followed, the election of the *parnas* needed to be confirmed by the provincial organization and the local Intendant.

Despite the progressive democratization of the electoral process in Metz, eligibility requirements for communal officers became increasingly exclusionary. By mid-century, the electoral college had been enlarged from 40 to 99 persons, composed of 33 from each of the three classes of the community and divided according to wealth. That body chose, by lot, 21 electors— 7 from each order—who in turn would choose the *parnassim*, ranging in number from 6 to 9. According to the 1752 *règlement*, in order to be eligible for the office of *parnas*, one needed to meet the following qualifications: to be in possession of the right to live in Metz; to have been married at least thirty years (twenty-two years if one had a rabbinic degree); to have a net worth of at least 5,000 crowns (which would place one in the middle order—the highest order was 10,000+); and to have previously served as administrator of the charity fund. With the broadening of the electoral base, more rigorous restrictions were applied to those wishing to serve in a public capacity. Property requirements were later raised to even higher levels, so that only the wealthier members of the community would be able to assume positions of leadership.[51] Rabbis would have been unable to meet these requirements unless they had become involved primarily in business.

Rabbinic Appointments and the Manipulations of Power

The history of rabbinic appointments in France offers a closer look at the workings of communal government and an entrée into the complex relations between the lay and religious spheres. Political, economic, and legal conditions varied from region to region, and this was especially evident in the system of rabbinic appointments. In Alsace lay leaders competed to control the rabbinate, believing that this would strengthen their economic influence and enhance their authority in communal affairs, whereas Metz leaders sought to protect the rabbinate—and the community itself—from such entanglements. Whether communities hired native or foreign rabbis had important cultural implications.

In the five cantons of pre-revolutionary Alsace, which included Upper and Lower Alsace, the territories of the bishopric of Strasbourg, the territories of the directory of the nobility of Lower Alsace, and the county of Hanau-Lichtenberg, grand rabbis assumed overall responsibility for religious affairs, judicial matters, contracts, marriage, and divorce. The two grand rabbis of the Upper and Lower Alsace were elected by an assembly of *parnassim* and delegates of the cities and most important *bourgs* of the region and were officially appointed by the king. In the bishopric of Strasbourg, the bishop received authorization from the king to name rabbis; in the lands of the directorate of the nobility of Lower Alsace, it was the directorate; and in the county of Hanau-Lichtenberg it was the prince of Hesse-Darmstadt. In smaller towns and villages of Alsace deputy-rabbis were elected by an assembly of householders. By law, these elections were to be confirmed by the regional rabbi and subsequently by the general *parnassim*; the election of the regional rabbi required the procurement of *lettres patentes* from the seignorial suzerain. From 1738, the three other cantons received authorization to appoint rabbis in their territories.[52] Various confirmation procedures offer evidence of the chain of authority that linked the royal government to village Jews, and of the hierarchical structure of the French rabbinate.

The nomination of the grand rabbi in Metz was made by a body of approximately fifty electors drawn from various sectors of the population, though most heavily from the ranks of community officials and the wealthy: (1) six communal leaders, either syndics or members of the administrative council; (2) the 18–20 members of the rabbinic tribunal, that is, all those who were eligible to be chosen as the *assesseurs* of the grand rabbi; (3) a total of 30 men selected by lottery from each of the three economic classes of the community. The *lettres patentes* of 1657 required that the choice be submitted to the approbation of the king.[53] In the duchy of Lorraine, of which much less is known, there was one regional rabbinate, based near Nancy. From 1737, when the office of grand rabbi was created, until the end of the century, there were only three rabbis, Nehemiah Reischer, Jacob Perle, and Jacob Schweich, who filled the position. Other rabbinic functionaries served in the rural countryside, thus forming a sub-rabbinate. The grand rabbinate of Lorraine was itself subordinate to the authority of the Metz rabbinate. It is not clear that there was a standing *beit din* in Lorraine; in some instances, the Metz *beit din* was called upon to adjudicate more difficult matters. A convocation of *parnassim* and community representatives, totaling thirty, elected the rabbi of Lorraine.[54]

Two principal models of succession predominated at the regional level. From the mid-seventeenth century, the Metz *kehillah* refused to consider the appointment of any rabbi with relatives in the city to the position of *av beit din*. In Alsace, where conditions were considerably more variegated, there was a general preference for rabbinic candidates who were native to the northeastern provinces. Metz's restrictions on rabbinic eligibility enabled the community to avoid many of the problems that typically accompanied rabbinic appointments in Alsace.[55] Intended to ensure that the rabbinate remain independent of special interests, this precautionary measure went hand in hand with the previously cited effort to define the office of rabbi more precisely during the first half of the seventeenth century and with subsequent efforts to distinguish the offices of *dayyan* and *parnas* more definitively.[56]

A dispute over rabbinic succession in 1625 prompted the Metz *kehillah* to adopt its noted policy against hiring local rabbis. R. Joseph Lévy, who had served since 1595 as grand rabbi (along with two colleagues) and *parnas*, strongly opposed the election of R. Mordecai (Maharam) Zey to the position of *dayyan* and member of the rabbinic council that would succeed his deceased father. Lévy argued on the basis of Jewish law that a judge who is related to the parties is disqualified. Overruled when the dispute was brought before the governor, Lévy left Metz for Frankfurt. Two important precedents nonetheless emerged out of the controversy. First, the *kehillah* decided after Lévy's departure that the idea of limiting candidates to those with no relatives in the city ought to be scrupulously observed, and Lévy's successor, R. Moses Cohen (1627–1632) of Prague, was the first to be imported from abroad to serve as rabbi of Metz. Second, the nomination of a foreign rabbi would henceforth require the king's formal approval. However, only during the rabbinic tenure of Moses Cohen Narol (1649–1659), a native of the Ukraine, was the new appointment policy formalized (the *lettres patentes* of 1657) and were the duties of the grand rabbi consolidated.[57] It was also from this point that Metz was able to attract several of the most distinguished rabbinic personalities in Europe to the position of *av beit din*, including Gershon Ashkenazi, Abraham Broda, Jacob Reischer,

Jacob Joshua Falk, Jonathan Eibeschütz, Samuel Hilman, and Aryeh Loeb Günzberg.[58] The Metz *kehillah*'s refusal to hire local rabbis did not extend to lower-level rabbinic positions, however. Various charitable foundations that were established for the education of poor children provided employment for scholarly relatives of the founders. One patron of Jewish education, Moyse Belin, who created a foundation that supported twenty-four poor children from Metz and Alsace, arranged for his son-in-law, R. Itzig Pousweiler, to head the local *kloiz* (a privately supported academy) and to receive a communal tax exemption.[59] Other positions, including rabbinic directors of the publicly funded *beit midrash* and assistant communal rabbis, were consistently filled by members of the local *kehillah*.[60]

Within the province of Alsace, patterns of succession varied from region to region. In the prefecture of Haguenau (Bas-Rhin), rabbinic appointments bore the imprint of the Metz *kehillah* for much of the century. Most of the rabbis serving the Haguenau community were either natives of Metz or had gone there to study in the renowned *yeshivah* (talmudic academy). R. Samuel Halberstadt, an immigrant from Prague, was named to the Haguenau post with the help of his mentor, Metz *av beit din* Jonathan Eibeschütz, under whom Halberstadt had studied in Prague.[61] His successor, Lazarus Moyses Katzenellenbogen, a son-in-law of Metz *av beit din* R. Samuel Hilman, and others, such as Aviezri Auerbach (to Bouxwiller), were attracted by the relatively good conditions in Alsace at mid-century. With the appointment of Katzenellenbogen, the direct connection to Metz resumed. Later, in 1805, the community invited Hirsch Katzenellenbogen, son of Lazarus, to return from Frankfurt an der Oder in order to assume the position of *av beit din*.[62] In the bishopric of Strasbourg (Mutzig), the position of *av beit din* consistently passed to sons-in-law, following the initial appointment of R. Aron and his son Loeb Aron (known as Loeb Elsass). Beginning with the 1784 appointment of Simon Horchheim, Loeb Aron's son-in-law, this pattern continued until after the mid-nineteenth century. In Upper Alsace, in the lands of the directorate of the nobility of Lower Alsace (Niedernai), and in the county of Hanau-Lichtenberg (Bouxwiller), the list of appointees included rabbis either born or trained in Metz, native Alsatians, and, on rare occasions, immigrants from central Europe. There were no instances in Alsace where the position of *av beit din* passed from father to son, which contrasted sharply with families of territorial *parnassim* that controlled such offices for generations.[63]

While natives of the region dominated the grand rabbinate of Alsace, lower-level rabbinic positions tended to be filled by immigrants from central Europe and Poland, at least through the first half of the eighteenth century. Rabbis elected by rural communities did not have any officially sanctioned standing, but their immigrant status nonetheless reflected an important cultural trend. Marriage and study frequently brought rabbis, teachers, cantors, *shohatim*, and *yeshivah* students to the region, while the appeal of larger communities at times induced some natives of Alsace and Lorraine to accept rabbinic positions in Germany.[64] Such rabbinic appointments attested to the unity characterizing the area from Metz to Prague, as did liturgical rites and the long list of shared religious customs reflecting the fluidity of movement and considerable cultural homogeneity of the region. The list of rabbis in the community of Rosheim, for example, included mostly foreigners (three of four), as was the case for nearly all of the schoolteachers, the cantor, and the assistant cantor. A similar trend may be noted in the Papal States, where most of the rabbis serving in the seventeenth and eighteenth centuries hailed from Poland, Prague, or other eastern localities.[65] The steady stream of eastern immigrants in search of better economic conditions and opportunities illustrates this phenomenon, but perhaps more important, it underscores the fact that until the mid-eighteenth century there were no community-supported institutions in Alsace or Lorraine—with the exception of the renowned Metz *yeshivah*—where young men could pursue advanced talmudic studies.[66] Most communities therefore depended heavily on the importation of talent from abroad. In the last decades of the *ancien régime*, however, owing to the increased availability of locally trained Torah scholars, there was a marked tendency to appoint native Alsatians to communal rabbinic positions as well.[67]

The overwhelming preference to hire native Alsatians, first for the grand rabbinate and only later at the communal level, attests to the powerful influence that the wealthy class was able to exert on the selection process specifically and on communal governance in general. Like French government appointments beginning in the mid-seventeenth century, rabbinic posts became available for purchase, as had been the case in Poland since the sixteenth century. During the Thirty Years War, and again from 1690, when France once more became immersed in decades of warfare, the royal administration was compelled to find new sources of revenue. Offices of various kinds, including clerical positions and municipal magistracies, were available for sale; these positions were life appointments and remained in families for generations. In 1704 it was decreed that lower-level magistracies would be brought under the same regulations.[68] The strong alliance between the rabbinate and the wealthy Jewish families who dominated local and regional politics was little more than a reflection of parallel trends within the higher Catholic clergy.

Corruption at the highest levels of communal leadership and the concomitant sullying of rabbinic prestige were invariably the result of such partnerships. Members of the families of the regional *parnassim* overwhelmingly dominated the highest rabbinic offices. Samuel Lévy, a son of *parnas* Cerf Lévy and son-in-law of *parnas* Abraham Mayer Schwab, was appointed rabbi of Upper Alsace before becoming treasurer for the duke of Lorraine. His nephew by marriage, Elie Schwab, gained his initial appointment in Haguenau thanks to the influence of his father, Jacob, a provisioner of services to the secretary of the *garde des sceaux* (justice ministry).[69] R. Samuel Sanvil Weyl was a son of *parnas* Baruch Weyl and brother of general *parnas* Jacob Baruch Weyl; and R. David Sintzheim, future president of the Napoleonic Sanhedrin and first grand rabbi of the Central Consistory, was a brother-in-law of Cerf Berr.[70] Issachar Carmoly (1735–81), a native of Ribeauvillé, married the daughter of Joseph Reinau, a wealthy banker, *parnas* in Soultz, and a syndic-general of the Jews in the lands of the bishopric of Strasbourg. Reinau succeeded in persuading the bishop to authorize the creation of a new rabbinic post in Soultz and arranged for his son-in-law to be named *av beit din*.[71] The extensiveness of this phenomenon, as well as its clear susceptibility to abuse—explains the contrasting Metz regulation that the *av beit din* be selected among candidates with no relatives in the community to avoid circumstances that were likely to comprise the independence of the rabbinate.[72]

As a consequence of the entanglement of the rabbinate in commercial affairs, competing Jewish factions routinely vied with one another to gain control over rabbinic nominations. Detailed evidence of a rift concerning the appointment of the territorial *parnas* in the seigneury of Ribeaupierre at the turn of the eighteenth century reveals some of the complexities surrounding rabbinic appointments and succession. In 1699 Prince Chrétien de Birkenfeld, the lord of Ribeaupierre, selected Baruch Weyl, a munitions supplier and financier, as the new territorial *parnas*. Weyl was authorized to direct the affairs of his coreligionists, serve as judge, impose fines, announce marriages, and respect seignorial rights when bringing Jews before tribunals outside the district of Ribeauvillé. However, on the basis of a complaint brought by Alexandre Doterlé (father-in-law of the previous *parnas*) and supported by the *parnassim* of Ribeauvillé, Bergheim, and Obernai, the Conseil Souverain prohibited Weyl from assuming the position. In the end, the Intendant confirmed the appointment of Doterlé, together with R. Samuel Lévy. The latter was subsequently elected rabbi of Upper and Lower Alsace by *parnassim* of the two provinces.[73] The battle between Weyl, supported by the prince,[74] and Doterlé, who had the backing of Lévy, was at once a struggle for control of the rabbinate and the accompanying right to provide goods for the army, as well as a clear indication of the continuing strains between royal and provincial authorities. Following the departure of Lévy in 1710, Baruch Weyl succeeded in regaining his former influence when his son Samuel Sanvil Weyl was elected rabbi of the Haute-Alsace.[75]

Driven by a seemingly insatiable ambition for power and money, several Alsatian rabbis aggressively sought to extend their authority across the region. Such was the strategy of R. Weyl and, in a more limited manner, Haguenau rabbi Elie Schwab.[76] Skillfully exploiting the failure of the *lettres patentes* of 1711 to specify which areas were under the jurisdiction of the grand rabbi, Weyl devoted much of his energy to expanding the spheres of his influence through the commercial dealings of his family, through the purchase of rabbinic offices, and by filling newly vacant posts. Precisely where the territorial boundaries of rabbinic jurisdiction were drawn was a key factor in the organization of Alsatian communities. It influenced procedures of appointing local *parnassim* and strongly affected commercial dealings. The complexities accompanying the definition and redefinition of areas under a particular authority can be observed clearly in the rabbinic career of R. Weyl. In 1713 the new *lettres patentes* procured from the king's advisor authorized Weyl to exercise the functions of rabbi in the lands and seigniories of the marquis de Chamlay in Alsace.[77] The following year, the Jewish communities in the abbey of Murbach were incorporated under Weyl's rabbinical jurisdiction, although in some localities Jews refused to recognize his authority. Two years later, the royal ordinance of 7 July 1716 confirmed his authority over all the Jews of Haute-Alsace.[78] Insofar as the county of Ribeaupierre was not included in the *lettres patentes* accorded by Louis XIV, Weyl proceeded to obtain authorization (in 1718) to exercise his functions in Ribeauvillé and Bergheim, the only two localities in the seigniory where Jews resided.[79] By taking advantage of family connections, he succeeded several rabbis upon their death (in Lower Alsace and in the bishopric of Strasbourg), and he deftly negotiated agreements with other rabbis in order to extend his jurisdiction over neighboring areas.

Weyl's ambitious efforts engendered a reconfiguration of the region's rabbinic jurisdictions, thereby forging a first step toward centralization in the *ancien régime*.[80] In 1722, following the death of R. Azriel Seligmann Bloch, rabbi of the territory of the directorate of the nobility of Lower Alsace, Liebmann and Mathis Weyl, *parnassim* of the Jews in the directorate, were able to have their brother appointed as Bloch's successor. Similarly, in 1731, following the death of R. Issachar Baer Wiener of the county of Hanau-Lichtenberg, Weyl obtained authorization to extend his jurisdiction to the bishopric of Strasbourg, an area that had also been under Wiener's authority. In 1738, Weyl agreed to withdraw his opposition to R. Elie Schwab's receiving *lettres patentes* on the condition that the latter not extend his rabbinic jurisdiction to the communities of Obernai, Rosheim, and Scherrwiller.[81] Evidence of subsidies that were paid to Baruch and Meyer Weyl, and through them to the rabbi, indicates that the seignorial interest in enlarging Weyl's jurisdiction was consistently motivated by financial concerns.[82] Weyl and his family were only too willing to comply, while the religious and spiritual domain within the rabbinic affairs was, by and large, neglected.[83] By the end of his career he controlled the rabbinate of Haute-Alsace, the lands of Klinglin, the abbey of Murbach, the county of Ribeaupierre, the county of la Noblesse-Immédiate, and the bishopric of Strasbourg. These developments show clearly that the map of communities corresponded to the demarcation of areas under rabbinic jurisdiction.

Whatever power accrued to the rabbinate as a consequence of its "unholy" alliance with the wealthy class was tenuous and impermanent, and was ultimately eclipsed by the progressive empowerment of the highly influential *parnassim*. From the 1730s and 1740s rabbinic predominance in communal affairs in Alsace-Lorraine was increasingly challenged by leading lay members. At the regional level, and to a much smaller extent in individual localities, *parnassim* began to assume duties formerly performed exclusively by rabbis, although this occurred later than in most *kehillot* of Europe. Territorial *parnassim*, who generally purchased their positions from the local seigneur, enjoyed far greater power than local officials and posed a greater challenge to rabbinic authority. Named by Alsatian dynastic rulers to direct, with the rabbis, the affairs of the Jews in the district of the seigniory, these territorial *parnassim* had functioned in the bishopric of Strasbourg since the mid-1600s and in the territories of the nobility, of Hanau, and the county of Ribeaupierre since the end of the century. They were on an equal footing with the rabbi with whom they shared power but were largely independent of conventional controls. Their status, resting on their economic influence and ability to bestow their offices to their sons, was most secure in areas where the princes defended their rights against the encroachments of royal power.[84] By contrast, the rabbis recognized that the source of their own authority was the monarchical regime.

Much of the conflict over rabbinic and communal appointments reflected chronic tensions resulting from the assertion of royal hegemony, on the one hand, and the struggle for independence in the provinces, on the other. The highly contested process of selecting a successor to R. Weyl in 1753 brought such stresses and strains to the surface in the community of Ribeauvillé. One of Weyl's sons-in-law, R. Jacob Wolff Gugenheim, a native of Obernai and resident of Ribeauvillé, was presumably the natural choice for the position; another candidate was Joseph Steinhardt, *av beit din* of Niedernai. Nevertheless, the two Alsatians were bypassed in favor of R. Süssel Moïse Enosch, a native of Frankfurt am Main, who was then serving as rabbi in Creuznach. Enosch owed his appointment to the efforts of his son-in-law, Lippmann Moyses, of the Upper Alsace region, who exercised much influence with government officials. Using various tactics, including economic pressure, defamation, deception, and manipulation of the election procedure, he succeeded in winning support for his father-in-law over the two other candidates.[85] In a *mémoire* to the Intendant of Alsace, Moyses argued that because the sizable Jewish population was under the authority of the prince, and since the rabbi was authorized by law to exercise civil jurisdiction over the Jewish population, it was in the interest of the prince to appoint a person of exceptional competence and experience. Enosch, not Gugenheim, he maintained, was perfectly suited for the position. Underlying Moyses's argument was the assumption that the authorities had a genuine and legitimate interest in ensuring that the appropriate candidate fill vacant rabbinic positions.[86]

Questions concerning the legality of Enosch's appointment were raised by R. Samuel Weyl's widow, Esther, and by her son-in-law, Gugenheim.[87] The main argument in their complaint centered on the claim that as a foreigner, Enosch was not sufficiently acquainted with the royal ordinances and the legislative acts of the Conseil Supérieur d'Alsace with which every rabbi would need to be familiar and, further, on his failure to provide any confirmation of his moral uprightness. The petitioners argued further that the appointment of Enosch was in violation of a standard electoral procedure requiring that when a rabbinic office became vacant, all of the *parnassim* representing each of the Jewish communities of the province were to be convened. Although there were approximately fifty Jewish communities in Upper Alsace, Lippmann Moyses convened only thirty of the fifty *parnassim* and then found reason to disqualify several more, reducing the number to sixteen. Using his economic influence to intimidate the electors, he had also purportedly insisted on an open vote instead of the customary secret ballot. Moyses thus succeeded in swaying the election in favor of Enosch.[88]

Quite ironically, the controversial selection of Enosch, the first non-native appointed regional rabbi in Alsace, was a turning point in the creation of an indigenous Alsatian rabbinate. Immediately after his arrival, a new *yeshivah* was formed in Ribeauvillé under his direction. While little is known of the *yeshivah* itself, its impact was far-reaching. The only extant roster of students at the Ribeauvillé *yeshivah* reveals its exclusively Alsatian character.[89] Virtually every one of the first dozen students who studied there went on to assume a major rabbinic position in Alsace, and others were trained to fill positions formerly held by immigrant rabbis. Following the lead of Ribeauvillé, several small *yeshivot* and *kloizen* were established in localities such as Bischeim, Bouxwiller, Ettendorf, Mutzig, Nancy, Niedernai, Jungholtz, Westhoffen, Rosheim, and Sierentz.[90] These academies contributed to the proliferation of advanced talmudic studies in northeastern France and, reinforced by the arrival of eastern immigrants, permitted communities to become moderately self-reliant in making rabbinic appointments.

The implications of this development were far-reaching. The new emphasis in rabbinic appointments corresponded closely to important transformations in Alsatian Jewry's regional consciousness and organization. As we shall see, the impetus toward centralization in the 1760s and 1770s reflected an awareness among community leaders that the solution to certain problems, such as the recruitment and training of rabbis, demanded a regional approach. In contrast to Metz, where communal authority had eroded considerably in the two decades before the Revolution, especially in the civil sphere, the creation of Alsatian provincial bodies reaffirmed rabbinic authority and the role of religion in communal affairs. Over the long run, these early signs of centralization and self-reliance adumbrated French Jewry's sharp break with the cultural legacy of eastern and central Europe in the half-century following the Revolution, setting the stage for the emergence of a distinct Franco-Jewish identity.

Chapter 2
Secularization, Consumption, and Communal Controls

If the autonomous *kehillah* was the last bastion of tradition, the strict regulation of public life would appear to be its most abiding feature. Each community determined modes of acceptable social and religious conduct by striking a balance between its recourse to the medieval rabbinic tradition, on the one hand, and the exigencies of public policy on the other. Recorded as by-laws in the communal register, the administrative protocols known as *takkanot ha-kahal* served effectively as the constitution of the community; their purpose was to maintain social and economic stability, preserve correct relations with the neighboring gentile population, and prevent the deterioration of religious and moral values. They drew their moral authority from the Talmud but were invariably shaped by the socioeconomic conditions and cultural mores of the surrounding society. These influences are discernible in regulations on the right of permanent residence, appointment procedures for communal leaders and functionaries, and taxation.[1] Seeking to define the norms and conventions of communal life as conceived by the communal leadership, the *takkanot* were enforced through an elaborate system of fines and penalties designed to safeguard the social and religious equilibrium.[2]

The foregoing characterization of the *kehillah*'s goals emphasizes the abstract structural dynamics of the typical Ashkenazic community. Building on this foundation, but with our lens focused closely on communal laws governing consumption, sexual mores, youth, and ritual life, I will reexamine the dynamics of social change in the century preceding the Revolution.[3] The investigation that follows centers on the mechanics of public policymaking, especially with respect to moral conduct and ritual observance, intergenerational tensions, and the relationship to the neighboring gentile population and culture. Comparing conditions in Metz and Alsace, we seek to understand communal legislation within its local and regional contexts. Ultimately, my objective is twofold. First, I will evaluate the relations between lay and rabbinic leaders, their relative power and modes of governance, and their use of legislation to address contemporary challenges such as conspicuous consumption, the misconduct and instability of youth, the blurring of hierarchies of social status, and declining moral and

religious standards. Second, proceeding from an analysis of changes in social behavior that are reflected in this legislation and contemporary
sources, we shall reconsider the question of the beginnings of modernity
and suggest that modernization, at least in its preliminary stage, was already underway well before the advent of civic emancipation.[4]

Secularization and Modernity

Ordinances aiming to restrict the use and display of extravagant items and
to limit the size and expense of religious celebrations were commonly enacted across the European continent by dozens of communities in Italy,
Spain, France, Germany, Poland, and Lithuania in the late medieval and
early modern periods. Their common purpose was to preserve the stability
of the social order and to maintain equilibrium in the relations between its
members and the neighboring gentile community. Although sumptuary
laws could find support in the Talmud for drawing a connection between
natural disasters and excessive indulgence, there is no body of rabbinic literature that consistently condemned luxury as immoral.[5] Reflecting a commitment to the wider societal struggle to control extravagance, Jewish
communities were faced with the immediate concern that ostentation
might arouse the envy and resentment of their gentile neighbors.[6]

The fact that the central themes of medieval sumptuary legislation were
repeated in the seventeenth and eighteenth centuries raises the question
whether the modern restrictions were simply a continuation of medieval
controls or were motivated by new conditions and concerns. Alan Hunt has
advanced the claim that the renewed restrictions on consumption were an
early instance of governmental regulation of public behavior, a phenomenon that in his view reflected the first stirrings of modernity.[7] The religious
and social controls enacted by the Metz *kehillah* mirror governmental efforts to confront the far-reaching demographic and socioeconomic
changes of the period. Medieval regulations were typically occupied with
the task of mediating between Jewish and general society, whereas modern
controls placed greater emphasis on internal affairs. Accordingly, neither
the *Pragmatica* regulations issued by Italian communities nor the *takkanot* issued in Cracow in 1595 specified any group or class.[8] However, the Metz
sumptuary laws aimed to preserve the existing social hierarchy and to exclude the younger generation from the communal power structure. The
Metz regulations did not draw their authority from the religious tradition
but were formulated in response to new social, economic, and political
conditions in the surrounding region and within the *kehillah*. Only rarely
did the modern *takkanot* have recourse to the prohibition of *ḥukkot ha-goi*
(gentile customs) to limit the adoption of gentile customs, even as gentile
fashion had made inroads among Jewish residents. These novel emphases
reveal blatantly secular concerns, offering the first signs of modernity.

The religious and social controls enacted by Jewish communities in northeastern France in the seventeenth and eighteenth centuries reflected the unmistakable tensions that were endemic to *kehillah* leadership. Lay-dominated governing bodies and rabbinic authorities regularly competed for legislative, judicial, and punitive powers, though formal cooperation normally prevailed. Lay leaders routinely enlisted rabbinic approval of communal legislation by requiring the resident *av beit din* to add his signature to theirs, and over the course of the Middle Ages the respective areas of responsibility were carefully defined. The rabbinate assumed primary responsibility for instilling spiritual values, providing religious instruction, offering moral exhortation, and interpreting the law and executing justice in the rabbinic court system. Lay leaders, for their part, assumed responsibility for fostering optimal material conditions essential to the moral and religious welfare of the community. The uneasy relationship between the lay and rabbinic realms is particularly evident in the formal struggle against popular religion and culture, efforts to control youth, and the regulation of consumption.

Anxieties about the dereliction of youths and excessive material consumption had been voiced regularly in the Middle Ages. The Catholic Church conducted its own vigorous campaign against popular religious culture, and similar concerns were recorded in medieval Jewish moralistic and pietistic literature as well.[9] From the sixteenth century, as Peter Burke has argued, the censure of objectionable conduct became the basis for systematic action at the communal level. Burke traced the development of the struggle to suppress deviant or unacceptable behavior through two stages: 1550–1650 and 1650–1800. Initially, the clergy led the charges, justifying its involvement mainly on theological grounds. The laity subsequently took over the battle, however, ultimately to pursue broader social goals.[10]

The schema set forth by Burke is very helpful for mapping the effects of laicization on Jewish life, but one major qualification is in order. Evidence of the semi-independent authority of the non-rabbinic leadership actually dates from the thirteenth century, and by the sixteenth century one can discern the emergence of a lay elite whose interests were distinct from, and often in direct conflict with, those of the rabbinate.[11] The creation of a professional rabbinate in the sixteenth century went hand in hand with the progressive empowerment of the laity. In larger communities the *av beit din* was not the exclusive judicial authority; groups of lay judges were elected to hear cases that did not require halakhic expertise. Recourse to lay tribunals not only encroached upon rabbinic authority but also weakened the influence of Halakhah in communal affairs, only confirming that it was the community that appointed the rabbi and possessed the exclusive power to enforce the law.[12] Developments within Jewish communities anticipated conditions in the absolutist state, whose emergence in the seventeenth century, Marc Raeff has argued, permitted the secular power to exercise its au-

thority in all spheres of public and private life. Lay control over public
morality, asserts Raeff, "proved more significant and came earlier than the
ideas of the *philosophes* in giving dynamic impulse to the process of modernization."[13]

Modern lay initiatives corresponded to the time-honored concern for social order in the public sphere, but as noted earlier, they did not draw their
authority explicitly from the Jewish religious tradition. Echoing the political trend noticed by Raeff, lay regulation of dress and consumption posed
a clear challenge to the rabbinate and to the authority of Halakhah,[14] although lay-rabbinic tensions certainly varied regionally. In seventeenth-
century Poland-Lithuania, for example, leaders of the Council of the Four
Lands enacted *takkanot* and had recourse to the *herem* without the express
approval of halakhic authorities, a tendency that was strongly contested by
the foremost rabbinic figure of the day.[15] In eighteenth-century Alsace lay
leaders were firmly in control of communal affairs, but they acknowledged
the authority of the rabbis in religious matters and as a moral force in the
areas of community administration and public life. Cooperation between
the two realms was an indication of the prevailing social and religious conservatism in the region. In Metz lay leaders had clearly gained the upper
hand over the rabbinate, whose political power and communal authority
had already begun to diminish by the late seventeenth century. Clear evidence of this trend is contained in the rabbinic contract extended to R.
Abraham Broda in 1708. The *kahal* defined the scope of rabbinical authority in no uncertain terms, especially with regard to the limits it set on
the rabbi's judicial independence. Of particular significance was the clause
empowering the *kahal* to issue legislation to correct a moral problem or to
prevent a religious infraction—areas formerly under the exclusive authority of the rabbis. The contract stipulated further that the *kahal* could require the *av beit din* to affirm his consent by formally pronouncing the
herem.[16]

Together, Raeff's assertion that the transformative character of the Enlightenment has been overstated and Hunt's reassessment of modern regulatory legislation challenge the standard interpretation of when European
Jewry entered the modern era. A similar revisionist claim had already been
advanced forty years ago with the publication of Azriel Shohat's *Im Hilufe
Tekufot* (The Beginnings of the Haskalah in Germany). Pointing to abundant evidence of behavioral changes in the early eighteenth century, including laxity in ritual observance, sexual immorality, adoption of the dress
and language of the surrounding culture, and a preoccupation with material comfort, Shohat argued that the advent of modernity substantially preceded the Enlightenment and the attainment of civic equality. Although
his data pertained almost exclusively to the elite of Ashkenazic society, he
presumed that these trends paved the way for the major transformations
that would occur later in the century. This position put him in direct con-

flict with Jacob Katz, who had adamantly argued that traditional society and culture remained largely intact until the last third of the eighteenth century. Katz stressed the primacy of ideological factors for determining whether changes in Jewish behavior signaled the beginning of a new era or were merely variations on the traditional pattern. In his view, violations of religious and social norms are significant only if they are consciously justified by a new value system inspired by external sources and rendered possible by the collapse of communal structures. Others pointed out that although the first stirrings of change may well have prefigured developments later in the century, Shoḥat had failed to show a clear connection between the two phases of divergence from traditional norms.[17] These methodological flaws notwithstanding, Shoḥat's definition of modernity in behavioral terms, to the extent that this implied attitudinal change as well, remains an attractive thesis, provided it can be correlated with broader social and cultural developments.

The evidence from France confirms a growing skepticism among historians concerning the ideological foundations of modernization and its presumed monolithic character. According to this view, the timing and intensity of Ashkenazic Jewry's encounter with modernity, especially in western and central Europe, were uneven and were shaped at the local level by varying political and economic factors.[18] In the case of Metz, new legislative initiatives reveal modernizing trends at the end of the seventeenth century, while contrasting developments in neighboring Alsace suggest that regional conditions, as well as urban-rural differences, slowed the pace and character of modernization considerably. Because consumption is an area where broad patterns of social and religious life intersect, communal efforts to regulate these trends offer valuable perspectives on issues of age, gender, and social status and their role in the modernization process. In early modern Europe, sumptuary laws were emblematic of efforts to stabilize the social order and strengthen public morality.[19] In the specific case of the Jews, social and religious controls evince two additional dimensions of Europe's transition to modernity. First, they contain evidence of the unique set of challenges facing a minority seeking to maintain its cultural distinctiveness while continuing to be part of the larger social and economic matrix. Second, modern regulatory efforts illustrate the process by which central elements of a religious tradition gradually underwent secularization.

The Sumptuary Laws of Metz

The *takkanot* issued by the Metz *kehillah* in the last decade of the seventeenth century reveal much about the dynamics of community legislation, internal politics and class divisions, celebrations marking various *rites de passage*, material culture, and relations between the Jewish population and the surrounding society. They also reflect the social impact of economic changes that had begun to affect the Jewish community and the region as a whole. The fact that restrictions on consumption in the 1690s were issued serially in five separate enactments over a seven-year period makes it possible to discern shifts in emphasis over the life of the legislation and provides the basis for comparing them to similar *takkanot* issued in the following century. Furthermore, direct and indirect evidence contained in the text of the statutes offers indications of how these regulations were received in the Jewish community.

Overall, the enactment of sumptuary laws by Jewish communities in southern France was a rarity. Henri Léon reported that the Bordeaux community imposed a series of laws that included restrictions on gold and silver jewelry and on fabrics embroidered with gold, but these controls were, at best, of short duration only. There is no evidence of corresponding regulatory measures in Bayonne,[20] which is likely due to the high degree of acculturation attained by the Sephardic community there. As an outgrowth of the *converso* experience, the notion of a restricted role for religion in everyday life and the accompanying effort to downplay overt elements of social distinctiveness explain the different path taken by French Sephardim. Though certainly not comparable to the far more advanced process of social integration that would unfold only in the nineteenth century, their acculturation was sufficient to render such laws pointless.[21] By contrast, Carpentras, one of the four southeastern communities that remained under the control of the pope since the thirteenth century, enacted a series of sumptuary laws in 1712, 1738, and 1740, after having issued several similar statutes in the previous century.[22] Typical of legislation elsewhere, the limitations placed on the size and extravagance of various festive meals marking a special religious occasion were motivated by economic and social concerns. In 1738 the same concerns were given new force: the *pinkas* records the enactment of highly detailed restrictive ordinances in the immediate aftermath of an earthquake. Communal leaders regarded the calamity as a warning "to search our deeds and investigate our ways, to return in full repentance to the Lord our God." This time, however, the regulations were submitted to the Bishop of Carpentras for his approval and were implemented only after the communal leadership had gained the approbation of R. Abraham Guedalia, a major rabbinic authority then visiting from the Land of Israel. Viewing the vicissitudes of nature as the impetus for religious-spiritual renewal, the Carpentras legislation exemplifies the premodern paradigm of luxury restrictions.[23]

The main thrust of the Metz sumptuary laws stands in marked contrast to the more sporadic regulations enacted in the south. Typical of the restrictions issued in many European *kehillot*, the Metz *takkanot* bore striking resemblance to the edicts enacted by governmental authorities, such as those pronounced at Saint-Germain on 18 November 1633. This law pro-

hibited many of the same fabrics and ornamentation that were to be included in the Metz ordinances. Although they may have been inspired by
the longstanding belief that excessive consumption violated the religious
virtue of modesty, the immediate context for the enactment of the Metz
laws was economic and political. Deteriorating conditions in France, particularly in the last dozen years of the seventeenth century, may account
both for the decision by Metz leaders to issue their far-reaching legislation
and for its progressive severity as well. Following the Revocation of the
Edict of Nantes in 1685, vast numbers of highly skilled Protestant craftsmen
emigrated. Some areas, such as Normandy, were virtually depopulated,
leaving the commercial and industrial projects of Colbert in ruins. A severe
agrarian crisis made itself felt in these same years, just as France became
immersed in war. At this juncture, in December 1689, Louis XIV responded
by issuing the *Déclaration portant règlement sur les ouvrages et vaisselles d'or et
d'argent.* Involvement in the War of the Grand Alliance (1689–97) further
strained the resources of France, producing an acute monetary problem
and the decline of maritime trade. Poor harvests in 1689–93 were accompanied by general economic stagnation that reached crisis proportions in
1693–94. Increasing numbers of vagabonds, a considerable decline in
births, and large-scale emigration were the most obvious signs of widespread destitution.[24]

Shortly after France entered the war, and only eight months after Louis
XIV ordered luxury restrictions, the Metz *kehillah* issued the first of its five
sumptuary ordinances.[25] At first blush, the regulations appear virtually
identical to those of earlier times. Restrictions on the weight of wine goblets, for example, echoed the disapproval of luxury so frequently recorded
in medieval *takkanot.*[26] The most prominent feature of the 1690 *takkanah*,
however, was the distinction it drew between the public and private domains. Restrictions on lavish clothing and jewelry aimed to avoid ostentation in the public domain while limiting its various manifestations to either
private settings or certain times and days.[27] These limitations were generally alleviated on the occasion of special religious ceremonies, on the Sabbath, and usually in the interior of the synagogue.[28] While expectant
mothers and young brides during their wedding week were permitted to
wear ornaments and clothing that were otherwise forbidden, they were not
allowed to sit at the entrances to their houses nor to stand or sit in front of
the windows for fear that this might attract undue attention. Restrictions
were also applied both to the playing of music in the street in celebration
of a wedding and to the manner of dress of any adult or young person invited to a ball in the city. Although it is not clear whether the purpose of
the sumptuary laws was to avert the envy of the city's gentile population, to
protect privacy, or to conceal the assets of the *kehillah* for fear that taxes
would be raised, the differentiation between the public and private spheres
represents, in its own right, an important indicator of modernity.[29] The

1691 law added a provision prohibiting married women and young girls from wearing fur around the neck, thereby remaining true to the 1690 provision permitting luxury, provided that it was not exposed.[30]

Regulations issued two years later indicate that concerns about gentile perceptions of Jews had grown noticeably. Responding to reports that numerous women were having their veils embroidered by local gentile tailors, the 1692 law issued more stringent restrictions prohibiting any man, woman, or child from bringing veils, bonnets, coat borders, or any other part of their dress to be embroidered by non-Jews. The new prohibition was necessary, the law explained, in order to prevent gentile dressmakers and suppliers from discovering that the gold used for embroidery was real and not imitation. Merchants were reportedly astonished at the Jews' display of luxury and wealth, complaining that their Jewish customers were rarely satisfied with the quality of fabrics and jewelry they received. In the estimation of community leaders, excessive permissiveness in the enforcement of the sumptuary restrictions had encouraged arrogance and extravagance, thereby aggravating Jewish-gentile tensions. Accordingly, the commission decided to extend for one year the 1690 restrictions on wearing veils of gold and pearls to women normally exempted when participating in a *fête de famille* rite, including midwives, godmothers, women who lead the bride to the wedding canopy, brides during their wedding celebration or on the following Sabbath, and mothers of a bar mitzvah.[31] Possibly out of concern that stylish women's clothing was a source of sexual distraction to men, and owing to the vagaries of fashion as well, women's clothing and ornamentation were regulated to a far greater degree than those of men.[32]

The course of legislation issued by the Metz *kehillah* reveals that the sumptuary laws corresponded closely to fluctuations in the French economy and reflected concern about the degree of interaction with the surrounding culture. As the economic crisis intensified in 1694, the community introduced harsher restrictions, reduced the amount of permissible jewelry, and removed several special exemptions and dispensations that had been suspended in 1692. Wearing prohibited clothing in the most private areas of the home was now forbidden, there were no longer any exceptions for coiffures (that is, for young girls), and a prohibition against boys or young girls wearing (ostrich) feathers or fur in their hats was added. The law also contained a new section listing restrictions on the number of guests that one could invite to events celebrating a circumcision, marriage, eve of circumcision, and the morrow of a wedding. No doubt born of the belief that large expenditures were economically unwise, these restrictions remained in force for nearly three years, until conditions improved.[33]

Only weeks after the conclusion of the Treaty of Ryswyk in September 1697, the Metz *kehillah* issued a set of revised laws that eased several of the more stringent measures introduced in 1694, while restating most of the restrictions that had been pronounced in earlier years. In its prologue, the 1697 law indicated that in contrast to the first sumptuary laws that had been received by the majority of the community as "fair and just," subsequent restrictions were widely ignored, so much so that "the pursuit of luxury increased each day among rich and poor alike." Clothing was routinely designed with silver, gold, and luxurious materials, and new fashions were adopted without concern for the prohibition against imitating gentile customs (*ḥukkat ha-goi*). Warning of "great inconveniences, even misfortunes" that could befall the community should members embrace foreign ways, the regulation underscored the dangers of arousing jealousy among their gentile neighbors, though never detailing what these dangers were. Attention to extravagance, especially with respect to celebrations, was undoubtedly motivated, in part, by a concern for the public image of the Jewish community.[34] Nearly from the start of the seventeenth century, local merchants had voiced dissatisfaction with Jewish competition, and following the establishment of the Metz *parlement* in 1633, Jews found themselves positioned precariously between conflicting royal and local policy interests. Reporting on regional conditions in 1697, royal intendant Turgot lauded the impressive achievements of Metz's Jewish merchants. The fact that they constituted "a kind of republic and neutral nation" enabled them to travel with ease and transport merchandise across national boundaries. But he also noted local complaints concerning their unfair advantage in procuring merchandise without delay and their readiness to sell at lower prices. The growing number of Jews and their impressive commercial success became a source of concern for local authorities; some even raised the possibility of curtailing future Jewish settlement in the region. However, by virtue of its crucial role in supplying the army with food and horses, the Jewish community was regarded favorably by the crown and was granted special privileges.[35] *Kehillah* leaders were nonetheless keenly aware of the dangers that accompanied this success.

Details concerning hairstyle and fashion that were included in the regulations, as well as the resistance these laws encountered, point to a heightened fascination with the surrounding culture.[36] In the estimation of the memoirist Glückel, this was a new development. "When I first came here [in 1700]," she wrote, "Metz was a very beautiful, pious community and the *parnassim* were all worthy men who verily adorned the council room. In those days not a man who sat in the council room wore a *perruque* [wig], and no one heard of a man going out of the *Judengasse* to bring a case before a gentile tribunal."[37] Although Glückel may well have overstated the level of piety that had prevailed in turn-of-the-century Metz, religious standards were undoubtedly in a state of flux. It is reasonable to assume that by enacting sumptuary laws in 1690, Metz leaders may have been expressing concern precisely for some of the changes that struck Glückel as odd. Significantly, however, the legislation proscribed only certain practices that community members had begun to embrace. Restrictions on fashion, for example, were applied in a selective manner, and young men and women were permitted to attend the Metz *bal* if invited, provided that their dress conformed to the communal regulations. Social intermingling with non-Jews was presumably not unusual, nor was it a source of undue anxiety for communal leaders, provided that outside the ghetto Jews remained clearly identifiable by their appearance.[38] Furthermore, the absence of explicit warnings against imitating non-Jewish customs or fashion in the first years of the legislation suggests that such trends had become both commonplace and, in all likelihood, impervious to communal regulation. Neither a knowledge of French nor a general familiarity with urban culture was at all exceptional among Metz Jews. Nevertheless, the appeal to the prohibition of *ḥukkat ha-goi* in 1697 appears to have coincided with a rise in Jewish-gentile tensions as the war ended. Evidence of social and economic interaction between Jewish and gentile tradesmen confirms the emergence of chronic social friction but also suggests that the Jewish community in late in seventeenth-century Metz was hardly insular.[39]

Consumption and Social Status

In contrast to the standard formulation of sumptuary legislation issued in early modern Europe, the Metz *takkanot* only hint at the reasons why it had become necessary to curtail consumption. In most instances, sumptuary laws aimed to regulate resources in a time of crisis or were symptomatic of a stagnant and protectionist mercantile economy. As stated in the preambles to typical legislation, sumptuary laws aimed to limit the outflow of cash resulting from purchases from abroad by restricting ostentatious consumption, for fear that excessive luxury would bring about economic ruin.[40] Similar concerns motivated Jewish communities. *Takkanot* issued by the Council of the Four Lands in the early 1650s, for example, endeavored to reduce spending in light of the dire economic conditions in the aftermath of the 1648–49 pogroms, much as the Poznan *takkanot* would aim to do in 1731[41] Although the Metz *kehillah* enacted its sumptuary laws in an era of war and economic crisis, it does not appear that conditions in the community itself warranted extreme measures. The last decade of the seventeenth century was an era of expanding commercial activity for the Jewish community, marked by a wider distribution of wealth and greater availability of imported fabrics. It is also conceivable that the *kehillah*'s decision to emulate governmental regulatory efforts by exercising economic self-restraint was not economic but political, possibly intended as an expression of solidarity and identification with the difficult economic plight of the French nation.

Developments within the community suggest that at the end of the century the Metz *kehillah* was in the throes of a major social and economic transformation. Its sumptuary laws were part of a comprehensive legislative effort to place all aspects of communal life on a firmer footing. Initiatives included the enactment of a compulsory elementary education law (1690),[42] the purchase of additional land for a new cemetery (1690),[43] and the publication of new guidelines clarifying court procedures and judicial practices (1694).[44] In these same years the community received a large endowment that ensured the viability of its talmudic academy (1695). These internal developments mirror the image of a growing and thriving community that is attested in external sources. From 1633 until the end of the century the Jewish population of Metz increased dramatically from approximately 350 to 1,500 individuals at a time when the general population declined due to the ravages of disease and warfare, and in the twelve years immediately preceding 1690 the Metz population increased 45 percent. The community enjoyed its greatest prosperity in the quarter-century beginning with the War of the Grand Alliance (1689) until the end of the War of the Spanish Succession (1715). In this period Jewish bankers provided large-scale financing and merchants supplied horses, grain, tents, and other provisions for soldiers in the Metz garrison. Recognizing the importance of the community to the military establishment and to regional trade, government authorities encouraged the growth of the Metz *kehillah* by permitting immigration from neighboring Germany, Switzerland, and other regions of France.[45] Signs of significant economic expansion in the region—and of rapid urban growth as well—were evident by the beginning of the eighteenth century—developments that were accompanied by the increased availability of luxury products and the growing number of luxury craftsmen.[46]

According to Hunt, seventeenth- and eighteenth-century sumptuary legislation was issued in response to three distinguishing features of modernity: urbanization, the emergence of class, and new constructions of gender relations. The increasing density of social life in the city demanded strategies enabling urban dwellers both to identify strangers and to protect and reinforce the prevailing hierarchical divisions of society.[47] Clothing and luxury, if misappropriated, could cause social confusion. Social harmony, it was widely believed, depended on the precise gradation of ranks; the use of luxury items by members of a lower station would be disruptive because this would contribute to the blurring of recognizable markers of social rank. Resting on the premise that consumption ought to correspond to rank, not means, sumptuary law would remain in force, if only in theory, until the Revolution introduced new rules based on function and freedom. Meantime, the transition from agrarianism to market economies characterized by international commerce, manufacturing, and free enterprise threatened the status quo, particularly as communities became increasingly receptive to cultural influences from the outside. In an era of dynamic social and cultural change, sumptuary law was exploited as an instrument of political power enabling leaders to preserve the hierarchies of social status.[48]

Communal leaders viewed the reinforcement of social divisions—whether based on age, gender, wealth, or position—as a central objective of the sumptuary legislation. The ranks of leadership were routinely filled by men of significant means, men who could afford to work and travel on behalf of the *kehillah* without receiving either monetary compensation or reimbursement.[49] Acknowledging these contributions, the sumptuary laws of the 1690s aimed to enhance the prestige of the community's elite members by exempting *parnassim* and *manhigim* (community leaders), as well as their wives, sons, and unmarried daughters, from most of the restrictions on jewelry and clothing. In 1694 and 1697 these exemptions were broadened to include permission to wear the largest wigs, whereas in 1690 all wigs were forbidden to young and old if they were longer than those worn by Catholic priests.[50] Additionally, *takkanot* dating from the beginning of the eighteenth century were especially protective of the status of leaders and reserved special synagogue honors for them. Eighty years later, even stronger efforts to emphasize class divisions were introduced. The 1769 *takkanah* contained provisions for synagogue protocol that were designed to underline the prominence of community leaders, and a more explicit correlation between financial status and the imposing of restrictions on jewelry and clothing was included as well. Thus, the number of guests one could invite to a wedding was unlimited when the dowry exceeded ten thousand livres. Measures aiming to differentiate sharply between the superior status of older, married men and the inferior status of younger, unmarried men were also added. The new emphases of the 1769 *takkanah* were consistent with the general tendency to stabilize prevailing hierarchies and social divisions most strenuously in periods of social dislocation. This, it would seem, was the primary purpose of the sumptuary laws in the mid-eighteenth century and far outweighed the purported moral concerns that were generally set aside in the case of the wealthy members of the community.

Certain regulations did transcend class distinctions, however, and may be rightly viewed as signaling a somewhat different emphasis. The 1769 law prohibited women whose husbands had a fortune of fifteen thousand *couronnes* or more from promenading on the Rhinport (the wharf along the Moselle) and in the interior of the *quartier* or in synagogues. These measures were similar to more generally applied restrictions against promenading while wearing *mantelettes* of muslin, of transparent light fabric, of thick linen (*toile mat*), or of silk. The fact that *mantelettes* woven of less costly fabrics could be worn anywhere, while on the Jewish street it was permissible to wear *mantelettes* composed of more expensive materials, including muslin and silk, suggests that leaders were still concerned about the ill-effects of conspicuous consumption.[51] Clearly, it was not extravagance per se that was deemed to be reprehensible; it was the untoward display of ostentation that posed a threat to both Jewish-gentile relations and the internal social order.[52]

Among the most important concerns facing communities in northeastern France, as elsewhere, was the age-old question of how to control the behavior of children and young adults.[53] Misgivings about the instability of youth served as the impulse for several different initiatives.[54] The Metz *kehillah* pursued the matter first within the framework of formal education in 1690, the same year it embarked on its sumptuary regulations. Comparable to the initiative undertaken in sixteenth-century Avignon,[55] Metz leaders enacted legislation making elementary education compulsory and regulating the hours of instruction, the duties required of teachers, and their salaries. This was part of an effort to extend communal authority over institutions that hitherto had been either independent or semi-independent. All fathers were to provide their children through the age of fourteen with tutors, under the threat of banishment. Children of the poor were to be taught at the community's expense and requests for assistance would be honored without conducting the customary investigation into the financial status of the applicants. In addition, the Metz laws required young men between the ages of fourteen and eighteen to study at least one hour per day. The detailed *takkanot* reveal the seriousness with which education was approached and illustrate how the communal dimension was present in the overall conception of the school, in the testing procedures, and especially in the penalties for noncompliance with the regulations. These penalties, including the forfeiture of a son's right of residence and monetary fines, show that the provisions of the compulsory schooling program were not limited to the educational domain but were interwoven with issues of social standing, personal status, and legal rights.[56]

Over the course of the eighteenth century, greater prominence was attached to hierarchies of social status than had been the case in the previous century. As we observed earlier, much of the focus of the legislation of the 1690s was on regulating extravagance in dress and jewelry worn by women, while additional distinctions were based on age and marital status. The 1690 law proscribed all coiffures in imitation of the styles of gentile women, except for girls under the age of eleven, who were permitted to wear coiffures *en cheveux*. Moreover, *peignoirs* were prohibited to all women, including girls over the age of eleven, and pleated coats were forbidden to all. The 1694 sumptuary law announced that all women over fifteen years of age, presumably irrespective of marital status, would be required to wear a coat and veil when attending synagogue.[57] According to the 1697 law, married women were prohibited from appearing in the synagogue without a veil. Young brides aged twelve, thirteen, or fourteen were excused from this law during the first year of their marriage, while one who wed at fifteen was free from wearing the veil for only three months. This dispensation,

though apparently an extension of the Mishnah's leniencies for a new
bride so that she would remain attractive to her husband, earmarked particularly young brides.[58] Married women were required to wear *manteaux*
(top coats) in the synagogue, irrespective of the time or day, but a new
bride received a special dispensation to enter the synagogue without a *manteau* for the first month after her wedding. Eighty years later, the requirement of wearing a coat would be applied more rigorously to men: heads of
households found promenading in the *quartier* without a *manteau* would be
disqualified from serving as electors of the community council.[59] Concerning restrictions on wigs, rings, or jewelry that were intended specifically for
youth, the Metz regulations were curiously silent.[60]

By mid-century a heightened emphasis on marriage as a marker of status
in the community can be observed in several new regulations. A sharp distinction between the standing of the unmarried and the married, and between younger and more established couples, is evident in the 1769
procedures governing eligibility for communal offices, the distribution of
synagogue honors, commercial freedom, and dress. To qualify for the office of *parnas*, according to the 1752 *takkanah*, one needed to have been
married at least thirty years (but only twenty-two years if one possessed the
title *haver*, indicating the completion of the first level of rabbinic studies),
in addition to several other residential and financial qualifications.[61] Moreover, several features of the 1769 *takkanot* indicate the degree to which
being unmarried was stigmatized. In an era when distinctions of all sorts
served as the basis of social status,[62] the highest synagogue honors were
usually reserved not only for older congregants but also for those who had
been married for many years. Unmarried men were generally not eligible
to obtain preferred seats, nor were they called to the Torah either on the
three pilgrimage festivals (Passover, Shavuot, and Sukkot) or on the high
holy days (Rosh Hashanah and Yom Kippur); young married men enjoyed
a slightly elevated status as they could be called to the Torah on the pilgrimage festivals but not on the high holy days. Certain important honors
were reserved for men who had been married for twenty years and possessed the title of *haver*, and medium honors were given to those combining the title of *haver* with six years of marriage, or twenty years without the
title.[63]

In the commercial realm, the *takkanot* distinguished sharply among boys,
bachelors, younger married men, and older married men. Boys under fifteen years of age were prohibited from engaging in commerce in the
community; if a boy violated this restriction before reaching the age of thirteen, he would be prevented from reading the Torah publicly on the occasion of his bar mitzvah, and any subsequent failure to obey this law would
be subject to a fine. An unmarried man was expected to yield to a householder (that is, a married man) if the two were selling their wares at the
same house.[64] Furthermore, the 1769 *takkanot* upheld legislation issued

earlier in the century (1728) that prohibited commercial dealings with either unmarried men or householders in their first two years of marriage.[65] These restrictions, though relaxed in the case of orphans and bachelors with the permission of their fathers, suggest that it was only after the initial period as man and wife, perhaps after they had begun to have children, that the marriage was considered stable and the husband was regarded as a full-fledged householder. In one instance in 1768, a Metz householder flouted the commercial prohibition and was therefore barred from participating in any religious activity in the two synagogues, including prayer, and was prevented from wearing the *schülmantel*.[66] Such were the tactics adopted by the Metz *kehillah* to protect the standing of householders from competition posed by individuals who were not yet established in the community.

The phrasing of other restrictions in the same *takkanot* suggests, however, that these broad social goals were rarely achieved. The community therefore sought to control rather than curb the dealings of the younger, less established residents. Any unmarried man conducting commerce in Metz, in the province of Lorraine, or in any province of France was required to pay to the inspectors 10 percent of his profits.[67] Moreover, no unmarried man, whether in possession of the right of domicile or not, could gain authorization to slaughter animals unless he maintained a business association (as a butcher) with a householder. The only exceptions to this rule were orphans, who were authorized to perform ritual slaughtering while still unmarried.[68] While the motivation for these regulations was clearly economic, they nonetheless reflect additional, ongoing efforts to preserve the social hierarchies of age and marital status.

In its approach to youth and class, the Metz *takkanot* of 1769 were more thoroughgoing than the earlier legislation. Controlling the behavior of youth, a recurrent theme in eighteenth-century legislation across the continent,[69] became an increasingly formidable task as the century progressed. In 1751, the community had established a central elementary school that formalized what had been, until then, essentially a tutorial program.[70] However, reports of truancy, accompanied by the fear of greater idleness and crime, prompted community leaders to issue new measures. From the 1769 communal *takkanot* we learn that some parents failed to send their sons to the school, and as a result boys of six or seven "promenade in the markets and street, each his own way, rejecting his obligations to God, and ultimately devoid of Torah knowledge and respect, he is no good for a trade; and as a result of this idleness he gets bored and becomes a brigand." As a preventive measure, the *takkanot* required that each boy study at least the two years before the age of thirteen; any boy who failed to do so would be barred from reading the weekly Torah portion in either of the two synagogues on the occasion of his bar mitzvah.[71] Parallel developments in Bordeaux suggest that the community there was facing similar problems. Until mid-century, the elders of the Nation showed no interest in community-wide Jewish education. But in 1760 Bordeaux leaders allocated considerable funds, drawn in part from a self-imposed tax on kosher meat, for the creation of a school. Their major objective was to control raucous children wandering the streets.[72]

Over and above the foregoing efforts in the educational realm, the 1769 Metz *takkanot* reflect the community's considerable concerns about adolescents, the disturbances they reportedly caused, and the ongoing struggle to prevent sexual immorality among unmarried men and women. Detailed enactments that barred young boys and girls, including valets and servants, from going out beyond the Jewish streets on the Sabbath and festivals point toward a serious problem that evidently had not concerned communal leaders in the 1690s. According to the new legislation, young people were not to visit the neighboring quarter (the *glacière*), much less venture beyond the gate of the city, except for the gate Chambière, until the end of the Rhinport (the *quai de la Moselle*). Extending along the river, from the Saint-Georges bridge to the Arsénal bridge, at the outer limit of the Jewish quarter, the Rhinport was evidently a point for young people to meet away from parental supervision, and may also have been a place to enjoy traveling entertainers.[73] Men were authorized to promenade with their wives and daughters along the *glacière* on Sabbath and festivals, but not beyond the limits of the Jewish quarter or outside the gate of the city. Unmarried men and women were specifically forbidden from promenading on the Sabbath and festivals on the Rhinport while dressed in a *robe*, even if they were accompanied by their parents and, moreover, were not permitted to go there on working days dressed in a *robe*. Also new to the mid-eighteenth-century Metz laws were *takkanot* that prohibited the practice of smoking tobacco on the Rhinport, both for householders and youths, evidently for fear that this borrowed custom might penetrate the community proper.[74] Women and girls were not permitted to promenade arm in arm "like a little chain" on the Jewish street, on the Rhinport, or any other place, at any time. As a meeting place for youth, the Rhinport offered an outlet for those seeking freedom from communal controls. With travelers and wares from afar arriving regularly, the port was a natural linkage and outlet to the wider world, and the dangers it posed were evident to the communal leadership.[75]

Growing concern about the sexual mores of young men and women prompted the enactment of several other *takkanot*. Stern warnings were issued against sexual contact between men and women engaged to be married, known in French society as *fiançailles*. In contrast to earlier communal legislation that was silent on this subject, the 1769 law prohibited betrothed couples from being in each other's company at night, even in the presence of a guardian.[76] In light of the apparent deterioration in the moral climate, stringent measures such as heavy fines and the public disclosure of such improprieties were now judged to be necessary. Legislation limiting social contact with servant girls is a case in point. The onus of responsibility was placed squarely upon servants who violated norms of sexual impropriety; they were to be denied the right to remain overnight in the community. Should a young servant girl become pregnant as a result of a liaison with a married man, both would be excommunicated and would forfeit their right to reside in the community for fifteen years. However, while the law added that the servant girl was also to be publicly shamed, no other measures were to be taken against the householder. The central role of gender notwithstanding, class weighed most heavily on how the community handled violations of sexual norms.[77]

Even social contact between men and women in less compromising circumstances was viewed with considerable alarm. For example, the 1769 Metz *takkanot* designated separate days for cemetery visitations,[78] as did several other seventeenth-century communities in central Europe. The *Hebra Kaddisha* of Triesch (1687) instructed the beadle to put an end to the "danger" of men and women mingling when the dead were carried to the cemetery, and the Prague community (1692) voted to halt "the disorder of women who jostle at each other at funerals and funeral preparations."[79] These sources reflect a range of concerns about the involvement of women in public ritual, the intermingling of the sexes at liminal moments, and the disorderly conduct of public rites.[80] Women, it has been observed, were widely viewed in early modern Europe as a fundamental source of disorder and were deemed most in need of discipline. The Metz community, for its part, adopted an even more restrictive measure prohibiting women from attending funerals entirely. This provision, undoubtedly a response to local concerns about declining standards of sexual morality, corresponded to R. Jonathan Eibeschütz's outspoken criticism of sexual libertarianism a quarter-century earlier. He had ruled that women were to arrange their annual cemetery visitations a day or two before Rosh Hashanah and Yom Kippur in order to avoid the morning before these festivals, which was normally reserved for men.[81] This ruling was but one of several initiatives undertaken by the Metz rabbi to influence communal legislation.[82] These and similar measures aiming to preserve the traditional character of Jewish life—and in some instances to introduce new, more rigorous standards than before—reflect the growing anxiety among communal leaders. Ultimately, their efforts proved to be ineffective against the impact of secularization and the increasing contact with the surrounding cultures.

Out of concern that children might choose to marry without first obtaining parental consent, the communities of southern France adopted extremely rigorous measures. The challenge to parental authority posed by clandestine marriage had emerged as a major societal issue in the era of the Protestant Reformation especially, and the phenomenon continued well into the modern period. Accordingly, numerous Jewish communal bodies from the 1520s prohibited marriages that were contracted without parental consent.[83] In Bayonne, a regulation (*ḥerem*) admonishing against the betrothal of a woman without the prior consent of her father was recorded in the community *pinkas* on 19 February 1700, though the interdiction clearly dated from an earlier period. It was reissued three years later by the *parnassim* "so that no one will take sexual liberties with the daughters of Israel." Marriage, the *parnassim* declared, was for the fulfillment of a divine commandment and not to satisfy one's sexual desire. The regulation received the assent of the Sephardic sages and rabbinic court of Amsterdam after Bayonne leaders turned to them for support. Later in the century (in 1779), the Avignon community issued its own statute (art. 16) warning that *kiddushin* (betrothal) without parental consent was null and void—even without a *get* (writ of divorce)—and that the witnesses were to be fined the sum of one hundred *écus*. This provision was not included in the *takkanot* of 1558, which only prohibited a man from leaving the city between the betrothal and the wedding.[84]

The legal ramifications of this enactment were subject to varying interpretations. R. Moshe Sinai of Carpentras insisted that rabbinic authorities could nullify the *kiddushin* (engagement) because the *takkanah* had been enacted by a *beit din* and by the *parnassim*, that it had the approbation of the Amsterdam rabbis, and that it fulfilled several additional technical halakhic requirements. R. Moshe de Rublis of Bayonne wanted to nullify the *kiddushin* on the basis of *dina d'malkhuta dina* ("the law of the land is the law"), because according to royal law no man less than twenty-five years of age could marry a woman without the consent of her father and his. However, R. David Meldola countered with the argument that *dina d'malkhuta dina* only applied to tax and civil law, but not in those areas governed by Torah law.[85]

No comparable legislation was enacted in the northeastern communities of France nor, for that matter, in any Ashkenazic communities across the continent. Communal restrictions in the area of marriage were limited to the reinforcement of rabbinic authority. In Alsace, Bamberg, Hamburg-Altona, and the Ashkenazic community of Amsterdam, for example, communal enactments stipulated that no one other than the *av beit din* or a *dayyan* of that locale was authorized to officiate at a wedding. This shift in emphasis was based on R. Moses Isserles' ruling against any nullification of the betrothal contract, known technically as *hafka'at kiddushin*. Furthermore, the Isserles ruling that upheld a child's right to marry the person of his choice remained dominant in Ashkenazic communities, but it clearly did not carry weight in the Sephardic orbit. Among Sephardim the emphasis was on subordination to parental authority, and the legislation was typically couched in rhetoric lamenting the declining standards of sexual morality. In Ashkenazic communities, clandestine marriage was viewed as a challenge both to the prevailing class system and to communal authority, and their leaders confronted the problem by threatening offenders with corporal punishment and coercive divorce. Issues of class and communal authority were much more contested there than among Sephardim, and these distinctions prefigured critical differences between Ashkenazim and Sephardim in the nineteenth century.

Controls in Rural Alsace: A Regional Approach

The uneasiness exhibited by Metz leaders was also apparent, though in a much different way, in the creation of a provincial organization for Upper and Lower Alsace in 1777. This development was doubtless an echo of the general impetus toward centralization in the two decades preceding the Revolution. Owing to the fact that all the communities in the region were evenly represented, the Alsatian provincial body contrasted sharply with the more modest models of centralization elsewhere in France. In the south, the Bordeaux community dominated the affairs of neighboring communities, as did the Metz *kehillah* in the province of Moselle. To be sure, Metz imposed its authority energetically on the outlying towns and villages of the province. Already in 1718 a royal law required nearby communities to contribute to the sums that Metz Jews paid for protection, and permission to tax these smaller communities was upheld by the government throughout the eighteenth century.[86] Moreover, smaller communities regularly turned to Metz to help resolve their disputes, insofar as they were expected to subordinate themselves to the authority of the Metz rabbinic court.[87] With the growth of the Jewish population in the countryside, the Metz *kehillah* implemented an economic policy that aimed to protect the interests of its own members.[88] In the province of Lorraine, the Jewish population was formally recognized as a single community. As a result, except in Nancy, the seat of the Lorraine rabbinate, there were no officially recognized rabbis or syndics, even in communities with sizable numbers of Jews, such as Lunéville and Sarreguemines.[89]

Conditions were far different in Alsace, and the regional initiative undertaken there was far more ambitious. The creation of an overarching provincial organization was the product of several developments that converged in the quarter-century preceding 1789. These included the dramatic increase in the Jewish population, dispersed in 182 settlements, most of which were so small that no local communal structure was feasible; the levy of royal taxes, which required regional officials who were directly responsible to the Intendant; the active involvement of Herz Cerf Berr, who was convinced that an improvement in the political condition of Alsatian Jewry depended on a reform of their communal structures; the recognition that the solution to certain problems, such as the recruitment of rabbis, required a regional approach to rabbinic training; and the realization that the centralization of Jewish life was consistent with the political aims of the monarchy.

The drive toward centralization began with the convocation of regional meetings at Niedernai in 1763, where statutes governing the appointment of deputies for Lower Alsace were issued in preparation for a subsequent meeting in Bischeim; subsequent meetings were held in Strasbourg (in 1776 and 1777) and Rosheim (1777).[90] In the same years, one observes the ascendancy of province-wide leaders who assumed responsibilities pertaining to the entire Alsatian Jewish population, and not just to the affairs of their own district. From the 1770s three of the territorial *parnassim*, Cerf Berr, Aron Meyer of Mutzig, and Lehmann Netter of Rosheim, each assumed the title *préposé général de la Nation Juive*, which was confirmed by the Intendant in 1777.[91] Assemblies representing the entire province of Alsace met first in Niedernai in 1777, then in Bischeim in 1780, and probably a third time in 1783. *Takkanot* addressed matters of common interest to communities throughout Alsace; these would need to be confirmed by the territorial assemblies of the seigniories, especially when they pertained to fiscal concerns. The Niedernai assembly—the best documented of the three—brought together the general and the local *parnassim* of the forty-two communities in the Upper and Lower Rhine. Its *takkanot* touched on many aspects of communal life, both civil and religious, combining the codification of older decisions and the introduction of new measures (for example, the creation of rabbinical colleges). Twenty-eight deputies, each one referred to as *parnas u-manhig*, were appointed to verify the accounts and to examine the proposed statutes. They were asked to submit their conclusions to the general *parnassim* and to the grand rabbis for their approval, and only then would they have the force of law.[92]

The legislative agenda in Alsace was more narrowly focused than in Metz, and controls were directed at a different set of concerns. Owing to the village character of Jewish life in Alsace and to the region's predominantly rural economy, there is no evidence of either excessive or conspicuous consumption, except among a handful of wealthy businessmen. Accordingly, sumptuary laws were never issued in pre-revolutionary Alsace, nor do the published *takkanot* evince any concern for class divisions. Nevertheless, the Alsatian leadership shared with Metz leaders a deep-seated anxiety about the challenges that threatened to undermine the social and religious status quo. The *takkanot* of Alsace differed from the Metz regulations in their assessment of the most serious challenges before the Jewish community. As in Metz, concerns about youth figured prominently in the Alsatian legislation, but these were motivated by apprehensiveness about the pervasive influence of the local village culture. Consistently, the *takkanot* of Alsace aimed to reinforce rabbinic authority and ritual observance. The Niedernai assembly of 1777 justified its legislative measures by asserting that they came under the rubric of *le-migdar milta* ("to stem the tide of immorality"); on this basis young men and women were prohibited from promenading together on Sabbaths and festivals, either within the city or beyond it, and were restricted in passing from one community to another unless it was to perform a religiously ordained act or was in accordance with the view of a halakhic authority.[93]

Steps were taken to prevent young people from practicing certain customs that were borrowed from the surrounding village culture and were therefore regarded by the communal leadership as improper. It prohibited the "unseemly practice" that when a bridegroom would arrive in the community before his wedding, the young men there would purchase on his behalf the honor of binding the Torah scroll during the synagogue service in exchange for which they would demand from him *portal*[94] (or money, according to Loeb) so they could eat and drink together. This custom, a variation on the widely practiced *charivari*, had been modified to accord with Jewish religious practice. Similarly, the custom of going to greet the bridegroom or bride on a horse was also prohibited, though the reason for the objection was not given, and the practice was punishable by a large fine. Historically, *charivari* functioned both as a mode of social control, expressing the animosity of the public toward those who broke time-honored customs and, paradoxically, as a protest against the prevailing social order. Jewish communal leaders in Alsace strenuously condemned such rites for their rowdiness and vulgarity, viewing them as a reflection of non-Jewish influence and as a sign of youthful rebellion against authority. The *charivari* was therefore declared "absolutely null and void," with the amount of a fine to be determined by the grand rabbi. Despite these objections, the *charivari* remained part of village life in western and central Europe well into the nineteenth century.[95]

Efforts to suppress dancing between men and women offer further evidence not only of the natural gravitation toward village culture but also of the concerns of community leaders regarding youth, sexuality, and what was viewed as excessive acculturation. Such restrictions, while certainly not new, were relatively rare before the sixteenth century;[96] in medieval Christendom dancing was commonly regarded as both immoral and in poor taste.[97] In a responsum issued by R. Joseph Steinhardt of Niedernai, several objections to dancing were advanced: it violated proper Jewish demeanor, and on the Sabbath and festivals it could lead to certain technical infringements. His strongest language, however, was reserved for mixed dancing on the grounds that it was likely to arouse immoral desires and lead to sexual impropriety. Steinhardt's own strenuous efforts to prevent dancing in Niedernai (ca. 1755) were directed at the youth in his community who objected to rabbinic interference and who informed against him to the government that had authorized their dance. Steinhardt succeeded in persuading the governor to permit the matter to remain under rabbinic control, though in at least one other community the government forced the rabbi to rescind the *ḥerem*.[98]

According to the protocol of the Rosheim meeting, dancing was frequently accompanied by quarrels and the desecration of Sabbath and festivals. The Rosheim assembly ruled that it would henceforth be permissible to dance only at weddings and on the preceding Sabbath (Shabbes Schenkwein).[99] At Niedernai the assembly reiterated a similar *takkanah* that had been enacted earlier by the general *parnassim*; however, in this case the *takkanah* referred explicitly to unmarried men and women, clearly voicing anxiety about the intermingling of the sexes and the general disorder it could cause. This prohibition, the assembly warned, was to be enforced rigorously: it would be announced in all the synagogues of the region in the name of the grand rabbis and in the name of the general *parnassim*; failure to abide by the law was punishable by a large fine. Furthermore, no man, married or unmarried, would be permitted to dance with a married woman, even at a wedding.[100] Such controls extended even to Metz, where originally the sole reference to dancing was the 1690 *takkanah* stipulating that those who were invited to *le bal* must adhere to the dress restrictions set forth in the regulations; the community later prohibited mixed dancing.[101] The particular case of Alsace shows that the primary aim of communal regulations was not to prevent the intrusion of non-Jewish customs and morality but rather to distinguish between acceptable and unacceptable circumstances for dancing.[102] The *takkanah* stopped short of categorically prohibiting unmarried men and women from dancing with one another, or husbands from dancing with their wives. Typically, communities limited dancing between the sexes to religious celebrations, evidently in order to mitigate its potential harm to public morality.[103]

The decisions of the assembly reaffirmed seignorial authority in external affairs and introduced uniform statutes intended to govern the internal life of the communities of Alsace in the following areas: election of communal *parnassim*; relative authority of local and general *parnassim*; internal policing; civil jurisdiction; rabbinic authority; taxation; higher talmudic education; record keeping; religious and social controls; social welfare; and regulation of inheritance. The assembly set down policy in each of these areas and served as a central authority empowered to enforce its rulings throughout the province.[104] Especially noteworthy among the *takkanot* is the hierarchical leadership structure that the assembly formalized with respect to general (that is, regional) and local *parnassim* and was later established as law by the 1784 *lettres patentes*. Local *parnassim* were responsible for internal matters: to convene assemblies to name the cantor or *bedeau*; to raise taxes for the salaries of communal functionaries; to police the synagogue, and to take the necessary measures in order to maintain order. The general *parnassim*, known as *les syndics des Juifs*, enjoyed extensive administrative powers, notable among them the collection of communal and royal taxes.[105]

Despite concerns about the deleterious effects of the surrounding village culture on Jewish life—or perhaps because of these anxieties—rural Alsace remained firm in its religious traditionalism, in sharp contrast to signs of eroding religious commitments in urbanized Metz. This difference is particularly noticeable in the status of the rabbinate. Until the Revolution, the *av beit din* was a central communal figure in Alsace, and where his authority may have eroded somewhat, the syndics made efforts to strengthen his position. This is evident in their endorsement of rabbis as conveners of local elections and as an authority whose approval was required before fines could be issued by the *parnassim*. Even more revealing is the reliance of the 1777 provincial decisions on the rhetoric of religion and rabbinic authority. The first article of the protocol stated that failure to abide by the *takkanot* was tantamount to a violation of "the law of our holy Torah, which has been transmitted to the august rabbis, *parnassim* and *manhigim*, and to the *shtadlanim* of the *Medinah*."[106] The system of fines used to uphold the authority of the *parnassim* required the approval of the *av beit din*, while the power to impose the *herem* against an individual who committed a religious infraction was contingent on the agreement of a rabbinic court. The *takkanot* also protected the exclusive authority of the rabbis in religious affairs. No one could issue rulings in matters of ritual law without the authorization of the *av beit din* of that particular province, and only the rabbi authorized in a particular locale could be approached with halakhic queries. Moreover, it was determined that once a resident consulted a rabbi on a halakhic question, he could not turn to a second rabbi on the same matter. Any person who violated this regulation would be fined and his house and utensils would be declared unkosher. The local *parnassim* were warned against authorizing any individual to conduct a wedding without written permission either from the *av beit din* or the *dayyan* of the *kehillah*. Finally, all *parnassim* were urged to attend synagogue mornings and evenings.[107]

While these provisions might be taken to imply a degree of religious laxity on the part of householders and communal leaders, they were also part of an effort to prescribe normative practice in Alsace. Concern about maintaining certain standards of religious behavior was present throughout the protocol, as indicated by the assembly's efforts to control the conduct of unmarried men and women, but this does not, in itself, imply a decline in the authority of tradition. Nevertheless, evidence of the intrusion of modernity in Alsace was met by the firm resolve of community leaders to revitalize the moral and religious foundations of Judaism. This is typified by the decision to create a central *beit midrash* for the entire province; efforts to fund the regional *yeshivot* of Sierentz and Ettendorf also continued unabated. Although there already were numerous *yeshivot* and *batei midrash* that offered opportunities to study intensively, community leaders of Upper and Lower Alsace believed that it was necessary to establish institutions where study could continue without interruption for up to three years.[108]

Within the context of the shifting balance of communal power, lay regulation of consumption and public morality posed a direct challenge to the

Metz rabbinate and to the authority of Halakhah, even when lay and rabbinic interests converged. For communal leaders, an overarching concern for the ordering of society emerged as a central value. In one instance at least, the idea received firm rabbinic approval as well. R. Ya'ir Ḥayyim Bacharach, who resided in Metz briefly in 1690, affirmed the right of communities to enact *takkanot* regulating behavior in areas beyond the boundaries of Jewish law and custom, while denying individuals the right to disobey if the legislation reflected the will of the majority of the community or its representatives. According to Bacharach, sumptuary laws were under the legitimate jurisdiction of the lay leadership either because they concerned an halakhically neutral sphere or because they functioned as a barrier to public immorality. Their ultimate justification, he asserted, lay in the fact that they were intended to sustain the collective body. With the emergence of the public interest as a value largely independent of halakhic constraints or religious justification, Metz witnessed the first stage of modernization, that is, laicization, nearly a century before the Revolution. In Alsatian communities, the penetration of cultural influences from surrounding villages and the indirect effects of economic modernization in the cities resulted in very modest social and religious changes there as well, but these can hardly be considered modernization.[109] The absence of sumptuary legislation in Alsace reflects the relatively impoverished and less urban nature of the region's communities and suggests, based on the comparison with Metz, that there is a correlation between economic condition on the one hand and religious and ideological change on the other.

The efforts of Jewish communal leaders in Alsace and Metz to respond to these changes were, as we have seen, quite dissimilar. Alsatian leaders endeavored to forestall the undermining of traditional religious life and consequently took action to bolster rabbinic authority. In Metz, communal controls also aimed to preserve the religious status quo, but the greater emphasis was on an unmistakably secular approach to the organization of public life. The ruling elite zealously guarded its authority, to the detriment of the rabbinate and younger householders. Communal legislation mirrored the dynamic changes of the early modern period, particularly the changing urban reality created by the economic and social consequences of the new mercantile culture. Although lay control over public morality—perhaps the most salient feature of the *kehillah* in this era—would eventually emerge as the dominant expression of communal governance in modern Europe, this did not lead, inexorably, to the demise of traditional patterns. Communal structures remained in place, and despite all the attendant tensions lay and rabbinic leaders continued to cooperate until the end of the *ancien régime*. These conservative trends notwithstanding, modern communal controls attest quite clearly to the emergence of significant social, cultural, and religious changes in Jewish society that anticipated the full-blown transformations of the nineteenth century.

Chapter 3
Ritual and Religious Culture in Alsace-Lorraine

Rituals observed during the *ancien régime* served discrete social and cultural purposes, though the two realms were hardly unconnected. Biblical and talmudic Judaism prescribed strict social separation from the potentially harmful cultural influences of neighboring peoples. This demand was amplified in medieval rabbinic literature to include restrictions on the consumption of food and wine prepared by gentiles, the appropriation of non-Jewish folkways and rituals, and the emulation of gentile dress. How rigorously these restrictions were applied and how successfully they limited the relations between Jews and non-Jews would depend on the intensity of social and economic relations in any particular locale. Recurrent complaints about the dangers of social intermingling and acculturation offer, on their own, little more than an echo of the anxiety routinely voiced by rabbinic leaders. But it is clear that over the course of centuries the rigorous demands and extensive details of Jewish ritual observance strengthened the long-established ethos of separation. Sabbath and festival observance, public prayer, religious education, and care for the dead encouraged the formation of separate Jewish communities and, as in the particular case of the dietary laws, served as markers of Jewish social distinctiveness. Social segregation could be sustained because it converged with the interests of ecclesiastical and lay authorities intent on keeping Jews socially apart.

The role of ritual in promoting a distinct national identity for Jews in the numerous lands of their dispersion has a long and fabled history. In the seventeenth century, ritual would emerge as a subject of fractious debate in discussions on the character of the Jews and their suitability as citizens.[1] The present chapter will consider an important yet hitherto little noticed aspect of the ritual system, namely, its role in the formation of a highly structured framework for the realization of the *vita religiosa*. This facet of ritual is intimately related to the realms of meaning, memory, and self-image. Beginning with the research of Gennep, anthropologists and students of popular culture have investigated the various systems devised by traditional communities to make sense of the world and of life's passages.[2] Ranging from religious practices that seek access to the supernatural to any

repetitive, formalized activity that expresses people's social interdepend-
ence, rituals are rules of conduct that guide behavior in the presence of the
sacred and in the domain of the profane. They are valuable sources of cultural history because their signs and symbols offer entrée into the underlying structures of thought that are so deeply rooted in the *mentalités* and
collective identities of group members.[3] The intricacies of ritual life resonated in the social arena as well, as we observed in the previous chapter,
especially in relation to class and gender. Attention to ritual will illustrate
both the breadth of the cultural orbit to which the Jews of Alsace-Lorraine
belonged and the first signs of an autochthonous French-Jewish culture
that would develop more fully after the Revolution. These trends diverged
sharply from the dominant patterns in southern France, where Jewish communities staunchly preserved their own liturgical and ritual traditions, as
the cases of Carpentras and Bayonne aptly reveal.[4]

In the two centuries prior to 1789, the rhythms of Jewish life in Alsace-
Lorraine were largely consistent with the patterns of traditional Ashkenazic
culture then prevalent in central Europe. Modes of Talmud study, rabbinic
peregrinations and appointments, religious customs, marriage patterns,
and liturgical rites indicate that toward the end of the *ancien régime* the area
stretching from Metz in the west to Prague in the east was still a unified cultural entity where the traditions of western Ashkenaz, as distinct from those
of Russia and Poland, were dominant.[5] With the growth of Jewish settlement in the west, these cultural patterns became more firmly entrenched
within a specifically French context. Nevertheless, fluid regional conditions
throughout most of the seventeenth century made it possible for students
in France and Germany to continue to travel to centers of Torah learning
in the east. Earlier in the century Asher Levy, for example, left Metz at the
age of fourteen in order to study in Prague;[6] two generations later, young
men were still traveling eastward. Tuvia Cohen, son of Polish refugee and
Metz *av beit din* R. Moses Cohen Narol, left Metz upon his father's death
(1659) to return to Poland, ostensibly to pursue talmudic studies. The fact
that he attended the University of Frankfurt an der Oder, completed his
medical training at Padua, and subsequently passed through Innsbruck,
Constantinople, and Broussa before finally settling in Jerusalem nonetheless confirms a pervasive trend to seize even distant cultural opportunities.[7]

Travel to far-off destinations in order to attain greater talmudic erudition
continued unabated in the early modern period. Budding scholars, often
driven by an insatiable spirit of adventure in their efforts to master the intricacies of rabbinic learning, moved freely between France and central Europe. The practice of leaving home to engage in Talmud study had been a
time-honored tradition for young scholars—including married men, on occasion—having received unfailing endorsement by contemporary rabbinic
authorities.[8] Young men typically began their studies at a local academy

and then continued at one or more of the major *yeshivot* in central Europe. R. Samuel Heller, son of the famed R. Yom Tov Lipmann Heller of Prague, relates in a memoir that in 1625 he was sent by his father to study in the Metz *yeshivah*, then headed by R. Mordecai b. Moshe Luria. After more than four years, Samuel returned to Prague, "as this was the custom then in these countries, that every *yeshivah* student, whether poor or rich, traveled exclusively by foot, with his clothing bundled on his shoulder and his staff in hand." Wandering from city to city, from *yeshivah* to *yeshivah*, these itinerant young scholars were instrumental in the diffusion of knowledge, *novellae*, books, and manuscripts and thereby served as vital links between centers of Torah study and areas of Jewish settlement. Ultimately, they helped forge a remarkable measure of cultural unity in the regions they traversed. The quest for prospective marriage partners was an additional, if not primary, reason for travel beyond the French borders, necessitated by the small size of Jewish communities in the northeast region. Whatever the precise motivation, these patterns gave expression to, and indeed facilitated, the bonds uniting northeastern France with territories to the east and testify to the dynamic character of this cultural universe.[9]

There is little doubt that the *yeshivah* was the institutional framework most directly responsible for nurturing the learned traditions and halakhic norms of rabbinic Judaism. Its impact on popular attitudes and conduct was decidedly more limited, as we shall see. Whatever its role in the shaping of Jewish culture, the fortunes of the *yeshivah* reflected, to a large degree, the general socioeconomic state of affairs. Owing to the prestige of the Metz *yeshivah* and to relatively secure conditions in Alsace-Lorraine, larger numbers of students were drawn to France in the early and middle decades of the eighteenth century. Though situated on the far periphery of the Ashkenazic world, late seventeenth-century Metz had achieved distinction as a leading center of Torah learning. Its *yeshivah* was well funded and its rabbis were celebrated scholars. Commenting on the relative importance of communities in Germany and Metz, a student of R. Jacob Emden asserted that the Fürth *kehillah* could not compare to Metz, as the latter was "second [only] to Frankfurt in size, quality, and as an ancient community, and its importance even exceeded that of the three communities of Altona, Hamburg, and Wandsback."[10] The prominence of the Metz *kehillah*, an outgrowth of the general economic prosperity in the region, contrasted sharply with conditions in Germany at mid-century. Whereas *yeshivah* students in Frankfurt complained of not being fed, and the Mainz community was forced to limit its support to four poor students, in Metz the student ranks from central and eastern Europe had swelled. The 1766 rabbinic contract of R. Aryeh Loeb Günzberg required the Metz *kehillah* to support twenty-five students; the number of foreign students was at least sixty in 1780.[11] After mid-century a dozen smaller talmudic academies were also es-

tablished throughout Alsace.[12] Although these institutions mainly served
the needs of the local and regional population, they nonetheless added significantly to the cultural vibrancy of the region and almost certainly to its
general attractiveness.

The biography of one Alsatian native vividly exemplifies the pattern of
movement and adventurism of his peers. Born in Ribeauvillé in 1735, Issachar Berr Carmoly first attended the local *yeshivah* and from there went
to Metz to study under the tutelage of R. Jonathan Eibeschütz. Three years
later, after completing the first level of rabbinic studies, he was invited to
Frankfurt am Main by his great-uncle, R. Jacob Poppers, the *av beit din*, to
continue his studies and become acquainted with the German branch of
the family. In Frankfurt, Carmoly studied under R. Jacob Joshua Falk,
renowned author of the *Penei Yehoshua*, but after a year returned to Metz
and resumed his studies with R. Eibeschütz and with R. Samuel Hilman,
Eibeschütz's successor, from whom the young scholar received the title Rav
Ḥaver. He proceeded to Fürth to study under R. David Strauss, subsequently returned to Nancy, and married the daughter of a wealthy *parnas*
of Soultz. Through the influence of his father-in-law, Carmoly was appointed *av beit din*, and some years later established a *yeshivah* in neighboring Jungholtz. He also authored numerous talmudic *novellae*, though most
remained unpublished.[13] His life typifies the patterns of Talmud study and
rabbinic appointments that prevailed in his day, and highlights how Alsace-
Lorraine had become a point of attraction for rabbis and students from the
east.

Several factors account for this development. First, in the early part of
the century Alsace-Lorraine witnessed a dramatic increase in its Jewish population, and the growth remained steady until the Revolution, while a relative decline in the population of Jews in the same period may be discerned
elsewhere on the continent.[14] By 1650 the Jewish population in Alsace increased to approximately 2,000 individuals, and by 1716 the population
rose to about 6,500. According to the census of 1784 there were 3,910 families in Alsace (19,624 individuals) and approximately 5,000 individuals in
the duchy of Lorraine. Although no exact figures are available, immigrants
from Poland, Bohemia, and Moravia filled the ranks of the rapidly increasing Jewish population. The Jewish population of Metz increased rapidly
from a meager four households in 1567 to 166 in 1678, 294 in 1698, and
480 in 1717. The latter figure represents nearly 3,000 individuals, which at
that time was approximately 7 percent of the total population of the city.
By the eve of the Revolution there were approximately 3,500 Jews in Metz
and the surrounding towns and villages.[15] Second, as we have seen, the
Metz community followed a tradition of appointing only rabbis who had no
family residing in the city, in an effort to ensure the independence of its
rabbinic leaders. By recruiting distinguished rabbis from afar, the community was able to enhance its prestige considerably. The occasional hiring of

immigrant rabbis seeking refuge in Alsace and Lorraine, though not a general practice, boosted the stature of those communities as well.[16]

Ritual, Popular Religion, and Kabbalah

The cultural significance of widely practiced rituals in the *ancien régime* may best be appreciated by what they reveal of the dynamics of ethnic heritage and identity, self-image, and memory. A full treatment of these themes demands a thorough investigation of several related issues as well, such as elite culture and folk religion, oral and print culture, and gender. The present state of scholarship on the history of the Jews in modern France cannot, at this juncture, sustain this ambitious research agenda. For now, it will have to suffice to consider those aspects of elite and popular religion that are relevant to the larger themes of our investigation; detailed sources pertaining to gender and religion in this period are more limited, and this important area of concern must await future investigation.

It is in the realm of religious custom and law that the strong attachment of communities of Alsace-Lorraine to the western Ashkenazic heritage was most apparent. Ritual life centered on divine worship, the study of the Torah, and the performance of acts of kindness. Broadly defined, worship included a system of divinely ordained rites (*mitzvot*) designed to position human nature, needs, and instincts in a religiously and spiritually meaningful context. Daily rites took the form of benedictions recited upon rising and before retiring, prior to partaking of food, and in advance of any obligatory act. Most rituals were performed in the home, which was considered the principal arena for divine service alongside the synagogue. Formal prayer and rites of passage such as circumcision, bar mitzvah, naming of children, marriage, and death were generally conducted in the synagogue because of their public nature. By its presence at such ceremonies, the community acknowledged and affirmed in each instance the passage to a new status. The central elements of synagogue worship positioned the biblical declaration of faith in the God of Israel, the conception of reward and punishment, the primacy of *mitzvot*, petitional prayer, and the public reading of the Torah within a framework devoted to the theme of redemptive history. In contrast to the domain of the home, where women were vitally involved in family rituals, active participation in the public ritual of the synagogue was limited to men.

Major and minor festivals played a crucial role in the life of the community. In addition to the Sabbath, the calendar listed three pilgrimage holidays (Passover, Shavuot, and Sukkot), the days of repentance (Rosh Hashanah and Yom Kippur), Ḥanukkah, Purim, the New Moon (Rosh Ḥodesh), and several fasts marking the destruction of the ancient Temple in Jerusalem. Originally conceived as agricultural festivals marking the beginning of spring, the summer harvest, and the conclusion of the harvest season, the pilgrimage holidays evolved into commemorations of important events in Israel's early history. The narrative focusing on the exodus from Egypt at the Passover seder was an especially paradigmatic rite of memory. Festivals and fasts provided a framework both for understanding contemporary developments in a national-historical perspective and for reassessing the significance of earlier events in light of the present. Ritualized remembering fashioned the national character of the Jewish people and forged its religious ideals. At the social level, the festivals fostered a strong collective identity by bringing ordinary people and elites together in common rituals.

The study of the Torah was viewed in the classical tradition as a devotional act comprising a balanced curriculum of Scripture, Mishnah, and Talmud. Medieval Franco-German practice modified this injunction in favor of the exclusive study of Talmud, whereas Sephardic authorities encouraged the broader course of study. Medieval and early modern authorities also debated whether Torah study ought to be combined with philosophical inquiry, mystical speculation, and other branches of knowledge such as the natural sciences and humanistic studies. Although the ideal of Torah study as a lifelong pursuit was incumbent upon all Jews, this was realized only rarely in practice. Women were generally viewed as exempt from the obligation to engage in Torah study, but there is abundant historical evidence of their involvement in the study of the Bible and those sections of the rabbinic tradition pertinent to ritual observance. With the possible exception of early modern Poland, where Talmudic learning had become relatively widespread, study remained an activity of a relatively small number. The performance of acts of kindness (*gemilut ḥasadim*), conversely, was grounded in a comparatively broad base of popular involvement. Rabbinic tradition derived its theoretical and practical dimensions from several biblical passages, concluding that one is enjoined to imitate God's moral attributes (*Sotah* 14a). Providing assistance to the needy was viewed as a crucial human-divine partnership in the perfection of the world. These efforts found expression in the creation of confraternities and societies for free loans, needy brides, visitation of the sick, burial, and consolation of the bereaved. Not infrequently, however, religious and moral idealism was compromised by financial strain, interethnic tensions, and an anti-poor bias that intensified in response to the growing number of beggars in the seventeenth and eighteenth centuries.

As in other traditional cultures, French Jews observed a host of rituals marking birth, marriage, and death. Such liminal moments were interpreted as times of crisis when individuals were exposed to demonic powers. Rituals aiming to counter these forces while warding off attendant fears and anxieties were abundant in the village life of rural Alsace and Lorraine, as they were in neighboring Germany. They were widely viewed as a means to impose order over chaos and as an antidote against exposure to the hazards of everyday life. Whether they also signify contact with popular religion and culture in the countryside is not at all clear. The fact that, as a rule, the Jews of early modern Alsace and Lorraine related to royal, regional, and municipal authorities with considerable trepidation, showed little interest in general culture, and had limited social interaction with fellow villagers and townspeople does not, itself, disprove the possibility of cultural influence. Instances of convergence between Jewish and general folk traditions have, paradoxically, occurred in periods when the social distance separating Jew and non-Jew was most pronounced. In northeastern France, Jews plainly shared with their non-Jewish neighbors an assessment of the world as a dangerous place controlled by mischievous spirits, but this perception need not have come from the outside. There are many possible sources of influence from within the Jewish tradition itself, as is evident from the pervasive belief in demonology, magic, and incantations that were "embedded in the rabbinic mind" and preserved in the concepts and imagery of the Kabbalah.[17]

Manifestations of folk religion in late medieval and early modern Ashkenaz emerged alongside the normative system of Halakhah. Initially transmitted orally, its ritual forms developed in response to the stresses and strains of daily life. Though conceivably distinct from text-based rituals of the rabbinic tradition, popular religious culture was rarely detached completely from literary sources. In due course, numerous protective rites and folkways coalesced with textual traditions, typically prompting the reinterpretation of biblical, midrashic, and talmudic sources. More often than not, the result was an amalgam of elite and popular religion, characterized not so much by internal dichotomy but by functional accord.[18] Childbirth is a case in point. In light of high infant mortality rates, bearing children was a particularly frightening experience. In eighteenth-century France, approximately 25 percent of newborns did not survive the first year, and more than 40 percent failed to reach the age of five.[19] According to popular belief, evil spirits dangerously lurked about mother and baby, and therefore the use of incantations and amulets, especially against Lilith, aimed to protect mother and baby. Emblematic of the region was the wearing of amulets of mineral and vegetable origin, the placing of a piece of iron in the delivery room as an anti-demonic device, the display of an article of the husband's clothing, and the tying of amulets made of snakeskin to the childbed.[20] To gain instruction in the preparation of amulets, including one for childbirth, men (and women) could typically consult *Sefer Raziel*, an especially popular manual published in Amsterdam in 1701 and reprinted nearly forty times. The book's popularity was no doubt enhanced by its traditional rabbinic style and air of authenticity, seeing as it drew upon Heikhalot and Merkabah mysticism, the literature of Hasidei Ashkenaz, and the mystical doctrines of pre-Lurianic Kabbalah.[21]

In a similar fashion, the custom of having pregnant women bite off the

tip of the *etrog* (citron) and recite special psalms to relieve the pain of childbirth drew upon talmudic and medieval halakhic sources linking the in-
gestion of the *etrog* with fertility. The custom thus gained legitimacy by
having been incorporated within the rabbinic tradition.[22] After giving
birth, women customarily remained in their homes for approximately
thirty days, refraining from performing such rites as baking *ḥallah*, lighting
the Sabbath candles, engaging in prayer, and reciting grace after meals. According to the book of customs compiled by R. Juspa Shamash of seventeenth-century Worms, the mother did not leave her house until the fourth
or fifth week after giving birth, attended by companions throughout the
period. From the onset of labor, a protective circle was symbolically marked
around the parturient's bed; each night, for the next four weeks, the
woman staying with the mother would wave an iron sword—symbol of the
biblical matriarchs—around the mother's head, reciting incantations to
protect mother and baby from demons. After approximately a month, the
mother would ceremoniously attend the synagogue. This ritual, which became popular only toward the latter part of the sixteenth century, bore
striking similarity to the Catholic rite of "churching." It points to the likelihood of social interaction between Jewish and Christian women; differences between them imply a conscious effort on the part of the Jewish
practitioners to separate their own ritual from the gentile rite.[23] Related to
this were several additional customs: the Wachnacht ceremony to ward off
evil spirits the night before the circumcision; the lighting of an oil lamp
(Jidschkerz) by women friends of the new mother three days preceding
and following the circumcision; and the Hollekreisch ritual, in which
adults and children gathered around the cradle of the newborn on the afternoon when the mother came to the synagogue for the first time, to as-
sign the baby a secular (*ḥol*) name. Despite their dubious origins, the latter
customs found their way into the *regimen vitae* and thereby gained considerable respectability in most quarters.[24]

Prayer books compiled in eighteenth-century Metz contain compelling
evidence of the fusion of elite and popular religious trends. Liturgical collections helped shape and sustain the traditional worldview of the Jews of
Alsace-Lorraine. The printed prayer book offered crucial guidance for the
attainment of ritual literacy and the deepening of religious belief. This is illustrated by the important role that prayer books played in the dissemination of kabbalistic customs and lore.[25] As in the case of the *siddur* published
in 1765, the Metz prayer books typically included entire sections of the kabbalistic *Tikkunei Shabbat* and selections from Lurianic *minhagim*, thus serving as a prime conduit for the diffusion of Lurianic Kabbalah.[26] Readers of
the Metz *siddur* were urged to perform a range of Lurianic practices such
as ritual immersion on each Sabbath eve and the study of the weekly Torah
portion with the corresponding sections of the *Zohar*. Passages from the
Zohar were adduced as support for wearing special clothing on the Sabbath

and for lighting the Sabbath candles. Also included were instructions concerning the attainment of the proper intention in Sabbath worship, especially when reciting the psalm for the Sabbath day, in order to neutralize or destroy the harmful husks of evil (*kelipot*); worshippers were also urged to focus on welcoming the *Shekhinah* (Divine Presence) when reciting the last stanza of the *Lekha Dodi* with the approach of the Sabbath. At the departure of the Sabbath, individuals were advised to read the entire Torah portion of the coming week, "because by so doing one beckons the abundance (*shefa*) of the approaching Sabbath."[27] In addition, assorted *tehinot* were reproduced in the *siddur*, including petitions for men whose wives were in labor. Instructions for the performance of the widely practiced *tashlikh* and *kapparot* penitential ceremonies were included as well—despite strong rabbinic opposition—thereby suggesting that the disjuncture between popular and elite religion was mostly theoretical.[28]

The proliferation of Lurianic rites and customs in eighteenth-century Alsace and Lorraine is attested by a wide array of evidence. A responsum written in 1718 by Metz *dayyan* R. Gershon Koblentz referred to a local group that assembled regularly for midnight vigils, according to Lurianic custom, in order to engage in ecstatic prayer, study, and mourn the destruction of Jerusalem. Unable to find fault with the practice, since the group constituted, in its own right, a "community," but still hesitant to lend his formal approval, R. Gershon recommended that the group refrain from meeting in the synagogue. His ruling was issued in deference to the local opposition that the pietists encountered. The opponents, clearly, could not be ignored, though the suggested change in venue evidently satisfied them.[29] Later in the century, a prayer composed in honor of Louis XVI and Marie Antoinette by the cantor in Niederhagental, Hayyim Plotsk, confirms the explicit penetration of Lurianic images and concepts into the formal synagogue ritual. The first part of the prayer is a typical appeal to God on behalf of the royal family;[30] this is followed by seven short petitions, similar in style and structure to the traditional prayers for rain and dew, requesting that God recall the merit of the patriarchs, prophets, and kings of Israel. Part 3, an entreaty to God to answer their prayers, contains the following language: "And in the merit of the holy names of this psalm [Ps. 20], and their vowels, words, letters, and meanings, will [God] protect us and destroy all of the thorns that encircle the supernal *Shoshanah*." By referring to the protective *"TaNTA"* that he enlisted to defeat the "thorns," that is, the *kelipot* that besiege the *Shekhinah,* the author employed familiar Lurianic imagery. An immigrant from Poland, Plotsk found both a receptive audience for these kabbalistic images in Alsace and a sympathetic ear in the rabbi of Sierentz, who formally approved the inclusion of the prayer in the daily service.[31]

Frequent autobiographical notations in R. Aaron Worms's *Me'orei Or* (Metz, 1789–1831) further confirm the proliferation of Lurianic rites in mid-eighteenth-century Alsace. Consisting of highly original and learned interpretations of talmudic and halakhic texts, *Me'orei Or* represents the single most extensive discussion of ritual practices observed in Alsace-Lorraine. Worms (1754–1836) was arguably the foremost rabbinic scholar in France in the revolutionary era, although he failed to gain a reputation comparable to that of his more senior colleague, R. David Sintzheim. Born in a village near Sarrelouis, he pursued his talmudic studies locally and later in the Metz *yeshivah* during the years when the renowned R. Aryeh Loeb Günzberg headed the institution.[32] He conceded that as a boy in the village of Geislautern, he felt the powerful attraction of Lurianic rituals and that he learned to recite kabbalistic prayers referring to the *parzufim* (the divine configurations) by heart.[33] Later, "when I served as a rabbi in the countryside and stayed in the villages, I observed the practice of twelve loaves according to the plain meaning of the midrash [Zohar]." In 1777 he composed a kabbalistic prayer book that included both commentary and detailed instructions for the execution of the zoharic *kavvanot* (mystical meditations); though never published, it signaled the depth of the author's preoccupation with Kabbalah.[34] Respectful of kabbalistic traditions even when they appeared inconsistent with Ashkenazic practice, his reverence for the *Zohar* and zoharic customs was unequivocal.[35] Worms frequently turned to the *Zohar* to authenticate either a custom needing a textual basis or a novel explanation that he had developed independently,[36] or to explain a talmudic passage in light of a difficult question of a later authority.[37] His deference for kabbalistic practices diverged substantially from the strident criticism voiced by major rabbinic figures of central and western Europe. R. Ezekiel Landau, R. Jacob Emden, and R. Jonathan Eibeschütz rejected the popular study of Kabbalah, opposed the dissemination of kabbalistic texts among the masses, and deplored the proliferation of kabbalistic practices. Their opposition was doubtless motivated both by fear that the nascent Hasidic movement might well precipitate the revival of a dormant Sabbatianism and out of concern for the possible distortion of the esoteric doctrines of the Kabbalah, as the introduction to R. Joseph Steinhardt's responsa, *Zikhron Yosef*, explicitly warned.[38]

Worms's disapproval of Lurianic customs assumed several forms. He insisted that the performance of most Lurianic practices was unwise because they were intended for *medakdekim kedoshim* (rigorously pious) but not for *beinonim* (ordinary individuals). He objected to the publication of the *Tikkunei Shabbat* and various kabbalistic formulae (for example, *leshem yihud* and *yehi ratzon*) that many recited before performing certain rituals, claiming that the Lurianic *kavvanot* were meant to remain unspoken. These, he asserted, were never intended for "*beinonim* such as us." In the *siddur* that he had compiled, Worms reported that he included "all the prayers according to the *Zohar* and [zoharic] *kavvanot*" but that he avoided "*kavvanat ha-yihudim ve-zivvugim*" (prayers for the unification of the divine emanations) because there were "none in our time who are worthy of [reciting] them, especially outside of the Land [of Israel]." On the basis of the foregoing distinction between zoharic and post-zoharic traditions, Worms was at once able to endorse kabbalistic modes of worship while urging his community to avoid Lurianic prayer.[39] In several instances he applied the argument concerning the elitist character of Lurianism specifically to rituals as well. Lurianic customs such as refraining from conjugal relations on the night of Shavuot or hiding the thumb during prayer were, in his view, intended for the spiritually elite only, not for the rank and file.[40] In the same vein, he regarded swaying during prayer (na'anuei tefilah) as a custom reflecting the profound kavvanot of the medakdekim but not the simple prayer of beinonim. His view was in direct opposition to the Hasidic interpretation, which likened a person's soul to a flame that flickers in the light; according to Israel Ba'al Shem Tov this image reveals how swaying, insofar as it causes arousal and enthusiasm, enables the soul to unite with the Shekhinah. Worms argued that prayer requires a state of physical serenity (menuḥat ha-guf) and, citing the Zohar and Ḥemdat Yamim, asserted that swaying is proper only when reading the Torah. He interpreted the silence of these same sources in reference to prayer, as well as the distinction drawn by early Ashkenazic authorities between swaying during study and prayer, as proof that body movement was meant to be limited.[41]

Although the main objection to Lurianic prayer was its elitist character, the general rejection of Lurianic rituals tended to be more substantive. They were inauthentic, Worms maintained, because they either lacked a talmudic foundation or were not mentioned in the Zohar.[42] Accordingly, he described the stringency transmitted in the name of R. Isaac Luria not to drink water before performing the havdalah ceremony at the close of the Sabbath as "fine for Hasidim, but not for us, because it is arrogant to act against the view of the Talmud and poseqim (halakhic authorities)."[43] In fact, he objected strongly to any practice that flouted the halakhic consensus.[44] He characterized the custom appearing in R. Isaiah Horowitz's Shenei Luḥot Ha-Berit, a book of sermons based on Lurianic doctrines, to observe additional fast days as an unauthorized invention. Similarly, he rejected the Lurianic practice of reading the Torah portion normally reserved for a public fast on the day preceding Rosh Ḥodesh (which followers of Luria treated as a mini Day of Atonement) and disputed the authority of the Lurianic nocturnal rituals (tikkun ḥaẓot) for lack of foundation in the Zohar.[45] Concerning another custom ascribed to Horowitz—to recite a biblical verse beginning and ending with the first and last letters of one's name at the end of the Amidah prayer—Worms used a different strategy. Since there was no basis for such a rite in either the Talmud or the Zohar, he averred, it was, technically, an unacceptable interruption. Nevertheless, for those who insisted on following the practice, Worms conceded that one could utter the verse after stepping back, immediately before reciting the *yehi razon* supplication at the very end of the *Amidah.* In cases such as this, when the custom had become popular and could not be easily defeated, Worms endeavored to reign in kabbalistic practices within the framework of Halakhah.[46] Worms's willingness to adopt an unorthodox interpretation of a zoharic custom, as in the case of the twelve loaves kabbalists require at each Sabbath meal, was consistent with this approach. He modified the Lurianic practice, preferring to divide the twelves loaves among the three Sabbath meals; only later did he discover that the modification had already appeared in *Yosef Omez.*[47] Worms's notion of authentic kabbalistic praxis was rooted in a *Zohar* that was stripped away from its layers of commentary.[48]

As in the case of Lurianic Kabbalah, the pervasive reliance on folk wisdom and accompanying expressions of popular piety were viewed in the west as inconsistent with the burgeoning rationalist tradition of the second half of the eighteenth century. This critical posture is plainly evident in Worms's efforts to discredit a host of customs based on superstition, misunderstanding, linguistic corruption, and textual error. His displeasure was part of a larger trend that dated from the early seventeenth century, with the composition of the *siddur* of Shabbethai Sofer of Przemsyl. The demand for more reliable versions of *siddurim* was clearly prompted by the need to correct errors and inconsistencies introduced and circulated by the invention of printing.[49] This need was more keenly felt in light of the migration patterns and greater geographical mobility in early modern Europe. Liturgical traditions that had formerly remained distinct now converged, and the growing accumulation of textual errors could no longer be overlooked.

Worms was one of several rabbinic and lay scholars for whom the notion of textual precision had become absolutely imperative. He strongly deplored errors that had found their way into the liturgy and devoted himself to correcting numerous instances of careless and incorrect pronunciation that had become commonplace among Ashkenazic Jewry. He also took exception to certain well-established liturgical formulations, asserting that their unintelligibility was the result of printing or copyist mistakes[50] or errors in understanding,[51] and objected to customs that had become prevalent in rural areas, such as the incorrect division of the Torah reading on Sabbath mornings.[52] He vehemently objected to liturgical imagery such as *Makhnisei Rahamim* ("Ushers of Mercy") and the *kavvanot* that were commonly recited during the sounding of the *shofar* because he was unwilling to countenance any prayer appealing to the intercession of angels.[53] In the case of the morning benediction *shelo 'asani goi* ("who has not made me a gentile"), Worms urged replacing it with *she'asani Yisrael* ("who has made me a Jew") because the scriptural connotation of the word *goi* was much broader than the conventional usage and included the nation of Israel as well. Accordingly, the expression *she-lo 'asani goi* could be viewed as nonsensical and, technically, an "unnecessary blessing." It is also not unlikely that heightened concerns about Judaism's attitude toward gentiles in postrevolutionary France added weight to this semantic argument and to the fact that the recommended change accorded with the time-honored rite in Worms and Frankfurt.[54]

Resting firmly on the primacy of reason, Worms's indisputably iconoclastic views were fueled by a sustained inquiry into the channels of ritual transmission. His method drew inspiration from the rationalist-halakhic tradition associated with Rav Hai Gaon and from his own great-grandfather, R. Gershon Ashkenazi, who insisted on discarding any practice that violated reason.[55] Commenting on the *Shulḥan Arukh*'s list of dangerous behaviors that one is obliged to avoid, Worms asserted that these directives were unfounded and therefore could be safely ignored, because "nothing may be invented following the era of the Talmud and midrashim." Although he may have overstated the preeminent authority of talmudic and midrashic sources, his stance routinely evinced an impatience with certain rituals of the medieval period and in this respect resembled several central arguments of the Protestant Reformation and early nineteenth-century liberal Judaism. In the specific case of the *kapparot* rite performed on the eve of Yom Kippur, Worms repeated the claims of R. Moses Nahmanides and R. Solomon Ibn Aderet that the ritual was an Amorite custom, and likewise condemned the *tashlikh* ceremony as a corruption of the zoharic practice of pouring water in order to recall the obligation of repentance. In this respect he distanced himself from the Lurianic embrace of the two ceremonies, a position that had wide ramifications.[56]

Central to this approach to ritual was an appreciation for the process of historical development. Elaborating on the gaonic claim that the purpose of certain restrictions was to frighten people to repent, Worms asserted that the *kapparot* and *tashlikh* ceremonies were invented in order to instill greater piety among the masses, before printing facilitated the wide distribution of ethical books (*sifrei musar*); the interweaving of biblical verses with these rites was intended to lend them a measure of religious authenticity that would otherwise be absent. Similarly, he was disturbed by the popular use of amulets for general protection, childbirth, and infertility, particularly "those clothed in rabbinic dress." While conceding that there were reliable talmudic remedies for various ailments, he asserted that access was no longer available to them because "the correct formulas and the correct intention have disappeared in our generation."[57] Clearly unable to impugn the authority of the Talmud, Worms effectively dismissed its medical doctrines as irrelevant.

These critical views extended to the realm of rabbinic authority as well. In contrast to colleagues who, in their struggle against modernity, armed themselves with broader powers, Worms considered such efforts an abuse of rabbinic authority. His objections centered on the overuse of the communal ban (*ḥerem*), frequently issued at the whim of rabbinic authorities

rather than out of concern for the public welfare. As an instrument of social and religious control, the ban had been formally suspended before
the Revolution, but its continued deployment by individual rabbis had become the target of ridicule, especially when it was issued to enforce the
copyright of newly published *siddurim* and *maḥzorim.* Infringement on authors' rights, Worms insisted, was a violation of the prohibition of *hasagat
gevul* (trespass), and therefore to impose the *ḥerem* in such cases was an halakhic blunder. The source of this criticism was a general uneasiness over
the potentially negative effects of rabbinic imprudence on the public
image of Halakhah.[58]

This latter concern, like the aforementioned expressions of dissatisfaction with certain ritual practices, went hand-in-hand with Worms's vigorous
reactions to the Haskalah's ridicule of traditional observance. He attributed the disrespect for such measures as rabbinic authorization to carry on
the Sabbath, and to take interest on loans (*eruvei hazerot* and *heter isqa*) to
ignorance and misunderstanding, which he believed could be overcome
with more careful explanation.[59] However, in other areas it is clear that
Worms did not dismiss the criticism of the *maskilim* as entirely lacking justification. He agreed that the inclination toward excessive stringency was a
distortion of the halakhic tradition.[60] For example, he was critical of those
who refrained from eating items baked from "*matzah* flour" as unnecessar-
ily pious because, from a strictly legal standpoint, once flour is baked as
matzah, no further leavening can occur. He conceded that at one time the
observance of this stringency may have been necessary in the case of thick
matzot, since they might contain grains of uncooked flour, but this was no
longer a problem.[61] He was also opposed to the formal sale of leaven
(*ḥametz*) to gentiles, a practice he labeled an "overwhelming deception."
The popular preoccupation with the sale of an entire storehouse of wheat,
barley, and crops, even though there was no actual leaven there, exemplified, in his view, a tendency to be stringent in inconsequential matters and
lenient in more serious ones.[62] In the case of delayed burial, a cause
célèbre for *maskilim* throughout Europe, Worms limited the prohibition
against leaving the dead unburied to cases of execution by the *bet din*, concluding that in all other instances greater caution ought to be exercised in
the examination of the deceased.[63]

Nor did customs that were enshrined in folklore escape criticism. Referring to the popular understanding of "Elijah's cup" customarily placed at
the center of the Passover seder table as a children's tale, Worms surmised
that the cup was originally intended as a large dispenser to facilitate access
to the wine by all assembled.[64] Over the course of generations, however, the
spiritual symbolism of the prophet Elijah displaced the original meaning of
the custom. Worms similarly denounced the recitation of the *kavvanot* accompanying the sounding of the *shofar*, remarking that "matters such as
this that have no foundation in the Talmud and *midrashim* [only] give

greater weight to the burden [of criticism] by those who mock (*ha-mal'igim*) [us]."[65] Worms's reference to *ha-mal'igim* reveals an awareness of the campaign mounted against certain rituals, while the fact that he responded to these attacks seriously may be taken as an acknowledgment that the criticism was not entirely unfounded. In his view, the criticism stemming from *maskilim* and reformers demanded of traditionalists higher standards of precision in the transmission and explication of ritual traditions, as well as a measure of self-consciousness that was previously unknown.[66]

Between Local and Regional Rites

The image of a unified geographical landscape of western Ashkenaz found expression in concrete halakhic terms. Joint efforts by communities on either side of the Rhine to resolve severe conflicts involving communal institutions and leadership offer further evidence of the degree to which northeastern France and Germany were virtually indistinguishable sectors of the same cultural and religious universe. From the seventeenth century, it was not uncommon for rabbis of the northeast region of France to consult with colleagues in Germany on halakhic matters. In one instance early in the century, internal opposition to the methods of governance and election of officers in the Jewish community of Frankfurt am Main resulted in a rift that could not be healed to the satisfaction of all parties concerned. Three rabbis—from Fulda, Hildesheim, and Metz—were invited to decide between the two parties. In the following century, the Frankfurt *beit din* itself was asked to give its judgment to resolve the bitter conflict between Rabbis Lehmann and Sintzheim. From these instances of collaboration, it is clear that major communities in Alsace and Metz not only belonged to the same world as those of western and central Europe but stood on equal footing as well.[67]

More explicit proof of regional unity is furnished by the example of the provincial *beit din* of the county of Hanau-Lichtenberg. Located in Bouxwiller (Bas Rhin), the authority of the *beit din* extended to twenty-eight communities on both sides of the Rhine.[68] For R. Joseph Steinhardt, who became *av beit din* of the Fürth community and head of its *yeshivah* in 1763 after having served in a similar capacity in the Alsatian community of Niedernai, proximity to the Rhine was the defining characteristic of the region and carried important implications for ritual observance. Responding to a query from Alsace, he asserted "that without any doubt, our land (*medinatenu*) is known as [that of] *benei Rheinus* (residents of the Rhineland), since the land (*ha-medinah*) is entirely along the banks of the Rhine," a definition that presupposed a measure of halakhic uniformity for communities throughout the region. Here, according to Steinhardt's usage, the term *medinah* had a broader connotation than the more commonly used reference to the communities of Alsace only. He evidently conceived of an expansive *medinah* to convey a sense of the wider juridical and ritual patterns in the region. In theory, then, the same customs concerning marriage and divorce, for example, would prevail, regardless of where in the Rhineland a particular ceremony, or dispute, had taken place.[69]

By employing the phrase *benei Rheinus*, Steinhardt's assertion of regional uniformity implied a continuous tradition going back at least four centuries.[70] Though intended to support his ritual and halakhic decisions, his assertion clearly could not be borne out historically. It should be noted, further, that the unity of northeastern France with Germany was undeterred by the diversity of *minhagim* throughout the region. A central feature in the world of medieval Ashkenaz, diversity was an expression of the importance placed on the cultural autonomy of the city (or town) and its environs. Differences between the liturgical rites of eighteenth-century Metz and those of cities in the Upper Rhine were no less significant than, for instance, those that divided Metz and Frankfurt.[71] In fact, in the case of Metz it has been observed that the community's orientation was not to the east but more to the north, toward Germany, and to a lesser extent toward Holland.[72] Overall, cultural pluralism was legitimized by the preference for local custom over regional uniformity, provided that it was consistent with the broad cultural and halakhic framework of the Ashkenazic tradition. It is thus clear from linguistic patterns, rabbinic appointments, liturgical traditions, and the general evidence of *minhagim* that Jewish life in Alsace-Lorraine was an integral part of a cultural and religious tradition that transcended the eastern border of France.

The halakhic underpinnings of these cultural and religious trends are evident in R. Worms's critique of broader developments in Jewish law. Worms argued that in his glosses to the *Shulḥan Arukh*, R. Moses Isserles had given undue weight to Polish *minhagim* and only insufficient attention to classical Ashkenazic sources; as a result, the customs he assembled were often inconsistent with usages observed in communities west of Prague. With this assault on Isserles's preeminence—virtually unquestioned by the mid-eighteenth century—Worms boldly endeavored to reclaim the western tradition to which Alsace-Lorraine and Germany had maintained strong historic ties. His efforts to rescue the classical Ashkenazic liturgy from its progressive abandonment and neglect in the preceding centuries were built on an explicit preference for the legacy of Rabbi Jacob Moellin (Maharil) of Mainz (ca. 1360–1427). In his words, "[W]e of Ashkenaz follow the Maharil . . . who is the quintessence of Ashkenaz."[73] Thus, against Isserles, he preferred the view of Maharil requiring the inclusion of the Priestly Benediction in the silent *Amidah*, provided there was a *minyan* present. Likewise, he insisted on the recitation of *Hallel* (Psalms 113–118) in the synagogue on the first nights of Passover, and he defended the standard Ashkenazic custom of substituting alternate benedictions on the Days of Awe for those normally recited throughout the year.[74] In order to authenticate Ashkenazic rites in an era when their validity was being challenged, Worms drew textual support from classical talmudic and halakhic sources. For example, he noted the clash between the custom in the Metz region to fulfill the obligation of *tosefet Yom ha-Kippurim*, that is, adding to the length of Yom Kippur, *before* the day actually begins, and "the Polish custom adduced by Isserles," to add onto the *end* of the fast day. Likewise, he objected to Isserles's claim that one may not recite the penitential *seliḥot* without a *minyan* and insisted that according to Ashkenazic usage as had been practiced in Alsace and Metz, the proper time to recite the evening prayers was before nightfall. Similar examples can be observed regularly in *Me'orei Or*.[75]

If the region's liturgical rites confirm that the Jews of Alsace-Lorraine viewed themselves as part of the broader heritage of western Ashkenaz, they also offer indications of a competing, local identity. The titles of two Metz prayer books, the *Seder Tefilah ke-Minhag Ashkenaz* (1765) and the *Maḥzor ke-Minhag Ashkenaz u-Folin* (1768), bear out clearly that neither one embodied the Metz ritual exclusively but embraced the broader Ashkenazic tradition. They contain all of the standard elements of the Ashkenazic liturgy, such as *Ma'arivim*, that is, poetic embellishments that were inserted, especially in the west, in the two benedictions preceding and following the festival evening Shema.[76] Distinctions between eastern and western rites are particularly evident in the Metz Yom Kippur *Maḥzor*. For example, only the first half of the alphabetically arranged *piyyut Ya'aleh* was recited in the west, in contrast to the custom in Poland where the *piyyut* was said in its entirety; similarly, the order of *Shome'a Tefilah Adekha* recited in Metz conformed to the western tradition. Conversely, certain *piyyutim* that were commonly recited in Poland, such as *Imru l'Elohim* and *Ma'aseh Elohenu*, were not included in the Metz editions.[77]

One feature of the Metz prayer books—the incorporation of the distinctive rites observed in Ashkenaz, Frankfurt, and Poland alongside the corresponding local *rituel*—calls attention to the wider cultural implications of liturgical compendia. The unusual format permitted the inclusion of liturgical variants likely to satisfy the needs of the diverse local population continually augmented by the ease of movement between France and Germany and by the growing presence of immigrants and yeshivah students from points further east. The Metz volumes evinced the sociocultural variegation and geographical mobility characteristic of large communities, and doubtless gained a decided market advantage over *siddurim* and *maḥzorim* that customarily incorporated only one or two variant rites.[78] In an era characterized by considerable population movement, it is also clear that liturgical variants functioned as markers of identity in heterogeneous communities. At the same time, the self-image of communities in northeastern France as culturally undifferentiated from their counterparts to the east was a clear reflection of general political and economic conditions. Until the collapse of the *ancien régime*, Alsace-Lorraine and Franche-Comté remained virtually detached from the interior of France because of customs restrictions, while trade with foreign countries was unhampered.[79] Smaller towns and villages were, as a rule, inclined to tolerate less diversity in ritual matters. Which liturgical rite a particular community might observe could depend on long-established tradition or, conversely, on the personal custom of the local rabbinic authority. The fact that mid-century Ribeauvillé adopted the *rituel* of Frankfurt following the arrival of its newly elected rabbi, Süssel Moïse Enosch, suggests that local traditions were not sufficiently entrenched to forestall innovation of this sort. By contrast, when faced with a similar situation in 1766, the community leadership of Metz firmly rejected an effort by Rabbi Aryeh Loeb Günzberg to alter the manner of reciting the *Aqdamut* hymn on the Shavuot festival because it contravened local custom. In Metz the custom was to recite *Aqdamut* immediately after the first verse of the day's Torah reading, in conformity with the view of Maharil, whereas Günzberg, like other rabbinic authorities, preferred that the hymn be read first in order to avoid an unnecessary interruption. Insulted by this rebuff, Günzberg refused to ever preach in that particular synagogue again.[80]

If only symbolically, the abrupt resolution of the Günzberg incident challenged the dominant paradigm of halakhic pluralism that reigned in western and central Europe.[81] The publication of a large core of commonly recited prayers and the inclusion of liturgical variants in the same volume had all attested to the broad religious culture in which Metz shared. However, the *siddurim* of Alsace and Metz also contain evidence of distinctive traditions that these communities steadfastly upheld. According to the earliest edition of *Seliḥot mi-kol Ha-Shanah ke-Minhag Elsass* (1691), the Alsatian rite originated as *minhag Colmar* and was observed by Rabbi David Sulzburg, *av beit din* and head of the *yeshivah* in Breisach.[82] Aside from this single collection of *seliḥot*, however, no other compendium of Alsatian liturgical traditions is extant, and there are no indications that a distinct rite was preserved. Conversely, while Metz knew of no distinct order of *seliḥot*,[83] clear evidence of local customs is interspersed throughout the series of *siddurim* and *maḥzorim* published by the local press. Copious notations indicated where the Metz customs diverged from the Frankfurt, Ashkenaz, Polish, or Amsterdam rite,[84] and detailed instructions guided the worshipper in the proper order of the *piyyutim*,[85] the correct manner of recitation (for example, where to begin, or if a *piyyut* is to be said responsively), and the replacement of commonly recited *piyyutim* with variants deemed preferable by local custom.[86] Several other practices were unique to Metz. The morning benediction *Magbiah Shefalim* was recited in Metz and in only a handful of other localities, though it was often identified as a specifically Metz custom.[87] In the case of deferred news of the death of a parent received on *ḥol ha-mo'ed* (intermediate days of a festival), the Metz practice was to wait until after the end of the festival before rending one's garment. This varied with the prevailing Ashkenazic custom to perform the ritual on *ḥol ha-mo'ed* for parents but not for other family members. In Poland, it was customary to rend garments for any relative who had died.[88] In a number of areas of Jewish law, Aaron Worms cited local traditions preserved in the writings of his father, R. Abraham Aberlé Worms, and his mentors, R. Isaac Netter of Bouxwiller and R. Leib Gugenheim.[89]

Rites of remembering further elucidate the construction of Metz Jewry's collective identity. A special memorial prayer composed by Rabbi Moses Cohen Narol, a refugee from Poland who was appointed *av beit din* of Metz in 1649, reveals an unusual effort to embrace the memory of Jews murdered in the Chmielnicki massacres. The adoption of the prayer by the Metz *kehillah* reveals the sense of intercommunal unity that pervaded Jewish consciousness; the author, using the metaphor of a single organism, asserted at the end of his elegy that "[all] communities are united as one person." Perhaps more remarkable than R. Narol's initiative, however, is the fact that the Metz community continued to recite the prayer twice a year for at least two centuries. Moreover, by choosing to remember the Chmielnicki victims on the Sabbaths preceding Shavuot and Tisha b' Av— the same Sabbaths when it was customary throughout Ashkenaz to recall the memory of the Crusader martyrs—the Metz community conflated the two catastrophes into a single rite of remembrance, incorporating it among other distinct rites performed locally. Of all the communities beyond Poland, only Metz and Venice recited elegies that were composed locally.[90] More specific to local history was the fast observed by Metz Jews on 25 Tevet to commemorate the anniversary of the burning of Raphaël Lévy, falsely accused of ritual murder in 1669.[91] The trope linking past suffering with contemporary deaths and persecution continued into the nineteenth century. In the *Yizkorbuch* (memorial book) of the Haguenau community the names of victims of the Damascus blood libel were recorded alongside the list of previous martyrs, beginning with the era of the Crusades. Similarly, the 1798 *Memorbuch* of Dornach (in Haute-Alsace) included memorial prayers for victims of religious persecution in Germany, Austria, Bohemia, Spain, Holland, and Poland, and for heads of *yeshivot*; special memorial prayers were also recited for Rabbenu Gershom, Rashi, R. Jacob Tam, R. Meir of Rothenburg, and R. Israel ben Petaḥiya, among others.[92]

In the Throes of Change

Conditions in Alsace and Lorraine were already in a state of flux approximately two decades before the Revolution. Following the tenure of Rabbis Eibeschütz and Hilman, the Metz *yeshivah* and community appear to have lost some of their prominence and to have entered a state of decline in the generation preceding 1789. The rabbinic contract offered to R. Samuel Hilman in 1751 expressed the hope that the rabbi-elect would be able "to restore the crown to its former glory"; in the contract offered to R. Aryeh

Loeb Günzberg in 1766 the *kehillah* demanded a twelve-year commitment from their rabbi, accompanied by penalties should he leave before the end of the term. It is not unlikely that the community's insistence on a lengthy commitment was motivated by concern over its ability to compete success-fully for distinguished rabbinic candidates.[93] According to Shlomo Lvov, author of a 1784 tract bemoaning the erosion in religious standards among Alsatian Jews, *yeshivah* students could no longer expect a good marriage proposal. Although this complaint was neither new nor limited to Alsace-Lorraine, the length of Lvov's tract, as well as its tone, exhibit a sense of ur-gency that other sources elsewhere do not contain.[94] We may assume that the students' loss of prestige was a reflection of the progressive decline of the *yeshivah* as a venerated communal institution.

While the faltering of the *yeshivah* was related to the dissolution of tradi-tional life in the west at the onset of modernity, regional conditions in Al-sace-Lorraine undoubtedly accelerated the process. Above all, economic factors contributed decisively to the eastward shift in the center of gravity of the western Ashkenazic tradition. Troubles in the Lorraine region, as seen in diminishing revenues and decreasing salaries in the second half of the eighteenth century, may explain Metz's Jewish population decline from 3,000 in 1714 to 2,000 in 1789, at a time when the general population of the city was increasing. The Metz *pinkas* also contains ample evidence of the *kehillah*'s progressive impoverishment. Thus, the *règlement concernant le droit de résidence* of 24 February 1780 indicates that economic troubles were increasingly problematic: "The times are more and more troubling and it is now necessary to erect ramparts to improve the condition of our holy community." Taxes and duties were heavy, and the treasury of the *conseil* was insufficient to meet its responsibilities. At the same time, the arrival of many young men to the community placed a strain on the scarce resources of local residents. Complaints that income did not keep pace with expenses (1772) were reflected in limitations on the number of foreign students ad-mitted to the *yeshivah* (1780) and in the *av beit din*'s approval of a request that money collected for the *yishuv* in Eretz Israel be used for local needs instead (1782).[95] In Alsace conditions were no better. From 1775 Stras-bourg saw its river trade decline, in favor of that of Mayence, resulting in a lower volume of sales to merchants in many Rhenish towns.[96] All of this was exacerbated by the influx of immigrants from Poland, most of whom were poor. The number of rabbis and their students exceeded the number of available positions, forcing many to migrate to Germany and Switzerland.[97]

Jewish culture in Alsace-Lorraine was hardly impervious to the changing economic conditions in the region, as the competition posed by German *yeshivot* across the Rhine suggests. By the last third of the century, talmudic academies in Frankfurt, Fürth, and Mainz attracted many students from the French territories, while far fewer went in the opposite direction. If the condition of the *yeshivah* in Ettendorf in 1786 was at all typical, enrollments were dangerously low in Alsace and some institutions may very well have been on the verge of collapse.[98] Naphtali Hirsch Katzenellenbogen, a grandson and student of R. Samuel Hilman in Metz, was sent to the *yeshivah* of Silesia following the death of his grandfather in 1765. In 1794 he was appointed rabbi of Frankfurt an der Oder, where he would remain until after the turn of the century.[99] Metz native Daniel Jacob Rottembourg, a student of R. Aryeh Loeb Günzberg at the Metz *yeshivah*, was sent to the Fürth *yeshivah* in 1782; after the completion of his studies he remained in Germany, assuming the position of rabbi of Boedigheim (Baden), until his death in 1845. Several accomplished Alsatian scholars also felt the attraction. R. Wolf Reichshoffen, *av beit din* in Bouxwiller and head of the Ettendorf *yeshivah* and Bouxwiller *kloiz*, was invited in 1786 to become rabbi of Mainz but in the end declined the offer. In a letter congratulating Reichshoffen on his decision "not to abandon his people and homeland," Ashkenazi leader Cerf Berr expressed strong sentiments of loyalty to the French province even before the outbreak of the Revolution.[100] R. Joseph Steinhardt, head of the *beit din* and *yeshivah* in Niedernai, could not resist a similar opportunity in 1763, despite his general satisfaction with conditions in Alsace. In his introduction to *Zikhron Yosef*, Steinhardt praised Alsace for its "learned and wealthy men who are God-fearing and pious, . . . who strive to maintain the Torah and to give it dignity, and maintain students appropriately." Nevertheless, he decided to leave Niedernai to become head of the Fürth *yeshivah* because, in his words, "God lifted my banner and my stature . . . and brought me here to the glorious community of Fürth, a great city of Israel, full of scholars and sages, students of Torah and the affluent who maintain them in honor and dignity, [and] this has increased the number of students who follow me."[101] The decision to leave for Fürth may be interpreted as further proof that in the *ancien régime* regional loyalty transcended political boundaries, but in this case the issue was primarily the relative attractiveness of the east over the smaller communities of Alsace-Lorraine. The fact that Fürth had become one of the largest and most important Jewish communities in Germany and was the site of the well-funded and prestigious *yeshivah* and an important Hebrew press as well were, without doubt, the critical factors in Steinhardt's decision.

Trends in Alsace and Metz thus represent two distinct frameworks in which the encounter of Jewish tradition and modernity can be observed. Alsatian Jews inhabited small towns and villages, having been prohibited from taking up residence in the cities of Strasbourg, Colmar, and Mulhouse. With little exposure to urban culture, rural Alsace remained firm in its religious traditionalism throughout most of the *ancien régime*. Even so, Alsatian leaders endeavored to prevent estrangement from the traditional religious lifestyle, and therefore made vigorous efforts to reinforce rabbinic authority and the centrality of religious values. It is noteworthy that the 1777 provincial decisions drew on the rhetoric of religion, stating that failure to abide by the *takkanot* was tantamount to a violation of Torah law.[102] The implementation of various communal procedures, including fines and punishments, required the approval of the *av beit din* and the rabbinic court. This ambitious regional initiative permitted Alsatian communities to address several of the demanding challenges posed by modernity, however muted it may have been.

Alongside the enactment of provisions aiming to bolster traditional observance in Alsace, certain changes in the leadership structure were just beginning to surface. In the last decades of the *ancien régime* a more pronounced distinction between internal community concerns on the one hand and external political affairs on the other had emerged. With the prospects of improvement in the political and legal standing of the Jews of Alsace and Lorraine, there appeared a cadre of new leaders whose influence in the community derived from their prominence in the general economy. Cerf Berr, a large-scale army purveyor, was the best known among a number of distinguished Jews who were able to intercede with the government on behalf of their coreligionists. Several of them were in close contact with leading figures of the Berlin Haskalah and were attracted to their ideology, and this enabled them to enlist the support of men such as Christian Wilhelm Dohm and Pierre Louis Lacretelle for improvements in the Jews' political and economic condition. Particularly from 1784, when the Jews' right to elect syndics was affirmed, these new *shtadlanim* came to be viewed by government officials—and by members of the local communities as well—as official representatives of the *Medinah,* and as such gained a measure of prestige that at least equaled, if not surpassed, the stature of the rabbis.[103] These changes were limited chiefly to the elite, however, and would not be felt in the daily lives of most Alsatian Jews for at least a half-century.

In Metz, despite the determined efforts of community leaders to promote strict allegiance and conformity to traditional Jewish observance through the range of social and religious controls at their disposal, indications of erosion in the religious lifestyle of the Jewish population intensified throughout the century preceding the Revolution. Paternity suits, extramarital pregnancies, and the adoption of the mores of the surrounding culture were noted regularly in the Metz *pinkas* and in the records of the *beit din.* The repeated condemnation of luxury and extravagance, first in the sumptuary laws of 1690–97 and subsequently in the 1769 *règlement,* suggest that these trends were on the rise and confirm the criticisms voiced by R. Jonathan Eibeschütz in the 1740s. His sermons regularly condemned the trend to adopt the preponderant fashion and modes of conduct common among their gentile neighbors. He criticized men who grew long hair, shaved, drank coffee, and attended the theater, and referred to "men and boys [who] wear fine clothing, curl their hair, wear 'gentile wigs' and look into the mirror to make certain that everything is in right, that none of the hair on their head is visible." Similarly, Eibeschütz complained of the tendency to conceal the ritual fringes (*ẓiẓit*) normally worn openly, and of those who wore "tiny *tefillin* hidden under their wigs, for from the day that wigs came into fashion . . . the Jews wore them as well." Also targeted for criticism was the time spent learning French, arithmetic, and dance to the detriment of Torah study.[104] It has been suggested that a parallel decline in the standards of religious observance accompanied the acculturation of Sephardic Jewry, insofar as the Bordeaux Talmud Torah curriculum did not include Mishnah or Talmud, heretical ideas were expressed unabashedly, and public infractions of Jewish law in areas such as dietary laws, family purity, and the Sabbath had become commonplace among the wealthy and the educated of the community. It has been further observed that Sephardic Jewry's modernized Judaism incorporated secular standards and values, particularly the notion of a more restricted role for religion in everyday life. These manifestations of change, however, need to be understood in the context of Sephardic culture and religious ideals, especially as they were molded by the *converso* experience.[105]

In contrast to conditions in southern France where a considerable degree of social and cultural equilibrium had been achieved, the situation in Metz appears to have become unstable and therefore of unending concern to the *kehillah* leadership. As compared with the *takkanot* of the late seventeenth century, the 1769 regulations were especially thoroughgoing in the restrictions they imposed. This severity mirrored the anxiety that Metz leaders felt about the dereliction of youth, the decline in sexual morality, and the blurring of social status; it also reveals how increasingly protective of their own authority they had become. Games of leisure and chance were also prohibited by the 1769 *takkanot*, which specifically targeted wagering on billiards or cards. Any person found playing these games in the city, quarter, or prison without the authorization of the community council— even at a distance of five hours travel beyond the gate of the city—would lose the right to participate in religious activities in the two community synagogues for a period of three years, even if this meant foregoing a family *fête*.[106]

A most significant response to these challenges was a series of initiatives undertaken by R. Eibeschütz to influence communal legislation. As we have seen, heightened concern about libertine sexual mores prompted lay and religious leaders to issue stern warnings against sexual contact between men and women engaged to be married. Eibeschütz had pledged in a Metz sermon that he intended to include a clause in the betrothal contract obliging couples to refrain from any physical contact until after the wedding. A quarter-century later the community issued a *takkanah* prohibiting betrothed couples from being in each other's company at night, under any circumstances.[107] Similarly, the community adopted a particularly stringent measure prohibiting women from attending funerals, in order to avoid excessive social contact between men and women. In light of Eibeschütz's outspoken criticism of sexual libertarianism—he regularly railed against sexual immodesty, excessive frivolity, and inappropriate physical contact[108]—it is not unlikely that communal leaders decided to issue such regulations in accordance with his views. Twenty-five years earlier he had ruled that in order to avoid the intermingling of the sexes, women were expected to arrange their visitations a day or two before Rosh Hashanah and Yom Kippur.[109] Eibeschütz noted several other instances where he tried to influence communal legislation, including additional efforts to limit social interaction of men and women and the allocation of communal funds for men to study Torah for the first five years of marriage. Hoping to elevate the general moral climate, especially by offering counsel to men on how to ward off sexual temptations, R. Eibeschütz urged Metz residents to engage in the daily study of moralistic works. He considered the hortatory sections of Isaiah Horowitz's *Shenei Luḥot Ha-Berit* to be especially effectual in this area and pledged to institute the study of a page of the work prior to each of his classes in Talmud and Halakhah, both within the *yeshivah* and in the community.[110] Though not all successful, these initiatives signal a considerable degree of cooperation between the lay and rabbinic branches at mid-century and, at the same time, reveal Eibeschütz's acknowledgment that ultimate authority was vested in the lay leadership.[111]

These efforts notwithstanding, the community council conceded at a meeting in 1772 and subsequently in a public pronouncement in 1776 that the preoccupation with luxury was on the rise. Five years later, it lamented a general decline in community discipline. Referring to a *takkanah* produced jointly by the *av beit din*, the preceptors, and the inspectors and distributed in the community, the council reported that "men no longer follow our laws."[112] While there is no reason to question the reliability of reports of halakhic deviations, caution should nonetheless be exercised in interpreting their significance. It is difficult to determine whether the violations recorded in the communal register had become increasingly common[113] or were still relatively sporadic, and there is no specific indication that these acts constituted an ideological assault on the authority of Jewish law or of the rabbis. Those who violated Jewish law conceivably viewed themselves as deviants from the normative tradition, in much the same way as earlier transgressors had. Nevertheless, the available documentary evidence suggests that at least from mid-century, the authority of tradition was in a somewhat precarious state and that these violations and excesses had become genuinely distressing to community leaders. For the Metz leadership, the overarching goal of maintaining the prevailing political and social structure of the community went hand in hand with efforts to uphold halakhic norms. As the barriers separating Jews and non-Jews were beginning to fall more quickly, efforts to control social, economic, and religious behavior proved to be ineffective.[114]

Evidence of tensions between the spheres of rabbinic and lay leadership became increasingly conspicuous over the course of the eighteenth century, especially as power shifted decisively to the laity. Already early in the century the preeminence of rabbis within the communal governing body had begun to ebb, as did rabbinic jurisdiction in civil affairs.[115] R. Jacob Reischer went so far as to concede, no doubt reluctantly, that the practice of establishing lay courts alongside rabbinic tribunals was acceptable from the standpoint of Halakhah.[116] Three decades later, R. Eibeschütz complained of legislation issued by the Metz *kehillah*, as in other Ashkenazic *kehillot*, that permitted litigants to go to gentile courts if both parties were in agreement. He confessed that he could not stop the practice because it had become so widespread. Upon his departure from Metz in 1750, the scope of rabbinic jurisdiction in civil affairs was more severely circumscribed.[117] Following a case involving a widow who appealed to the Metz *parlement* after she received an unfavorable ruling from the local *beit din* in 1759, Jewish authorities were forbidden from imposing the *herem* on individuals who went to French courts. Efforts to persuade the *parlement* that civil jurisdiction was inseparable from religious authority and that without the *herem* the rabbis would become powerless ultimately proved unsuccessful. In 1777, although rabbinic jurisdiction in civil affairs was again confirmed by the king, it was subsequently limited by the *parlement* to those instances when Jews chose of their own accord to submit to Jewish courts.[118]

R. Aryeh Loeb Günzberg's rabbinic contract offers even clearer evidence of the rabbinate's subordination to the *parnassim*, the shrinking of its jurisdiction, even in the religious sphere, and the limiting of its judicial independence to matters of relatively minor importance. The contract stipulated that should the *parnassim* decide to enact an ordinance to correct or prevent a religious infraction, the *av beit din* would be required to join them in the pronouncement if so instructed, whereas his own power to issue the *herem* or a prohibition was contingent on their prior approval. Even his freedom to authorize other individuals to officiate at a wedding ceremony depended on first obtaining permission from the appropriate communal officials.[119] In much the same way, the local rabbinic *beit din* was required to operate according to general regulations set forth by the community. Clearly, every religious rite or ceremony was regulated in accordance with communal authorization.[120] The decline in the civil and religious authority of the Metz rabbinate exemplified the crisis that had begun to be felt in western and central European communities.

Conclusion

The cultural history of the Jews in Alsace-Lorraine prior to the Revolution may be regarded as a struggle between two competing forces: pan-Ashkenazic culture and indigenous Alsatian culture. Initially, the fluid movement between France and eastern Europe was evident in patterns of Talmud study, rabbinic appointments, halakhic rulings, religious customs, and liturgy. In Metz, the pan-Ashkenazic trend dominated throughout the *ancien régime*, though signs of a local identity were beginning to become evident in the last third of the eighteenth century. In Alsace an evolving regional consciousness was already well in evidence at mid-century. With the creation of the first Alsatian *yeshivah* in Ribeauvillé in 1753, a native rabbinate began to emerge and, concomitantly, it proceeded to free itself of commercial entanglements. Over the course of the ensuing decades, at least a dozen communities in Alsace followed the lead of Ribeauvillé and saw the establishment of small *yeshivot* and *kloizen*. These academies contributed to the proliferation of advanced talmudic studies in northeastern France, enabling communities to become moderately self-reliant in making rabbinic appointments. This new development anticipated French Jewry's sharp break with the cultural legacy of eastern and central Europe in the half-century following the Revolution and prepared the groundwork for the emergence of a distinct Franco-Jewish identity in the nineteenth century.

On the basis of aggressive efforts to preserve the highly stratified social structure of the pre-revolutionary communities, there emerges a vivid portrait of Jewish life at the end of the seventeenth century. In Metz, communal regulations were designed, on the one hand, to maintain the internal equilibrium threatened by a steadily rising population, a widening gap between the generations, an emerging sexual libertarianism, and the blurring of class distinctions; on the other hand, they aimed to reduce tensions between the community and the neighboring gentile population. These developments may be traced to the end of the seventeenth century, and by the early eighteenth century they were well underway. The legislation reveals clearly that the intermingling between Jews and gentiles had become fairly commonplace—certainly more than is normally assumed—and that this state of affairs was not particularly distressing to communal leaders. By mid-century the Metz *kehillah* appears to have entered a state of crisis, certainly before the influence of the Enlightenment could have been felt. There one can observe the emergence of the public interest as a value largely independent of halakhic constraints and religious justification. A veritable hallmark of modernity, lay control over public morality would become the dominant expression of communal governance across the continent. In Alsace, efforts to develop a centralized regional structure in the 1760s and 1770s confirm that leaders there, like their counterparts in Metz, had embraced the idea of rigorous social and religious controls. However, in contrast with Metz, rabbinic authority in Alsace remained a vital force that was fully acknowledged by lay leaders. Corresponding to wider trends in France, the initiatives undertaken in Metz, and later in Alsace, typified a first stage in the unfolding of modernity, a quasi-governmental effort to shape society and to set public policy. They were born of the belief that tougher standards of order would counterbalance the potentially disintegrative trends associated with urbanization, rapid population growth, and the increasing access to and affordability of luxury items. These efforts were entirely consistent with autonomy, and in fact rested on its wide-ranging authority.

A second stage of modernization, indicated by the dissolution of communal autonomy, occurred as a direct outgrowth of the state policy of leveling down corporations and was accompanied by a growing dissatisfaction with traditional authority and mores. In Metz, this was noticeable in the last decades before the Revolution.[121] There, eroding standards of religious observance and a weakening of rabbinic authority in the 1770s and 1780s were evident well before the Jews of Alsace-Lorraine formally surrendered their communal autonomy in exchange for citizenship. In 1759 the Metz *parlement* had already withdrawn the right of the Jewish community to issue the *herem*; a quarter-century later the second *lettres patentes*, issued in July 1784, prohibited Jews in Alsace from marrying without special permission from the king, while rabbis were warned not to perform marriage ceremonies unless they first received royal authorization. Clearly, the latter decree aimed to limit the size of the Jewish population; however, it also confirmed the authority of the *parnassim* and reaffirmed rabbinic jurisdiction in all litigation involving Jews.

At the end of the *ancien régime*, French Jews were divided into several distinct social and cultural frameworks that would substantially affect their encounter with modernity in the nineteenth century. The Sephardim of Bordeaux and Bayonne typify the "port Jews" of other localities such as Amsterdam, Bordeaux, Hamburg, Livorno, London, and Trieste. Shaped by state efforts to promote maritime commerce, such Jewish communities were valued for their contributions to the common good, and they were therefore not expected to submit to the process of radical transformation that was demanded of their Ashkenazic coreligionists. Moreover, because of the religious and cultural diversity that was characteristic of port cities, the Jewish population encountered less hostility than elsewhere. Their economic utility, imbued with the moral dimension of virtue, made it possible for Jews to be included in the civic realm without needing to undergo political emancipation. By contrast, Alsace and Metz prefigured the emergence of two divergent social contexts where emancipation was to unfold. Well into the nineteenth century, the cultural dynamics of the village and the city would contrast with one another profoundly, each with its own requirements for meeting the demands of citizenship.[122]

Part II
Revolution, *Régénération*, and Emancipation

Chapter 4

The Ordeal of Citizenship, 1782–1799

Heightened anxiety within the Jewish communities of France in the last years of the *ancien régime* grew in anticipation of the turbulent changes widely expected to transform society at large. Jews encountered pressing demands from diverse quarters to redefine their relationship to the society around them and prove themselves capable of meeting new and unprecedented obligations to the *patrie*. In the minds of many, this would require a reformulation of Judaism in dramatically new terms and would involve a new attitude toward the Jewish past and a reprioritization of Jewish commitments. For the Jews, as for their fellow countrymen, the French Revolution came to constitute the primary myth of origin and the birthdate of a new existence. On 27 September 1791, two years after the storming of the Bastille and the Declaration of the Rights of Man and of the Citizen, the French National Assembly voted to admit the Jews of Alsace-Lorraine to citizenship. Subsequent generations would recall this momentous event as a turning point of extraordinary magnitude and would view themselves as compelling evidence of its transformative power. Their memories tended to be dominated by images of celebration and glory, comparing the Revolution to the Sinaitic revelation and referring to it in messianic-redemptive terms. Not surprisingly, the many setbacks suffered by the generation of 1789 were largely absent from these recollections, while only meager appreciation for the complexities introduced into Jewish cultural life can be detected in the half-century following the Revolution. A sweeping conviction that history was surging forward, colored by a pervading optimism, credited the Revolution with ending centuries of degradation, legal discrimination, and exclusion from the mainstream of society. From 1789, as so many would attest, the destinies of France and the Jews became one, and would remain inseparable.[1]

The historical record, however, reveals a much more complex picture. Civic equality came at a heavy price and only after an arduous and demanding struggle. In the end, citizenship was granted on the condition that Jewish communities surrender their special privileges of communal autonomy and rabbinic jurisdiction in civil affairs. Nevertheless, although these two concessions would ultimately prove highly repercussive, their impact was felt neither immediately nor uniformly. For most of France's Jewish population the Revolution introduced no abrupt changes. Residence patterns, the range of occupations, and the rhythm of religious life remained largely unchanged for the vast majority of French Jews in the following two or three generations. Likewise, rabbinic leadership, though its authority was undeniably curtailed by the loss of civil autonomy, continued to exercise influence in religious and communal affairs for much of the nineteenth century, while within French society anti-Jewish hostility persisted unremittingly for an even longer period. Whatever the uncertainty concerning the tangible effects of the Revolution, however, the eventual triumph of its ideals assured the mythic Revolution pride of place in the consciousness and memory of French Jewry.

The role of the Revolution as an agent of change in modern European society is still fiercely contested even after two centuries. According to the conventional view, the Revolution is one of history's great pivotal events, an upheaval that triggered decisive changes in political, social, and economic life, first in France and subsequently in the rest of Europe. All vestiges of feudalism were swept away, peasants were freed from ecclesiastical tithes and seigneurial dues, and free trade was established throughout the territories under French control, while autonomous corporations were abolished, local and provincial privileges were curtailed, and a new democratic tradition emerged. An equally powerful tendency to minimize the historical significance of the events of 1789 has taken two principal forms. Georges Lefebvre concluded that the economic impact of the Revolution, particularly with respect to agrarian reform, had been greatly overstated. For others, the pace of modernization, and not the Revolution, was identified as the decisive factor. Data cited by Maurice Agulhon and Eugen Weber concerning the steadfast traditionalism of vast sectors of the rural population throughout most of the nineteenth century suggested that the effects of the Revolution were hardly perceptible in the countryside. A second trend, even more damaging to the standing of the Revolution than the first, emphasized the high degree of continuity between the pre- and post-1789 eras. Alexis de Toqueville insisted that political life in the *ancien régime* embodied democratic ideals and that the ideas of the Enlightenment were an essential part of the Revolution. Similarly, François Furet discovered that opposition to the corporate regime was already well established in voluntary organizations of the pre-revolutionary period. Others, pointing to extensive indications of political and social change before 1789, argue that modernization may well have been interrupted, ironically enough, by the Revolution. To this last argument, Simon Schama added the claim that the legacy normally associated with the Revolution was already represented at the highest levels of French society before 1789. The "great period of change," according to Schama, "was not the Revolution but the late eighteenth century."[2]

Developments over the course of the nineteenth century confirm that

Jewish life in France was dramatically transformed both in objective terms and with respect to self-understanding. Previous research has failed, however, to determine precisely what function the Revolution served in this transformation and how critical its mythical dimension was to the process. To be sure, neither the erosion of the economic role of the Jews in the Alsatian countryside nor advances in social integration and mobility in urban centers stemmed directly from the Revolution. Likewise, state efforts to promote social and cultural reform, such as those set in motion during the Napoleonic regime, were hardly limited to France but were widespread in central and western Europe.[3] Only on the basis of a comparison of developments in France and beyond its borders during the first half of the nineteenth century will it be possible to assess the distinctiveness of French Jewry's response to the challenges it encountered and to identify those aspects of its struggle that it shared with Jewish communities abroad.[4]

Where, then, may the impact of the Revolution be discerned? In the next several chapters we shall focus on the internal, cultural dynamic of France's Ashkenazic Jews—concentrated mainly in Alsace-Lorraine and Paris—and on the pace of their transformation. By "transformation" I refer to the aggregate metamorphosis produced by urbanization, economic development, and industrialization. However, my chief concern is not the socioeconomic change per se but with the progressive refashioning of traditional values in the encounter with secularization, modernity, and non-Jewish ideas and symbols.[5] We shall observe the dynamics of this process on several levels: the authority of religious leaders and institutions; attitudes toward integration into the surrounding society; and efforts to reexamine the texts and to reassess the knowledge formerly limited to traditionalist interpretation.

How quickly this transformation occurred is an equally crucial question. In the century preceding the Revolution, modest transformations affecting communal governance, the provenance of rabbinic culture, and the religious behavior of the urban elite were already evident. Politically, the Revolution paved the way for the civic enfranchisement of the Jews, but the pace of social and cultural change proceeded rather lethargically as compared to the vigorous transformation of large sectors of German Jewry in the latter third of the eighteenth century and the beginning of the nineteenth century. Religious and educational reform, the emergence of a modern rabbinate, and the development of modern Jewish studies are among the most conspicuous areas that lagged far behind developments across the Rhine. In accounting for this difference, I will suggest that the Revolution unleashed forces that disrupted Jewish communal life for nearly two decades—including acute anti-Jewish hostility, deteriorating economic conditions, religious persecution, the emigration of an entire generation of *yeshivah* students and rabbis, and the closing of schools, synagogues, and the two Hebrew presses. A severe communal crisis in the aftermath of 1789 left its bold imprint on the religious and communal leadership, on patterns of Jewish culture, and on the pace of modernization for most of the nineteenth century. Their communal structures in disarray, the Jews of France were unprepared for the difficult new challenges they faced as French citizens.[6] Ironically, instead of launching the modernization of the Jews of the northeast, the French Revolution seems, at least in the short term, to have slowed the process that had already begun a century earlier.

The foregoing should not be taken to imply that the impact of the Revolution was at all insignificant, however. The long-term effects of the delay were quite extensive and ought to be viewed as endemic to the Revolution's legacy, even if they were not noticeable until much later. As this and the next several chapters will suggest, the Revolution may best be approached within a broad chronological framework as the first and indeed the most important in a series of events that together left an indelible mark on Jewish consciousness. We shall therefore track the impact of the Revolution over a period of several generations, through its principal stages of development. What unites the Napoleonic Empire, the Bourbon Restoration, and the July Monarchy with the Revolution is a shared commitment to the ideals of 1789, a commitment that came to be expressed in accordance with the particular emphases of each ensuing political regime. At each juncture, the question of Jewish civic equality and social integration remained inextricably linked to the revolutionary ideals, subject of course to continuing reinterpretation.

At the Threshold of the Revolution

Of all the long-term cultural developments to have resulted from the revolutionary upheaval, the most important was the progressive break with the tradition linking the Jews of Alsace-Lorraine with communities of central and eastern Europe. Evolving over the course of a half-century, this transformation manifested itself in the construction of a distinct Franco-Jewish identity that became most conspicuous during the Bourbon Restoration and July Monarchy. This identity was shaped by political and social forces that were native to France, including the abiding link between the Revolution and the bestowal of citizenship, the urgency of socioeconomic *régénéra-tion*, the effects of the severe communal crisis of the 1790s on ensuing generations, and the creation of centralized communal institutions under Napoleon.

Evidence of change in the religious and cultural identity of French Jewry can be traced to the political and intellectual ferment immediately preceding and following the Revolution. In the last years of the *ancien régime* the place of the Jews in the impending new order was reconsidered. Central to all discussions concerning the suitability of the Jews for citizenship was the question whether the observance of Judaism and Jewish law was compatible with prevailing notions of reason, morality, and, ultimately, the exercise of civic duties. Overall, a negative assessment of Jewish culture and religion appears to have been virtually endemic to Enlightenment thought, despite its overwhelming commitment to religious tolerance and humanism. Even Baron de Montesquieu, whose passionate denunciation of the Spanish Inquisition and praise of biblical Judaism were cited frequently by advocates and defenders of Jewish emancipation, strongly condemned the "poverty" of rabbinic literature and its adverse effects on the Jewish character. In fact, these views corresponded closely to those of the harshest critics, most notably Voltaire and the Encyclopaedists.[7] The major area of disagreement revolved around the question of whether the Jews could be redeemed from the corrupting effects of their religious heritage and, if so, what steps would need to be taken to realize this goal.

Echoing the Enlightenment's critique of Judaism, even the most ardent supporters of the Jews conceded that centuries of oppression had left a lasting and devastating impression on Jewish behavior.[8] Though most would grant that the Jews were scarcely to blame for this regrettable state of affairs, there was no denying the reality, whatever its cause. But neither were they entirely relieved of responsibility for the moral corruption and antisocial conduct that was routinely, if only implicitly, imputed to them.[9] Fanciful rabbinic readings of the Bible ostensibly epitomized this moral degeneration. Armed with "sophistic artistry," the rabbis distorted the pristine morality of Mosaic law and made "narrow-minded and petty regulations" the quintessence of the Jewish religion.[10] Widely viewed as exuding an ethos of social separatism and prejudice toward non-Jews, the ceremonial laws were obstacles to true piety.[11] This assessment of classical Judaism, especially its moral implications, was an amalgam of many of the arguments advanced by the most severe critics of Jewish culture. What distinguishes the end of the eighteenth century from the earlier period was a new willingness to reconsider the political status of the Jews despite these deeply held prejudices. Impassioned pleas for Jewish civic equality were accompanied by the expectation that in time the Jews' social and religious ethos would be thoroughly transformed.[12]

In the decade preceding the Revolution, as the idea of a contract between the state and its citizens gained increasing currency, civic obligations were endowed with an importance akin to sacred duty. Accordingly, the title *citoyen* was deemed inconceivable for any person whose religion impeded the fulfillment of duties necessary for the maintenance of the state. This idea was expressed as an undisputed political axiom. Most of the debates on the Jewish question, from the 1780s to the middle of the nineteenth century, centered on whether the Jewish religion was an impediment to full *régénération*. Opponents of Jewish emancipation advanced the argument that the ritual practices of Judaism were obstacles to full participation in the life of the country, much as Graeco-Roman authors in antiquity had assailed Jewish exclusiveness and ridiculed the Sabbath as a day of utter idleness.[13] Modern critics maintained that agriculture was not a feasible means of livelihood in light of traditional Sabbath restrictions, while the alleged prohibition in Jewish law against fighting on the Sabbath cast doubt on the usefulness of the Jews in time of war.[14] Citing several historical and legal sources, among them an opinion by Moses Mendelssohn, Dohm refuted this claim, asserting that military service was fully sanctioned by the Jewish religion.[15] Later, Grégoire and Mirabeau repeated this defense of Jewish law against opponents of Jewish emancipation in the National Assembly.[16]

Efforts to defend the Jewish religion did not go unqualified, however. Advocates of civic equality routinely conceded that Jewish religious practices needed to undergo certain modifications—often this meant the creation of a deritualized Judaism—so that Jews could become genuinely good citizens.[17] In some respects, certainly, partisans of Jewish emancipation were beset by the same reservations concerning the suitability of Jews for citizenship that troubled their opponents. The difference concerned the significance attached to the widely acknowledged difficulties posed by the Jewish religion. Those who supported emancipation maintained that these difficulties were not of sufficient magnitude to preclude the bestowal of civic rights. In fact, nothing short of emancipation would, in their view, produce the desired improvement of the Jews. Dohm imagined that within several generations Jews would practice an enlightened, purified form of Judaism, not unlike Deism. He believed that as soon as Jews were accepted as members of general society and would make its interests their own, "they will reform their religious laws and regulations according to the demands of society. They will go back to the freer and nobler Mosaic Law, will explain and adapt it according to the changed times and conditions, and will find authorizations to do so alone in their Talmud."[18] Grégoire also expected the Jews to observe a more modern form of Judaism once they were emancipated; he even stated explicitly that he envisioned the process of emancipation as a transitional phase leading to their ultimate embrace of Christianity. Until then, he asserted, civic equality would provide opportunities for broader education and freedom from the excessive authority and influence of the rabbis.[19] Emancipation, then, was conceived not only as freedom from restrictions imposed by society but also as an internal process of liberation from the traditional Jewish behavior and mores that western society found objectionable.

The foregoing observations and criticisms are representative of the challenges facing the Jews in their struggle to be accepted as citizens of France. By participating in these discussions, communal leaders and *maskilim* assumed the important task of demonstrating that their coreligionists were entirely capable of fulfilling the duties of citizenship and the more loosely defined obligations related to sociability. But more than this, their writings articulate the reformist vision that their supporters had outlined only vaguely. Their proposals, which included criticism of the rabbinic leadership, appeals for the elimination of moneylending, the assertion that Jews were obligated by their religion to love members of other faiths, and recommendations for educational reform, bear striking similarity to views advanced by *maskilim* elsewhere. The claim that Judaism was incompatible with modern life, coupled with the indictment of the Jews' purported moral inadequacy, furnished an opportunity for Jewish writers to give careful consideration to the implications of citizenship and to advance a range of proposals concerning *régénération*. Over the course of approximately twenty years, ending with the convocation of the Napoleonic Sanhedrin in 1807, the participation of Jewish communal leaders and intellectuals in these public discussions produced new conceptions of communal organization and leadership, as well as a clarification of attitudes toward the state and its gentile citizens. Although one can argue that the Sanhedrin simply restated positions already articulated by Franco-Jewish leaders in the previous two decades, its real significance, as we shall see, lay not only in its reaffirmation of French Jewry's commitment to the terms of citizenship but in transforming the views of individuals into official policy for the Jewish community at large. In these, the formative years of the emancipation debate, the foundation was established for what came to be known in the 1830s as *le mouvement régénérateur*.

Those French Jewish leaders who publicly debated the socioeconomic, cultural, and political implications of emancipation identified closely with the Berlin Haskalah. While the promise of a "neutral society" founded on humanistic and rational principles undoubtedly deepened the frustration with the cultural limitations imposed by ghetto life, the Haskalah movement in Germany drew on internal concerns as well. Criticism of *pilpul* (casuistry), advances in talmudic study, and interest in Hebrew grammar, philosophy, and science were already present earlier in the eighteenth century, preparing the ground for the fully developed movement associated with Moses Mendelssohn and his circle. In the last third of the century, especially as *maskilim* became acquainted with the major writings of the *philosophes*, they subjected traditional Jewish society to a critical reevaluation according to new criteria such as the primacy of reason, the aesthetic ideal, the universal brotherhood of man, and economic productivity. Haskalah aimed to produce a generation of Jews capable of taking their place in the new order as productive and loyal citizens. To accomplish this goal, a new Judaism was substituted for the old, one that was refashioned to correspond to the social, cultural, and political underpinnings of emancipation. Traditional restrictions on social intercourse with non-Jews were deemed incompatible with the concrete demands of citizenship and its wider implications. In their writings and through their activism on behalf of educational and communal reform, the *maskilim* constructed a new vision of the ideal Jew and of the relationship of Jews to general society. Conscious of the alleged liabilities presented by traditional Judaism, Jewish intellectuals developed strategies to advance the process of cultural and social integration by adjusting Jewish religious and social teachings to the cultural norms of European society. Emphasizing the rationalist tradition of Judaism and its integrationist ethos, the *maskilim* mounted energetic efforts against the rabbinic establishment, which they viewed as the embodiment of cultural obscurantism and excessive political power. Critical of religious and social traditions that were purportedly the product of superstition and persecution, radical *maskilim* distinguished, as did Deism, the divine core of religion from variable customs.[20]

Conditions in France precluded the emergence of a dynamic Haskalah movement as in Germany. Owing to the relatively small Jewish population, legal restrictions on residence and mobility, and widespread anti-Jewish hostility in the rural countryside, most of France's Jews remained in a state of social and cultural isolation, set apart from the great changes that were taking place in enlightened Europe. Small clusters of *maskilim* in the principal centers of Sephardic and Ashkenazic life represent exceptions to this general pattern. Bordeaux produced several distinguished men of letters, including Jacob Rodrigues Péreire, known for his work with the deaf; Isaac de Pinto, author of important essays on finance; and Louis Francia de Beaufleury, a writer on issues of social welfare.[21] In Alsace-Lorraine, a handful of Hebrew poets and publicists, among them Moses Ensheim, Lipmann Moïse Büschental, and several rabbis, gained notoriety. Notwithstanding these modest literary achievements, the French Haskalah remained in the shadow of the Berlin movement.[22] More revealing evidence of shifts in Jewish consciousness is evident in the work of several men whose intellectual commitment to Haskalah was interwoven with an active participation in the political struggle for emancipation. In each instance, writers defended Jewish claims to citizenship while also offering concrete proposals for the reform of Jewish institutions. The sharpest differences concerned the scope of the reforms they envisioned.[23]

Metz native Isaïe Berr Bing (1759–1805), who combined a vigorous involvement in local community affairs and in the Berlin Haskalah, struck a balance between the defensive posture and reformist spirit. His translations of Mendelssohn's *Phaedon* into French and Hebrew and Judah Halevi's *Song of Zion* from Hebrew into French were among his more significant works. In addition, he served on the editorial committee of the *Décade philosophique*, which contained many of his literary compositions, including a French translation of Lessing's *Nathan the Wise*. Bing was later appointed to the Malesherbes Commission (1787), a body instructed to study the status of French Jewry and its possible emancipation.[24] His most important contribution to the public discussion of the Jewish question was a letter refuting *Le cri du citoyen contre les juifs*, a pamphlet that appeared during the

Metz prize essay contest. Quoting Voltaire to substantiate his anti-Jewish polemic, the author portrayed the Jews of Alsace as an irretrievably flawed nation whose distinguishing characteristics were leprosy, fanaticism, and usury. He proposed that the government transport them to a large tract of uncultivated land where they might be regenerated through agricultural labor.[25] Although the Metz *kehillah* was able to convince the city's *parlement* to suppress the pamphlet soon after it appeared, Bing nonetheless felt compelled to answer its allegations, precisely because many had been drawn from the French Enlightenment.[26] Responding first to the charge that the Jewish religion offers its adherents the exclusive path to salvation, Bing emphasized that all men will partake of divine bliss, provided they observe the Noahide laws, and declared "that our principles oblige us to love you as brothers, and to perform for you all the acts of humanity that our position permits us."[27] The more difficult issue was the subject of usury, an accusation frequently raised by critics to discredit the ethical foundation of the Jewish religion. Bing conceded that Jewish law permitted Jews to lend on interest to gentiles while prohibiting the same from their fellow Jews; however, he insisted that in light of Judaism's positive attitude toward the non-Jew, this distinction could scarcely be motivated by an aversion to strangers as was commonly asserted.[28] Still, the question of usury, particularly when it was formulated in moral terms, demanded a carefully crafted elucidation of the law.

Moneylending had long been viewed as the quintessence of Jewish character deficiency. Images of "bloodsucking" Jews who intended to victimize the Christian population through economic oppression were commonplace in the literature, sermons, art, and public disputations of the Middle Ages, and these persisted, though to a lesser degree, in the early modern period. Moral concerns were also the subject of internal debate in medieval halakhic and philosophical literature.[29] It was only in the late eighteenth century, however, as the prospects for citizenship improved, that moneylending became a defining issue in Jewish-gentile relations. Bing approached the problem from two decidedly different angles. Initially, his effort to defend the practice was blatantly apologetic. Lending on interest, he insisted, ought to be regarded as an economically valuable service to those in need of credit, provided that the rate of interest was within "normal" limits. This stipulation rested on the assertion that *neshekh*, the biblical term referring to interest, had been incorrectly translated as "usury."[30] However, the absence of any explicit reference in the Bible to rates that may be considered either "reasonable" or "usurious" suggests that Bing interpreted the biblical terminology in light of contemporary social and economic thought. The fact that in these same years French jurists had proposed the legalization of moneylending and the regulation of the maximum rate of interest may very well account for his distinction between interest and usury. Be that as it may, Bing endeavored to prove that society's denunciation of the Jewish law of moneylending was unwarranted because the Bible never expressly endorsed usury.[31]

The moral problem posed by the laws of moneylending demanded a more innovative interpretation. Bing's claim that lending on interest was an honorable profession in light of its economic and social utility only explained the permissibility of taking interest from non-Jews. Concerning the injunction against charging interest to fellow Jews, he emphasized two fundamental considerations. The first aim of the law was to preserve the communal-national identity of the Jews. Differentiation in the ethical standards applied to Jews and gentiles was intended to remind Jews of their common origin and to promote among them a familial spirit.[32] This same suggestion would later emerge in the decisions of the Paris Sanhedrin, where the purpose of the law was formulated in the following terms: "to draw closer between them the bonds of fraternity, to give them a lesson of reciprocal benevolence."[33] The second reason for the injunction was socioeconomic: its goal was to mold the Jews into an agrarian people devoted to the cultivation of their land. The Bible's detailed agricultural laws, especially the legislation governing the cancellation of debts in the sabbatical year, were adduced as the strongest evidence for this theory. Moreover, the prohibition against taking interest from fellow Jews was motivated, according to Bing, by important moral considerations. The "commercial spirit" was a dangerous, corrupting force, leading first to an excessive concern with riches and luxuries and ultimately to an "austerity of *moeurs.*" Finally, taking into account the widespread skepticism concerning the economic usefulness of the Jews, Bing argued that the ancient aversion to moneylending was proof that Judaism unequivocally preferred productive occupations. "Far from permitting us to engage in usury," he concluded, "our law took all possible precautions to remove the circumstances which could lead to it."[34]

Resting primarily on biblical imagery and selective citation, the foregoing argument amounted to a virtual repudiation of moneylending. Bing exhibited no comparable effort to consider the reform of Jewish ritual life, however. In direct response to the Enlightenment critique of Judaism, he declared that "if scrupulous observance of the prescriptions of our religion appear to you as superstitious, I admit openly that we are. And we will stay this way in spite of the progress of fashionable philosophy, with its aversion for the ceremonial and for everything which it cannot touch physically and immediately." This was a forthright expression of trust in his coreligionists' ability to participate as full-fledged members of society without throwing off the yoke of Jewish law. He urged his coreligionists to remain loyal to their ancestral faith, declaring that should an improvement in their condition not materialize, they must be prepared to "live, suffer, and die as Jews." It nevertheless should be noted that Bing did not consider the Jews entirely blameless for their social segregation. Like *maskilim* elsewhere, he singled out the use of Yiddish as an obstacle to social integration, claiming that it epitomized the mistrust that the Jews felt toward their non-Jewish neighbors. Moreover, this "unintelligible jargon" was an obstacle to scientific and cultural advancement, and its continued use would perpetuate the Jews' social and cultural estrangement. But overall, underlying the optimism that characterized Bing's views was the belief that once the barriers separating the Jews from general society were lifted, integration would proceed in due course: "Experience will show that two nations, who live under the same climate, between whom there is a sort of political equality, and whose religions are based on the same moral principles, cannot differ essentially neither in *capacité* nor in character."[35] The Jewish problem was thus viewed exclusively in terms of its social and economic parameters; its solution would require the removal of residential and occupational disabilities in order to prepare the way for normalization within general society.

A more ambitious work, one that bridged the apologetic and reformist agendas, was *Apologie des Juifs* by Zalkind Hourwitz.[36] The author, a Polish Jew employed as an interpreter of oriental languages at the Bibliothèque Royale in Paris, had originally submitted his essay to the 1785 Metz contest and was awarded a prize together with Abbé Grégoire and Adolphe Thiéry. In the spirit of Dohm and Grégoire, Hourwitz advocated the liberalization of laws governing land purchase, commerce, entrance into liberal professions and trades, and public education.[37] His first objective was to defend Judaism against the charge that its doctrines were incompatible with the exercise of civic duties. But in contrast to Bing, Hourwitz focused on the Enlightenment's social critique of Judaism, especially as expressed in the allegations of Jewish chauvinism, immorality, and social exclusiveness.[38] His method, characteristic of a growing tendency among *maskilim*, drew a sharp distinction between biblical and talmudic Judaism. Hourwitz stressed biblical Judaism's commitment to humanistic-universal values, as exemplified by its tolerance for the non-Jewish resident of the Land of Israel and elaborated in greater detail in the Talmud. More significantly, however, in an effort to silence his critics, he maintained that the political laws of Judaism were no longer in force and exerted no influence whatsoever on contemporary Jewish mores. Jews were required to pray for the welfare of the state in which they resided and to abide faithfully by its laws.[39] As for the charge of social exclusiveness, Hourwitz argued that neither of the two most commonly cited examples—Jewish dietary restrictions and the prohibition against intermarriage—was designed to preclude normal relations with non-Jews. In the case of the dietary laws, he defined their meaning narrowly in terms of ingredients and preparation but rejected any implications for remaining socially apart from non-Jews. On the question of intermarriage, Hourwitz limited the prohibition to those pagan nations mentioned explicitly in the Bible. Building on the medieval distinction between gentiles and pagans, Hourwitz concluded that Mosaic law prohibited only unions with the latter; the Talmud's extension of the prohibition to include all gentiles, he insisted, was only to avoid domestic inconvenience. This argument was glaringly apologetic and could hardly be construed as a serious defense of Jewish law.[40]

In Hourwitz's estimation, the successful transformation of the Jews would require a genuine willingness on their part to reform their communal organization and economic behavior. The Jews bore responsibility for their degraded and isolated condition, but during the initial stage of reform it would be necessary for the government to exercise control over Jewish affairs. He recommended that his coreligionists be prohibited from moneylending and that there be closer supervision of their commercial activities.[41] The extension of rabbinic authority beyond the synagogue was, in his mind, the most severe obstacle to reform. Referring to the rabbis' failure to meet the religious needs of the laity as dictated by the changing social and cultural reality, as well as their obscure teachings of intolerance, he went so far as to call for the elimination of the institution of the rabbinate entirely.[42] Accordingly, although the *Apologie* enjoyed a distinctly positive reception in enlightened circles, it was viewed disdainfully in the established Jewish community. Metz leaders were most disturbed by Hourwitz's scathing criticism of their regime, his antipathy for rabbinic Judaism, his sarcastic description of religious extremism, and his willingness to dismantle some of the social barriers separating Jews and non-Jews. In Bordeaux, there were objections both to the prominence that Hourwitz attached to Jewish vices and to the commercial restrictions that he proposed. On the other hand, the failure to denounce Hourwitz's negative characterization of Jewish ritual practices may be a reflection of the limits of Sephardic concern at that time.[43]

The disjunction between the positive and negative reactions to the *Apologie des Juifs*, and Hourwitz's own vacillation between *apologia* and the search for radical solutions, underscore the fundamental tension inherent in the work. His ultimate goal was to prove that the Jews were capable of participating fully in the envisioned new order. He could therefore defend the Talmud while revealing considerable antipathy for rabbinic Judaism and contemporary rabbinic leadership. This typified the Haskalah's distinction between essential and nonessential elements within Judaism. He joined those who urged fundamental changes in the social, cultural, and economic life of French Jewry and, further, urged greater governmental supervision and controls. Combining a defensive posture with an unabashedly critical perspective, the *Apologie* exemplified a new tendency only beginning to emerge in his day. Here was an attempt, on the one hand, to present Judaism as an "enlightened" religion that showed no signs of incompatibility with contemporary conceptions of reason, morality, and sociability. On the other hand, the fact that the Jews deserved to be tolerated did not diminish their own obligation to eliminate certain social, cultural, and economic abuses that would only impede their participation in modern society.

Régénération: The Underpinnings of Change

With the outbreak of the Revolution and the accompanying promise of a new world soon to be born, Jewish leaders encountered difficult challenges on two separate fronts. Most immediate was the political battle for civic equality, which was conducted at the French National Assembly, in the press, and behind the scenes; the second involved an internal debate concerning the nature and scope of the transformation demanded of Jews by gentile critics and supporters alike. Bridging the two struggles was the idea of *régénération*, the foremost expression of Jewish accommodation to the prospects of civic equality. Strikingly similar to proposals advanced by *maskilim* in communities such as Berlin, Koenigsberg, Hamburg, and Prague, *régénération* rested on the prevailing assumption that a dramatic improvement in the socioeconomic and cultural mores of the Jews was necessary before they could become productive members of the larger society. What distinguishes the shaping of Jewish identity in France from parallel developments in central and western Europe, however, was the profound impact of civic equality and the accompanying demand for social integration—*égalité* and *fraternité*—on Jewish consciousness. The promise of civic equality—and its eventual realization—set French Jews apart from their coreligionists abroad. In the social and political milieu of post-revolutionary France, the ideas of *égalité* and *fraternité* imbued the long-awaited transformation with an uncommon sense of urgency. Jews were continually reminded that *régénération* was a sacred obligation upon which the bestowal of civic equality had been conditioned, and members of the Jewish communal establishment quickly internalized this view.

A rudimentary awareness of the implications that civic emancipation augured for the Jews of France was evident in the first reactions to the Revolution. The Ashkenazic leadership displayed unequivocal enthusiasm for the prospects of civic equality, and the Revolution enjoyed wide support, as the enlistment of more than one hundred Jews in the National Guard, including several rabbis, indicates.[44] But leaders also exhibited considerable anxiety over the surrender of communal autonomy. Initially, Ashkenazic leaders could not conceive of a Judaism that was independent of communal controls, and they therefore sought to maintain the juridical and religious status quo. Following the passage of the Declaration of the Rights of Man, Jewish delegates from eastern France petitioned for full citizenship while affirming their right to autonomy. Shortly thereafter, in a joint petition with the Jews of Paris, the Ashkenazim formally dropped their insistence on the retention of autonomy, but several months later, in response to an anti-Jewish speech given by the Bishop of Nancy, de la Fare, one last attempt to retain the old communal structure was made. De la Fare had argued that the Jews were aliens in French society. Their moral commitments and ritual obligations precluded the fulfillment of civic duties and made it inconceivable for them to hold positions in the magistrate or municipality.[45] Berr Isaac Berr (1744–1828), a syndic from Lorraine who had emerged as the leading Jewish spokesman for Ashkenazic emancipation, proposed that the Jews of Alsace-Lorraine voluntarily forfeit the right to hold public office in exchange for the right to maintain communal autonomy, including rabbinic jurisdiction over civil affairs. Until the ultimate bestowal of citizenship in September 1791, Berr remained ardently opposed to the dissolution of the autonomous Jewish communities.[46]

The old guard's preference for communal autonomy over full citizenship did not have undisputed backing, however. In August 1789 dissenters from Lunéville and Sarreguemines questioned the wisdom of preserving the autonomous framework, but the most outspoken challenge came from Berr's nephew, Jacob Berr of Nancy. The younger Berr accused his uncle of wanting to perpetuate Jewish estrangement from French society. Echoing the views of Zalkind Hourwitz, he vilified the "despotic regime" controlled by rabbis who were vested with both religious and civil powers.[47] Berr's appeal for the repudiation of autonomy recalled the declaration that the Jewish delegation of Bordeaux had pronounced at the National Assembly in January 1790. The delegation dissociated itself from the Jews of Alsace, Lorraine, and the Trois Evêchés who "aspire to live in France under a special regime, to have laws peculiar to themselves, and to constitute a class of citizens separated from all others."[48] As Clermont-Tonnerre had declared earlier, the retention of a pre-revolutionary status at the expense of civic rights was inconceivable: "The Jews should be denied everything as a nation, but granted everything as individuals; they must disown their judges, they must have only ours; they must be refused legal protection for the maintenance of the supposed laws of their Jewish corporation; they must constitute neither a state, nor a political corps, nor an order; they must individually become citizens; if they do not want this, they must inform us and we shall then be compelled to expel them. The existence of a nation within a nation is unacceptable to our country."[49]

Formulated by an ardent proponent of Jewish emancipation, this statement of the conditions of citizenship confirms that the Jews of France could have expected no better terms. Aware that his plan had little chance of being accepted, Berr declared adamantly that "if we must no longer remain as a community, if we must sacrifice our civil laws in order to be registered with the national law; if, in the end, the revolution which was so fortunate for all Frenchmen, only increased our misfortune, then we prefer a thousand times death over acquiescence; we will obey, but we will persist in demanding justice from the National Assembly, the plenitude of the rights of man."[50] In the end, the Ashkenazic leadership, following the example of the Sephardic communities eighteen months before,[51] set aside its proposal to retain autonomy.[52]

Following the admission of the Ashkenazic Jews to citizenship, Berr became an outspoken enthusiast of the new status. In a public letter congratulating his coreligionists on the morrow of the National Assembly's vote, Berr presented his vision outlining the nature and obligations of citizenship.[53] Most striking was the author's characterization of the newly won status in deeply religious terms, as a modern-day redemptive experience, a reenactment of the liberation from ancient Egyptian slavery: "We have not deserved this wonderful change by our repentance, nor by the reformation of our manners: we can attribute it to nothing but to the everlasting goodness of God. . . . He has chosen the generous French nation to reinstate us in our rights, and to operate our regeneration, as, in other times, he has chosen Antiochus, Pompey, and others, to humiliate and enslave us."[54] The prophetic theme detailing the enlistment of various nations as tools in the execution of divine will was applied to revolutionary France but with one important difference. Now the French nation had become instruments in the long-awaited reversal of Israel's bleak fortunes. Berr's exuberance was expressed in vivid language reminiscent of the Passover Haggadah: "[A]nd what bounds can there be to our gratitude for the happy event! From being vile slaves, mere serfs . . . we are, of a sudden, become the children of the country, to bear its common charges, and share in its common rights."[55]

If the representation of the Revolution in biblical terms was intended to justify the surrender of communal autonomy, there appears to have been an even more essential purpose: inherent in the bestowal of citizenship was a responsibility on the part of each Jew to prove himself worthy of the new privileges. The Jews of France would need to undergo a process of collective self-examination and remorse before being able to embark prudently on the path that lay ahead. Berr asked his coreligionists "to conform to their wishes . . . [to] let us examine with attention what remains to be done, on our part, to become truly happy, and how we may be able to show, in some measure, our grateful sense for all the favors heaped upon us."[56] Introspection and self-examination thus framed the concept of citizenship in even more compelling terms. With his admission that "we ourselves know how very deficient we are" in respect to the qualifications of citizens, Berr introduced the language of repentance to underscore the urgency of acquiring those qualities necessary for participation in general society. Civic equality constituted an unprecedented expression of confidence in the Jews, one that required corresponding dedication to social and cultural transformation.[57]

Citizenship demanded that French Jews seize every available opportunity to "give signal proofs of glowing patriotism." This would be accomplished not through ritual reform, which Berr and others rejected,[58] but by forging spiritual and physical bonds to the state, by "divesting ourselves entirely of that narrow spirit, of Corporation and Congregation, in all civil and political matters not immediately connected with our spiritual laws; in these things we must absolutely appear simply as individuals, as Frenchmen, guided only by a true patriotism and by the welfare of the nation."[59] Hoping to allay concerns about the surrender of autonomy, Berr insisted that the disadvantages of a separate community far outweighed its advantages. Social exclusion, arbitrary taxes, collective responsibility and guilt for the actions of individuals, and being deemed unworthy of participation in civic affairs were among the ignominies endured by the Jews during the era when they enjoyed autonomy. Berr concluded that the civic oath of allegiance was simply "a renunciation of those pretended privileges and immunities [which] were only relative to our state of slavery." By stressing the connection between the humiliation of noncitizenship and the privileges of autonomy, Berr aimed to minimize the significance of the dissolution of a separate community. Nevertheless, despite this momentous shift, Berr certainly did not concede that Jews ought to surrender their sense of community. The maintenance of a communal structure was essential, as it would facilitate the establishment of institutions designed to carry out the proposed *régénération*. A voluntary community would administer modern schools, provide services for the elderly and the poor, and oversee the collection of funds. Communities would continue to maintain their rabbis, but rabbinical authority would be limited to the areas of religious custom and ceremony.[60] Convinced that citizenship would one day supplant religion as the basis of *fraternité*, Berr envisioned the rapid eradication of anti-Jewish prejudices. He rejected any notion of incongruity between religious obligations and civic duties, as the two spheres were, in his view, complementary. This idea would reemerge as a central argument at the Assembly of Jewish Notables.[61]

Evidence of the compatibility of republicanism and Judaism may be observed in a particularly fascinating and dramatic moment in Metz Jewry's early history as citizens. In October 1792 the community gathered in its main synagogue to conduct a *fête civique* in response to the triumph of the republican armies at Thionville. This enthusiastic reaction to its new status permitted the community to identify with the French nation, to interpret for itself the significance of recent developments in its own history, and to express thanks for divine assistance. The ceremony consisted of a procession of soldiers and a discourse delivered by the Grand Rabbi Uri Phoebus Cahen extolling the bravery of the defenders and emphasizing the duties to the *patrie*; it culminated with the congregational singing of a Hebrew poem, accompanied by an orchestra, to the melody of the "Marseillaise." Composed specially for the occasion by Moses Ensheim, the poem used biblical imagery and motifs to interpret the events of the Revolution. The virtues of the Revolution were vividly portrayed in stark contrast to the injustices of the oppressive monarchy, evocatively referred to as *malkhut haresha* ("the regime of evil") and equated by Ensheim with idolatry; the victory of the republican armies recalled Isaiah's prophecy concerning the overthrow of Babylon. Perhaps more important, the new social values of the Revolution, including *sensibilité*, transparency, *fraternité*, citizenship, patriotism, citizenship, and *régénération* are represented in the biblical idiom in order to confer sacral status upon them.[62]

The use of the term *régénération* to characterize the transformation of the Jews suggests that the process of change was considerably more complex than many had initially envisioned, or were even aware. First applied to the Jews by Pierre Louis Lacretelle in 1775, *régénération* entered the vocabulary of the Jewish question in 1788 only after it became the central focus of the Abbé Henri Grégoire's *Essai sur la régénération physique, morale et politique des Juifs*.[63] While the thrust of Grégoire's argument for improving the legal, economic, and social status of the Jews parallels that of Dohm and Mirabeau, his precise motivations in advancing their "regeneration" are still the subject of scholarly debate. All agree that he had faith in the ability of non-Western peoples to regenerate themselves and thereby join the ranks of "civilized nations." The controversial passage in Grégoire's *Essai* refers to what may be termed the "ultimate" aim of emancipation: "L'entière liberté religieuse accordée aux Juifs sera un grand pas en avant pour les réformer, et j'ose le dire, pour les convertir."[64] There seems to be no question that Grégoire envisioned the eventual conversion of the Jews to Christianity and that he regarded their improved treatment and civic emancipation as laying the groundwork for that eventuality. Precisely how he intended to realize that vision is not clear, however.

While one can resolve the difficulty, in part, by ascribing either mystical or messianic significance to this text, it is my sense that one may legitimately attribute more than mystical meaning to Grégoire's plan without necessarily concluding that the *abbé* had concrete missionary intentions. In his considerable writings he suggested that the successful regeneration of the Jews, like that of other peoples, would depend on their adoption of Christian (and European) values.[65] This should not surprise us. Over the course of the revolutionary years, the religious significance of the word *régénération* would continue to inform its usage. According to the 1690 edition of the *Dictionnaire Universel*, "*régénération* is accomplished by baptism, when a pagan converts."[66] Grégoire could not ignore the fact that in the classical Christian tradition *régénération* signified spiritual renewal and rebirth, and there can be no doubt that with this meaning in mind he applied the term to the disconsolate plight of the Jews.[67] It is in this sense that he expected the Jews to gradually become convinced of the superiority of Christianity through political and cultural *régénération*.

Under the impact of the Revolution, the term would be secularized in much the same way as other religious symbols and concepts.[68] The French emphasized the role of their nation as the Redeemer of mankind. In a proclamation made on 21 February 1793, the convention entrusted the armies with the following sacred mission: "If you are victorious . . . nations will embrace each other, and, ashamed of their longstanding error, they will forever extinguish the torch of war. You will be proclaimed saviors of the fatherland, founders of the Republic, regenerators of the universe."[69] The Revolution thus appropriated *régénération*, attributing to it a secular-messianic significance. In the spirit of revolutionary rhetoric, *régénération* would come to represent the basis of a new faith in the future of humankind, led by France of the Revolution. Philippe Sagnac vividly characterized the faith in the regeneration of French society as "a powerful sentiment that communicates an infinite energy—infinite like religion itself." It was "an act of faith," a "synthesis of spiritual elements," and a universal "religion."[70]

In *régénération* the French saw the promise of a new era unencumbered by the failings of the past. It embodied the vision of a social and cultural revolution that would complete the work begun in 1789.[71] The fact that *régénération* was applied to the Jews is proof of the comprehensiveness and ambitiousness of that dream. Nevertheless, the shared use of the term *régénération* in general and Jewish writings ought not conceal the widely divergent thinking on what it entailed. For the French, *régénération* was a break from the past, a rejection of a national history marked by corruption and degeneration. The belief that nothing was worth preserving explains the Revolution's early radical character.[72] Accordingly, French expectations for the transformation of the Jewish population were far-reaching. Owing to the links between *régénération* and Revolution, the anticipated metamorphosis of the Jews was framed in extraordinarily compelling terms. Its religious, patriotic, and universalistic character served as the primary impetus and conceptual foundation for tackling the Jewish question directly.

For Jewish leaders, *régénération* represented a less radical proposition. It signified not an outright rejection of traditional values and norms but the act of restoring to its original state that which had become corrupted over the course of centuries. The success of this restorative process would require careful historical investigation in order to distinguish between the essential and nonessential elements of the Jewish religious tradition. For the following two or three generations, discussion of the long-awaited socioeconomic and cultural transformation would be framed principally in religious terms, owing to the consensus shared by virtually all members of the community on the need to invoke the authority of Judaism in support of their respective visions. The notion of "tradition," though reinterpreted and redefined throughout the nineteenth century, would endure as the linchpin of Jewish identity in France and suggests that use of the term *secularization* may be an unsatisfactory characterization of French Jewry's ideological transformation. More striking is the markedly conservative conception of tradition espoused by French Jews in the face of swift and dramatic changes in modern society. Explanations for this restraint have proposed that French Jewry's achievement of civic equality without a prolonged political struggle made religious accommodation unnecessary.[73] The present analysis takes a different approach, concentrating on developments within the Jewish community in the revolutionary era and after. A new Franco-Jewish consciousness emerged very deliberately, apparently slowed by well-established social and cultural patterns that prevailed during the *ancien régime* and that continued to influence the nature of Jewish identity in the nineteenth century.

Régénération Delayed: The Crisis of the 1790s

Ironically, even the relatively slow progress made on the ideological level far outstripped practical efforts at implementation. Leaders of the first generation of emancipated Jewry failed to translate their commitment to *régénération* into a concrete program of action. Their failure was due, in large part, to a delay in the transformation of French Jewry—a development that would have far-reaching consequences for much of the nineteenth century. From a comparative perspective, the regeneration of Jewish life in the northeast provinces proceeded at an exceedingly slow pace. The Jews of Alsace-Lorraine remained largely isolated from the effects of modernization already underway in central Europe at the end of the eighteenth and early nineteenth centuries. Throughout Bohemia and Moravia, and to a large extent in Hungary, Galicia, and Bukowina, state-sponsored normal schools were established in the 1780s, and within a decade thousands of Jewish children had already attended these institutions. Great strides were also made with respect to vocational training. In Kassel, for example, the Gesellschaft der Humanität, founded in 1802, assumed responsibility for encouraging Jews to learn artisan trades. Frankfurt's 1807 regulations allowed Jews to learn and pursue trades, and the director of the Philanthropin school resolved to indenture suitable students with Christian masters, and to do the same for non-students as well. Toward the same goal, the Society for the Promotion of Industry among the Jews of Prussia was chartered in 1813, following the Judenedikt of 1812. These developments in Jewish schooling and vocational training in the Habsburg Empire and Germanic lands in the last third of the eighteenth century offer striking examples of advanced socioeconomic and cultural transformation achieved independently of political emancipation.[74] Modernization clearly preceded the emancipation of central European Jewry.

The situation was far different in France. No modern Jewish schools were established until the early years of the Bourbon Restoration, and no sustained effort in the active encouragement of greater productivity can be discerned until after 1820. The educational program advanced in 1782 by Berlin *maskil* Naphtali Herz Wessely, in *Divrei Shalom ve-Emet*, though available in a French translation, remained a theoretical proposition only and would not be implemented until several decades later.[75] Although the immediate improvement in legal standing heightened the expectation of far-reaching changes, the transformation of the Jews in France lagged far behind that of their coreligionists to the east. Even two decades after the Revolution the Central Consistory complained that less than 10 percent of Jewish children in Alsace were able to attend public schools, while in Lorraine, according to the prefect of Vosges, only a slightly higher proportion—20 percent—attended such institutions.[76] In the economic sphere change was quite slow in coming. Movement away from commercial activity, especially petty trade and moneylending, was uncommon, thus serving to buttress conservative trends.[77] For the vast majority of Jews in France, emancipation preceded modernization.

Three general factors account for this delay. First, the surrounding society in eastern France was at a very low cultural level, and the pace of modernization there was exceptionally slow. The persistence of a traditional orientation was manifested in community organization, family, schooling, religious ritual, and in the remarkably tenacious attachment to *patois*. Owing in part to the general view that Alsace-Lorraine was still outside the mainstream of French social and political life, relatively little effort was directed at the modernization of rural populations until the last third of the nineteenth century when the spread of government-sponsored communication and transportation systems succeeded in bringing the modern world into the village.[78] Until that point, most Jews of Alsace-Lorraine, like their gentile counterparts, lived in rural districts where social conventions were dominated by religious tradition, still insulated from many of the social and cultural forces at work in urban areas. Although the Jews of eastern France displayed an impressive commitment to learning French and underwent urbanization more rapidly than their non-Jewish neighbors, the continuation of traditional cultural and social patterns was invariably a product of the general environment in which they lived. Among Jews in rural communities, even well into the nineteenth century, apprehensiveness concerning the dangers of modernity severely limited the effectiveness of separate Jewish regenerative institutions. Fearing the effects of secular studies and the difficulties of remaining religiously observant, many were reluctant to send their children to modern Jewish schools or institutions for vocational training. The endurance of Yiddish as a spoken language, the comparatively high birthrate, the relatively slow movement to the cities, and the rejection of religious reform provide further indications of just how strong the grip of tradition remained.[79]

A second factor contributing to the slow pace of change was the hostility Jews encountered in the immediate aftermath of the Revolution and the bestowal of civic equality. The Revolution unleashed forces that were damaging to Jewish interests and would disrupt Jewish communal life for nearly two decades. It is not without great irony that this aggression was more vehement than anything they experienced in the previous century. Whether this was due to the essential illiberalism of the Revolution or resulted from the ill-preparedness of French society to embrace the new principles of 1789 is still the subject of historical debate.[80] Prior to the Revolution, relations with the general population had been governed by a longstanding tradition of legal disability. The *péage corporel* (body tax), residence restrictions, and stringent economic regulations had been renewed periodically throughout the *ancien régime*, and indeed the 1784 decree eliminating the *péage corporel* met with resistance from the general populace.[81] If the Revolution represented a genuine break with this legacy of hostility and exclusion as far as the Jews were concerned, it is nonetheless clear that its liberal ideals failed to gain popular approval. In July 1789 after news of the Revolution had reached the countryside, anti-Jewish riots broke out in twenty Alsatian communities. Estimates have between 1,200 and 3,000 Jews injured, while the number fleeing to Basel and Mulhouse may have been nearly 1,000. According to Zosa Szajkowski, however, the riots must be viewed in their larger context: Alsatian farmers, frustrated by the delay in the passage of the law granting them ownership over the land they were working, directed their violence against the nobility, the church, and, in some instances, even against Protestants. Jews, too, were victimized, although in most communities where Jews lived there was no violence. Riots were concentrated in Upper Alsace; outbreaks were reported in Nancy and Metz, but they were not as serious.[82] Whether or not we view the riots as having targeted Jews specifically, there is no denying their severe effects. Violence continued into the autumn months and was renewed in at least one town, Scherwiller, after nearly a year of relative calm.[83]

Instances of anti-Jewish discrimination and exclusion were not at all uncommon in the early 1790s. Insistent that "the National Assembly had set aside indefinitely the decision regarding the civil status of the Jews of Alsace," the Directoire du Bas-Rhin affirmed the decision of the Osthoffen municipality in 1790 to deny Jews the benefits of citizenship. The right to settle in numerous localities such as Habsheim, Sierentz, Bischheim au Saum, Winzenheim, and Lingolsheim also encountered local opposition.[84] In Strasbourg the municipality only permitted Jews to take the civil oath after a full four months had elapsed following the passage of the law of citizenship,[85] while in Bischeim the mayor prevented a group of Jews from voting in an election for justice of the peace.[86] In Haguenau the Jewish population continued to suffer the indignity of the *péage personel*, were threatened with expulsion by the first *tribun revolutionnaire*, and in some instances, as late as 1796, were required to provide military lodging as a condition of gaining citizenship. Although the expulsion of the Jews from the

city turned out to be nothing more than a threat, the *péage corporel* did survive at least until 1796.[87] In Metz in 1792 the municipal council and the military authorities suppressed riots against Jews soon after they began,
causing little harm.[88] The varied expressions of hostility toward the Jews in
the aftermath of the Revolution were, nonetheless, more than simply a
relic of the *ancien régime* that had persisted despite the new legislation. Anti-
Jewish hostility was clearly intensified by opponents of the new order.[89]

In the early 1790s popular resistance to Jewish rights was accompanied
by government interference in internal Jewish affairs. In Fegersheim and
Odratzheim, for example, the municipalities either prohibited the local
rabbi from performing several marriage ceremonies or refused to issue a
marriage license.[90] Actions such as these relied on the prohibition against
marrying without the permission of the king as their pretext. In at least one
case the Directory instructed the municipality not to prevent the couple
from marrying, however.[91] In 1791, Benjamin Hemmerdinger, rabbi of the
Jewish communities that were formerly part of the directorate of the nobility of Lower Alsace, asked the government authorities to intercede on
his behalf. Having failed to receive his salary for two years, he turned to the
Directory of the Lower Rhine for assistance. Accordingly, the Directory ordered the communities to pay the rabbi the sum that he was owed.[92]

While the two aforementioned factors point to the failure of the Revolution to overcome the powerful forces of conservatism that prevailed in the
ancien régime, a third reason for the delay in the modernization of French
Jewry was a direct result of the Revolution itself. The upheavals of revolution and war severely aggravated economic conditions in a territory where
crude industrial and agricultural technology prevailed. Ultimately, the
elimination of the feudal order and the introduction of agrarian reforms
would transform the French economy, but the short-term economic effects
of the Revolution were disappointing. As a result of this economic stand-
still, Jewish army purveyors continued, for the next quarter-century, in the
role they had played before the Revolution. Ultimately, the transformation
of Jewish economic activity would depend on macrocosmic changes in industry, agriculture, and banking.[93] For the largest number of Jews in Alsace-
Lorraine, economic devastation was the most immediate consequence of
the Revolution, as is illustrated by conditions in Metz in 1791–92. In an impassioned plea directed at Jewish communities throughout Europe, Metz
leaders described the rampant poverty that had overtaken their community. New customs restrictions and the enforcement of laws regulating
moneylending had become overbearing. Many were without food, while
Torah scholars, formerly maintained by community funds, could no longer
be supported. Less than a year after the bestowal of civic equality, the community had fallen deeply into debt and was threatened with expulsion.[94]
This situation was by no means limited to Metz. For many wealthy Jewish
families in the northeast, the Revolution was the cause of financial ruin.

Isaïe Berr Bing, for one, lost two-thirds of his fortune, while many others experienced similar difficulties.[95] Beyond the obvious fiscal impact, the widespread confiscation of property and the loss of fortunes aggravated the already difficult conditions in the post-revolutionary era.

During the Reign of Terror the situation deteriorated dramatically. The *kehillah* fell into a state of disorder, while many who observed Jewish rituals openly became the victims of a general assault on established religions. In Alsace-Lorraine the Jewish religion was persecuted relentlessly: synagogues and *yeshivot* were either closed down or in a state of disarray, cemeteries were desecrated, Torah scrolls were publicly burned, *shehitah* and circumcision were prohibited, and Sabbath observance was punished as a crime. At Dijon the Jacobin club demanded the suspension of ritual slaughter, and at Besançon Jews were denounced for their distinctiveness. Memories of the trauma and persecution suffered during the Terror, including evidence of public ridicule of beards and sidelocks, the wearing of *zizit* and head coverings, and the performance of *shehitah,* have been preserved in published works, manuscripts, and oral traditions.[96] In perhaps the most vivid surviving account from these years, R. David Sintzheim described the burning of Torah scrolls and holy books, the closing of his *yeshivah,* and his own wanderings in the introduction to his collection of *novellae, Yad David.*

It was the year 1794, when the days of remembrance, the days of anger, arrived. The Lord opened His treasury and produced the instruments of His anger, and we said: we have been condemned. Were it not for the Lord's mercy on us, we would nearly all have disappeared and been lost, as they had proclaimed that they would destroy all the books written in Hebrew. Our numerous faults caused some *sifrei Torah* and precious books to be burnt, and precious treasures were then pilfered. I had to hide my books. In this period of trouble and anger, those who know the ways of the Talmud stopped traveling and the ways of Zion were desolate. The doors of the Temple were closed to study and to prayer. I could not even study a single chapter of a well-known Mishnah. I was in exile and moved from city to city, from border to border. Finally the Lord took pity on His creatures, and freed the land from the evil beast. The anger disappeared and everyone returned to his home in peace.[97]

The publishing history of R. Aaron Worms's multivolume *Me'orei Or* also mirrored the disruptive effects of the Reign of Terror. *Me'orei Or* was one of only a handful of works of rabbinic scholarship published in France in the revolutionary era. The first three volumes appeared in the early 1790s, but publication ceased abruptly as the Hebrew press in Metz was forced to close its doors.[98] During the height of oppression in 1793–94, Worms set his own unpublished manuscripts afire, evidently for fear they would fall into the wrong hands.[99] His colleague in Metz, Rabbi Ouri Phoebus Cahen, reported that in 1793 he had hurried to publish his *novellae* before trouble arrived.[100] By the end of the century, the institutional and cultural foundations of Jewish life were left in shambles, while the policy of economic exploitation during the Napoleonic regime further diminished the

prospects for communal rehabilitation. Worms did not return to his erstwhile project for twenty-five years, when he resumed publishing *Me'orei Or*
in 1819.[101]

Others, such as R. Jacob Meyer of Niedernai, were imprisoned, while R.
Simon Horchheim of Mutzig was arrested and nearly executed for violating
the order prohibiting Sabbath observance.[102] Among the most poignant
recollections is one describing R. Jacob Gougenheim of Haguenau, who
was ordered to turn the keys of the synagogue over to the authorities of the
city and was thereafter prohibited from bearing the title "rabbi." Forced to
terminate his rabbinical functions in year II (1793–94), the Jews of Haguenau were forbidden from gathering to pray, until the order was overturned
by a decree in 1795.[103] According to one Jacobin observer, the expulsion of
the Jews from Strasbourg was justified because "they substitute *cupidité* for
love of the *patrie*, and their ridiculous superstitions for reason." The solution, he concluded, demanded nothing less than "la régénération guillo-
tinière."[104] Significantly, recollections of persecution tended to be the least
prominent in nineteenth-century French Jewry's collective memory of the
Revolution.

While the situation was not nearly as acute in the southern communities,
Jews did suffer there as well from the revolutionary upheavals. Some, such
as members of the Crémieux family of Carpentras, were imprisoned. A petition to the Chambre des Deputés submitted by several Jews of l'Isle-sur-
Sorgues in 1820 contains a rare description of the difficulties experienced
by the communities of Comtat Venaissin. Following the termination of the
Jewish communities of the Comtat, the government seized their property,
which included two large cemeteries, two synagogues, and all the liquid assets. The synagogues of l'Isle and the street where members of the community had lived were destroyed, while the synagogue of Carpentras was
stripped of all its magnificent ornaments and was subsequently turned into
a club. Later, in year VIII, the Carpentras building was leased by the Régie
des Domains and remained so even after the government had reinstated
Jewish worship in localities where it had been disrupted and had returned
synagogues to the control of the Jewish religious authorities.[105]

As a result of the deterioration of conditions in Alsace-Lorraine, an entire generation of *yeshivah* students and rabbis left the region and immigrated to Germany where they pursued their studies. Loeb Sarassin, a
native of Bischeim, had attended the local *yeshivah* until it closed in 1796;
he subsequently left for Germany to study at the *yeshivot* of Mayence,
Mannheim, and Frankfurt am Main, only to return to France in 1813 when
he was appointed rabbi of Ingwiller. Similarly, Rabbi Samuel Wittersheim
of Metz settled in Westphalia after having been ruined financially by the
Revolution and remained there until 1813 before returning to Metz. Others were not as fortunate in returning to their native land. Rabbi Abraham
Isaac Lunteschütz saw the collapse of the *yeshivah* he directed in Westhof-

fen, lost his fortune, and was imprisoned during the Reign of Terror. Failing to find a position in France, he was later selected as rabbi of the communities of Endigen-Lengnau, Switzerland.[106] The cumulative impact on the rabbinate was profound. Until 1840 virtually all of the rabbinic positions in France were still occupied by men who had been trained in German *yeshivot.*[107]

Problems did not disappear with the Terror. Various sources point to the persistence of public ridicule, continued discrimination, and widespread persecution well into the nineteenth century. According to a letter sent in 1806 to the Minister of Cults by four Bas-Rhin delegates to the Assembly of Jewish Notables, anti-Jewish sentiment in the villages was spirited; local clergy reportedly were responsible for stirring the general populace to violent acts directed against the Jews and their property.[108] Not surprisingly, relatively few Jewish families ventured beyond the surety of their communities. In Metz, according to the Prefect of Moselle, only twenty-nine Jewish families had left the ghetto.[109] The result was the preservation of an unmistakable social distance between Jews and their gentile neighbors in the villages, at least until mid-century. The economic hardship caused by the Infamous Decree of 1808 further depleted the ranks of Jewish communities across Alsace-Lorraine, only aggravating the emigration pattern that had begun in the 1790s. In general, the leadership appears to have been demoralized by these developments.[110]

The disruptive effects of the Revolution and the Reign of Terror on Jewish communal life and leadership presented formidable obstacles to the implementation of regenerative proposals. In several communities in Alsace-Lorraine, such as Haguenau, Hegenheim, Metz, and Mutzig, the rabbinate remained vacant until 1808, schools and synagogues were closed, and the two Hebrew presses, in Metz and Lunéville, ceased operations. As a result, the Jewish population of the northeast was not able to organize itself to meet the new challenges that faced them as French citizens. Owing to the crushing effects of the Terror on community institutions, as well as the turmoil that disrupted Jewish life in general, the Jews of Alsace-Lorraine found themselves in the throes of a severe communal crisis that was to leave its mark on Jewish life throughout France for much of the nineteenth century. The state, for its part, was preoccupied with first establishing and then consolidating its power during the 1790s and therefore took little interest in the transformation of the Jews. In fact, aside from initiating the administrative reorganization of French Jewry in 1808, the state refrained from intervening in Jewish affairs as was done in the Habsburg Empire, where legislation preceded and prompted social change.[111] This tendency was reinforced by the belief that the natural forces of modernization and civic equality would yield the desired results.

Despite the many disturbances, it was not uncommon for Jewish communities to function as they had prior to the Revolution and for French authorities to relate to the Jews as members of collective bodies. As far as the Jews themselves were concerned, there was no alternative framework that could guarantee continuity in the essential areas of Jewish life, especially in an era of social and political turmoil. Continuity with the pre-revolutionary modes of communal organization also made it possible both to record the Jewish *état-civil* and to meet ongoing fiscal obligations. It was therefore in the interest of local authorities to encourage and support the perpetuation of the pre-revolutionary communal system, especially by preserving the authority of communal leaders. Although communities were required to surrender judicial autonomy in the civil sphere, private litigation in the early years remained under rabbinic jurisdiction; community officials were elected as before. The situation was to change in 1795 with the passage of a law abrogating obligatory taxes for religious activities. While this legislation undoubtedly undermined the enforcement of internal discipline, communities continued to function in order to maintain the basis of Jewish life and to collect taxes needed to pay debts owed by the former communities, debts the new regime failed to nationalize as in the case of all other communities.[112] Unable to function at more than the most minimal level, Jewish communities of Alsace-Lorraine remained in a state of crisis until the Napoleonic regime undertook its own reorganization program. Until then, and even after, the much-heralded program of *régénération* would remain virtually stillborn.

Chapter 5

Religion, State, and Community: The Impact of Napoleonic Reform

Over the course of the nineteenth and twentieth centuries, the persistence of anti-Jewish discrimination and the occasional outbursts of violence against Jews coexisted alongside France's steadfast commitment to their civic equality. This unwavering pledge has endured because the emancipation of the Jews has remained interwoven with the revolutionary legacy. Their experience in modern France has nonetheless involved an unceasing struggle to balance the competing demands of religion and state. Efforts to resolve this struggle, with all its implications and paradoxes, are at the heart of modern Jewish consciousness. Its evolution has been guided by the progressive interpretation of the legacy of 1789—in effect a hermeneutic that was profoundly influenced by political and social forces within the Jewish community and beyond. In the years following the Revolution, the Jews of France became noticeably more conscious of their public image, especially as opportunities for social interaction with non-Jews increased. The achievement of citizenship in 1790–91 did not quell continuing doubts about the wisdom of this decision. Extensive discussions of the Jewish question during the first half of the nineteenth century produced shifts in the Jews' self-image, persuading some to embrace French culture more vigorously, while others concluded that defiance of this trend was the better response. It is also clear from the various terms used in reference to emancipation—*émancipation intérieure, émancipation industrielle, émancipation civile*, and *émancipation politique*, to name only a few—that Jewish communal and intellectual leaders had developed an appreciation for the complexities of emancipation and understood that for it to be realized fully, the process would unfold only in phases.[1]

The Napoleonic years represent a critical period of transition when efforts to transform French Jewry were undertaken in accordance with a new vision of the Revolution. With the conclusion of the Concordat in 1801, Napoleon Bonaparte determined that relations between the state and religion ought to be cooperative, not hostile. However, the initial terms of mutual respect and recognition that characterized the agreement with the pope were not honored beyond the first few months. Napoleon greatly limited the rights and powers of the church with respect to the nomination to bishoprics; registration of births, deaths, and marriages; and in the training of clergy. Once the state asserted its authority over Roman Catholicism, it introduced parity among the major religions by enacting laws for the public regulation of the Protestant community and by assuming responsibility for clerical salaries.[2] Judaism was subsequently granted the status of an officially recognized religion alongside Catholicism and Protestantism. Although a quarter-century would pass before Jewish clergy were salaried by the state as Catholic and Protestant ministers had been, the principle of parity advanced the legal status of French Jewry in an unprecedented manner. The idea and its realization would exert extensive influence on their political and cultural orientation. What is more, the aggressive efforts of the Napoleonic regime to shape domestic policy rested on a novel understanding of the function of the state in promoting societal reform.

By the first years of the nineteenth century it had become evident to most everyone familiar with the "Jewish question" that the pace of regeneration had lagged far behind expectations; the buoyant spirit that permeated Jewish writings in the early revolutionary era waned precipitously. Nevertheless, enthusiastic support for the emperor at the turn of the nineteenth century, prior to the unveiling of his policy initiative vis-à-vis the Jews, points to the awakening of deep national sentiment in diverse quarters of the Jewish community. A profusion of literary creativity, dominated especially by Hebrew poetry, flourished within a cadre of rabbis and in the small circle of French *maskilim*. Rabbis Jacob Meyer, Abraham Cologna, and Netanel Wittersheim each published poems honoring the emperor. Hebrew and German poetry exalting Napoleon and his military prowess sprang from the French Haskalah, which counted Moses Ensheim, Elie Halévy, and Lipmann Moïse Büschental among its leading figures. Several poems composed by Halévy in particular reflected an effort to identify with the military campaigns undertaken by the regime. In "Ha-Shalom," composed in 1801, Halévy praised France using terms typically reserved for the Land of Israel; on the occasion of several battles he wrote prayers that were recited in the Paris synagogue.[3] Likewise, the enthusiasm that manifested itself during the Napoleonic regime found expression in a liturgical innovation at the Sabbath morning public service. The traditional prayer *Ha-Noten Teshu'ah la-Melakhim*,[4] in which Jews appealed to God to grant to the head of state victory and dominion over his enemies, was replaced by a composition authored by R. Abraham Cologna, of the Central Consistory, in 1808. The new prayer, called *Elohim Ḥayyim*, a stately, poetic hymn in rhymed verse, was considered to be more appropriate for choral accompaniment. Substantively, although the two prayers each concerned the glory and triumph of the king, the newer prayer omitted the section asking God to incline the heart of the king and his counselors to have mercy on the unhappy fate of the Jews and to hasten their deliverance in Zion. Such elements were doubtless viewed as out of step with the patriotic devotion and universalist strivings of the new era.[5]

One should nonetheless not overestimate the significance of this literature. Although the works appearing in these years reflected an unmistakable yearning to identify with the state in times of crisis, they belong, more correctly, to the literary genre of the early Haskalah era; they contain no evidence of a new Jewish consciousness. In the first years of Napoleonic rule, the Haskalah remained a received ideology that *maskilim* in France appropriated from Berlin with only minor modifications. In the decade following the Revolution, enthusiastic literary productions were the predominant Jewish cultural expression, while no well-defined prescription for Jewish modernization was proposed.

Traces of a revolutionary consciousness reminiscent of the optimism displayed immediately before and after the Revolution can nonetheless be detected in a pamphlet that appeared in Paris in 1806, as the Assembly of Jewish Notables prepared to convene. Published by Simon Mayer, the brief tract was issued in response to an essay by Louis de Bonald charging that the Jews could never attain genuine political equality or integration in French society as long as they refused to accept Jesus as the messiah. The state, Bonald asserted, was Christian, and citizenship was therefore the exclusive privilege of those who adhered to Christianity. Vehemently denying Bonald's claim that Jews failed to recognize the laws of the state, Mayer expressed the view that political emancipation would lead naturally and directly to their integration within French society. Mayer boldly asserted the right of Jews to defend their honor, but his confidence in the capacity of the legal and political system to achieve "la réunion de tous les Français" evinces a largely naïve assessment of the difficulties inherent in social integration. His naïveté was typical of the small group of Parisian Jews who remained not only unconvinced of the urgency of establishing separate Jewish institutions but ideologically opposed to it as well.[6]

Others reassessed their initial optimism and offered an amended plan for *régénération*. Berr Isaac Berr, for one, realized that in setting forth his vision for Jewish life in the emancipation era, he had failed to consider the various social and religious forces that were likely to slow the pace of modernization. Fifteen years later, on the eve of the convocation of the Assembly of Jewish Notables, Berr took a more sober view. In his *Réflexions sur la régénération complète des Juifs en France*, he explained that the persistence of anti-Jewish prejudices not only impeded the process of Jewish social integration but also impacted negatively on Jewish self-perception. The recreation of a communal organization under official auspices would remedy these problems by serving as much-needed proof of the government's commitment to the principle of religious equality. Equally important was the role that such an organization would play in easing the formation of regenerative institutions under Jewish sponsorship and direction. Berr had come to the realization that in spite of its political achievements, French Jewry was still ill-prepared for the obligations that citizenship demanded they fill. In his view, the Jews would embark on the road to modernization only under the watchful eye of an enlightened Jewish leadership whose authority had received the full endorsement of the government. Nevertheless, no genuinely significant efforts to come to terms with the new social and political order in revolutionary France would materialize until after the full thrust of the Napoleonic reforms had become apparent.[7]

Since citizenship was granted with the implicit understanding that *régénération* would soon be carried out, the progress of Jewish modernization became a matter of public debate in the post-revolutionary era. To most gentile observers, emancipation produced only modest adjustments in the socioeconomic condition of the Jews. The removal of legal disabilities resulted in some changes in their residence patterns; they began settling in regions where formerly few or no Jewish inhabitants had lived. Strasbourg, for example, became a major Jewish population center, as did Paris; in Metz, on the other hand, a diffusion of its population into neighboring villages reflected economic expansion in the region. Nevertheless, although these residential shifts resulted in a Jewish presence in forty-four *départements*, as compared to only ten on the eve of the Revolution, the relative size of most new communities remained quite small. The greater tendency was to concentrate in cities with already existing Jewish populations. Migration tended to be in the direction of towns and cities in Alsace-Lorraine, as well as in the Bordeaux-Bayonne region. The inclination to move in groups resulted in an even greater concentration than before.[8] Occupational changes were less pronounced still. For the most part, Jews tended to use their new opportunities to vary and extend their traditional occupations. Commercial activities became more diversified with the availability of new markets, and some participated in the purchase of nationalized property, but this was primarily for speculation. Due to a combination of factors, mainly the lack of economic motivation to shift occupations and the reluctance of Christian masters to accept Jewish apprentices, the greatest concentration of Jews remained firmly entrenched in moneylending, peddling, and petty commerce.[9]

The failure to furnish convincing evidence of social and economic regeneration was invariably taken by critics to confirm earlier qualms concerning the advisability of emancipation. It was widely observed that emancipation had contributed little to the regeneration of the Jews. Impatience with patterns of Jewish integration in the post-revolutionary era was related, at least in part, to the emergence and growth of nationalism. Having transformed the embryonic forms of national consciousness of the early modern period into a genuine nationalism, the French Revolution substituted loyalty to the state for allegiance to the monarchy, and faith in the ideals of liberty and equality for identification with the church. The revolutionary movement conceived of the nation as the totality of its inhabitants, as the realization of Rousseau's conception of the general will. Symbols such as the flag, the anthem, and the revolutionary festivals were concrete signs of the growing national feeling.[10] The emergence of strong national sentiment, however, only added to the uneasiness about the social integration of the Jews. Reservations concerning the alien nature of the Jewish people, a concern heard frequently at the National Assembly and voiced repeatedly in the ensuing decades, rested firmly on the envisioned social and cultural amalgamation of diverse sectors of the population. In light of the Jews' disappointing record of socioeconomic improvement since the Revolution, some concluded that the bestowal of citizenship may have been premature, while others, in upholding Jewish emancipation, sought avenues for an acceptable transformation of Jewish life.

Emblematic of the complaints lodged against Alsatian Jewry is a pamphlet published in 1806 by Louis Poujol, a Parisian lawyer originally from Alsace. The author assembled data aiming to help the government determine whether citizenship ought to be maintained or temporarily withdrawn from the "German" Jews. The "Portuguese" Jews, according to Poujol, were entirely different. Economically, they were honest and productive, and the mores they practiced resembled those of the larger French nation. As far as the Jews of Alsace were concerned, the question depended on their readiness to abandon deeply rooted patterns of behavior. Poujol reviewed Jewish involvement in moneylending and concluded that the popular animosity, discriminatory legislation, and numerous expulsions that the Jews experienced ought to be viewed as legitimate responses to their immoral practices. And in light of the fact that the Jews continued to practice usury even after economic restrictions had been removed, he maintained, citizenship ought to be temporarily withdrawn so that exceptional legal measures could be justifiably invoked. Beyond its economic implications, usury epitomized the alien nature of the Jews. Their alleged failure to partake of public ceremonies and military obligations, as well as their unwillingness to participate in agriculture and trades, were taken as proof that they were unprepared to pay their debt to state and society. Their profound hatred of Christians made them dangerous enemies of the state; world domination, as promised to them by their religion, was their only true aspiration.[11]

The problem, in Poujol's view, was that the Jewish religion prescribed a value system and a lifestyle that were in absolute opposition to the general interest. His recommendations were therefore not limited to the strict regulation of their economic activity, as others had insisted, but extended to the realm of religious reform as well. He criticized the Sabbath restrictions because they rendered the Jews utterly useless to the state, and he therefore appealed for the reconciliation of these laws with requirements of various occupations. The dietary laws were, in his estimation, detrimental to the relations between Jews and non-Jews and should therefore be abrogated. Hebrew and Jewish studies were irrelevant and incompatible with the *moeurs*, customs, and education required for the common good. The Talmud, more than any other field of study, contained precepts that contradicted the principles of simple morality. Poujol's plan was straightforward: once divested of their peculiar customs and mentalities, the Jews would ultimately be assimilated into French society; only their manner of worship would distinguish them from other Frenchmen.[12]

Though devastatingly critical, Poujol's observations reflect a cautiously optimistic faith shared by government officials in the efficacy of reform. This is what impelled Napoleon to address the failures of Jewish emancipation and regeneration so dramatically. Ironically, the underpinnings of a new social and political vision on the part of the Jews were first set down precisely when their envisioned transformation was perceived to be at its lowest ebb. Government intervention in Jewish communal affairs during the First Empire was prompted by growing disappointment in the socioeconomic regeneration of Alsatian Jewry, but it also reflected the new role that was envisioned for the state in the pursuit of social reform. The Napoleonic program to transform the Jews was a radical departure from the policies pursued during the fifteen-year period following the Revolution. Emancipation had become synonymous with freedom from state interference, but it is evident from conditions in central Europe that intervention was critical to the success of modernization because the state could exert its coercive powers upon the Jewish community. The Napoleonic regime inaugurated a period of rehabilitation of Jewish life ravaged by a decade of violence and turmoil. Although Napoleon's exceedingly hostile views toward the Jews culminated in severe limitations on their economic freedom, he nevertheless took important steps to secure legal guarantees for their civic equality. This policy was consistent with his general plan to consolidate the changes conceived by the Revolution.[13] Napoleonic legislation defined the structure of Jewish communal life and the relationship of Jews to French society, while the convocation of the Paris Sanhedrin demanded that Jewish leaders rethink the relationship of Judaism to the state. Although the First Empire was clearly a political and economic setback for the Jews in the short run, the institutional achievements of the regime proved to be of enduring significance. The ideals of *égalité* and *fraternité* found expression in three spheres representing the fusion of the legacy of 1789 with successive interpretations: (1) the subordination of religion to the state; (2) administrative centralization; and (3) civic equality and the legal parity of religions. Each of these areas represented a major contribution to the reshaping of French-Jewish identity, and although their effects would not be evident immediately, their repercussions would be felt throughout the modern period.

Religion and State

Emboldened by his success in defining the respective spheres of influence of church and state, Napoleon sought clarification of Judaism's position vis-à-vis civic duties by convening an assembly that could speak authoritatively for the Jewish population of his empire. The decision to convene the Assembly of Jewish Notables owed its origins to a fateful meeting in January 1806 between Napoleon and Alsatian farmers in Strasbourg, following the emperor's return from Austerlitz. Persuaded by complaints that their progressive impoverishment was the result of heavy indebtedness to Jewish moneylenders, Napoleon came to view the Jews as the "vilest of all nations." Their unique circumstances justified the sort of government action ordinarily considered illegal. In a report to the Council of State Napoleon argued that "it is necessary to consider the Jews as a nation and not a sect . . . a nation within a nation,"[14] and he demanded that they be judged "according to political and not civil law."[15] Over the next several months, he concluded, against the nearly unanimous opposition of the legislative section of the Council of State, that exceptional legal measures were necessary in order to put an end to Jewish usury and to the humiliation of the French nation.[16] In a report to the emperor, the Minister of Religions Portalis conceded that it may not have been "advisable to proclaim them citizens without investigating if they could or even wanted sincerely to become so." Given their unique circumstances, he argued, "it would not be unreasonable or unjust to submit to particular laws a type of corporation, which, on account of its institutions, principles and customs, remains constantly separated from general society."[17]

Together, the dramatic convocation of the Assembly of Jewish Notables and its reconstitution early in 1807 under the portentous name "le Grand Sanhédrin" represented a thinly veiled effort to pressure Jewish leaders to acknowledge that strict adherence to Jewish law precluded the fulfillment of duties incumbent upon them as citizens of the state and as members of society at large. The delegates were doubtless aware that the attainment of citizenship depended on the satisfactory resolution of the competing demands of state and religion. It is therefore widely assumed that under such circumstances it was virtually impossible to represent the demands of Halakhah honestly and forthrightly. The responses of the Assembly of Jewish Notables are generally presumed to be a classic case of *apologia*, clearly intended to construct a positive image of Judaism vis-à-vis the general world at almost any expense. In the most extreme case, the assembly's pronouncement on the feasibility of intermarriage according to Jewish law appears to have been nothing less than a rebuff of the halakhic tradition.[18]

In the analysis that follows, we shall reconsider the prevailing evaluation of the Sanhedrin by carefully examining the conceptions of gentiles and gentile culture that had emerged among a number of respected halakhic authorities in the two centuries preceding the Paris convocation. Evidence of a fundamentally positive view of gentiles in the halakhic literature of the period was, by the turn of the nineteenth century, considerable, suggesting that the much-maligned Paris body did not deviate from the Jewish legal tradition to the extent that is generally assumed.

The much-vilified attribute of social exclusiveness that had come under attack repeatedly in the revolutionary years was purportedly the product of two grave flaws in Judaism's legal system. First, as Portalis had asserted, it combined "the religion, the political and the civil laws, the habits, the manners, and all the customs of life."[19] According to Napoleon himself, the problem lay in the failure of Judaism to distinguish between religious and political laws. Religious prescriptions were, he admitted, of an eternal character and therefore immutable; Judaism's political provisions, however, applied to the era when Jews had resided in their own land as an independent nation. However, since Jewish civil law no longer enjoyed any contemporary application, the newly constituted Sanhedrin had "the mandate to abolish all atrocious laws . . . that could only apply to Jews living in Palestine."[20] Behind this claim lay an argument for a more restricted role for religion in society. Shared habits, customs, and symbols were viewed as agents of national cohesion and unity, whereas religion was limited to matters of conscience. The interrelation of the religious and civil domains in Judaism was fundamentally foreign to the new political culture of France and was therefore considered intolerable by republicans. For their part, Jews had traditionally understood religion to have a crucial role in the regulation of social life. By accepting the premise that there were two independent sources of law, many "enlightened" Jews broke, consciously or not, with traditional Judaism of the pre-revolutionary era. Second, the contention that the Jewish religion upheld a dual standard of morality that freed Jews, in their relations with gentiles, from ethical obligations routinely required in dealings with fellow Jews threatened to undermine the emancipation project in its entirety. Judaism's authorization of usurious rates of interest on loans to non-Jews was taken as proof of its professed hatred of the non-Jew and, generally, of its policy of moral duplicity.[21] Though hardly novel, these accusations produced an acute sense of urgency in the revolutionary era.

Inspired by the belief that government intervention was the best hope for restoring economic stability in Alsace, Napoleon issued the Imperial Decree of 30 May 1806, which declared a moratorium on all debts owed to Jews by noncommercial farmers of the northeast. Economic rehabilitation was not the emperor's chief concern, however. Jewish lending practices were understood to be symptomatic of a more fundamental problem—the questionable suitability of the Jews to fulfill the obligations incumbent upon them as French citizens. Economic circumstances in the northeast made it clear "how urgent it is to revive sentiments of civil morality among those who profess the Jewish religion in the countries under our jurisdiction, sentiments which have, sadly, disappeared among a very great number of them due to the state of degradation in which they have languished, a state which it is not at all among our intentions to maintain nor to renew."[22] In Napoleon's view, the transformation of the political status of French Jews demanded intensive efforts to remedy the allegedly deficient "sentiments of civil morality" to which the Jewish population still stubbornly adhered. He therefore proceeded, in the second section of the Imperial Decree, to order the convocation of a Jewish assembly empowered with legislative authority to resolve the question of the incompatibility of Judaism and civic duties once and for all.

The tactical success of the plan to transform the Jews of the empire demanded that the full endorsement of their leaders first be secured. Napoleon sought formal reassurance that the Jews of the empire were committed to the French civil code and to his program of broad social integration. Twelve questions, focusing on marriage and divorce, attitudes toward non-Jews, civic duties, rabbinic authority, occupational restrictions, and moneylending, were brought before the assembly. The ultimate goal, as made clear by Napoleon, was to "reconcile the beliefs of the Jews with the duties of Frenchmen, and to transform them into useful citizens, in order to remedy the evil to which many of them apply themselves to the great detriment of our subjects."[23] To accomplish this objective, the emperor convened another body in 1807—the Sanhedrin—to formally ratify the assembly's responses and place "on equal footing with the Talmud, as articles of faith and principles of religious legislation."[24] A careful look at Napoleon's correspondence reveals that the emperor's ultimate objective was the total assimilation of French Jewry and, failing that, to achieve the means to impose rigorous state control over the Jewish population. One dispatch, written immediately before the convocation, contained a list of the specific answers that he desired, confirming that he expected of the assembly nothing short of an endorsement of intermarriage, a clear affirmation of the "brotherly" relationship between Jews and other Frenchmen, and an explicit prohibition of usury. More concretely, Napoleon entertained the idea of requiring one of every three marriages involving Jews to be with a Frenchman, while he envisioned that military conscription would effectively bring the Jews into the orbit of French culture and mores.[25]

Undoubtedly aware of the dangers implicit in the Napoleonic initiative, the delegates to the assembly divided into two principal factions—those whose worldview approximated the ideology of the Haskalah movement and those who adhered to a traditional halakhic orientation. Despite their differences on the authority of Jewish law and tradition, however, the two groups reached a general consensus on how an ethos of tolerance and respect for non-Jews ought to be formulated. This should not be surprising. Members of each faction were aware of the prevailing social and political realities in the early nineteenth century, and each acknowledged the need to fulfill the obligations that that the status of citizenship entailed; civic duties, such as military service, were the most obvious and tangible requirements. Liberal members of the assembly were firmly committed to a broadly conceived universalism and were therefore prepared to break with what they understood to be Judaism's overly parochial view of the world beyond the borders of the Jewish community. The traditionalist delegates, despite their full confidence in the superiority of Judaism over other faiths, naturally followed the teachings of the more tolerant rabbinic authorities of the late medieval and early modern periods. To view French society with contempt was scarcely plausible. In light of the political, social, and economic transformations that had altered the character of Jewish life in the west, and taking into consideration the expectation that the Jews would become part of the larger social framework, they were prepared to consider a new foundation upon which Jewish-gentile relations could be based.[26]

Throughout its deliberations, the assembly displayed an unequivocally positive attitude toward the primacy of the state and strongly endorsed Judaism's compatibility with civic duties. It denied that any aspect of Jewish religious law, for example, marriage and divorce, contravened the laws of the state. The reason for questions concerning the realm of personal status is clear: in France marriage was the specific arena where the conflict between religion and state was first waged. In 1792 marriage was brought under the auspices of the civil authorities and Jews were required to abide by the new law, which invalidated the legal standing of the Jewish marriage ceremony. Nevertheless, because the National Assembly had not yet established protocols for non-Catholic unions, Jews continued for some time to marry and divorce "according to the laws of Moses and Israel."[27] Napoleon went a step further, instructing rabbis not to perform the marriage ceremony without proof that the civil ceremony had already been performed before a government official. The Assembly of Jewish Notables confirmed that the state's role in establishing the legal validity of a marriage took precedence over Jewish law.[28] Though permitted in biblical Judaism and not expressly forbidden by the Talmud, polygamy had been formally prohibited since the synod of Rabbenu Gershom in the eleventh century. On the matter of divorce, the delegates stated that while "repudiation is permitted by the law of Moses . . . it is not valid if not previously pronounced by the French code." With this answer the assembly then proceeded to underscore the fundamental principle that guided Jews in all their dealings, that is, that the law of the state is undisputed: "In the eyes of every Israelite, without exception, submission to the prince is the first of duties. It is a principle generally acknowledged among them, that, in every thing relating to civil or political interests, the law of the state is the supreme law."[29]

The possibility of marriage between Jews and Christians was doubtless the most challenging issue facing the delegates, and it was here that progressive and traditionalist views diverged so widely that no agreement could be reached on a single formulation. Instead, two distinct answers were combined. The first part reflected the position that intermarriage with Christians was not expressly forbidden by biblical law. Accordingly, the prohibition was limited to the seven idolatrous nations of ancient Canaan only and did not extend to adherents of modern monotheistic faiths such as Christianity.[30] The second part referred explicitly to the opinion of the rabbinic delegates. It stated that in spite of the foregoing technical permissibility of marriage with Christians, the rabbis could not lend their support to such unions. Their response accentuated the ritual requirements of the marriage ceremony, which they argued were indispensable to the religious validity of the union. From the standpoint of Jewish law, then, marriage uniting a Jew with a Christian was not a recognized union. The rabbis did concede, however, that such marriages were valid civilly and that a couple so united could dissolve the union without the need for a religious divorce.[31] Even more significant, the rabbis resigned themselves to the fact that individuals were now free to live well beyond the authority of Jewish law. Nevertheless, by combining two answers into one, the delegates appeared to balance the widely divergent demands of Jewish law and contemporary French culture.

It is important to note that in the case of intermarriage, as in other areas as well, the decision of the Sanhedrin varied substantially from the response of the assembly of Jewish Notables. Regrettably, differences between the texts produced by the two bodies have been largely ignored. All in all, the assembly's responses were more deliberative in tone and reflected a wider range of views than the Sanhedrin, which was predominantly a rabbinic body. In decision 3 the Sanhedrin stated that although a mixed marriage created *civil* obligations, it was, from a religious standpoint, a prohibited act and the *kiddushin* were invalid.[32] As for the highly unorthodox formulation in the first part of the assembly's response, it appears to have been little more than a rhetorical ploy intended to curry favor with the Napoleonic commission; it offered no *legal* dispensation from the traditional prohibition against intermarriage.

The failure to notice this distinction has led many historians to exaggerate the delegates' general failure to represent the positions of Jewish law and tradition faithfully. Additionally, the assembly's effusive declarations of patriotism and brotherhood, especially, have been routinely understood as having broken with inviolable assumptions concerning the collective destiny of the Jewish people. In spite of the intense pressure to which members of the assembly were subjected, it is not at all clear that they either intentionally misrepresented or offered a tendentious reading of Judaism's view of the state and its gentile citizens. Their responses generally fell within the broad range of the Jewish legal tradition, though they invariably rested on certain opinions that were, certainly in the case of marriage, unconventional. Moreover, a more sympathetic reading of the Sanhedrin is amply supported by two bodies of pertinent evidence that historians have either overlooked or underestimated: (a) literature referring to the status of gentiles in Jewish law in the era leading up to the French Revolution; and (b) the published writings of Rabbi Aaron Worms, an important Metz halakhic authority who had served as a leading delegate at the Assembly of Jewish Notables and as a member of the Sanhedrin.

Before surveying this literature, we shall note three sources that offer additional perspective on the Sanhedrin. The first are the written responses of Rabbi Ishmael Ha-Kohen of Modena, a contemporary Italian halakhist who was invited to participate as a delegate but was unable to attend because of his advanced age. Left in manuscript, these private views were published for the first time thirty-five years ago. They reveal that the positions advanced by the assembly delegates corresponded closely to the views of at least one contemporary halakhic authority who was free of the intense political pressures felt in Paris.[33] Second, in a letter to Rabbi Baruch Jeiteles, *av beit din* of Prague, Sanhedrin president Rabbi David Sintzheim expressed satisfaction at having successfully resisted all challenges to the integrity of Jewish law. Third, a more convincing indication of respect for the way that the body performed its difficult task may be adduced from a eulogy pronounced by Rabbi Moses Sofer following the passing of Sintzheim in 1812. Sofer, the undisputed champion of Hungarian orthodoxy, praised Sintzheim for having maintained halakhic standards under extreme pressure. Although no details are provided, one may assume that such an uncompromising opponent of religious reform as the Ḥatam Sofer would not have praised Sintzheim undeservedly on so crucial a matter.[34] Clearly, however, neither of these two last sources is entirely free of bias.

Gentiles in Early Modern European Halakhic Literature

The sixteenth through the eighteenth centuries witnessed the emergence of substantial common ground between Jews and non-Jews, especially as mirrored in the halakhic literature of the period, though recent historical research suggests that this was not the case in Germanic lands.[35] Before proceeding, we shall first consider the range of ethical obligations toward gentiles within classical halakhic sources. The claim that in Jewish law there was a fundamental inequality between the status of Jew and non-Jew gained considerable notoriety with the publication of Johann Andreas Eisenmenger's *Entdecktes Judentums* in 1699.[36] Although the book was riddled with intentional distortions and errors, it succeeded in calling attention to legal inequities in the areas of theft, robbery, return of lost property, and deception. In *Bava Qama* 113b, for example, the prohibition against withholding money (*osheq*) was limited to fellow Jews only, based on the wording of Leviticus 19:13, "You shall not oppress your fellow" ("lo ta'ashoq et re'akha"). *Re'akha* is understood in this instance, as in most others, to refer specifically to Jews.[37] Maimonides, however, saw the withholding of money earned as the equivalent of robbery and ruled that the one (*osheq*) is prohibited like the other (*gezelah*).[38] Even so, the position of Maimonides is exceedingly complex as regards the scope of the prohibition of robbery and more generally with respect to the status of gentiles in Jewish law.[39]

Historically, several key arguments for prohibiting the mistreatment of gentiles emerged in the classical tradition. The talmudic discussion in *Gittin* 61a defined Jewish-gentile relations within the framework of reciprocal interaction. It is clear that the extensive list of ethical obligations vis-à-vis gentiles was mandated for the sake of social stability, mutual responsibility, and the promotion of peace (*mippnei darkhei shalom*). To these largely prudential-ethical concerns Maimonides offered a more positive reason why the abuse of gentiles was objectionable. According to Hilkhot Genevah 7:8, one who cheats the idolater performs an abhorrent act—an act of *avel*—that was condemned harshly in Deuteronomy 25:16: "For all that do such things, even all that act unrighteously, are an abomination unto the Lord thy God." In his *Commentary on the Mishnah*, Maimonides elaborated this idea further, asserting that no form of "falsification, trickery, deceit, fraud, or subterfuge is permitted; of the idolater they said it is prohibited to deceive any person, even the idolater, especially in a matter that could cause the name of God to be desecrated . . . [or] will foster in a man degenerate character traits, qualities which God abhors, like those who perform them, as is written, 'even all that act unrighteously.' "[40] Enlarging on *Hullin* 94a, Maimonides here linked the specific proscription against deception (*genevat ha-da'at*) with the general prohibition of the desecration of the divine name (*hillul Hashem*) and defined the latter in terms of its inexorable moral implications.[41]

Distinctly different from the Maimonidean view was the approach of R. Menaḥem ha-Me'iri of fourteenth-century Provence. Me'iri established a new principle of ethical obligation toward non-Jews, based on the premise that adherents of monotheism were ethically responsible and therefore deserved to be considered as peers. More than any of his predecesors, he formulated a clear distinction between idolaters and those he called "nations restricted by the ways of religion." This distinction permitted a rigorous classification of *halakhot* that applied to the low standing of gentiles in the ethical system of Judaism, on the one hand, and the removal from that inferior category all those who were members of a monotheistic faith. Concerning the return of lost property and the prohibition of robbery, Me'iri argued that the principle of inequity did not apply to "nations restricted by the ways of religion," who were to be considered as full-fledged Jews.[42] Moreover, he argued that those gentiles who were restricted by the ways of

religion ought to be included in the term *amitekha* ('your fellow'), therefore entitling them to ethical treatment comparable to that of a Jew. His
principle extended to the ban on excessive profit, equal compensation for
property damage, and equality of punishment for bloodshed. The result,
theoretically at least, was the collapse of many of the traditional distinctions
between Jew and gentile in the civil—though not ritual—realm.[43]

Although the vast majority of Me'iri's writings were unavailable until the
twentieth century, his contributions to the idea of tolerance were known to
some medieval authorities and indirectly influenced the evolution of Jewish legal thought. In the writings of several early modern halakhic authorities, the essence of his approach frequently appeared together with the
view of Maimonides, combined into a single, comprehensive view. For the
latter, the fulfillment of ethical obligations toward non-Jews, even idolaters,
was essential for the perfection of one's moral character, irrespective of
who the beneficiary might be. Fundamentally inner-directed, the Maimonidean view contrasted with Me'iri's outer-directed approach, which
centered on the identity and status of civilized gentiles and their entitlement to equal treatment.[44] These two distinctly different viewpoints each
found expression in the positions of respected halakhic authorities in the
early modern period.

Important structural changes not only account for the transformation of
Jewish political status in modern Europe but also triggered significant cultural shifts as well. In the last decades of the seventeenth century, expanding commercial activity in western and central Europe set the stage for
major changes in the Jewish community, as is evident from the wider distribution of wealth and greater availability of imported fabrics and other
luxury products. The transition from agrarianism to an economy based on
capital investment, international commerce, manufacturing, and free enterprise went hand in hand with urban growth,[45] creating novel opportunities for Jews to become involved in a wider range of activities in general
society. New commercial venues encouraged greater interaction between
Jews and non-Jews, which, in turn, accounted for the proliferation of questionable business practices. Concern that deception against gentiles would
cause harm to the Jewish community was perennially voiced within the context of warnings of *ḥillul Hashem*. However, increasingly in the seventeenth
and eighteenth centuries condemnation of such behavior as "ugly deeds"
on their own account, and not simply for the dangers they posed to the Jewish public, can be found in the halakhic literature.[46]

The legal writings of Rabbi Moses Rivkes of seventeenth-century Lithuania stand out with respect to their heightened concern with ethical justice
in dealings with non-Jews. In *Be'er ha-Golah*, his commentary on *Ḥoshen
Mishpat*, Rivkes affirmed and reaffirmed the medieval legacy of ethical
teachings. He echoed Maimonides's warning that the mistreatment of gentiles would be injurious to Jewish character development, and he cited tra-

ditions strongly commending exemplary behavior toward idolaters, such as the return of lost property, "in order to sanctify the Name and glorify Israel, so that they will know that they [the Jews] are men of faith."[47] His comments also manifested the clear distinction between pagan and civilized nations that figured so centrally in the halakhic system of Me'iri. Rivkes affirmed that the Halakhah had intended to exclude only idolaters from the category of those deserving ethical treatment, "but not the peoples under whose protection we are exiled."[48]

Evidence of a more positive orientation toward contemporary gentiles and gentile culture is contained in several responsa authored by R. Ya'ir Ḥayyim Bacharach of seventeenth-century Worms. He viewed Christianity as a non-idolatrous religion[49]—certainly not an uncommon position in his day—but went several steps further than his predecessors. In one ruling, a responsum on abortion, Bacharach referred to moral values that he believed were shared by Jews and Christians. Bacharach was asked to rule on the halakhic feasibility of abortion in the case of a woman who had become pregnant during an adulterous affair. Despite his having reached the conclusion that abortion was, in theory, halakhically permissible, Bacharach refused to grant authorization to terminate the pregnancy because of "a clear consensus [minhag] between us and them [the Christian community] in the interest of curbing promiscuity and immorality."[50] His positive evaluation of German legislation and of the law-abiding tendencies of contemporary gentiles is evident in a ruling on legal extradition. Most halakhic authorities were reluctant to deliver Jewish criminals to general courts because of the tense nature of Jewish-gentile relations, the extensive anti-Jewish discrimination, and the injustices that Jewish defendants were likely to face in the non-Jewish court system. Nevertheless, in the seventeenth century one may discern a growing effort to build upon medieval talmudic law. In two separate responsa, Bacharach concurred with the famous ruling of R. Joel Sirkes permitting extradition to gentile authorities. As a clear response to concerns about fairness in the general justice system, Bacharach distinguished sharply between the anti-Jewish prejudices rampant among the masses and the enlightened views of the governing bodies. He based these arguments on the presumption that a non-Jewish court was capable of conducting an honest investigation and reaching a just verdict.[51]

The foregoing developments in the realm of Halakhah corresponded to changes in Christian and Jewish iconography in early modern Europe. Evidence of a new sense of religious tolerance, despite ongoing tensions, had become more common in central and western Europe. Christian portrayals of Jews had begun to soften the severely negative anti-Jewish stereotypes of the medieval era, preferring to depict them in a more humane and objective manner. No less significantly, in a departure from the earlier tendency to emphasize the Jews' alien character, Christian art had begun to focus on Jewish religious rites. The depiction of daily life in Johannes

Alexander Böner's paintings suggests that Jewish-Christian interaction was not a rarity and that Christian interest in Jewish celebrations, such as weddings, was keen; his work gives expression to the emergence of a public arena where sectarian tensions did not prevail. In the same period, Jewish art aspired to portray to Christians both the inner world of Jews and the public face of Judaism as a rational religion deserving of respect.[52]

Two facets of the responses advanced by the Assembly of Jewish Notables suggest that the body was perhaps more conservative than has hitherto been assumed. Conceptually, the assembly did not break any new ground, as virtually each of the substantive issues discussed at the Assembly of Jewish Notables—intermarriage, Judaism's attitude toward non-Jews, rabbinic authority and moneylending—had already been debated by government officials or by Franco-Jewish leaders in the years immediately preceding the Revolution and during the subsequent debate on citizenship.[53] In fact, the Malesherbes Commission, in the course of inquiring into the feasibility of Jewish citizenship in 1787, first addressed many of the same issues with respect to both Sephardic and Ashkenazic communities. Initially, seven questions were formulated to clarify Judaism's position on divorce, choice of occupations, and rabbinic authority, among others. Subsequently, a slightly longer questionnaire, consisting of thirteen questions, was submitted to the Bordeaux delegates. These included questions about Sabbath restrictions, moneylending in Alsace-Lorraine, military service, and the status of syndics.[54] A comparison between the twelve questions posed by Napoleon and those taken up by the Malesherbes Commission indicates that after twenty years the issues defining the Jewish question remained largely unchanged. Although political conditions had changed dramatically during the two decades, the decision to convene the Sanhedrin represented a direct challenge to the fact of Jewish emancipation. In effect, the delegates were asked to formally reaffirm their coreligionists' acceptance of the original terms upon which citizenship had been granted in 1790–91. The 1806–07 deliberations belonged to the discourse of the preceding twenty years, as indicated by the fact that the old guard, consisting of French *maskilim*, community leaders, and rabbis, were all well represented among the delegates to the convocation.[55]

Second, it has now become clear that crucial halakhic positions adopted in Paris were forged under the influence of R. Aaron Worms of Metz.[56] The halakhic writings of Worms, arguably the foremost rabbinic scholar in Alsace-Lorraine in the emancipation era, provide the basis for a more complete analysis of the Paris deliberations. A student of R. Aryeh Loeb Günzberg, author of the widely acclaimed *Sha'agat Aryeh*, Worms played a key role at the Paris meetings. His halakhic discourse on gentiles in Jewish law, which he delivered to fellow delegates at the assembly, is mentioned in several sources but was never included in the official transactions. Fortunately, Worms decided to publish a summary of the address amid his talmudic *novellae* twenty-five years later, in the final volume of his magnum opus, *Me'orei Or*. Contained in this discourse are the underpinnings for the assembly's declarations of loyalty to France and her citizens, though, as one would expect, Worms's presentation was far more nuanced. The fact that throughout his presentation he never referred to the potential harm that the mistreatment of gentiles could bring upon the reputation of the Jewish community—the concern for *ḥillul Hashem*—is consistent with the new direction taken by the early modern halakhists cited earlier.

Four central claims were at the core of Worms's address. He opened with an appeal to morality, referring first to the biblical identification of *avel* with cheating others (Lev. 19:35), then to Maimonides's unqualified objection to deceitful behavior. His second argument reflected an appreciation for advances in the legal system of post-revolutionary France. French society's rigorous commitment to the ideal of legal equality virtually erased earlier distinctions in the status of gentiles and Jews.[57] It followed that Jewish law could scarcely maintain inequitable standards in its ethical system. Legal parity was closely related to Worms's third claim concerning the important differences between the status of idolaters and Noahides. By disassociating contemporary non-Jews from the pagan nations of antiquity, Worms was able to set aside talmudic sources permitting what modern society viewed as unethical behavior. In the concept of Noahides, he found a talmudic analogue to the law-abiding gentile citizens of modern Europe who were bound by a moral code proscribing murder, theft, and lechery. Worms thereby placed himself squarely within the liberal tradition advanced by Me'iri, though the latter was unknown to him. "Only among the nations of antiquity were there true heretics," Worms asserted, "[but today] there is no distinction between Jew and gentile"; "we are obligated to physically save the gentiles of today, and their money is prohibited as is any Jew's." Like Me'iri, Worms insisted that the talmudic warning (in *Sanhedrin* 76b) against returning a lost object to non-Jew "does not apply to the nations of the world in our day. One announces their lost objects, as in the case of a Jew."[58]

Worms's final argument was predicated on the ideological and social foundations of the Revolution. His vision appears to have been modeled after the Aristotelian *societas civilis*, a community of citizens bound together as free and equal participants and whose ethical responsibilities are grounded in the principle of reciprocity. These ideas governed Worms's selection of sources and the interpretations he chose to highlight, particularly those reflecting a broad universalist thrust. For example, he cited the position advanced in *Seder Eliyahu Rabbah*, against *Bava Qama* 111b, that the proscription "lo ta'ashoq et re'akha" (Lev. 19:13) was the basis for banning the use of property stolen from a gentile (*gezel ha-goi*). From there he proceeded to demonstrate painstakingly that each time the term *re'a* (fellow) appears in biblical texts, its intended referent is humanity at large.[59] This line of reasoning corresponded to the efforts of talmudic sages and Maimonides to apply the Torah's injunction against deception to Jew and gentile alike.[60]

Elaborating on the distinction between idolatrous and monotheistic nations that relegated much of talmudic law to desuetude, Worms applied the general principle to lending money on interest. He went well beyond his predecessors, adopting an independent position where no precedent could be found. With respect to moneylending, even Me'iri could find no justification to overlook the essential difference between Jew and gentile with respect to moneylending and therefore did not apply his principle of "nations restricted by the ways of religion." Worms, however, averred that interest on loans extended to "a believing gentile is only permitted in accordance with the law of the land, [while] interest from a Jew is permitted by the partnership of *heter isqa*." This formulation reflected the central claim of Worms's Paris address: that Jewish law envisioned the establishment of virtual parity between Jews and gentiles in the civic arena. The case of moneylending reveals the great importance attached by Worms to regulating the scope of halakhic permissibility within limits imposed by *dina d'malkhuta*.[61]

Considered from the standpoint of Worms's other halakhic writings, the aforementioned views reflect a keen sensitivity to the pressures stemming from modernity. For example, he permitted haircuts in the afternoon preceding the Passover holiday,[62] although the practice was routinely prohibited according to most authorities. Citing a lenient tradition concerning those who feared adverse effects on their livelihood, Worms asserted that "in our day it is not customary to go out in long, unkempt hair among the gentiles, who also do not resemble those of former times." Hardly limited to the economic argument advanced by medieval halakhists, Worms's ruling was grounded in the dictates of early nineteenth-century French society and culture and their implications for Jewish-gentile relations. This, we may assume, was also the basis for his ruling permitting men to go bareheaded.[63] These and similar decisions suggest, in contrast to the considerable number of cases of ritual law where Worms ruled stringently, that in his estimation normative Jewish behavior in the civil sphere ought to be governed by a flexible approach to Halakhah.[64]

It is evident from the responses of the Assembly of Jewish Notables that the delegates relied heavily on the argument that Christians ought to be excluded from the category of idolaters.[65] The demands of the emancipation era were far more challenging, however. If the Jews of France were to maintain their position in post-revolutionary society, they would need to dispel all notions of religious superiority and social exclusiveness routinely attributed to Judaism. Still lacking, however, was a general principle justifying positive relations with non-Jews. The assembly arrived at such a formulation first by asserting, particularly in its answers to questions four, five, eleven, and twelve, that loyalty to the state and its citizens was the highest category of religious devotion. Further, the delegates affirmed that "France is our country, all Frenchmen our brothers, and this glorious title, while honoring us in our own eyes, becomes a pledge of which we shall never cease to be worthy."[66] The delegates were thus willing to concede that a redefinition of brotherhood was required in light of the new social and political reality of post-revolutionary France. The bonds of fraternity could no longer be defined solely in terms of religious affiliation; citizenship had emerged, above all else, as the principal basis for uniting members of the French nation. Accordingly, the Jews of France declared themselves "Frenchmen of the Mosaic persuasion."[67]

This declaration did, in theory, signify a revolutionary departure from the assumptions underlying the collective identity and destiny of the Jewish people, but its real significance should not be overstated. Not all sectors of western Jewry understood citizenship in these terms nor did they all redefine the nature of their affiliations according to the assembly's pronouncements. Most, in fact, would continue to maintain the strongest attachments to their coreligionists, in France and abroad, for most of the century. The social and cultural barriers that continued to separate Jew and Christian, particularly outside of the major urban centers where traditional associations were more easily preserved, inevitably reinforced the ethos of Jewish solidarity. Members of the assembly were undoubtedly aware of the tenacity of these social realities but also understood the urgent need for clarification of the role of Jewish law in the modern state. At the apparent expense of traditional Jewish solidarity, they affirmed French Jewry's allegiance to the *patrie* by asserting that they would fight Jews of other countries with which France was at war.[68]

Still to be resolved was the question of whether the theoretical compatibility of Judaism with duties toward the state and its citizens could accommodate the Jewish law of moneylending. After initially attempting to neutralize the overwhelmingly negative evaluation of moneylending, much as Isaïe Berr Bing had argued nearly twenty years before, the assembly tackled the much tougher issue of the alleged double moral standard. In this area, too, the delegates followed Worms's lead. The assembly emphatically denied the allegation by asserting that Jewish law was unconcerned with the identity of the borrower. Crucial to this argument was the distinction it drew between two types of loans, commercial and charitable. The delegates asserted, as did Worms, that there was no practical distinction between Jewish and gentile borrowers. Their contention rested on the premise that in Jewish law there were two categories of transactions, commercial loans and charitable loans. In discussing the case of commercial loans, where interest was permitted, the delegates based their argument on the fiction of the *heter isqa* explained by Worms, though they made no explicit reference to it. Through this legal device, designed to circumvent the prohibition of taking interest from a fellow Jew, interest became a share in the profits that accrued in the temporary business "partnership."[69] Building on the twin claims that the right to charge interest depended on the religious faith, not affiliation, of the borrowers and that the purpose of the loan is determinative, the assembly argued that the Jewish law of moneylending reflected virtual parity between gentile and Jew. Interest, even among Jews, was therefore lawful in commercial operations, as it was for gentiles.[70] In the case of charitable loans (that is, those intended for food, clothing, or shelter), the assembly argued that interest was forbidden, whether the borrower was a Jew or a gentile. Finally, the assembly endeavored to present the foregoing legal interpretation as consistent with the plain meaning of Deuteronomy 23:21, the source text for the prohibition against taking interest from a fellow Jew. Because the verse makes no explicit reference to Jews but only proscribes the taking of interest from "your brother" [*aḥikha*], the delegates declared that the term *aḥikha* ought to be understood broadly to refer to all fellow French citizens.[71] By so doing, the Paris body virtually erased the difference between Jewish and gentile borrowers. This conception of brotherhood—defined by citizenship, not religious affiliation—represented a most serious challenge to Jewish identity in the modern era.[72]

Because the assembly had no official standing in the Jewish community, Napoleon ordered the convocation of a religious body charged with the task of converting the responses to the twelve questions into authoritative doctrines "that would be placed next to the Talmud and [would] thus acquire, in the eyes of all Jews in all countries for every century, the greatest possible authority." Like the ancient Supreme Court in Jerusalem after which it was named, the Grand Sanhedrin was composed of seventy-one members, though only two-thirds were rabbis. On 4 February 1807 the Sanhedrin met for the first time, and over the course of five weeks issued decisions that were binding both from the standpoint of French law and Halakhah. The body sought to define the relation between Jewish law and the modern state without altering any rituals or doctrines of Judaism. More far-reaching in the long run was the distinction that the Sanhedrin drew between the political and the religious realms of Judaism:

Let us declare, then, that the divine law is complete, [and that] the precious inheritance of the community of Jacob contains [both] religious provisions and political provisions; that the religious provisions are by their nature absolute and independent of circumstances and times; that this is not the case for political provisions, that is, for those that made up the government and were destined to direct the people of Israel in the land of its inheritance, when there was a king, high priest, and magistrates; that these political provisions can no longer be applicable now that Israel no longer forms a national body.[73]

The separation of the two realms profoundly imprinted itself on the consciousness of French Jewry during the next several decades. This was accomplished thanks to the persistent efforts of the consistorial leadership to make the Sanhedrin decisions a regular part of the Jewish school curriculum and to require that every child be examined by the departmental grand rabbi before becoming a bar or bat mitzvah.[74] Evidence of the impact of the depoliticization of Judaism and, generally, of the importance of the Sanhedrin is also found in school curricula, in the views of scholars such as Salomon Munk and Adolphe Franck, and in rabbinic sermons and writings throughout the nineteenth century. By mid-century the idea was strongly endorsed by broad sectors of the Franco-Jewish community.[75]

The Paris Sanhedrin owed both its prominence and notoriety to the role it played in endorsing the revolutionary concept of *fraternité* as the exclusive mediating principle between the Jewish religion and French society. It drew upon the Mendelssohnian proposition calling for cooperation between Judaism and the secular state and, as we have seen, on a halakhic tradition that viewed non-Jews in a favorable light.[76] The Paris body affirmed that seemingly irreconcilable conflicts between the religious obligations of Judaism and the duties demanded of citizens by the state were to be resolved in favor of the latter, since loyalty to the modern state was defined as a supreme religious value. Not all French rabbis agreed on the religious status of patriotism, however. Some worked vigorously to infuse emancipation with religious significance; others had misgivings about how far the practical halakhic implications of republican Judaism might be taken.[77] Leaving nothing to chance, the newly formed consistory would soon take measures requiring rabbis to emphasize the lessons of the Sanhedrin in their sermons, while the text of the decisions was reproduced in every textbook approved for use in Jewish schools. For the Napoleonic regime, as for Jewish communal leaders, the Sanhedrin provided the authoritative interpretation of emancipation; its answers and doctrinal decisions formed a new and central text for subsequent generations.

Enveloped in stunning drama and steady publicity—and subjected to acute political pressure—representatives of French Jewry had no choice but to focus their attention on weighty matters of great substance. Historically, the Sanhedrin was the first *public* organization of Jews to articulate a positive attitude toward the state and its gentile citizens and to draw a clear distinction between the national and religious components of Jewish identity. Considering the fulsome rhetoric and hyperbolic style demanded by the occasion and in view of its halakhic background and social historical context, the Sanhedrin may be said to have voiced a far more moderate position than is normally assumed. Changing conceptions of gentiles and gentile culture in the preceding two centuries, including a growing respect for gentile law and a progressive disassociation from certain discriminatory views of gentiles, permitted the rabbinic leadership that assembled in Paris to draw boldly on those classical traditions it felt corresponded to the new conditions facing emancipated Jewry. But equally important, the Sanhedrin, following R. Aaron Worms's lead, was careful to maintain a sharp distinction between the ritual and civil spheres. The civil sphere encompassed the full range of Jewish-gentile relations and duties to the state, whereas the ritual sphere, it was agreed, remained largely inviolate.

Despite the delegates' unequivocal declarations of patriotism and brotherhood, and despite the religious reassurances provided by the Sanhedrin itself, the government's confidence in the ability of the Jews to undergo self-reform faded quickly. On 17 March 1808 the emperor issued three decrees: the first two decrees established the consistory system for the organization of French Jewry. The consistories were to enforce the decisions of the Sanhedrin through education and surveillance. In the third decree, Napoleon evinced a radically different approach to the Jewish question, probably in deference to the intense anti-Jewish sentiment among the Alsatian peasantry. In seeking to put an end to Jewish moneylending in Alsace, the Infamous Decree, as it was later called, nullified all debts owed to the Jews by soldiers, minors, and women, and cancelled any loan granted at a rate of interest beyond 10 percent. These laws also prohibited any movement of Alsatian Jews to other *départements* and forbade Jewish immigrants from settling in Alsace. Finally, the decree forbade the Jews from supplying replacements for military service, though this was commonly practiced throughout France. The provisions of the decree were to remain in force for a period of ten years and could be extended further if the conditions that brought it into being persisted.[78] With the 1808 decree, emancipation suffered a major setback. French Jewry was denied the rights constitutionally guaranteed to French citizens and was once again expected to prove itself worthy of citizenship. Whatever the motivation behind the imperial decree, whatever its goals, the result was the establishment of French Jewry as a separate body, subject directly to the will and authority of the emperor. Special legislation, enacted in a humiliating fashion against this one group, signified the return of the Jews of France to a pre-revolutionary status.

Quite apart from the debates themselves, it is important to emphasize that the decisions of the Sanhedrin shaped the discourse of modernization for decades to come. This is most apparent in its iconic image as having defined the limits of the transformation that French Jewry needed to undergo in order to be worthy of the title *citoyens*. The absence of any explicit mention of religious reform, either in the questions addressed to the assembly or in the assembly's responses, confirmed for contemporaries and their descendants that political loyalty and a commitment to social integration alone were the basis of French citizenship. Even fifty years after the convocation, the authority of the Sanhedrin was still in force among all sectors of the community, although its deliberations invariably invited conflicting interpretations. Religious reformers and staunch conservatives alike found in the Sanhedrin's decisions clear proof to bolster their respective positions. For all intents and purposes, however, the Sanhedrin removed the question of ritual reform from French Jewry's communal agenda and thus undercut the movement to reform the Jewish religion.[79]

In the end, the Sanhedrin played a crucial role in shaping a distinct Franco-Jewish identity. Delegates from all corners of the French empire came together in common purpose to address the issues put before them by Napoleon. Cultural, ethnic, and religious differences were bridged, and a tenuous unity was forged. In the process, local leaders such as Abraham Furtado of Bordeaux and Rabbi David Sintzheim of Strasbourg were transformed into prominent national leaders. Their messages were no longer intended for their former constituencies alone but were directed at the broader population of French Jewry.[80] By reconfirming French Jewry's acceptance of the terms of citizenship, the Sanhedrin was instrumental in setting down the rudiments of an ideology of emancipation; this would prove essential to the ideological and programmatic foundations of *régénération*. These important developments stemmed from the Napoleonic effort to institutionalize the ideals of 1789, although they were manifested only much later. During the quarter-century following the Revolution, virtually no Jewish initiative, either communal or otherwise, was taken in response to the enormous changes that had transformed France. But the foundation for a new vision shared by all sectors of French Jewry, irrespective of ethnic heritage, geographical origin, or religious orientation, was secured. In the century-long debate over the challenges posed by emancipation, the founding premises and myths established in Paris served as the starting point for all future discussion.

The Establishment of the Consistory and Its Functions

Serving as the new organizational framework for the Jewish communities of post-revolutionary France, the Consistoire Israélite came into being through the convergence of Jewish and governmental interests. Following the creation of the Protestant consistorial system in 1802, Jewish leaders sought governmental authorization and assistance in forming a comparable organization. It had become clear after the turn of the century that without a formal communal framework, the continued viability of Jewish life in France would remain gravely imperiled. With its religious, social, and educational institutions in decline and its rabbinic leadership virtually paralyzed by the atmosphere of intolerance toward the Jewish religion, disorder had begun to reign in many communities, making it virtually impossible to manage day-to-day affairs. Moreover, solutions for the ever-present problems of begging and idleness demanded a collective response only possible at the communal and intercommunal levels.[81]

This vision of a revamped Jewish communal organization accorded closely with the Napoleonic policy of centralization and control. In the view of the emperor and his advisers, the envisioned transformation of the Jews required nothing less than aggressive government intervention in internal Jewish affairs. Precipitated by the growing disappointment in the socioeconomic regeneration of Alsatian Jewry, the Napoleonic program rested on a new view of the primacy of the state in the promotion of social reform and thus constituted a radical departure from the policies of the previous fifteen years. Emancipation had been broadly conceived to signify freedom from state interference; both Jewish leaders and non-Jewish observers alike had assumed that the natural forces of modernization and civic equality would yield the desired transformation. Developments in central Europe reveal that the state was the driving force in the modernization process wherever its coercive powers were exerted upon the Jewish community. At a time when this transformation was perceived to be at its lowest point, Napoleonic legislation redesigned the structure of Jewish communal organization in the hope of redefining both the relationship of Jews to French society and the relationship of Judaism to the state.[82]

At the instruction of the emperor, a committee consisting of three government officials and a nine-man council selected from the Assembly of Jewish Notables drafted a plan that was subsequently adopted by the entire assembly and ratified by Napoleon in 1806. Two years later Jewish communities of the empire were organized in consistories that closely resembled the model used for the Protestant population. The imperial decree of 17 March 1808 ordered the formation of a synagogue and consistory in each department with a Jewish population of two thousand or more. Initially, seven consistories were formed in France, in the departments of Haut-Rhin, Bas-Rhin, Meurthe, Moselle, Seine, Gironde, and Bouches-du-Rhône. An eighth consistory was established in Saint-Esprit in 1846, and a ninth in Lyon in 1857. At the administrative helm sat the Central Consistory in Paris. The departmental consistories were originally composed of a grand rabbi, one additional rabbi, and three lay members; members were elected by twenty-five notables chosen by the government from among the wealthiest and most respected Jews. The Central Consistory was originally composed of three grand rabbis and two laymen. However, a series of legislative enactments in the first half of the nineteenth century altered the proportion of rabbis to laymen in favor of the latter.[83] The trend toward lay domination, together with the predominance of the most affluent of the community, was the most salient feature of the consistory system, evident in its ideology and programs. These efforts to centralize the administration of Jewish communal life proved to be of enduring significance throughout the nineteenth century.

Reconfirmed by every government regime throughout the century, the consistorial system was the sole framework that was authorized to administer internal Jewish affairs and to represent Jewish concerns before the government. From the outset, the state assumed a role as an active partner in the supervision of Jewish communal life. Over the course of the century, this role grew increasingly more involved, as the consistory became a virtual arm of the state. According to article 12 of the *règlement* of 10 December 1806, the consistories were charged with three principal functions: (1) community administration, which included maintaining order in synagogues; overseeing the administration of particular synagogues; fiscal control, including the raising and use of sums intended to cover the expenses of the *culte*; construction, organization, and supervision of synagogues; and supervision of charitable organizations, schools, and *kashrut* (dietary laws); (2) regeneration (the term that became synonymous with the socioeconomic transformation expected of French Jewry); accordingly, the consistories formed committees to eliminate begging, organized societies to encourage vocational and agricultural training, and supervised Jewish schools; and (3) policing tasks, which involved exercising surveillance over the behavior of the Jewish population. The consistories were to ensure that rabbis offer no interpretation of the law that failed to conform to the Sanhedrin decisions and were to make certain that no prayer assembly was formed without expressed authorization. Each of these areas included routine bureaucratic tasks as well as specified duties intended to advance the government's plan to modernize the Jews.[84]

In sharp contrast to the medieval *kehillah*, the consistory worked to promote the modernization of Jewish life in accordance with prevailing notions of civic morality, industrialization, and civility. For consistory leaders, the realization of this goal depended on the assertion of consistorial authority in virtually every area of public life and over the entire French-Jewish population. Because this objective was not easily accomplished in the provinces, emphasis on a centralized approach came to be regarded as strategically essential and was reinforced by the emergence of the state as a framework for collective action and consciousness. The consistories' programs echoed governmental efforts to impose centralization on the general populace, while the highly valued theme of unity inspired the invention of certain ritual ceremonies such as the *initiation religieuse*, the quest for a fusion of the Ashkenazic and Sephardic liturgies into a single rite, and the attempt in 1856 to ratify halakhically acceptable religious reforms for communities throughout France. To the extent that unity was successfully realized, the achievement represented a significant departure from the mentality of the *ancien régime* where local and regional forces were paramount.[85] In most instances, however, "unity" was still a reflection of the mythic Revolution and would remain elusive for much of the century.

Empowered to collect and disburse funds, the consistories assumed control over communal institutions, including synagogues, cemeteries, schools, vocational societies, and charitable organizations. Likewise, they were responsible for hiring religious functionaries, for authorizing the building of synagogues, and for administering local religious affairs. The battle against private prayer meetings was unrelenting, lasting for a half-century. Mutual aid societies, which preserved the structure of the traditional confraternities (*ḥevrot*) and staunchly resisted submission to the consistorial monopoly, insisted on maintaining their private *minyanim*. This, the consistories claimed, resulted in a loss of revenue to the consistorial synagogue; no less important, it gave the appearance that the dignity and authority of the consistory was under attack. Each of the consistories therefore tried to prevent private *minyanim* from meeting, but their success in this area was only partial. The persistence of these *ḥevrot* and the refusal to respect the monopoly in other areas, such as ritual slaughtering, reflects a deep-seated dissatisfaction with consistorial authority and raised the question of whether the consistory was truly the exclusive framework for the organization of Jewish life in France.[86]

Despite the constant tension between consistorial authority and local autonomy, the consistories were able to achieve considerable success in controlling local affairs in the *chefs-lieu*, that is, the cities where the departmental consistories were based. In the outlying towns and villages, however, the consistories faced a more difficult situation. Seeking control over the solicitation of funds in local communities and underscoring the duty of community members to support communal and regional institutions (such as the *école de travail* of Strasbourg) were high on the consistory's agenda. Consistory-appointed delegates to the local community, known as *commissaires surveillants*, presided over the local commission to elect rabbis, cantors, and other community functionaries, and bore responsibility for tax collection and issuing annual reports, enabling the consistory to control the local budgets. Moreover, the consistory saw in the *commissaire* a progressive influence on the village population. Communities, for their part, demanded the freedom to make budgetary and fund-raising decisions on their own without consistorial interference and frequently protested the imposition of religious guidelines that seemed foreign by local standards. Opposition to the role played by the *commissaire surveillant* was a clear expression of the strong desire for autonomy from consistorial control. In the aftermath of the 1848 revolution the consistorial monopoly became weaker.[87]

Independence from consistorial control assumed other forms, including the creation of extra-consistorial bodies for the administration of the synagogues (in Metz and Bordeaux), the formation of confraternities, and the regenerative programs undertaken without consistorial involvement. Particularly in Alsace-Lorraine, the *ḥevrot* served as an alternative framework to the consistory, fulfilling needs of religious piety, study, philanthropy, and fellowship. They were governed in accordance with strict regulations. As for *régénération*, proponents questioned the consistory's ability to serve as the spearhead for educational and vocational transformation, and thus most efforts in these areas resulted from private, not consistorial, initiatives.[88] Even when initiatives were undertaken independently, however, the consistories eventually provided the necessary organizational framework and support.

Two areas that were not specifically prescribed in the original legislation—the protection of Jewish rights and religious modernization—eventually came under the purview of consistorial responsibility and became the subject of intense public debate. Over the course of the nineteenth century, these two issues revealed the deep divisions within French Jewry. Concerning its role of protector, the consistory undertook to act on behalf of French Jewry as a whole, watching governmental legislation closely to ensure fairness. It was also called upon to defend its constituents, collectively and as individuals, against antisemitic injustices. However, the consistory's record in this area was uneven and was occasionally criticized for being overly conservative and ineffective. This criticism eventually gave rise to frustration and alienation, and in 1860 the Alliance Israélite Universelle was established to address the problems facing Jews abroad and, to a lesser extent, within French society.[89] The formation of the Alliance attests to the limits of the organized community in responding to external challenges.

Questions concerning the role of the consistory in religious affairs were brought to the attention of the public between the years 1839 and 1844. In 1839 the Central Consistory proposed a plan to reorganize its administrative constitution. Most notable among its features was the proposal to give lay members of the consistories ultimate authority in religious matters. Article 24 would grant the consistory exclusive power to make ritual reforms as it saw fit and to determine which prayer books and textbooks would be used in synagogues and schools. Invited to comment on the draft proposal, the departmental consistories were nearly unanimous in criticizing the Central Consistory's usurpation of rabbinic authority. Critics were apprehensive about the implications of lay domination of the rabbinate, centralization of power in the Central Consistory, and the creation of a rabbinic hierarchy. Rabbis and orthodox laymen in the northeast provinces were most vehement in their opposition to the plan. Their vigorous efforts, which included formal protests to the Ministry of Religions, public petitions, and various publications refuting the claims of reformers, succeeded in modifying some of the more controversial provisions of the plan. When finally published in 1844, the ordinance included several provisions that balanced the potentially unchecked drive for reform. It included communal rabbis in the *notabilité*, thus giving them a voice in the selection of Central Consistory members; it required the approbation of the Central Consistory grand rabbi before any textbook could be used in Jewish schools; and it confirmed the authority of the grand rabbi in specifically religious matters. The consistory's proposed powers of censure, suspension, and dismissal of consistorial rabbis were also limited by the 1844 ordinance, stipulating that action in these areas could be taken only in accordance with the opinion of the local consistory and the grand rabbi. Although the ordinance did contain provisions for the increased participation of lay members in the Central Consistory, the law fell short of its goal of investing the laity with unchecked powers to institute ritual reforms.[90] The powerful trend toward lay domination, together with the cooperation of progressive rabbis, nevertheless enabled the consistories to introduce several reforms of a moderate nature: *initiation religieuse*, the abolition of sale of religious honors in the synagogue; the modernization of funeral ceremonies; and the regulation of circumcision procedures. These reforms were related to the improvement of the aesthetics of synagogue worship, or reflected administrative centralization, but they did not reflect any doctrinal changes.[91]

One of the principal areas that the consistories targeted for reform was the rabbinate. Efforts to exercise control over the rabbinate were motivated by ideological and practical considerations. Rabbis were believed to be the major obstacle to reforms that were judged to be crucial to the emerging Franco-Jewish ethos. Lay proponents of *régénération* argued that if rabbinic authority could be brought under control, ritual and synagogue reforms would be implemented more effectually. The recasting of the rabbinate into a modern force capable of leading the Jews of France forward would depend on establishing minimal rabbinic qualifications, modernizing rabbinic training, creating a rabbinic hierarchy, and revamping the process of rabbinic selection and dismissal. In each of these areas the cooperative efforts of the French government and the Central Consistory were evident from the beginning. In 1829 the Central Consistory created a rabbinic seminary in Metz; the institution subsequently moved to Paris (in 1859) where rabbis were more suitably trained to handle the challenges of the new era.[92] The 1839 project for consistorial reorganization fixed attention on the surveillance and censure of rabbis, the procedure of suspension and filling vacancies, terms of office, election procedures, and eligibility for various levels of rabbinic posts.[93]

Two central themes of the proposed legislation—lay domination of the rabbinate and the notion of a rabbinic hierarchy—each greatly alarmed traditionalists. The latter, especially, was of concern because its implications were so very concrete. A hierarchical structure within the rabbinate would permit the consistory to achieve its goal of surveillance and censure at every level. Many challenged the right of the Central Consistory grand rabbi to censure departmental rabbis, or of departmental rabbis to censure community rabbis, but rabbinic hierarchy was nonetheless retained in the 1844 *ordonnance* and would not be debated after this. Instead, new efforts to revise the law in accordance with the spirit of the 1848 revolution rekindled the earlier debate on centralization and the lay domination of the rabbinate, adding to these the issues of universal suffrage and direct elections. In Paris, both in the departmental and central consistories, the lay leadership favored limiting suffrage to a small, elite group to whom decisions on the major issues of communal policy would be entrusted, while in the southern and northeastern provinces the adoption of universal suffrage was preferred, albeit according to some consistories, in stages. Nevertheless, the 1853 decree determined that the elections of communal rabbis and grand rabbis would remain under consistory control. Departmental grand rabbis were to be elected by the local consistory, voting together with twenty-five *notables* chosen by universal suffrage, and communal rabbis were to be appointed directly by the consistory. In other words, the revolution of 1848 left the election procedures followed by French Jewish communities virtually unchanged. By 1862 departmental grand rabbis were no longer chosen in their own districts but were selected from among three nominees submitted by each consistory to the central body.[94] More revealing is the fact that rabbis never elected their own leaders; rabbinic selection was lay-imposed and lay-dominated. Efforts by the Metz consistory in 1850 to reinstitute general elections for the rabbi of the Sarreguemines district were thwarted by the Central Consistory. In 1853 the Central Consistory withdrew from the communities the right of selecting their own rabbis and gave this authority to the departmental consistories.[95]

Each of the areas emphasized in the Napoleonic reforms—centralization, subordination of religion to state, and parity among the major religions—penetrated the consciousness of French Jewry and found institutional expression in the consistorial system. As the sole recognized framework for the administration of internal Jewish affairs and as the body representing Jewish concerns before the government, the Consistoire Israélite became the foremost instrument in the realization of the government's plan for regenerating the Jews. The consistory evinced administrative centralization, adamantly and successfully rejecting any effort to compete with its authority. Despite the persistence of divisions over regionalism versus centralization, tradition versus reform, and unity versus diversity, all institutions under its control tended to be pluralistic and, therefore, moderate. Driven by pragmatic considerations above all else, those responsible for religious, educational, and social policy were committed to the goal of forging an ongoing modus vivendi among the various constituencies making up the Jewish population of France.

Chapter 6

The "Jewish Question" During the Bourbon Restoration

With the restoration of the Bourbon Monarchy in 1815, an era of renewed confidence in France's commitment to its revolutionary heritage began to reverberate distinctly within the Jewish community.[1] In the political arena and at the communal level, French Jewry displayed a consciousness of the dramatic changes precipitated by the Revolution and a vitality that contrasted sharply with the lethargy of the preceding twenty-five years. The 1816 ordinance on primary education provided the legal foundation for the establishment of modern Jewish schools in the spirit of the Haskalah; the first Jewish periodical to appear in French, *L'Israélite français* (1817–18), was published; a central rabbinical seminary was created; the Hebrew press in Metz resumed its work after nearly two decades of inactivity; and the first steps in the emergence of modern Jewish scholarship were taken. These developments signify a conspicuous departure from the cultural patterns of the *ancien régime*. The discontinuity and disruption triggered by the Revolution and the subsequent upheavals of the 1790s account for a progressive break with the tradition linking the Jews of Alsace-Lorraine with territories to the east. Slowly, a distinct Franco-Jewish identity, driven by powerful political, economic, and cultural forces set in motion by the Revolution itself, crystallized and was fortified by the return to France of rabbis and *maskilim* who had emigrated to Germany during the Napoleonic years. Whether the repatriation of members of French Jewry's intellectual elite was a reaction to deteriorating conditions in central Europe or signified an expression of faith in France is difficult to ascertain. In the case of R. Lion-Mayer Lambert, who returned to Metz from Frankfurt in 1816 with no rabbinic position awaiting him, it was widely assumed that his decision was motivated by loyalty to his native land.

The Public Debate

Public discussion of the Jewish question in the years following the adjournment of the Sanhedrin was discouraged by the tight grip of the emperor and came to a virtual halt. Only with the defeat of Napoleon in 1815 did the Jewish question again come to the attention of the public. The deterioration of the Jewish condition in central Europe, in those territories where emancipation had been granted and subsequently withdrawn, stimulated new interest among the French. It was also inspired by the impending renewal of the 1808 decree in the early years of the monarchy and developed into a broader consideration of the Jewish condition in France. Charles-Joseph Bail, formerly responsible for the administration of the Bonapartist Kingdom of Westphalia, published the first book of the post-Napoleon era to decry the intolerance and legal discrimination directed at the Jews of Frankfurt, Hamburg, Lubeck, and other free cities. The ensuing debate on the compatibility of Judaism with the duties of citizenship extended for several years, focusing on French Jewry's slow transformation. Concerns about purported obstacles posed by the Jewish religion were voiced routinely, although the spirit of these discussions was generally constructive.[2] Figuring most prominently in these discussions was the Paris Sanhedrin. Widely commended for having defined the proper relationship between Judaism and the state,[3] the body was also a source of frustration in the following decade because it accentuated the vast distance between the theoretical potential for change and the resistance that obtained in reality. Ironically, the Sanhedrin inspired a new genre of criticism. Jews were commonly taken to task for failing to behave according to the "noble sentiments" of loyalty to the *patrie* that the Paris assembly had articulated.[4]

Most detractors attributed the failures of French Jewry to the alleged shortcomings that plagued Jewish legislation. In the case of Bail, critics accused him of overlooking these deficiencies, claiming that by so doing, he had become an apologist for the Jewish religion. Accordingly, in a second edition of *Des Juifs au dix-neuvième siècle*, the author retreated from his unconditionally positive view of Jewish emancipation. Now conceding that Jewish ritual law impeded the process of social integration, Bail called for the implementation of moderate reforms as a prerequisite to the enjoyment of full social equality. This demand was realistic, he insisted, because ritual was less than crucial within Judaism.[5] But not all criticism was so benign. In a work titled *De l'incompatibilité entre le Judaïsme et l'exercice des droits de cité*, former Jacobin leader Agricole Moureau argued that Jewish law was incompatible with the modern state because its claim to be of divine origin outweighed any temporal obligations in society. As long as it was defined in divine terms, Jews could not be expected to serve state or society faithfully. Moureau also maintained that the mentality of the Jews had been adversely affected by a legal system that required its adherents to remain separated from the mainstream of society. Having been virtually enslaved to their own legal system, they were unable to aspire to a higher political and social morality, and thereby became strangers to the public spirit and welfare.[6] According to many observers, the crux of the problem was that Judaism constituted at once a religious and social system originally designed for the administration of a theocratic state—a "state within a state"—while all the medieval corporations had been dissolved. In order to protect its adherents from unwanted religious and cultural influences, Jewish legislation proscribed various degrees of social contact between Jews and non-Jews, ranging from casual encounters to intermarriage. In virtually every aspect of Jewish life and thought—whether dietary laws, ceremonial rites, or education—critics observed an exclusiveness that violated contemporary notions of brotherhood.[7]

More devastating than the charge of exclusiveness was the insistence that the Jews were an uncivilized people. Through its ascent toward reason, *civilisation* represented the advance of humanity away from the primitive state of barbarity, ignorance, and servitude. Rooted in an abiding optimism and faith in the future, the French Revolution inspired an unprecedented receptivity to these ideas. It drew strength from and lent credence to the philosophy of progress and the idea of the infinite perfectibility of man. The process of perfection, argued François Guizot, is two-pronged, directing itself at man's external condition and at his internal, personal nature as well. Improvements in social and material well-being therefore require corresponding intellectual and spiritual development, including religious beliefs, philosophical ideas, the sciences, letters, and the arts. In the case of France, *civilisation* was understood to be the basis of large-scale social reform of those sectors of the population that were culturally disadvantaged. Defined largely in moral terms, this mandate for reform was applied to the Jewish question, widely viewed as a case of severe cultural disparity and inferiority. If Jews were to become part of *la grande famille française*, then their time-honored religious and cultural legacy would need to be thoroughly reevaluated, and much would, ultimately, need to be discarded. In short, full emancipation involved experiencing the processes of civilization and modernization as a single transformation.[8]

In the absence of a consensus on how the regeneration of the Jews might be accelerated, the Société des Sciences, Agriculture et Arts of Strasbourg sponsored an essay contest in 1824 to stimulate public discussion. Contestants were to address themselves to two questions: "(1) To determine the most appropriate means to enable the Jewish population of Alsace to partake of the benefits of civilization; (2) To investigate whether the factors that estrange members of this population from society are at all the product of superstition and the obstinacy to persevere in the ancient customs that time and changes in the political situation should have [already] modified."[9] The Société explained that it was motivated by a desire to assist Alsatian Jewry, first by awakening the dormant seeds of perfection and then by publicizing the various means of assistance that could be provided by the general population. An award of 300 francs was earmarked for the author of the essay judged most useful in the regeneration of the Jews.[10]

One can hardly fail to notice the unmistakable air of condescension that riddled all aspects of the contest. The program announcing the competition portrayed the Jews as an uncultured people living among European nations whose high level of civilization was attributed to the positive influence of Christianity and to the general impact of the arts and sciences. By positing a sharp contrast between the superior culture of Europe and the primitive customs of this "Asian" nation—steadfast in its mores and religious tradition, estranged from neighboring peoples in the countries in which they reside—framers of the contest implied that the work of regeneration was far from complete. The first question was predicated on the assumption that the Jews of Alsace were bereft of civilization, and the second proposed that the Jewish religion was the source of the Jews' estrangement from French society and civilization. Characterized as "superstitious," Judaism's religious practices were presumed to have produced a separatist, isolationist mentality that was principally to blame for the social and cultural destitution in which the Jews found themselves. Their adherence to the ceremonial law was deemed to be out of step with contemporary mores.[11] Nevertheless, despite the rather bleak assessment of the Jewish condition, the general outlook was certainly more optimistic than at the Metz contest of 1785. In the 1820s *régénération* was viewed as an attainable objective. Accompanying the essay questions were several additional points that the Société asked prospective authors to consider. The first concerned whether the Sanhedrin decisions might assist the Central Consistory in pursuing regeneration. Second, the Société asked whether ritual reforms embraced elsewhere in France and Europe could be introduced in Alsace. Third, the Société inquired as to whether a reconciliation of Jewish and state holidays was possible according to "the essential dogmas of Mosaism."[12] Together, the two published questions and the three guiding suggestions reveal the contours of the debate and its essential parameters.

Three of the four *mémoires* submitted to the evaluation commission were judged to be suitable for consideration by the Société.[13] The wide-ranging discussion of the practical means of regenerating Alsatian Jewry—in the essays submitted to the competition and in other works published in the same years—addressed issues of ritual reform, economic transformation, and educational reform, among others. Invariably, the question of exceptional legislation directed at the Jewish population came again to the forefront of French political debate. The more conservative critics of the progress of Jewish regeneration argued that special legal measures would force the Jews to be rehabilitated. This idea, of course, was not new. In 1808 severe restrictions on the economic activity and mobility of French Jewry were instituted, except in the case of the Jews in Bordeaux and in the *départements* of Gironde and Landes. By the end of the ten-year term, few thought that the legislation would be extended. Napoleon, the author of the law, was in exile, while the 1815 Charter of the Bourbon Monarchy reaffirmed the principle of civic equality for all Frenchmen. Nevertheless, although an attempt in 1817 to renew the 1808 decree was defeated, a number of writers continued to recommend strict supervision of the movement and occupational freedom of Alsatian Jewry. Both punitive and rehabilitative impulses were behind the range of appeals for special legislation.[14]

The argument used most often to defend exceptional legislation was the alleged alien nature of the Jewish people and their religion. This was similar to the reasoning employed in the National Assembly by opponents of emancipation. Since the Jews were viewed as "outside of the population" and "voluntarily outside the common law,"[15] and insofar as Jewish law was "contrary to [the laws] of the country," special legislation was not considered discriminatory but conceived as an act of strict justice.[16] For some, the position of the Jews on the periphery of society explained their failure to exercise reciprocity in their dealings with fellow Frenchmen. Moureau, for example, insisted that the voluntary exclusiveness of the Jews, expressed most blatantly by the incompatibility of their laws with the duties to state and society, called for corresponding legal exclusion from certain privileges. He explained that as human beings, Jews could not be denied the *droits de l'humanité* (the rights of humanity). However, the *droits de cité* (the rights of citizenship) are granted conditionally to those who fulfill fundamental civic obligations. Moureau went so far as to suggest that every French Jew be required, annually, to take the medieval oath *more judaico* as proof of loyalty to the *patrie* and its laws.[17]

In one instance, the issue of exceptional legislation was linked explicitly to the purported failure of the Jews to abide by the decisions of the Sanhedrin. Betting de Lancastel, a *sous-préfet* in the Haut-Rhin district, argued that the Jews were unjustified in citing in their own defense the 1815 charter's promise of freedom of religion and equal protection for members of all faiths. He insisted that the charter protected only the Jewish religion as interpreted by the Sanhedrin, not the "cult of prejudices" that most Jews continued to practice; he therefore concluded that those who failed to accept the decisions of the Paris assembly could rightfully be subjected to special legislation without violating the constitution. In short, exceptional legislation was justified on the grounds that the continued special status of the Jews warranted it, while general society required it for its own self-protection.[18] Even the author of the prize-winning essay, Arthur Beugnot, was an advocate of such legislation, though this was certainly not the main thrust of his proposals. By contrast, the evaluation commission recorded its objection to special legal measures. Conceding that the Jews of Alsace were in a deplorable state of moral degeneration, the commission nonetheless felt that Beugnot had exaggerated the evils he attributed to them and therefore rejected the contention that contemporary Jews were identical with those of past generations. It argued that the Jews had indeed benefited from advances in French law and had made important strides in becoming civilized, as evidenced by the promising effects of education, their greater participation in agriculture, and improved relations with Christians. These modest achievements, then, were clear proof of a positive relationship between legal equality and the eradication of Jewish vices. In the view of the commission, and increasingly for most observers, the goal of civilizing the Jews would therefore not be served by exclusion from common law but through the work of local institutions.[19]

Proposals for the creation of new institutions aiming to advance the regeneration of the Jews occupied the most conspicuous place in the essays written in the 1820s. Despite various efforts to justify exceptional legislation, it appears that reliance on the repressive powers of the state was no longer seen as a viable solution, and indeed, no serious proposals to enact similar laws were thereafter advanced. Rather, a variety of projects aiming at the diversification of Jewish economic life in Alsace appeared in response to the acknowledged need for change. Some dealt with the problem of directing the Jews toward productive occupations, most notably agriculture and industry, while others maintained that the problem of Jewish usury had reached excessive proportions because of the absence of dependable sources of credit. One suggestion, advanced by the secretary of the Strasbourg Société, Amédée Tourette, centered on the creation of a Jewish communal credit institution that would be supported by affluent Jews and supervised by community officials.[20] Betting de Lancastel supported the creation of a similar institution for the protection of the general population of Alsace, where the continued role of the Jews as creditors posed an allegedly grave danger.[21] Tourette, however, regarded the plan for credit reform as having a different purpose. He envisioned Jewish participation in a public credit institution as contributing to an improvement in their public image, as this would offer them the opportunity to display moral uprightness.[22]

The Bourbon Restoration's most comprehensive plan to regenerate the Jews was advanced by Arthur Beugnot, a lawyer, senator, and delegate to the National Assembly. Hardly unacquainted with the Jewish question, he had participated in an essay contest sponsored by the Académie des Inscriptions et Belles-Lettres (in 1821) on the status of the Jews in medieval France, Spain, and Italy. Together with J. B. Capefigue and G. B. Depping, Beugnot was accorded honorable mention by the Académie, and his essay was subsequently published under the title *Les Juifs d'Occident*. The work focused first on the injustices and nature of the intolerance suffered by Jews throughout their history. Beugnot challenged the idea that the degradation of the Jews was a theological imperative, concluding that the countless instances of social and religious maltreatment of the Jewish people simply contradicted Christian teaching.[23] Conceding that the charge of Jewish antisocial behavior was accurate so long as the hope to rebuild Jerusalem persisted, he averred that now that this hope was, for all practical purposes, shattered, Jews could be expected to live sociably within French society.

The much-vilified crime of usury could no longer be viewed as a sign of antagonism, because by modern standards it had become a respectable activity. Like many of his contemporaries, Beugnot expressed admiration for the social and political genius of Mosaic law, the role played by Jews in the development of European commerce, and their important contributions to the field of philology and oriental languages. However, Beugnot's favorable judgment of the Jews' historical experience and cultural achievement stood in marked contrast to the denigration of rabbinic Judaism that periodically surfaced in his work. Although he showed admiration for the grammatical works and lexicons that Jews contributed toward "the progress of the human spirit," he considered rabbinic learning to be "frivolous" and advised Christian scholars to separate the "truly useful research" from the "talmudic rubbish" (*fatras*).[24] Accordingly, it is not surprising that the proposals he put forward in the 1824 essay contest only expressed in concrete terms his pronounced misgivings about the cultural value of traditional Judaism.

Beugnot had full confidence in the Jews' capacity to direct their own *régénération*, provided that this was carried out under the aegis of governmental supervision. Convinced that the consistorial system was ineffective, he proposed the establishment of a *société israélite d'Alsace*, either to augment the body formed under Napoleon or to replace it. It would be divided into five *comités*, each responsible for a specific area of supervision, including the general studies curriculum; the publishing of school textbooks; the development of an experimental farm; vocational education and employment; and charitable affairs on behalf of needy Jews.[25] The second part of the Beugnot essay was devoted to the subject of ritual reform and the modernization of the rabbinate. Echoing a criticism often heard in the Jewish community, Beugnot derided the poor training that French rabbis received, as this rendered them incapable of providing instruction in the religious doctrines contained in the decisions of the Sanhedrin. Accordingly, he proposed the establishment of a new rabbinical seminary in Strasbourg to prepare rabbis for their diverse obligations.[26] Only graduates of French secondary schools with a *bachelier ès lettres* degree would be eligible for admission. A well-rounded curriculum consisting of biblical studies, rabbinic theology, oratory, and ethics, in addition to Talmud, would, in the author's mind, counterbalance the exclusive emphasis on rabbinics at the Metz *yeshivah*. On this point in particular the evaluation commission concurred with Beugnot's vision of the importance of transforming rabbinic training.[27]

Criticism of Jewish ritual was rarely motivated by purely religious concerns. It reflected an awareness of the social and economic implications of Jewish exclusiveness, which, critics claimed, was encouraged and sustained by the detailed corpus of Jewish law. Beugnot's plan for religious reform included a demand for the convocation of a new Sanhedrin that would revise

those religious dogmas and moral principles that underlay the social estrangement of the Jews, on the one hand, and prescribe concrete changes,
on the other. As an example, Beugnot cited the calendar of Jewish religious
holidays as an obstacle to normal business relations with Christians and to
the hiring of Jewish workers in gentile shops. As a partial solution to the
problem, Beugnot suggested that the Jewish Sabbath be moved from Saturday to Sunday, in accordance with Christian practice. Arguing that the
rabbis had originally fixed the day of the Sabbath not according to chronological considerations but as a counterpart to the Christian day of rest and
owing to apparent uncertainties in the astronomical calculations, he suggested that the transfer of the Sabbath to Sunday could be carried out without fear of actually violating Jewish law.[28] Also targeted for reform were
those rituals that allegedly precluded Jewish social integration. Some writers, such as Tourette, cited the Jews' refusal to intermarry as the greatest
obstacle to their integration. Beugnot reserved his most severe criticism for
Jewish dietary laws because they impeded "la fusion sociale des Juifs." The
elimination of these restrictions was not, in his estimation, an unjustified
demand since he viewed them as paradigmatic of the many religious
customs and ceremonies that were invented by the rabbis to replace pentateuchal prescriptions. Rabbinic laws represented, paradoxically, precedents for ritual innovation that lent legitimacy to the contemporary
enterprise of reform; conversely, they themselves were only late revisions of
biblical legislation and were therefore of questionable validity, at best. Accordingly, Beugnot called on the Consistory to announce to its members
that the prohibition of certain foods had originally been motivated by political and hygienic considerations, but now that these motives were no
longer necessary or justified, the time had come to abandon them.[29]

Though never published, the prize-winning Beugnot essay was representative of the general climate of opinion on the Jewish question in Restoration France. It incorporated the range of views that prevailed among
government officials and public figures, and it systematized many of the
proposals that had been published in the previous decade. The underlying
assumption was that traditional Judaism and its institutions were fundamentally incompatible with the demands of contemporary civilization and
would, inevitably, continue to exert corrupting influences on the Jewish
people unless reforms were introduced. Despite repeated evidence of condescension and condemnation, the most striking element in the literature
on the Jewish question in this period was the universally shared faith in and
commitment to change. Dissatisfaction with the state of emancipated Alsatian Jewry was pervasive and virtually uncontested, and on this basis writers
demanded wholesale changes in compliance with the prevailing social,
economic, and cultural ethos of revolutionary France. Over the course of
the 1820s, efforts aiming to realize the elusive economic, social, and cultural regeneration of the Jews gained wider support. In contrast to the pre-

revolutionary period, it was now the Jew qua citizen who was obliged to become civilized and "to never isolate his interest from the public interest, nor his destiny . . . from the destiny of the grand family of the state."[30]

Greater emphasis on the social dimension of emancipation thus rested on a fundamental principle of the Revolution: that citizenship was a public and political expression of an idealized, extended family. Repeated references to *la grande famille française*, both in Jewish and gentile sources, attest to the spread of the Revolution's social doctrine. In fact, the expectation and demand that the Jews become absorbed into the French "family" had been voiced decades earlier, even before the Revolution. Abbé Grégoire had emphasized the membership of the Jews in *la famille universelle*, but this was an argument for their humanity, not their being Frenchmen. The transition from human to French would require active encouragement on the part of men of good will.[31] Napoleon was of the opinion that the Jewish problem would be solved, in the end, through intermarriage, and this view was repeated regularly by French writers, bureaucrats, and other public figures throughout the next half-century. The ultimate aim of emancipation, then, was the incorporation of the Jews within the French nation as indistinguishable elements of a single harmonious entity. Throughout the first two decades of the nineteenth century gentile writers criticized the Jews for failing to avail themselves of the generous invitation offered to them. Seeking to explain this failure, virtually all competitors in the 1824 Strasbourg essay contest concluded that the Jewish religion obstructed the *rapprochement* of the Jews with French society and civilization.

This indictment was so pervasive that Jewish intellectual and communal leaders reached many of the same conclusions as their gentile counterparts, though the negative assessment of Jewish life also evoked a new critical responsiveness to the much-debated issues of Jewish modernization. Jews did not experience the acute trauma of emancipation in the immediate aftermath of the Revolution and the bestowal of civic rights, but only with the passage of several decades when normal participation in French society became possible. Increased attendance at French secondary schools and universities became evident only after the demise of Napoleon. Many of the younger generation measured solutions to the Jewish question not by expressions of loyalty to the state nor according to the outworn discourse concerning the performance of civic duties, but by the extent and scope of social integration. They demanded thoroughgoing religious reform, including the abandonment of the Jewish dietary laws and Sabbath observance in order to facilitate what was widely referred to as *la fusion sociale*.[32] For Léon Halévy and Olry Terquem, the elimination of the *la rituel asiatique* in Judaism would lessen the distance between Jew and non-Jew and ultimately effectuate the *fusion* mandated by the Revolution.[33]

Not everyone within the Jewish community could agree that social fusion was the functional equivalent of emancipation. Rabbi Abraham Cologna of the Central Consistory protested the use of the term in the following strongly worded observation: "Let no one speak to us any more of 'fusion,' away with these vague expressions, let us call things by their names: it is only a matter of civil and political association, which has nothing and which can have nothing in common with belief in the messiah who has come or who is still to come."[34] For Jewish intellectuals in Paris, and for the affluent as well, *fusion* denoted the dream of social acceptance that had long eluded realization. But for the most radical among them, the goal of *fusion* was to be pursued not by abandoning one's Jewish identity but by first rethinking the fundamental ideas of Judaism. Though undeniably extreme in his views, Terquem (1782–1862) did not endorse intermarriage as some gentile observers proposed. He viewed the alienation of Jewish intellectuals in Paris as symptomatic of a larger problem, namely, the failure of Judaism to adapt itself to the new conditions in post-emancipation France. He warned that unless ritual reforms were introduced, the situation would continue to deteriorate. These views were clearly unacceptable to the vast majority of French Jews, and as we shall see, evoked considerable protest.

Terquem was the first French Jew to publicly address the question of religious reform in a systematic manner, and he was largely responsible for bringing the issues to the attention of the public. A native of Metz, he received a traditional education and then pursued secular studies at the *école centrale*. Moses Ensheim may have assisted the young Terquem in preparing for his *école polytechnique* entrance examination; Terquem later occupied the chair in theoretical mathematics at the *lycée* in French-occupied Mayence until 1814 and then moved to Paris where he became librarian at the Dépôt d'Artillerie. He also served on the faculty of the *école centrale rabbinique* as a teacher of elementary sciences. Best known for his *Lettres Tsarphatiques*, a series of twenty-seven pamphlets and letters published over a period of twenty years, Terquem brashly advocated radical changes in Jewish religious life. Although his efforts had yielded few concrete results by 1841, when he withdrew from the arena of religious controversy, there can be little doubt that his writings set the ideological stage for subsequent reforms.[35]

Aiming to accelerate the entrance of Jews into the mainstream of French society, Terquem urged the reform of those rites that impeded the process of *fusion*. Accordingly, he scrutinized biblical and talmudic traditions in light of contemporary notions of civilization, spirituality, and justice, hoping that his conclusions would encourage a reappraisal of Judaism's role in the nineteenth century and, in turn, provide justification for certain essential ritual reforms. Relying on massive historical and legal evidence, Terquem concluded that Judaism was an imperfect religious and social system. Many *régénérateurs* would reach the same conclusion. It was their contention, however, that rabbinic Judaism had corrupted the ancient purity and simplicity of Mosaism. Terquem took a different tack, claiming that

Mosaism had not freed itself entirely of pagan influences.[36] He argued that most pentateuchal ritual prescriptions were borrowed from Egypt, albeit with certain modifications, and reserved special contempt for the adoption of the priestly cult and sacrificial order.[37] Terquem went further, blaming rabbinic literature for having distorted the plain meaning of the Bible. He considered it undeserving of the scholarly attention it received, while he also ridiculed those sections of the Talmud that formed the major portion of the curriculum at the *école rabbinique.*[38]

The case for reform drew upon the Deist distinction between religion and ritual. While the former was an immutable moral and spiritual essence, the latter was an imperfect representation of the sacred, subject to variable conditions such as climate, mores, and political status. Accordingly, when any one of these elements varies, the *culte* must undergo corresponding modification and adjustment. Claiming that he had no intention of tampering with the essence of the Jewish religion, Terquem directed his attention to those external manifestations that had already undergone substantial modification throughout the course of history.[39] His concern with the external forms of the *culte* points to the widening gap between France of the eighteenth and nineteenth centuries. In contrast to the Deists and the *philosophes,* Terquem acknowledged that the ethereal ideas of the spiritual world required concrete forms of expression. While rituals such as prayer, festival observances, and commemorative rites may well have originated as concessions to human frailty, they were, in his view, essential to the ultimate purpose of religion: the perfection of human moral sensibilities.[40] This view explains Terquem's near obsession with ritual reform, an idea that was virtually unknown in the eighteenth century. In effect, Terquem went one step beyond the Enlightenment by applying the notions of progress and the perfectibility of man to the domain of institutional religion. Central to his argument was the claim that the Jewish religion had failed to keep pace with political, social, and economic transformations set in motion by the French Revolution. Judaism had somehow escaped the dominant influence of European civilization and remained unscathed in its *accoutrement asiatique.*[41] Terquem bemoaned the fact that despite advances in the civil and political realms, "we [Jews] are the most backward in the religious sphere, thanks to our present consistorial organization."[42] The time had come, he maintained, to adapt religious ritual to the demands imposed by civilization and citizenship.

More than any other rite, circumcision was portrayed as an affront to modern European culture. Terquem's aversion to the "asiatic" ritual is illustrated by the following: "If I were to tell you that, in a certain country, there exists a population which attaches a religious importance to mutilating, to slashing, to lacerating the weak creatures as soon as they enter life, to submitting them to so painful an operation that sometimes death follows it . . . with no protest ever being raised in favor of the victims, if I let you

guess the country, would not your ideas naturally point to an African country, inhabited by some savage race? Such is not the case. It concerns our *patrie*, France, and a notable segment of its inhabitants."[43] The fact that cases
of syphilis, tuberculosis, and diphtheria had been linked to circumcision
only added to the urgency of reform. Terquem demanded the elimination
of two aspects of the operation that had been adjoined to the biblical ritual
by the Talmud: *peri'ah* (tearing of the edge of the mucous membrane with
the thumbnail) and *meẓiẓah* (sucking the blood). He also insisted that *mohalim* undergo certification by a medical faculty. Convinced that the findings of contemporary medical science far outweighed the narrow
perspectives of the Jewish tradition, he looked forward to the eventual
eclipse of rabbinic Judaism, because "the authority of the Talmud ceases
where the rights of humanity begin." Concern for health was not the only
issue, however. Although Terquem did not go quite as far as Voltaire, who
ridiculed circumcision as an example of the meaninglessness of ritual, his
irreverence is characteristic of the man. In anticipation of opposition to his
proposed reforms, Terquem recommended that government authorities
enforce his proposed guidelines.[44]

Citizenship also imposed demands that would necessarily impinge on
Jewish religious observance. Many of the arguments concerning the incompatibility of Judaism with civic duties that had dominated discussions
of the Jewish question in the revolutionary period occasionally resurfaced
later on, serving as added justification for reform. Terquem advocated a
fundamental reorientation—a *rapprochement*—toward the Christian population, citing the problematic *Kol Nidrei* prayer and *Shefokh Ḥamatkha* passage in the Passover Haggadah as representative of hateful, antisocial
sentiments.[45] He argued that these prayers ought to be expunged from the
liturgy as proof of Judaism's willingness to join general humanity. More
concretely, he proposed that in those instances where traditional religious
observance encroached on the obligations of citizenship, as in the case of
the Jewish Sabbath, the main source of conflict ought to be modified.[46] He
maintained that the restrictive Sabbath laws posed an obstacle to the Jews'
economic integration into French life by requiring them to be idle two days
of the week. The Paris Sanhedrin, according to his unconventional reading, had provided a religious dispensation to anyone receiving vocational
or military training or engaged in occupations that might require the violation of traditional Sabbath restrictions.[47] Going a step further, he asserted
that because of mounting economic and social pressures, both the working
and educated classes of Jews found themselves excluded from public worship. He urged communal leaders to acknowledge the reality of nonobser-
vance by allowing Jews whose occupations did not permit Saturday
observance to celebrate the Sabbath on Sunday, the "national day of rest."
An appeal to hold Sabbath services on Sunday, in French, was meant not to
supplant the Saturday service but only to supplement it. Answering his crit-

ics, Terquem declared that he had no intention of secularizing Saturday, since "this secularization is in operation without me." His avowed purpose was to salvage Sabbath observance in some alternative form for the emancipated Jew because the combination of Saturday and Sunday as days of rest was an insurmountable difficulty for many.[48] This was dangerous, he insisted, because Christian biblical societies engaged in missionary work were making their greatest inroads among the Jewish indigent. The morality of the family and its spiritual safety, Terquem argued, depended on its economic well-being.[49]

To be sure, these sensationalist arguments for religious reform rested on a set of assumptions that were far too radical for the vast majority of French Jews and were anathema to the leadership as well. Ultimately, Terquem held the leadership of the Jewish community responsible, claiming that the consistories "embrace antisocial and separatist passions; they protect worm-eaten opinions, the superstitious practices of the ignorant, degenerate class, but they do nothing for the enlightened, liberal, industrial class."[50] Embodying all the old values of the pre-revolutionary era, the consistorial system was unmercifully identified with the forces of reaction. The major obstacle to reform was, in his view, structural: as long as authority was vested solely in established institutions, there was no hope for change.[51]

Terquem's proposals were an impassioned response to the indifference, radical assimilation, and renunciation of Jewish identity that had begun to gain attention in the 1820s. A number of cases of apostasy in this period suggest that the final decision to convert came in the aftermath of bitter personal disappointment and as a response to profound skepticism concerning the ability of the Jews to ever achieve *fusion sociale* as long as they remained Jewish. Théodore Ratisbonne, for one, concluded that there was a fundamental, unbridgeable incompatibility between Judaism and French citizenship. He was strengthened by the realization that French society was not religiously neutral but Christian. Ratisbonne had served as secretary of the Société d'Encouragement au Travail en Faveur des Israélites du Bas-Rhin. In a *mémoire* he composed in 1824, he had advanced recommendations for reform that aimed at realizing the vision of *fusion sociale*. Until his conversion in 1827, he was active in the work of the Société d'Encouragement. According to Ratisbonne and fellow converts Isidore Goschler and Jules Lewel, their involvement in Jewish communal affairs was undertaken at the insistence of their mentor, Louis Bautain, as a preparatory step before undergoing baptism. In fact, it appears that for most, the decision to convert was not inconsistent with their commitment to *régénération*, as Ratisbonne himself affirmed: "It is my Christian faith that brought me to renounce the pleasures of life in order to consecrate myself to the *régénération* of my brothers."[52] Terquem could certainly not countenance the equivalence asserted by Ratisbonne between conversion and *régénération*. He undoubtedly viewed the case of Ratisbonne as proof of the dangers implicit in inaction. Although he could boast no tangible results for his efforts, he had succeeded by the end of the 1830s in bringing the issues of reform to the attention of the community and in generating public discussion within the leadership of the Jewish community. The actual work of modernizing the Jewish religion would ultimately be taken up by men who defined Jewish identity in more traditional terms.

Reconstruction of Jewish Life: Ideological and Institutional Changes

Under the Bourbon Monarchy, French Jewry discovered unprecedented opportunities to participate in the mainstream of French society and culture, though in these years such developments were restricted to urban centers, especially Paris. As admission to institutions of higher learning became feasible and as a small number entered the liberal professions, the process of acculturation slowly moved forward. It is clear that the pressures of professional and social advancement were, for many, taxing, while the intellectual and cultural challenges to traditional Jewish identity were difficult. They encountered a society that demanded of them full integration but displayed considerable ambivalence about their joining its ranks. A variety of responses to the complex dynamics of social integration in these years, particularly to the extensive criticism described above, are evident in the political activity, institution building, and intellectual life of French Jews, and in new constructions of religious identity among those who had concluded that traditional Judaism was incompatible with the social and political demands of citizenship.

The first evidence of a Jewish consciousness of the dramatic changes precipitated by the Revolution may be discerned in the realm of politics. In 1817 the first French-language journal of Jewish affairs, *L'Israélite français*, appeared, offering a valuable index of the new political outlook of French Jewry. The journal was the product of efforts to thwart the extension of the residential and economic restrictions of the 1808 Infamous Decree beyond its original ten-year term. Already in 1814 the Conseils Généraux of the Haut- and Bas-Rhin had demanded that the 1808 regulations remain in force, apparently fearful that the new regime might permit the law to expire. Aware, then, that an attempt would undoubtedly be made in 1818 to reintroduce the discriminatory law, Jewish leaders had begun to lay the groundwork for the political struggle early in 1816. Arguing that the 1808 law was a violation of the status of the Jews as citizens, representatives of the five *départements* making up Alsace-Lorraine were able to win support among public officials. A year later, with the publication of the journal in Paris where the matter would ultimately be decided, the Paris Jewish community assumed a leading role in the struggle. Relying on *L'Israélite français* to bring the issues before the general and Jewish public, Paris leaders succeeded in galvanizing the support they needed to defeat the petition.[53]

Underlying the political orientation of the French-Jewish elite was the conviction that full emancipation would be achieved only with a total dedication to improving the public image of French Jewry. This view was expressed repeatedly throughout the pages of *L'Israélite français*. The fact that literary and intellectual affairs were largely subordinated to the practical concerns of a population unsure of its future only supports the contention that in the first years of the Restoration Jewish leaders were preoccupied with the political challenges facing their communities. The new Franco-Jewish spirit, then, assumed a predominantly political character, marked by an abiding faith in the ideals of the French Revolution. Significantly, once the battle against the renewal of the 1808 *règlement* was successfully completed, the new journal lost its raison d'être and ceased to appear.[54]

Efforts to establish Jewish primary schools where children were to receive secular and religious instruction in accordance with modern pedagogical techniques came to fruition beginning in 1818 when the first such institution was opened in Metz. By 1821 twelve Jewish public schools, all consistent with the educational philosophy of the Haskalah, were established in the seven departmental consistories. The history of Jewish education has received more attention than most other aspects of Jewish life in nineteenth-century France, and there is no need to repeat the findings of that research. Insofar as our interest here concerns the timing of this development, however, several observations are in order. The new Jewish schools were created after nearly thirty years of discontinuity, and their objectives were defined in relation to vastly different conditions than those that prevailed in Germany when the movement for educational reform began. In late eighteenth-century Germany enlightened Jewish schools founded by *maskilim* were intended as vehicles for either progressive social change or more radical restructuring of Jewish values. Their beginnings coincided with the crisis in religious authority that was then enveloping German-Jewish communities.[55] The French schools, by contrast, were much more conservative, insofar as their mission was to serve the goals of regenerating the Jewish community. Frequently the products of individual or private initiative, the schools were in full harmony with the publicly articulated goals of *régénération* and therefore received the unqualified support of communal leaders. Because rabbis were full partners in the community leadership structure, they could hardly afford to be antagonists of the movement for educational modernization. Rabbinic involvement was crucial for whatever success these ventures enjoyed, owing to the central role of the rabbi and the synagogue in Jewish life, particularly in Alsace-Lorraine. No less important, the communal rabbis were a consistently conservative influence on the character of school reforms.[56]

The activity surrounding the creation of a rabbinical seminary in 1820, though less familiar than that of the primary schools, furnishes an especially instructive example of the new trends. Employing the same method of fund-raising used several years earlier to establish the Metz primary school, the founders of the *école talmudique de Metz* solicited broad support through individual subscriptions.[57] Carefully crafted and highly evocative, the Hebrew appeal for support contains the following description of the rueful state of affairs in Metz:

On account of the distress of the times, the Torah is forsaken, abandoned to the side, and no one inquires after it. Everyone has gone his own way, turning to the vanities of this world, placing trust in the idols of silver and gold, while impassive about the eternal world. Nearly lost is the wisdom of God. . . . Anguish filled our loins, as we recall how the splendor of Israel was cast off. Alas, how desolate is our community, formerly in Israel the joy of the entire earth, and the home of outstanding scholars (*ba'alei terisin*) and robust leaders (*ba'alei qarnayim*). Torah and greatness are complementary.[58]

Dramatizing the urgency of the situation by drawing on images of Jerusalem following its destruction, this elegy for the former glory of the Metz community prescribed a clear course of action. If the community owed its past reputation to the mutually sustaining partnership of scholarship and power, it was now imperative for leaders to revive this alliance. The author(s) of the appeal maintained that neither Torah scholarship nor "greatness" could be fully realized without the other, and therefore the creation of a new rabbinical school was a vital community project.

While the attempt to recall and restore the glory of the acclaimed Metz *yeshivah* is evident in the placement of the school in the original *yeshivah* building, it is clear that the founders of the new institution envisioned a very different direction. Their intention was "to form a school enabling Jewish youths to rise from one level to another, ascending upon the ladder reaching heavenward, so as to be nourished by the Talmud and *poseqim* and even by the other essential subjects, *derekh eretz* (general studies), will the young then satisfy their hunger, to find favor and understanding before God and men." The influence of the Haskalah, which placed emphasis on graduated education and on the importance of *derekh eretz*, is especially apparent here. Moreover, in contrast with the period preceding the Revolution when entrance to the *yeshivah* was limited to the very best students only, the nineteenth century witnessed a dramatic liberalization of admissions standards, permitting any student "who has an open heart" to study there. On the basis of reports dating from the 1830s and 1840s it may be concluded that the *école centrale rabbinique* (founded in 1829) continued in this vein.[59]

In addition to the trend toward popularization, the modern rabbinic facility in Metz evinced two salient qualities of post-revolutionary France. First, for all intents and purposes, the establishment of the Metz rabbinical school put an end to the many local *yeshivot* that had reopened or were founded anew in the first decades of the century. This network of small academies corresponded, at least organizationally, to the pre-revolutionary pattern. In time, the *yeshivot* across Alsace-Lorraine eventually fell victim, as did other local academies in Europe, to the dominant forces of centralization set in motion by the state and supported by Jewish partisans of reform. Second, the rabbinical facility attracted French students only and in this respect reflected, perhaps even strengthened, the distinctively French identity of the Jewish citizens of France. In the first class of matriculants in 1829, ten of the eleven students were born in Alsace-Lorraine, and the eleventh, though born abroad, was a resident of France. Thirty years later, as the school prepared to be transferred to Paris, it was reported that all 109 students who had attended the institution during the years 1829–59 had been French citizens.[60]

Revived shortly before the end of the Napoleonic regime in 1813, the Hebrew press in Metz was influenced by the disruptive effects of the preceding two decades on Jewish cultural and intellectual life and guided in its work by the opportunities that became available during the Bourbon Restoration. From its inception in 1764 until its doors were closed in 1793, the Metz press published fifty-two titles that included biblical commentaries, tractates of Talmud and *novellae*, responsa, liturgical compilations, Hebrew calendars, two volumes of Haskalah literature, and one Hebrew grammar. The list of published works was heavily weighted on the side of classical Torah scholarship, clearly intended for a learned and religiously observant public. A comparison with the list published after 1813 reveals a vastly different circumstance. Among the thirty-eight titles that appeared between 1813 and 1843, only a handful of works of traditional talmudic scholarship were published. The vast majority of publications can be classified in the following categories: *siddurim* and *maḥzorim* (9), textbooks and catechisms (10), and calendars (9). Particular emphasis was placed on translations of Hebrew texts, in the first years into German and later into French. The post-1813 list was intended, without doubt, for a public that had seen a decline in its knowledge of Hebrew and a reduction in the number who were either capable of or had an interest in traditional rabbinic learning. Moreover, the absence of any titles composed by foreign authors, the gradual disappearance of references in the liturgy to variants on the broader themes of Ashkenazic tradition, and the persistence of local Metz rites all point to the emergence of an independent Franco-Jewish consciousness.[61]

The new involvement in modern Jewish scholarship exemplifies, in a striking manner, French Jewry's evolving perspective on emancipation and tradition. Though undeniably inspired and nurtured by the example of the German *Wissenschaft des Judentums* movement, the roots of Jewish scholarship in France are more correctly located in an entirely different social and intellectual framework. For German Jewry, *Wissenschaft des Judentums* was the product of the failure of political emancipation. In France Jewish scholarship emerged not as a response to anti-Jewish hostility but as an expression of confidence in the prospects of emancipation. Its character was shaped by a small group of intellectuals who were secure in their Jewish identity and observance. Its development was slow, principally because of the small number interested in the subject matter. Notwithstanding the powerful influence of the German example, the nascent French movement of *la science de judaïsme* developed a special character that it owed primarily to the constellation of local forces. Ultimately, the degree to which Jews were received into the general circles of scholars, as well as Jewish perceptions of the dangers posed by the continuing Christian imprint on French culture, would determine the direction and character of Jewish scientific research in France.

The singularity of Franco-Jewish scholarship, particularly its relationship to emancipation, evolved in two successive stages. Initially, Jewish and Christian scholars were drawn together by a common interest in Hebrew language and Semitic texts, despite the chasm still separating Jews from the mainstream of French society in the first decades of the century. Scholarly collaboration between Jews and Christians in the early 1820s was cut short by the resurgence of Catholicism in 1824, while the quest for social acceptance and equality lost much ground. Not until after the 1830 Revolution, however, was there a revivification of Jewish membership in learned societies and a resumption of regular scholarly collaboration. In the July Monarchy Jewish scholarship entered its second stage and assumed an entirely different character.[62]

As in the case of modern Jewish scholarship, radically new forms of Jewish identity originated during the Bourbon Restoration, but it was only in the July Monarchy that they attained their fullest expression. The flight from traditional identity, for example, was evident in several celebrated cases of conversion to Christianity, in a small group that joined the Saint Simon movement, and in the early efforts to remove religious obstacles hindering social integration. These alternative expressions of identity certainly do not represent a numerically significant trend to abandon the Jewish community and tradition. However, they do underscore the importance of investigating the complex relationship between emancipation and integration in order to attain greater insight into the Jewish encounter with modernity.

Part III
Transformations in Jewish Self-Understanding

Chapter 7
Scholarship and Identity: *La Science de Judaïsme*

In a letter to Leopold Zunz in the fall of 1822, French orientalist Sylvestre de Sacy predicted that the important work of *Wissenschaft des Judentums* would never gain the appreciation it deserved in France because the Jewish community there showed so little interest in intellectual affairs.[1] Two decades later, commenting on the failure of French Jews to embrace ritual reform, as did their German coreligionists, Abraham Geiger went a step further, holding the paucity of Jewish intellectual life responsible for the disappointing lack of progress in the realm of religion. With impassivity rampant, he was convinced that only a movement devoted to the scientific study of Judaism could save French Jewry from the portentous effects of indifference. In accordance with de Sacy and Geiger's views, the achievements of French Jewish scholarship have been commonly dismissed as inconsequential, at best only a faint echo of the more celebrated and undeniably more important trends that prevailed across the Rhine.[2] There is no doubt that the disintegration of French universities, both in the aftermath of the Revolution and as a direct result of Napoleonic policy, was a limiting factor in the development of modern Jewish scholarship.[3] It is also abundantly clear that French Jewish scholars were never entirely free of German influence. In the revolutionary era, Moses Mendelssohn and the Berlin circle that formed around him profoundly inspired French *maskilim* such as Zalkind Hourwitz, Isaïe Berr Bing, and Berr Isaac Berr. During the Napoleonic regime especially, this relationship of intellectual indebtedness to German Jewry would intensify. Continuous contact with German scholars, together with the training received at German universities, fostered among French Jewish intellectuals a greater awareness of the methods and objectives of the nascent *Wissenschaft des Judentums* movement, influencing their work in several important areas.

The two regnant assumptions concerning Franco-Jewish scholarship—its meager value and its distinctly German provenance—prove to be unreliable, however, when examined carefully. Geiger's judgment has gone unchallenged because the scholarship produced in France before the mid-nineteenth century is still largely unknown to most students of the period. The second claim—that modern Jewish studies was without roots in

French soil but was imported from central and eastern Europe by immigrant scholars and only came of age in the 1860s—ignores the body of work
produced in France, beginning in the third decade of the nineteenth century.[4] It will become clear that Franco-Jewish scholarship, though certainly
not autonomous, developed an independent character reflecting the matrix of political and intellectual issues peculiar to France.

Patterns of Jewish scholarship in nineteenth-century France offer a valuable perspective on the complexities facing Jews in the emancipation era.
Accompanying the process of legal emancipation was a progressive liberation from the intellectual constraints of the Jewish tradition. In response to
unprecedented demands to fulfill the duties of citizenship and to become
part of *la grande famille française*, scholars took the lead in redefining the
meaning of Jewish tradition and history. Toward this end, Jewish intellectuals appropriated the methods and tools of modern scholarship and
began to subject classical Jewish literature to critical examination. Clearly
the direct and natural outgrowth of ongoing secularization, the critical-
scientific approach was generally adopted wherever religious authority had
weakened. It emerged not only as a novel interpretive mode for the explication of ancient and medieval texts but also as a new source of prestige for
those able to meet the scholarly standards set by the general academic community. In this way, modern scholarship served as a vehicle by which intellectuals were able to attain power and influence within the Jewish
community. In the case of Germany, their efforts resulted in the forging of
a close relationship between critical scholarship on the one hand and the
struggle on behalf of emancipation and religious reform on the other.[5] The
work of Leopold Zunz, like that of Abraham Geiger and Zacharias Frankel,
was motivated by a desire both to prove the worthiness of Jews as citizens
and to substantiate the claims for ritual change. The first of these goals was
rooted in the conviction that the Jews' social and political status was a function of the level of intellectual respect accorded to Judaism. The second
goal, the modernization of Jewish religious practice, though undoubtedly
related to the first, was largely an internal issue on which the German Jewish community was deeply divided.[6]

The fact that these motivations were less prominent than in Germany
does not at all diminish the efforts of modern French scholars to deal with
the cultural and intellectual implications of emancipation. As French citizens, they may have felt less compelled to respond to many of the political
pressures facing their coreligionists elsewhere. But a host of social, cultural,
and religious tensions that were endemic to the modernization process—
and not necessarily linked to the process of legal emancipation per se—informed the entire modern history of the Jews in France. Two issues were
especially significant. First, a growing interest in reexamining the texts and
traditions that had formerly been restricted to traditionalist interpretation
had begun to surface even before the prospect of full civic equality was in

view. Second, the dialectical tension between the particular and universal—perhaps the most abiding cultural question for modern Jewish identity—reverberated loudly in many areas of Jewish cultural expression. These tensions are particularly evident in the work of modern Franco-Jewish scholarship. From its emergence in the revolutionary era to its maturation at mid-century, Jewish scholarship assumed a decisive role in the construction of a new Jewish identity. In this chapter, we shall analyze the ideological and intellectual trends in modern Jewish scholarship through its various stages of development. However, before examining the accomplishments of this movement, we shall first consider changes in the world of traditional rabbinic scholarship.

The World of Rabbinic Scholarship in Transition

Intimations of a critical approach to traditional Judaism were evident well before the publication of modern scientific studies in the nineteenth century. The transition to works that broke with the methods and underlying assumptions of the Jewish tradition was invariably slow, however, and often difficult to detect. For centuries, much of traditional scholarship rested on a firm foundation of rational inquiry and rigorous argumentation, despite Ashkenazic Jewry's oscillation between rationalistic and antirationalistic pursuits, between receptivity to external influences and a tendency toward insularity. In the writings of R. Solomon Luria of sixteenth-century Poland, for example, one encounters exacting criticism of the talmudic text, and the halakhic writings of R. Ya'ir Ḥayyim Bacharach of seventeenth-century Worms offer clear evidence of a highly rational approach to law and custom. R. Moses Isserles, R. Mordecai Jaffe, and R. Yom Tov Lippmann Heller exemplified a positive orientation toward philosophy, which Isserles termed "the legacy of our fathers." If the rationalist tradition was not continuous, there is at least sufficient evidence to suggest that by the late eighteenth century the new critical spirit that had emerged in the writings of individual rabbis and *maskilim* had more than a leg to stand on.[7]

In the specific case of Alsace-Lorraine, indications of change in traditional scholarship are somewhat more obscure. In part, this may be ascribed to the meager scholarly attention that this literature has attracted. It is compounded by the nature of the literature itself, which typically exhibited little interest in contemporary affairs and historical events. With its focus on the clarification, interpretation, and elaboration of issues found in the Talmud, medieval commentaries, and the codes, rabbinic scholarship assumed a style—consciously or not—that promoted the pretense of timelessness. One glaring example of independence from the hegemony of rabbinic tradition is buried in the talmudic scholarship of R. Aryeh Loeb Günzberg, the *av beit din* of Metz from 1766 to 1786 and famed author of *Sha'agat Aryeh*. Based on an independent analysis of the phrase *ad ha-yom ha-zeh* ("to this day") (1 Chron. 4:42), R. Aryeh Loeb disputed the talmudic (*Bava Batra* 15a) attribution of authorship of the Book of Chronicles to Ezra the Scribe. According to Günzberg, Ezra copied sections from earlier books, and therefore some of the references appearing in the text were already outmoded by the time he had completed his work. The many contradictions in the text itself, as well as the various inconsistencies with the Book of Ezra, led Günzberg to conclude that Chronicles was the product of human ingenuity. It was to this work of editing, Günzberg concluded, that the Talmud referred when it identified Ezra as the "author" of Chronicles.[8]

By sheer volume alone, the highly original talmudic and halakhic *novellae* published by Metz grand rabbi Aaron Worms offer a substantially more striking illustration of the new critical spirit. Structured as a running commentary to the Talmud and *Shulḥan Arukh*, the seven-volume *Me'orei Or* sought to discredit practices that were rooted in superstition, linguistic error, or corrupted texts.[9] His sustained efforts to reconstitute the authentic Ashkenazic ritual corresponded to a parallel interest in classical traditions that typified the Enlightenment and Romanticism. Though fully consistent with the medieval rabbinic tradition of comparative source analysis and rigorous argumentation, one can discern in *Me'orei Or* the utilization of methods that had become popular in the Enlightenment era as well, including text emendation,[10] consultation of manuscript sources that differed from standard printed documents,[11] and a skeptical assessment of medieval compilations of *minhagim*.[12] Worms routinely compared the Isserles glosses on the *Shulḥan Arukh* with parallel formulations contained in his *Darkhei Moshe* commentary to the *Tur* in order to establish the more authoritative ruling.[13] His interest in Kabbalah is most evident in the role he ascribed to the *Zohar* either as a formative influence in the development of Halakhah or as simply an integral part of the discourse on custom and law since the appearance of the *Shulḥan Arukh*. In either case, he succeeded in clarifying the origins of many Ashkenazic rituals while also displaying a critical-historical approach to Kabbalah.

Alongside Worms's affinity for the critical style of the Haskalah were his strenuous efforts to respond to its periodic ridicule of traditional Jewish practice.[14] Unlike most defenders of rabbinic tradition, he eschewed apologetics and instead took what might be considered the improbable position that the Haskalah was not entirely incorrect in the criticism it leveled against established rites. The thrust of this critique, as Worms understood it, demanded of traditionalists higher standards of precision in transmitting ritual practices and in explicating their underlying principles. Failing to correct errors and corruptions that had crept into the ritual system would only compromise the integrity of the religious tradition in the eyes of the public. This approach is what endeared Worms to French *maskilim*, proponents of moderate religious reform, and practitioners of *Wissenschaft des Judentums.* Their judgment was doubtless rooted in the belief that Worms's worldview constituted a reversion to a rational and enlightened traditionalism rarely found among contemporary rabbinic personalities.

Clearly focused on the legal-exegetical issues that had been debated in study houses over the course of centuries, *Me'orei Or* exemplified the hermeneutical conventions and modes of analysis characteristic of early modern talmudic scholarship. But it addressed itself as well to internal challenges threatening to weaken the infrastructure of the halakhic system. The invention of printing, westward migration, and greater geographical mobility each, in its own way, contributed to a dangerous fragmentation of views, a growing multiplicity of ritual practices, and a decentralization of authority. What set *Me'orei Or* apart from the more standard talmudic and halakhic *novellae* of the eighteenth century was its concern for these larger issues. The voluminous halakhic and kabbalistic literature that appeared in the two centuries following the publication of the *Shulḥan Arukh* had become a source of considerable confusion for scholars and laymen alike.[15] Worms concluded that in order to forestall these potentially disintegrative and erosive trends it had become necessary to affirm and reinforce the primacy of the *Shulḥan Arukh*.[16] His efforts are noteworthy in light of the principled opposition of many Ashkenazic authorities to codification.[17] According to R. Elijah b. Solomon Zalman, the Gaon of Vilna, hierarchy within the legal tradition was established by the relative antiquity of rabbinic texts; he therefore rejected the principle of *halakhah ke-batrai* ("the law follows the later authorities"), which had come to dominate decision making in medieval Ashkenaz.[18] While Worms, too, was unwilling to be guided by this legal concept, he nonetheless concluded that the *Shulḥan Arukh* had exhibited exemplary faithfulness to the talmudic tradition and that its rulings were generally more reliable than those of earlier or later authorities.[19]

The central assumption governing this approach was the strong preference accorded to talmudic sources over the medieval halakhic tradition. Worms objected vehemently to the elevation of late medieval and early modern authorities to the status of talmudic sages and insisted that their language did not warrant the exacting scrutiny normally reserved for biblical and talmudic literature. Medieval halakhic works were, fundamentally, exegetical texts that must remain subordinate to the Talmud.[20] Despite differences in their appraisal of the *Shulḥan Arukh*, Worms and the Gaon of Vilna shared the conviction that the halakhic system had, by their own day, veered off its original course. This assessment, undoubtedly shared by others,[21] implied that Judaism faced an internal crisis arising from the growing multiplicity of ritual practices—themselves frequent distortions of classical traditions. Israel Zamosc, an older contemporary of the two, maintained that the problem could be traced to the deleterious effects of *pilpul.* Others, such as R. Shlomo of Chelm, R. Yeḥezkel Feivel, and Barukh of Shklov, denounced the exclusive focus on talmudic study, convinced of the importance of exposure to science.[22] In the case of Worms, there is not only no evidence that he had studied secular subjects, but he explicitly warned against engaging in their study: "[T]he fear of sin exists only among those who study Mishnah and Talmud; those who draw near to other subjects distance themselves from the yoke of heaven and abandon prayer."[23] His view of philosophy and philosophers was equally negative,[24] comparable to the attitudes of R. Solomon Luria and the Gaon of Vilna, while the idea of religious reform was utterly foreign to him.[25] For Worms, and for the French *maskilim* as well, this situation demanded the restoration of the Halakhah to an earlier, uncorrupted stage.

Worms's detailed halakhic defense of the *Shulḥan Arukh* centered on the animadversions of its two leading commentators, R. Abraham Gombiner's *Magen Avraham* and R. David Halevi's *Turei Zahav*.[26] Setting out to analyze and ultimately discredit their criticisms, Worms identified weaknesses in their arguments, as well as routine oversights and inconsistencies. His criticism of the *Magen Avraham* pointed to (a) its failure to encompass *minhagim* observed in the west,[27] (b) its uncritical use of the kabbalistic tradition when challenging a ruling of Isserles;[28] (c) its having overlooked a crucial source;[29] and (d) an occasional blurring of the distinction between rabbinic and Torah law, resulting in unjustified leniencies.[30] Likewise with respect to the *Turei Zahav*, Worms cited weaknesses that were largely methodological, including (a) the failure to compare Isserles's glosses to the *Shulḥan Arukh* with parallel formulations in the *Darkhei Moshe*, resulting in a tendency to misconstrue Isserles's position;[31] and (b) a repeated failure to examine Isserles's glosses closely and carefully, as in the case of whether to remove one's *tefillin* before the Musaf (additional) service (*O.H.* 25, n. 15), so that the criticism was predicated on a misreading of the focus of Isserles's gloss.[32] Many of these failings originated, in Worms's view, in Gombiner and Halevi's reliance on R. Mordekhai Jaffe's *Levush Malkhut*, a sixteenth century code-commentary that had challenged the hegemony of the *Shulḥan Arukh*. According to Worms, Jaffe had strayed from the normative halakhic tradition, and his work, riddled with errors, exerted undue influence on early modern interpreters of Halakhah.[33] To counter difficult questions posed by either the *Magen Avraham* or the *Turei Zahav*, Worms typically returned to the Talmud to find an explicit source to support an alternative reading or to discover an unnoticed distinction or nuance that resolved the problem.[34] His efforts on behalf of the *Shulḥan Arukh* were not defensive at all but were devoted to clarifying the method or rationale that underlay its legal rulings.[35]

The burgeoning literature of Lurianic ritual practices constituted an equally formidable challenge to the *Shulḥan Arukh*. Entirely aside from its theosophical implications, Lurianism called into question the authority of the halakhic tradition as interpreted by medieval sages and assembled in the major codes. As the mythic image of the Isaac Luria gained in strength, propelled by the wide diffusion of hundreds of compendia of kabbalistic rites that were published or reprinted in the second half of the eighteenth century, Lurianic practices grew in popularity and stature.[36] Worms harbored halakhic reservations about certain of these developments but endeavored to balance the practical demands of both Halakhah and Kabbalah while continuing to view the *Zohar* with the utmost seriousness. In this he was not alone. The most pronounced examples of this phenomenon, characterized by Scholem as "orthodox anti-Sabbatian Kabbalism," were the *kloiz* in Brody (Galicia) and the circle that formed around R. Nathan Adler in Frankfurt am Main. Enthusiasts embraced the principle elements of ecstatic prayer according to the Lurianic tradition and performed kabbalistic rites that constituted a clear departure from *minhag* Ashkenaz. Elsewhere, major halakhic authorities evinced a lesser-known tendency to embrace kabbalistic praxis and doctrine, but unlike Hasidism, this inclination remained both private and eclectic.[37] Several of the rites observed by the Frankfurt pietists or by other non-Hasidic kabbalists are mentioned in *Me'orei Or*, either approvingly or without critical comment, as were works such as *Ḥemdat Yamim* and *Sha'arei Zion*.[38] It nonetheless remained for Worms to articulate a sense of order among the disparate voices and traditions vying for authority in Ashkenaz. Among Sephardic kabbalists such as R. Ḥayyim Joseph David Azulai, the authority of the *Shulḥan Arukh*, or at least of Karo, had become subordinated to that of the Luria,[39] and this development further exacerbated the challenge posed by Kabbalah.

As the emergent Hasidic movement gained in strength, the *Zohar* figured more prominently in the discourse of ritual practice; in the process, the apparent preeminence of Kabbalah over normative halakhic rulings became even more pronounced. In Worms's view the most effective response to these challenges was to wrest the *Zohar* from the control of Hasidism by demonstrating that it belonged to the normative legacy of Ashkenaz.[40] As a result, the explication of talmudic passages and halakhic themes in *Me'orei Or* was noticeably broader than most *novellae* published in central and western Europe in the eighteenth and early nineteenth centuries.[41] Several different approaches can be discerned among Worms's efforts to resolve the competing authority of Halakhah and Kabbalah.[42] First, Worms defined the relationship of the *Zohar* to the Talmud as primarily exegetical, as is evident from his treatment of the talmudic tradition in *Berakhot* 5b, "one who places his bed between north and south will merit male children." In accordance with Rashi's explanation, the *Shulḥan Arukh* (*O.H.* 3:6) ruled that "it is forbidden to sleep between east and west with one's wife at one's side." Against this, R. Menaḥem Azariah de Fano ruled in accordance with the *Zohar* that it is obligatory to place one's head in the westerly direction, while R. Joel Sirkes, author of the *Bayit Ḥadash*, stipulated that one's head must be in the east and one's feet in the west. Insofar as neither the talmudic source according to Rashi nor the *Zohar* according to de Fano could be dismissed, Worms sought a more flexible reading of the talmudic passage. He made use of a passage in *Zevaḥim* 62b to show by analogy that the language in *Berakhot* was not unequivocal, and enlisted a theory of conception propounded by scientists (*ḥakhmei ha-meḥkar*) in order to prove that the wording of the Talmud could accommodate an interpretation akin to that of the *Zohar*. Once these steps were taken, Worms concluded that the de Fano-*Zohar* reading was correct and that Rashi's literal interpretation would therefore need to be set aside. To resolve the apparent contradiction between the two authoritative sources, he approached the *Zohar*—or more correctly, de Fano—as an exegetical source that clarified the meaning of the talmudic tradition.[43]

The disjuncture between Halakhah and Kabbalah was due to the fact that the *Zohar* was not "discovered" until the end of the thirteenth century. Owing to its presumed canonical status in rabbinic Judaism, however, one could hardly dismiss its numerous discrepancies from the normative ritual tradition. Accordingly, halakhic authorities were often unclear how to proceed; in some instances they decided that the normative tradition was incorrect, as the example of the beds illustrates. That the north-south direction had become standard practice simply testified, according to Worms, to the vast influence of the popular *Iggeret Ha-Kodesh*. Since the author of the thirteenth-century marriage manual—widely assumed to be R. Moses Nahmanides—could not have known the *Zohar*, Worms concluded that the author had misunderstood the passage in *Berakhot* and he, in turn, misled subsequent generations. The case of the *Kol Nidrei* rite suggests that in some cases an erroneous practice was formally instituted as a *minhag*. Historically, opinions have diverged over the precise halakhic function of the rite—whether it was used to invalidate vows taken in the past or those yet to be pledged. According to Rav Sa'adia Gaon, R. Asher b. Yeḥiel, and R. Jacob b. Asher, *Kol Nidrei* was a form of retroactive annulment. R. Jacob Tam, however, argued that the standard version of *Kol Nidrei* contravened the accepted rules of annulment, and therefore emended the text in order to conform to the anticipatory cancellation of vows prescribed by the Mishnah. Worms insisted, contra R. Tam, that the original version of *Kol Nidrei* employed the past tense, as found in the *Raaya Mehemna*, and he suggested that a special rabbinic ruling dating from the tannaitic period must have been overlooked by the Geonim because the *Zohar* was unknown to them. Worms's attempt to resolve the problem is instructive: "I certainly know that a *minhag* practiced since the days of Rabbenu Tam cannot be changed . . . however, had R. Tam been aware of the words of R. Simon bar Yoḥai, he [R. Tam] would not have uprooted an ancient custom." Although Worms recommended a compromise urging individual worshippers to recite the *Kol Nidrei* both in the past and future tenses, he nonetheless ruled that the public service must preserve the text of R. Tam. This example shows that even when it was evident that the *Zohar* was the more authoritative source in a particular instance, the fact that it became known only *after* the medieval ritual was formally institutionalized undercut any subsequent revisionist effort.

Emphasizing that it was through an accident of history that medieval authorities were unaware of the *Zohar*, Worms argued that there was no real divergence between the opinion of the *Zohar* and that of Halakhah.[44] In the case of ritual washing at the end of a meal (*mayyim aḥaronim*), however, Worms advanced a different argument. Those authorities who viewed the practice as purely hygienic—and therefore as no longer obligatory—had so concluded not because the *Zohar* was unknown to them but on the basis of their own halakhic calculations. But if the *Zohar* were indeed known, how could it be set aside? Worms adduced a passage from the *Raaya Mehemna* suggesting that the status of *mayyim aḥaronim* was uncertain and would ultimately be determined by the conventional methods of halakhic decision making. Therefore, according to Worms, by deciding that the practice was not obligatory, the Tosafist ruling was consistent with the view of the *Zohar*.[45] Viewed as an exegetical text, the *Zohar* emerged in Worms's system as an exceptionally authoritative source, though ultimate authority rested with Halakhah's rabbinic interpreters.

In each of the foregoing examples, Worms offered an interpretation of the *Zohar* that was impervious to the vast influence of Lurianic Kabbalah. The case of ritual handwashing in the morning reveals a genuinely critical view of Lurianic exegesis of the *Zohar*. The sixteenth-century *Tola'at Ya'akov*, in the name of the *Zohar*, referred to the failure to wash one's hands immediately upon rising as a capital offense—a position that contradicted the view of *Berakhot* 60b where the subject of handwashing was discussed only after the morning benedictions. The standard codes and commentaries— the *Tur, Beit Yosef*, and *Shulḥan Arukh*—adopted the approach of R. Solomon b. Aderet (Rashba), who related to handwashing both as preparatory to prayer and as signaling the new cycle of ritual activity that one begins each morning. The formulation in the *Zohar*, and more pointedly in *Tola'at Ya'akov*, presumed that one became defiled during the night because it was then that the soul experiences death. Spiritual impairment (*ruaḥ ra'ah*) of this sort needed to be removed—at the moment the soul is reborn—by ritual handwashing. In Worms's view, the crucial argument against the *Tola'at Ya'akov* was that its source in the *Zohar* could not be located, and its claim was therefore rendered groundless. Here, then, no effort was made to reconcile the differing views attributed to the *Zohar* and the Talmud, but instead the argument turned on the reliability of the talmudic-halakhic tradition as compared to the disputed authority of Lurianic Kabbalah.[46] Worms's frequent characterization of Lurianic practices as superogatory was typically, if paradoxically, accompanied by a direct challenge to their legitimacy because they lacked either a talmudic or midrashic basis, on the one hand, and were not mentioned in the *Zohar*, on the other.[47]

Me'orei Or offers a striking illustration of how traditional learning in the late eighteenth and early nineteenth centuries began, rather tentatively, to embrace elements of the new critical spirit. It conformed to the conventions of Ashkenazic *novellae*, having subordinated itself almost entirely to the talmudic or halakhic texts it sought to explain. Rarely did it give attention to general problems or themes. Its impressive halakhic erudition, terse style, and cryptic allusions suggest that *Me'orei Or* was intended for Worms's rabbinic colleagues and veteran students of Talmud and Jewish law. Its aim, as in the case of *novellae* generally, was to elucidate passages and specific issues on which there had been considerable divergence of interpretation, and this included efforts to explain apparent inconsistencies between the talmudic-halakhic tradition and the *Zohar*. Assumptions concerning the undisputed authority of the written and oral traditions were central and unquestioned, while the utilization of secular disciplines was entirely absent from the work. Nevertheless, despite its unflinching commitment to the fundamentals of the Jewish faith, *Me'orei Or* represents an unmistakable—if faint—echo of the new critical spirit of the Enlightenment. Worms's theory of *minhag* reflected the centrality of the textual tradition. Text, not practice, was what authenticated *minhag*. In *Me'orei Or* Worms sought to reconstitute a halakhic Judaism that had become, by his own day, a rarity. Worms's work conceded implicitly that something had gone awry with the tradition. What is perhaps most remarkable about the progressive character of *Me'orei Or* is that it contains no evidence of influence from the outside. It is also important to bear in mind that the crucial shift in attitude toward study and practice had emerged well *before* the Jewish community was torn apart by denominational struggles.

Taken together, the foregoing elements exhibit a critical independence that endeared Worms to French proponents of Haskalah and moderate ritual reform. His refusal to participate in the *Eleh Divrei Ha-Berit* manifesto protesting the Hamburg Temple reforms, his support for reciting prayers in French, his willingness to reduce the number of *piyyutim*, his criticism of customs rooted in popular superstitions, and his staunch advocacy of socioeconomic modernization were all taken as evidence of sympathy for the reformist agenda. Moreover, by joining the National Guard at the outbreak of the Revolution, he publicly affirmed that Halakhah was compatible with civic responsibility, love of the *patrie*, and the emerging cultural and social ethos of modern France.[48]

Portents of Change: Haskalah and *Ḥokhmat Israel*

The first signs pointing to the scientific study of Judaism in France were evident in the literary endeavors of *maskilim* in pre-revolutionary Alsace-

Lorraine. Intellectual productivity resounded with the clear echo of the Berlin Haskalah. The careers of the handful of individuals who maintained a close personal association with the German Haskalah follow a familiar pattern: their traditional Jewish education was, typically, supplemented by their own acquisition of classical and modern European languages and by an interest in secular studies. They earned their livelihood as private tutors, teachers, and businessmen. The various programmatic essays and *apologia* authored by members of the small cadre of French *maskilim* anticipated many of the changes that would soon transform the Jewish community. Hand in hand with their political activism were efforts to translate literary, educational, and philosophical productions composed in Berlin into French and Hebrew. Among the most noteworthy for their involvement in the scientific study of Judaism were Berr Isaac Berr, who translated Naphtali Herz Wessely's *Divrei Shalom ve-Emet* into French in 1782; and Isaïe Berr Bing, who translated Mendelssohn's essay on the immortality of the soul, *Phaedon*, into Hebrew in 1787 and published a French translation of Jedaiah Bedersi's *Beḥinat Olam* in 1794. These works exemplify the transfer of German-Jewish culture to France while underscoring that the early French Haskalah remained a received ideology that *maskilim* appropriated from Berlin with only minor modifications.[49]

Also connected to the Berlin Haskalah was a small number of Hebraists whose poetry attests to the powerful impact of the Revolution on Jewish consciousness. The best known of this group include Moses Ensheim (1750–1839), Lippmann Moïse Büschenthal (1784–1818), and Elie Halévy (1760–1826). The goal of bringing the fruits of German-Jewish scholarly creativity to the attention of French Jewry remained constant for decades, as exemplified by Olry Terquem's French translation of S. Y. Rapoport, *Toldot Rabbenu Sa'adia Gaon*, which originally appeared in Hebrew in *Bikkurei Ha-Itim*. Historical writing, however, tended to be motivated by a desire to portray the Jews to the general public in the most positive terms, and as a result, scholarship was subordinated to the broadly defined political agenda of emancipation and social integration. Two examples of this genre include Léon Halévy's *Résumé de l'histoire des Juifs modernes* (1828) and L. M. Lambert's *Précis de l'histoire des hébreux depuis le patriarche Abraham jusqu'en 1840* (1840). One exception to the Ashkenazic domination of Franco-Jewish scholarship in the early nineteenth century was Joseph-Cohen Moline, originally of Bordeaux, who translated some of Solomon Ibn Gabirol's poetry into Hebrew.[50]

More directly linked to the emergence of modern Jewish studies in France, however, was an indigenous scholarly trend that can be observed in the work of young scholars who were active after the turn of the century. Armed with extensive classical learning, they were also imbued with a clear, though perhaps unconscious, reverence for systematic, critical thinking. They applied the scientific method cautiously to the classical texts of Judaism, frequently following leads that had been suggested decades, even centuries, before. Also characteristic of these early efforts was an inclination to investigate works beyond those normally consulted in traditional circles. Although the number engaged in these endeavors was still very modest, their work is historically significant because of its unmistakable similarity, both thematically and methodologically, to scholarly undertakings inspired by the new historicism in western and central Europe and because they laid the foundation for more far-reaching scholarly advances later in the century. I refer to them as "forerunners" because the social and cultural world to which they belonged was still largely intact. Evidence of the transition from traditional to modern scholarship may be observed especially in the areas of Bible, liturgy, and Hebrew language.[51]

Several works composed in Comtat Venaissin embody many of the changes that typify the scientific-critical approach to classical texts. Mardochée Crémieux (1749–1825) of Carpentras published a two-part work titled *Ma'amar Mordechai* (Leghorn, 1784–1786) on the *Shulḥan Arukh*, in which he noted errors and omissions of the leading halakhic authorities in previous centuries.[52] His nephew and son-in-law, Moïse Crémieux (1766–1837) of Aix, was a prolific author whose thirteen-volume *Ho'il Moshe Be'er* (Aix, 1829–36) contained six volumes devoted to a detailed explication of Comtadin ritual and liturgy,[53] and six volumes of notes to Abraham Ibn Ezra's commentaries on the Pentateuch (1833–1836). The latter's exegetical writings epitomize Spanish Jewry's commitment to contextual analysis and naturally came to be favored by Sephardic scholars and *maskilim* in the west. Although Ibn Ezra fully accepted the authority of the rabbinic tradition in the realm of biblical interpretation, he nonetheless acknowledged that *peshat* (literal meaning) could at times exist parallel to and independent from rabbinic exegesis.[54] Whether Crémieux's interest in Ibn Ezra was a reflection of the new cultural and intellectual climate is not clear, though Ibn Ezra's unorthodox style would certainly provide an opportunity to expound on any number of grammatical, syntactical, or literary issues that other commentators did not emphasize to the same degree.

The preoccupation with correcting faulty liturgical texts was a conspicuous expression of the new critical spirit that had first penetrated the ranks of traditional Ashkenazic Jewry in the eighteenth century. The expanding number of *siddurim* and *maḥzorim* that drew on a heightened concern for textual precision, linguistic accuracy, and grammatical exactitude were consistent with contemporary intellectual developments in the west. Despite the parallel concerns, however, it is clear that the new prayer books were not composed in direct response to the eighteenth century's reverence for science. As a literary genre, corrected *siddurim* had already become widely known, first with the composition of the *siddur* of Shabbethai Sofer of Przemsyl in 1617, followed by several similar undertakings in the seventeenth and early eighteenth centuries. The production of more reliable versions of the liturgy was clearly prompted by the need to correct the textual errors and inconsistencies that became widely circulated by the invention of printing. A renewed emphasis on Bible, grammar, and systematic thinking in the sixteenth and seventeenth centuries both aggravated the distress concerning printing errors and furnished the technical skills needed to address the problem.[55]

Having spanned nearly the two centuries preceding the French Revolution, the concern with liturgy was hardly novel. Under the impact of several factors, activity intensified in the eighteenth century. Migration patterns and greater geographical mobility brought together various liturgical traditions that had formerly remained distinct; the growing accumulation of textual errors could no longer be overlooked; the ignorance of authentic traditions was unprecedented; and individuals emerged for whom the notion of textual precision had become intrinsically important. In France, Moïse Israel Biding (1775–1841) was among the first of several scholars to address the problem of faulty liturgical texts. Like many young men of late eighteenth-century Alsace-Lorraine, he went abroad to study, in his case to the Frankfurt *yeshivah*, before returning to his native Metz to work as a schoolteacher and as a proofreader at the Hebrew press. It is likely that Biding acquired an appreciation for Hebrew grammar and secular studies from his teacher, Moses Ensheim, the French *maskil* and tutor of Moses Mendelssohn's children. By the 1830s his imposing erudition had gained him prominence as "le premier hébraïsant de notre époque."[56] As one who was absorbed in the intricacies of liturgical poetry, Biding was very disturbed by the deprecation of the *piyyutim* and their authors that had become common among the high-ranking members (*benei aliyah*) of the Jewish community. His use of the expression *benei aliyah* was, in all likelihhod, a reference to men who had been exposed to the Haskalah's critical view of the *piyyutim* and of other elements of traditional observance. In the hope of reversing the fortunes of the *piyyutim*, he sought to restore the original texts so that they would conform to each author's intended meter. This would involve correcting the many corruptions that had crept into the liturgical literature by using the most reliable manuscripts available.[57] Drawing heavily on his vast knowledge of biblical phraseology and midrashic sources, Biding devoted himself to explicating the highly allusive style of each *piyyut* and to establishing the proper pronunciation.[58] By applying modern linguistic tools in an unpolemical fashion, Biding and others were able to draw on science in the service of religion.

At this stage in the development of *la science de judaïsme*, there was still no conflict between modern scholarship and traditional methods. The new critical spirit flowed evenly from the rigors of rabbinic learning, with perhaps a renewed interest in textual exactitude its main distinguishing characteristic. Those *maskilim* who reached adulthood in the era of the Revolution were, for the most part, ritually observant and *yeshivah* educated; their efforts were largely devoted to applying the new methods to traditional texts and to the advancement of elementary education.[59] The production of new *siddurim*, such as Biding's commentary on the *piyyutim* of the Rosh Hashanah *maḥzor* (Metz, 1817), therefore became a major desideratum, aiming to meet the prevailing standards of grammatical precision in the general scholarly world while remaining loyal to Jewish tradition. Biding's work was of the highest quality, in several respects considered even preferable to that of Wolf Heidenheim, the leading figure in the field of *maḥzor* commentary in the nineteenth century (1800–1805).[60] Like Heidenheim's commentary, the Biding *maḥzor* ought to be viewed as one of the early exemplars of *ḥokhmat yisrael*, as it was built on a foundation of impressive linguistic expertise and encyclopedic knowledge of midrash. With the intensification of the struggle over religious reform in the following decades, however, a new generation of scholars sought to discredit the same *piyyutim* by showing that they were grammatically corrupt and linguistically deficient.[61]

Renewed rabbinic and lay scholarly interest in Hebrew grammar and philology in the first half of the nineteenth century mirrored the profusion of Hebraic studies in general French society and appears to have been a bridge between the old and new scholarly trends. New grammatical theories and efforts to reconstruct corrupted texts were the main focus of eighteenth-century Hebraists François Masclef, P. Houbigant, and Pierre Guarin, while similar involvement on the part of Jews, such as Jacob Joseph b. Meir Sofer,[62] was still a rarity before the Revolution. Interest in Hebrew texts and grammar grew stronger after the turn of the century, first among prominent orientalists such as Sylvestre de Sacy and Auguste Pichard, and subsequently among rabbis and *maskilim*.[63] Rabbinic publications in the field of Hebrew concentrated on systematizing the presentation of grammar as a reference tool for teachers and students. Among the most widely used were Lion-Mayer Lambert, *Abrégé de la grammaire hebraïque* (Metz, 1820); Marchand Ennery, *Dictionnaire hébreu-français* (Nancy, 1827); Samuel Dreyfus, *Abrégé de la grammaire hébraïque* (Mulhouse, 1839); and Salomon Klein, *Nouvelle grammaire hébraïque, raisonnée et comparée* (Mulhouse, 1846). Primarily intended to instill greater enthusiasm for the study of the Hebrew language, these works cannot be taken as an endorsement of the objectives of *Wissenschaft*, though they do contain some hints of the new critical spirit. Few rabbis were willing to touch the potentially explosive questions raised by historical research. Lay scholars whose first publications were devoted to the Hebrew language include Moïse Biding's *Em la-Mikra* (Metz, 1816), Samuel Cahen, *Cours de lecture hébraïque* (Paris, 1824), and Adolphe Franck, *Meliẓ Leshon Ivrit* (Paris, 1833).

Biding's work, which was devoted mainly to proper vocalization and reading, was not only the most exacting of its kind, but it also offered the most thoroughgoing critique of the field of Hebrew language pedagogy.

Lamenting the progressive apathy toward the rules of pronunciation, and reading, manifested in textbooks of earlier times, Biding was highly critical of recent books composed for those who were knowledgeable in science and linguistics, works that failed to distinguish between rules of reading and modes of pronunciation, on the one hand, and the many other rules of vocalization (*nikkud*), on the other.[64]

Ideological and Intellectual Trends in Modern Jewish Scholarship

Until the mid-1820s, there were virtually no signs of any ideological rift separating traditionalist from more modern scholars. However, during the following decade, as the new movement of modern Jewish scholarship in France came of age and struggled to define its own identity, the question of precisely how the Mendelssohnian legacy ought to be interpreted would become a highly controversial issue in France, signaling the distinction between Haskalah studies and the beginnings of *Wissenschaft*.[65] Reflecting the larger social, political, and intellectual milieu of mid-nineteenth-century France, modern Jewish scholarship was motivated both by ideological considerations and a new, critical approach to sacred texts. In order to understand how the intellectual and ideological foundations of modern Jewish scholarship developed, it will be first necessary to establish what social structures made this possible.

The various expressions of scholarly engagement with the sacred texts and traditions of Judaism offer evidence of the continuing efforts of French Jewish scholars to come to terms with the impact of emancipation. While it cannot be denied that modern Jewish scholarship in France and Germany shared many common traits and, further, that the German *Wissenschaft des Judentums* movement exerted considerable influence on the small circle of scholars in Paris and Metz, Jewish scholarship west of the Rhine emerged largely in response to social and intellectual forces that were of a local or regional nature. In the case of German Jewry, *Wissenschaft des Judentums* was as much an expression of the failure of political emancipation as it was a reflection of the powerful impact of nineteenth-century scientific historical method on German Jewish scholars. The reversal of the political achievements of the Jews following the demise of Napoleon, triggering an intensification of anti-Jewish rhetoric, hostility, and physical violence in the ensuing years, set the stage for an unprecedented response to the challenges of modernity. With the creation of the Verein fur Kultur und Wissenschaft der Juden in 1819, a concerted effort was made to eradicate the negative image of the Jew by emphasizing the universal values of Judaism. Most members of the Verein were not ritually observant and saw their involvement in the group as a way of strengthening their attenuated ties to Judaism; several ultimately converted to Christianity.[66] Subsequently, Abraham Geiger and Zacharias Frankel each, in his own way, sought to correct some of the distorted images of Judaism by studying the sacred texts critically, ultimately seeking to strengthen the case for religious reform. Perhaps only Leopold Zunz, of all the major German Jewish scholars, abandoned the "overtly present-minded religious rationale for *Wissenschaft des Judentums*," to use Michael Meyer's formulation.[67]

Owing to the impact of the Revolution and the attainment of citizenship, the work of French Jewish scholars was free of the urgency felt in Germany to fashion a Judaism that would strengthen the entitlement to civic equality. Its dominant forms, nonetheless, corresponded to the social and cultural tensions associated with the experience of emancipation, ranging from confidence in the prospects of full civic equality and social integration to concern over the serious complexities inherent in those processes. Population size was also a distinguishing factor. The character of modern Jewish studies in France was shaped by a small group of intellectuals who were secure in their Jewish identity and observance; its development was much slower, both because of the very modest size of the group and the relatively limited interest among the Jewish population. Undeniably, trends in German-Jewish scholarship influenced the nascent movement of *la science de judaïsme*. Owing to the woeful condition of Jewish institutional life brought on by the Reign of Terror, particularly the demise of schools and *yeshivot*, significant numbers emigrated to neighboring Germany to avail themselves of study opportunities. Among these émigrés were men who would become major figures in the scientific study of Judaism following their return from Germany after the collapse of the Napoleonic regime. The time spent in Germany permitted contacts with leading *Wissenschaft* personalities such as Zunz and Jost, contributing considerably to the character of Jewish scholarship in France. Ultimately, however, local cultural conditions in France, the degree to which Jews were received into the general circles of scholars, and the perception of the dangers posed by the continuing Christian imprint on French society would exert the greatest influence on Jewish scientific research.

Modern Franco-Jewish scholarship developed in three stages, corresponding roughly to three distinct periods in the political history of France. Changes in regime had either made new scholarly initiatives possible or ran parallel to developments already at work in the social and intellectual realms. The three periods may be divided as follows: (1) stage 1 (1815–30): transitional era; (2) stage 2 (1830–48): intellectual/ideological foundations were set, and scholars were able to place a Jewish imprint on scholarship; and (3) stage 3 (1848–): modern Jewish studies became grounded institutionally.[68] For the present, we shall limit ourselves to a discussion of the first two stages, which together constitute the formative period of *la science de judaïsme* in France.

Initially, Jewish and Christian scholars were drawn together by a common interest in Hebrew language and Semitic texts, despite the chasm still separating Jews from the mainstream of French society in the first decades of the century. With the creation of the Société Asiatique in Paris in 1822, Jews and Christians were able, for the first time, to participate in joint scholarly ventures. This opportunity, however, was short-lived. Owing to the resurgence of Catholicism, bolstered by the accession of Charles X to the throne in 1824, Jews lost ground in their quest for social acceptance and equality. New exclusionary measures curtailed many of the advances of the preceding years, including the feasibility of Jewish-Christian collaboration. From this date, no new Jewish members were admitted to the Société Asiatique, and those who had joined earlier were entirely inactive during the last five years of the Restoration.[69]

As a direct consequence of the liberal political climate of the July Monarchy, Jewish scholars were able to resume their membership in the Société Asiatique and to develop new areas of scholarly collaboration with non-Jews. Concomitantly, Jewish scholars who had trained in central Europe were beginning to arrive in Paris. Three distinguished orientalists, Salomon Munk, Albert Cohn, and Joseph Derenbourg, for example, were educated in German and Austrian universities before coming to France.[70] By the mid-1830s, the noticeable concentration of Jewish and gentile scholars devoted to the scientific study of classical Jewish texts gave impetus to more frequent scholarly exchange and cooperation. Abbé Jean Baptiste Glaire, author of a Hebrew dictionary, collaborated with Adolphe Franck in the publication of a Hebrew chrestomathy and annotated translation of the Pentateuch, titled *Torat Moshe* (Paris, 1835–37). Sylvestre de Sacy published an extract of *Taḥkemoni*, with translation and notes, in the *Journal asiatique*.[71] Several years later a colleague, Eugène Boré, published "Une séance du Taḥkemoni" with help from Munk, who was then serving as curator of oriental manuscripts at the Bibliothèque nationale. Other examples of Munk's collaboration with French scholars include the assistance he provided to a cooperative project on the Druse together with de Sacy, the help he gave astronomer J.-B. Biot for the latter's work on Abulafia in 1843; and his general support of Ernst Renan, who preceded him as professor of Hebrew and Syriac literature at the Collège de France. It is reported that Renan met regularly with Munk when they both were employed at the Bibliothèque nationale and that he consulted periodically with other *Wissenschaft des Judentums* scholars as well.[72] Philologist Auguste Pichard also drew upon Munk's expertise, as is apparent in the publication, translation, and annotation of *Sefer Lekah Tov* and the Book of Enoch.[73]

Munk's research in Islamic and Jewish philosophy, together with his painstaking efforts to elucidate oriental manuscripts, epitomizes the pursuit of scholarly research in both Jewish and general French contexts. Born in Glogau (Silesia) in 1803, Munk was a prodigious scholar who edited the *Dictionnaire de la conversation*, the *Encyclopédie des gens du monde*, and the *Encyclopédie nouvelle*, and in this manner established personal contact with members of the Académie Française and the Institut de la France. Between 1834 and 1838, in addition to assisting numerous scholars in their research, he published nearly a score of articles in *Temps* on biblical, Persian, and Sanskrit literature, several studies in the *Journal asiatique*, and biographical studies of selected thirteenth-century French rabbis in the *Histoire littéraire de la France*. Other Jewish scholars shared Munk's dedication. Gerson-Lévy, champion of Jewish educational and moderate religious reform, was centrally involved in the general intellectual life of his native Metz, first as editor of *L'Indépendant* and then as a founding member of the Académie de Metz. Similarly, Samuel Cahen, Jewish educator, director of the Bible project, and editor of the *Archives israélites*, collaborated in the *Encyclopédie des gens du monde*.[74]

The critical study of the Kabbalah pioneered by Adolphe Franck (1809–1893) offers a vivid illustration of the new scientific trends that had become prevalent before mid-century. Trained in philosophy and philology under Victor Cousin, Franck was appointed to the chair of classical philosophy at the Collège de France. But it was his work on Jewish mysticism, *La Kabbale ou la philosophie religieuse des hébreux*, that established his academic reputation. Focusing on literary problems, theosophical issues, and comparative philosophy, he ventured to explicate the origins and ideas of the Kabbalah on the basis of scientific method. He discerned Chaldean and Persian influences, leading him to conclude that the *Zohar* was an ancient text. Franck's emphases contrasted sharply with the concerns of Aaron Worms. Worms was not interested in external influences or questions of authorship but was drawn to literary and conceptual issues, distinctions between zoharic and Lurianic Kabbalah, and implications for ritual authority. Like Salomon Munk, who studied the relationship between the mystical and philosophical traditions of the Middle Ages, Franck found in the Kabbalah a model of cultural and intellectual cross-fertilization. The careers of Franck and Munk plainly exemplified a dual commitment to the particular and the universal, which was now both desirable and possible in post-revolutionary France. Their work rested on the conviction that the study of Jewish civilization demanded the milieu of world cultures, nurtured by and integrated within the intellectual traditions of European society. Grounded in judicious scholarship, their universalism was clearly reinforced by the legal, political, and social advancement of Jews in French society.[75]

During this second stage, scholars undertook three major ventures: the French Bible project; the creation of the *Archives israélites*; and the study of Judaism under Islam. Each of these areas illustrates how the intellectual and ideological aspects of Jewish identity in post-revolutionary France converged. In the ideological realm, proponents of *régénération* in the 1830s and 1840s called for a reversal of the historical process responsible for the degeneration of the Jewish religion. Historical inquiry would emerge as central to their scholarly program; in fact, the term *régénération* itself signified an appreciation for the forces of historical development. According to the early nineteenth-century definition, *régénération* was "action to reconstitute in its original state that which had undergone decadence and regression."[76] At the same time, it rested on the premise that human history progresses steadily in a continuous movement toward a future far superior to the present or the past. The idea of progress presumed a connection among scientific, technological, and material advances on the one hand and the realization of concrete social and moral objectives on the other. In the view of French Jewish scholars, a Judaism restored to its pristine state would be more amenable to the demands of contemporary civilization.

Complementing the ideological thrust inherent in these efforts, a critical approach to sacred texts emerged as an outgrowth of the new scholarly traditions in France. Two trends, source criticism and comparative history, characterized this development, together representing a significant departure from traditional learning and from the scholarship of the transitional period. The first was founded on the premise that the classical sources of Judaism ought to be approached utilizing the same methods that were then being applied to ancient texts of other traditions. Summarizing the view of modern students of religion, Salomon Munk defined the duty of the scholar, as distinct from the theologian-philosopher, as the pursuit of truth without any concern for the theological or philosophical implications of scientific inquiry. This view was based on the idea that genuine religious sentiment is impervious to the critical examination of sources and is in no danger of being undermined by the conclusions that may follow. It was supported by a tendency among modern scholars in the field of theology and philosophy to underscore the centrality of "essence" over "form."[77] By the third decade of the 1800s, Jewish scholars had begun to appropriate the methods and tools used in the burgeoning science of antiquities—philology, anthropology, and archaeology. Utilizing the work of Germans such as Eichhorn, Ewald, De Wette, Gesenius, Hitzig, and Rosenmüller, most often to the total exclusion of the French, Jewish scholars in France strove to examine Judaism within a broader literary and cultural framework.[78]

More far-reaching than source criticism, however, was the application of comparative historical method to sacred texts. The idea of investigating ancient laws, customs, and political institutions had already gained wide currency through the writings of Montesquieu, Diderot, Voltaire, and Hume, among others. Inquiries into the political and moral underpinnings of "the spirit of a nation" was an important, albeit primitive, contribution to what Peter Gay has termed "a scientific history of culture."[79] Strongly influenced by the example of the *philosophes*, the early *maskilim* approached the Jewish religion using the rational categories established by the Enlightenment, concluding that the scientific study of Judaism required attention to its various stages of development. Although the Bible, talmudic literature, and the medieval codes were seen from this perspective,[80] it was rationalism, not historicism, that was at the heart of Enlightenment and early Haskalah thought. Only in the nineteenth century did historical consciousness come to replace rationalism as the foremost medium for the interpretation of human culture.[81] In his discussions of Abraham and of Israelite enslavement in Egypt, for example, Salomon Munk presented background material drawn from ancient Mesopotamia and Egypt in an effort to contextualize the patriarchal and Israelite narratives. In the case of the priestly code of Leviticus, emphasis was placed on parallels to the customs in the ancient Far and Near East,[82] and it was likewise shown that the Israelite system of levirate marriage had also been practiced among ancient Indian tribes.[83] The implications of this approach—and generally the utilization of historical method in determining the various layers of development of Judaism—were offensive to traditionalist sensibilities and invariably perceived as an assault on the primacy, uniqueness, and authenticity of the Torah.

The rift between traditionalists and modernists was especially evident in biblical studies, a particularly sensitive area of scholarship to which modern Jewish scholars in France devoted their primary efforts. In 1831 the first volume of a new French Bible translation and commentary appeared under the direction of Samuel Cahen; it was completed over the course of two decades.[84] Modeled after Moses Mendelssohn's *Biur*, the French translation project was an ambitious attempt to develop an alternative to classical biblical exegesis. In France, as distinct from Germany, Jewish scholars concentrated on biblical studies while exhibiting virtually no scholarly interest in the field of rabbinic literature. In Germany the vast majority of scientific works focused on rabbinic Judaism, with the exception of a handful of biblical studies authored by Zunz, Geiger, and Frankel. The question why the focus of research in the two countries was so dissimilar has puzzled historians of the past century. According to Max Wiener, the traditionalism of German Jewish scholars precluded the scientific investigation of biblical texts. Considering the unabashedly reform orientation of *Wissenschaft* scholars there, this explanation appears highly unconvincing. Elsewhere, I have suggested that because the school of biblical criticism in Germany was dominated by Protestant scholars whose research evinced prejudice and even hostility toward the Jewish religion, German Jewish scholars were apprehensive about engaging in biblical studies for fear that their work might be discredited through its association with harsh critics of Judaism.[85] Furthermore, it appears that biblical studies would not prove as valuable as critical research in post-biblical and rabbinic Judaism, insofar as the latter could be easily enlisted to lay the foundations for religious reform.[86] In France, the possibility of dialogue and cooperation between reformers and the rabbis precluded unrestrained assaults on the Talmud, in spite of the fact that the former concurred with their German colleagues on the evolution of Jewish law. Thus, although the Bible project was thoroughly consistent with the new intellectual milieu of nineteenth-century western Europe, no such enterprise was undertaken by Jewish scholars in neighboring Germany.

Owing to their relative freedom from the political and intellectual constraints on the critical study of the Bible, and because they labored outside the sphere of intense controversy, French Jewish scholars were able to address issues on which German Jews had remained silent. Salomon Munk, for example, treated the various questions concerning the documentary hypothesis dispassionately, refuting most of its claims while accepting the idea, in principle, of human authorship of certain parts of the Pentateuch.[87] It is equally clear that the prime importance placed on cultural adaptation in France strongly influenced Jewish scholars to enter an area of research consistent with prevailing intellectual trends. Accordingly, they chose to direct their energies to biblical, philological, philosophical, and anthropological research. Preferring the literalist school of medieval biblical interpretation to the rabbinic-homiletic approach, modern scholars sought to reawaken interest in and appreciation for Hebrew grammar, referring to comparative Semitics and literary context to explain difficult words and phrases. Their reverence for the exegetical methods of Abraham Ibn Ezra and David Kimhi, among others, signifies the widening gap separating rabbinic and lay scholars.[88] This is evident, as well, in the range of sources brought to bear on the biblical text. Volumes of the new translation regularly included important scholarly studies, such as the first part of Munk's French translation of the *Guide of the Perplexed*, which were intended to serve as a scientific companion to the biblical text. Other relevant texts of medieval and modern commentaries were frequently translated and published along with the corresponding book of the Bible. The Isaiah volume, for example, included the preface to Isaac Abarbanel's commentary, while the Ezekiel volume also contained portions of the *Guide* and an excerpt from Zunz's opus on rabbinic sermons. Various ancient and modern translations of the Bible were consulted as well, including the principal variants of the Septuagint and the Samaritan texts of the Pentatueuch.[89] Its substantial reliance on midrashic exegesis notwithstanding, the Bible project represents a considerable departure from the early modern homiletical tradition in Ashkenaz.[90]

We may now turn to the question why those Jewish scholars who had succeeded in penetrating French academic circles decided to devote themselves to the more narrowly conceived Bible project. The answer may be found, in part, in the timing of its conception. The initial decision to undertake this translation was made in 1829, during the period when Jewish scholars were still excluded from academic circles. It is not unlikely that as a result of the assault on the legacy of the Revolution and the accompanying experience of social exclusion Jewish intellectuals were driven more tightly together and that the project permitted an opportunity to form their own learned society. In light of the strong Christian orientation prevailing in French biblical scholarship, Cahen's initiative may very well have constituted an attempt to wrest the Bible from Christian dominance and place it squarely within the province of Jewish studies. In fact, from the outset, the Bible project encountered the rancor of Christian critics who took aim not only at its pervading rationalist method but also at its failure to embrace the views of Christian interpreters. The editors of the *Archives de Christianisme* went so far as to blame Cahen for the success of rationalism in France, taking him to task for his anti-dogmatic and anti-Christian excurses.[91]

According to Munk, who took up Cahen's defense, contemporary rabbis shared the underlying theological conviction that inspired the Protestant journal. Like their Christian counterparts, the rabbis purportedly viewed reason as the enemy of faith; accordingly, they considered Cahen's biblical commentary an egregious attack on traditional Judaism.[92] Rabbi Salomon Klein of Colmar, the most vocal French critic of the *Wissenschaft des Judentums* movement, characterized the new trend with the following: "There have arisen in the land a new group of men who do not place their trust in the truth of faith, but have followed the desires of their hearts. They have vented their disgusting spirit upon the Torah, which they have not accepted as from Moses, and now will do the same to the Talmud."[93] In response to opposition of this sort, the Bible translation represented a sustained effort to articulate an intellectual alternative to rabbinic dogmatism. The decision to undertake the project was undoubtedly reinforced by the realization that even French liberals such as Vinet, Constant, de Broglie, and Guizot continued to identify French civilization with Christianity, despite their declared commitment to the separation of church and state.[94] The Bible project thus gave expression to the particularistic interpretation of emancipation. On the other hand, the appearance of the first volume of the translation ironically coincided with the ordinance of 1831 that finally accorded the Jewish religion full parity with Catholicism and Protestantism by recognizing Jewish clergy as employees of the state. In the more favorable political climate of the 1830s, the Cahen Bible became a concrete expression of optimism about the future course of emancipation. Two distinct sets of demands, corresponding to the two pivotal facets of emancipation—the particular and the universal—were deemed integral to the dynamics of Jewish life in nineteenth-century France.

Alongside their efforts to recast the Bible within a multidisciplinary framework, Jewish scholars addressed issues that were pertinent to the ritual character of Judaism and the accompanying discourse of religious reform. In its attitude toward Jewish law, critical scholarship started from the premise that Halakhah had undergone several stages of development. Far from being immutable, as many traditionalists would claim, Halakhah had been influenced by a variety of forces (economic, cultural, and political). In the view of critical scholars, the halakhic rigor of medieval Judaism had developed in response to the wretched conditions of Jewish life, and that with the advent of civic equality, it now became possible, indeed imperative, to remove the abuses that had accrued to the Jewish religion, especially its "asiatic" forms. According to Samuel Cahen, ignorance of the history of the *minhagim* was the greatest obstacle to the regeneration of Judaism: "One would be surprised by the number of customs we have borrowed from foreign nations. Many presume that these date from antiquity, but the majority is very recent. The most useful work that one could undertake will be to do for the entire religion what Zunz has done for the liturgy." The distinction between a religion and its ceremonies represented the common ground shared by critical scholarship and ritual reform. Invariably, members of the small cadre of critical scholars were vocal proponents of religious reform. In contrast with Germany, few were practicing rabbis; they were employed variously as book dealers, teachers, manuscript curators, editors of journals, and, later, as university professors.[95]

History was frequently enlisted in order to discredit laws and customs that presumably grew out of superstition, were deemed overly stringent, or appeared to contradict the findings of modern-day science. Aiming to provide a forum for the scholarly examination and public discussion of ceremonial laws and customs, Samuel Cahen and his fellow *régénérateurs* founded the *Archives israélites de France*, a monthly journal, in 1840. As the journal's editor, Cahen set a moderate tone, urging scholars to research the conditions that had engendered the large number of purportedly outmoded ritual practices. The *régénérateurs* routinely cited rabbinic texts as proof that the idea of ritual reform had been endorsed throughout the course of history by eminent authorities and that evolutionary change was intrinsic to the halakhic system. It was here that scholarship and ideology converged. The oeuvre of Franco-Jewish scholars was enlisted to strengthen the claim that *régénération* ought to be conceived in religious as well as social terms. In the end, they demanded the elimination of prayers, ceremonies, and laws that were no longer in step with the political freedom that French Jews now enjoyed. Ironically, the same scholarly program that argued for ritual change actually counterbalanced the drive for radical religious reform, by dint of the overriding concern to examine the history of laws and customs objectively.[96]

The impact of Islamic civilization, especially medieval Arabic philosophy, on Jewish culture became an abiding interest of French Jewish scholars from the 1830s onward. Their exceptionally valuable contributions in this area are beyond the scope of the present work; however, we ought to consider why the study of Judaism under Islam was pursued so ardently. Salomon Munk's French translation, careful annotation, and introduction to Maimonides's *Guide of the Perplexed* is the best known and most important scholarly achievement in this area, and his *Mélanges de philosophie juive et arabe* (1855) remains a remarkable display of classical erudition and painstaking research that far exceeded other works in the field. The latter included a French translation of *Fons Vitae*, appearing as *La source de la vie*, accompanied by scholarly notes and analysis; an extensive essay on the principal medieval Arabic philosophers; and a historical survey of medieval Jewish philosophy. Munk's discovery that the real identity of Avicebron, the author of *Fons Vitae*, was Solomon Ibn Gabirol, the Spanish Jewish poet and philosopher, furnished a stunning example of a philosophical work, composed by a Jew, that was a major influence on thirteenth-century Christian philosophy, though its impact on Jewish thought was negligible. Such a discovery could only embellish the image of a Jewish minority whose cultural worth was repeatedly challenged by the host society.[97]

Modern scholars of Judaism were convinced that medieval Sephardic civilization represented an instructive paradigm for integrating Jewish and general culture. Munk himself would regularly stress the indispensability of studying Jewish thought within its general philosophical context, a theme that underlay all of modern Jewish studies.[98] Islamic texts were found to be especially useful in resolving a variety of difficulties encountered in the study of ancient Israelite religion. This new scholarly direction was doubtless linked to French colonial politics as well, insofar as France had become involved intricately with societies in North Africa and the Near East. These developments laid the groundwork for the creation of a chair in Arabic and Semitic languages at the *école rabbinique* of Metz, which, in turn, strengthened the idea of transferring the school to Paris where future French rabbis would benefit by their proximity to leading centers of oriental scholarship.[99] With the move to Paris, a new chapter in the history of *Wissenschaft* opened, now with the unprecedented participation of the French rabbinate.

Conclusion

The course of Jewish scholarship in France in the revolutionary era and in the following half-century offers an important index of the forces that shaped Jewish identity in modern Europe. Even before the onset of unprecedented political and social changes, Jewish scholars struggled to define their relationship to the legacy of Jewish tradition. The cumulative impact of rationalism, skepticism, and modern methods of textual criticism prior to the Revolution may be observed in the emergence of a reassessment of the religious and cultural legacies that the new world had inherited from the past. Though limited, there are examples of a pre-revolutionary stance that anticipated the source-critical approach of nineteenth-century scholars. Aaron Worms's clear preference for the authority of talmudic and midrashic sources over medieval rabbinic writings mirrored the preeminence of classical antiquity in Enlightenment thought, and it provided the leading criterion by which accretions to the halakhic tradition were to be judged. Against the invention of rites and the introduction of Lurianic customs, Worms argued that they not only violated the standards of reason but that "matters such as th[ese] have no foundation in the Talmud and *midrashim.*" Equally significant in the crystallization of his thinking vis-à-vis the Jewish tradition was the importance of a centralized halakhic authority. In this respect, his views were consistent with one of the dominant forces of the revolutionary period. Concerned that a host of changes that had begun to transform the face of early modern Jewry now threatened the faithful transmission of the halakhic tradition through ritual fragmentation and decentralization, Worms endeavored to reconstitute the authority of the *Shulḥan Arukh* as an agent of unity for communities across the continent. Although religious rituals were, historically, a form of cultural variegation that was resistant to halakhic uniformity, Worms also viewed them as susceptible to the historical ruptures, shifts, and transformations that eroded the authority of Halakhah during the two centuries preceding the Revolution.

While virtually every aspect of this criticism had its roots in the vast halakhic literature of the medieval and early modern periods, the fact that they were all assembled together in *Me'orei Or* in the revolutionary era is proof that Worms constructed—whether consciously or unconsciously—an enlightened traditionalism grounded in the intellectual underpinnings of his day. A close reading of *Me'orei Or* suggests, then, that the image conceived by the Haskalah, though certainly incomplete, was not entirely inaccurate. While Worms's world—both in terms of learning and practice—was clearly circumscribed within the "four cubits of Halakhah," it appears that several key elements of his outlook constituted a reversion to a rational, enlightened traditionalism that was a rarity in his generation. Qualities such as his independence of mind, his refusal to follow tradition uncritically, and his insistence that customs with no textual basis or rational foundation be discarded all corresponded closely to the religious ideology of the Haskalah and contain faint echoes of the new critical spirit of the Enlightenment. What the *maskilim* apparently failed to understand was that the *Me'orei Or* was representative of the longstanding dialectic of tradition and innovation and that its critical views were counterbalanced by an unflinching commitment to the fundamentals of the Jewish faith. Although there is no evidence of a new conceptual approach to the problematic aspects of the halakhic tradition, in *Me'orei Or* we do have an indication that the concerns voiced by *maskilim* and reformers were judged to be compelling by at least one major halakhic authority. Moreover, an appreciation for the process of historical development is also evident in an embryonic form, at least as far as the halakhic and kabbalistic traditions are concerned. These were only the very first steps anticipating the beginning of critical rabbinic scholarship in the modern era.

In contrast to the German *Wissenschaft des Judentums* movement, French

Jewish scholarship does not appear to be a product of political turmoil and intellectual ferment, nor a response to traumatic discontinuity. The founders of the French Bible project regarded their work as a natural continuation of the Mendelssohn *Biur*; their reliance on German biblical criticism was, in their view, a natural extension of Mendelssohn's pioneering work. These disparities with the German model may explain the general lack of interest in *la science de Judaïsme* in France. Assuming that the number of subscriptions is a reliable index of readership, the French Bible project enjoyed very limited success. In some years the published list of subscriptions included as few as twenty names. Writing in 1847, Samuel Cahen conceded that the Bible project's lack of popularity was due to the general indifference of French Jews, exacerbated by the fact that the critical method employed was not widely used in the scholarly and literary world of France, nor among Jews in other countries.[100] Nevertheless, according to German theologian Heinrich Paulus, the rational explication of the Bible had made more progress among the Jews of France than of Germany, where there was "too little esteem for antiquity" among the "so-called enlightened."[101]

Irrespective of how one assesses the success of such scholarly endeavors, the scientific study of Judaism mirrored deep divisions within French Jewry over how much of modern culture it ought to embrace. Reflecting an unshakable optimism in the prospects of social and cultural integration, scholarly work promoted, in its initial stages, increased contact and collegiality with non-Jews while it championed the universal ideals of Judaism. In time, gestures signaling confidence in the unrestrained advance of emancipation became more sober. Referring to the general lack of support for his work, Samuel Cahen lamented that "nos services, nos efforts régénérateurs sont devenus pour nous réellement un titre d'exclusion."[102] By mid-century, in the face of growing challenges stemming from the academy, the church, and socialist critics, *la science de judaïsme* embarked on a course emphasizing anew the particularity of the Jewish tradition.

Chapter 8

Rabbinic Authority and Ritual Reform

The battle lines separating reformers and traditionalists in nineteenth-century Europe are commonly assumed to be clear and well defined. From 1817, with the establishment of the New Israelite Temple Association in Hamburg, the nascent Reform movement broke progressively with the normative halakhic tradition. Almost immediately, reformers encountered vehement resistance and criticism on the part of their traditionalist opponents. Appalled by each of the proposed liturgical and synagogue reforms, stalwart defenders of orthodoxy argued that change of any sort threatened to undermine the integrity of Halakhah and the authority of its rightful interpreters.[1] While the conflict was undeniably fierce, it has now become clear that the common ground shared by conservative and liberal interpreters of the Jewish tradition was far more expansive than is normally assumed. The social, cultural, and philosophical forces of modernity in the west affected all sectors of the Jewish community, producing a dangerous attenuation of Jewish loyalties in the case of most and significant shifts in consciousness even among the staunchest guardians of tradition.[2] Like proponents of religious reform, traditionalists struggled with the difficult challenges of modernity, and although the two movements disagreed fundamentally on how these issues ought to be approached, they were each confronted by the spectre of rampant assimilation, religious apathy, a sharp decline in ritual observance, and the erosion of rabbinic authority.

These challenges, and the struggle over religious reform in particular, gave expression to the ambiguities inherent in the emancipation of western European Jewry. During the Bourbon Monarchy, the debate still centered on determining which elements of the Jewish tradition were obstacles to or were in harmony with the status of Jews qua citizens. In 1831 a consistorial commission in Strasbourg proposed liturgical and ritual innovations that anticipated the reform agenda of the following decade. Assigned the task of "researching the obstacles that continue to oppose the complete regeneration of Alsatian Jewry," the commission concluded that the failure of regeneration was related to several problematic aspects of ritual practice.

The commission proposed three categories of religious reform. The first concerned the enhancement of the aesthetic dimension of public rituals.

This included synagogue and funeral decorum, the elimination of the sale of honors, and the introduction of weekly preaching. The second category related to the introduction of a representative role for religious functionaries that would, in effect, supplant the participatory nature of synagogue rites. This initiative would authorize the rabbi or *ministre officiant* to recite the *kiddush* or take the *etrog* (citron) on behalf of all those in attendance and, in so doing, to discharge their individual religious obligations. The third category of reform was the reduction in the total number of prayers and the elimination of passages that were viewed as hostile to other faiths. Among the rituals that were earmarked for discontinuation were the prohibition against drinking gentile wine (*yein nesekh*), the periodic prohibitions against shaving, the second days of festivals, and Tisha b'Av observances. This category also included the establishment of a ceremony of religious initiation for girls and the easing of restrictions on minor holidays. Together, these proposals represent an effort to pattern the synagogue after the Protestant mode of worship and to remove rituals that purportedly contributed to the social alienation between Jews and gentiles.[3]

Although the Strasbourg initiative proved somewhat premature and ultimately abortive, it offers an indication of the mentality that had only then surfaced among the modernizing elite. At that point, with the exception of Terquem's *Lettres Tsarphatiques*, criticism of traditional Judaism was rarely voiced publicly in France. However, in the late 1830s when the Central Consistory underwent a major legislative overhaul, questions of ritual reform and rabbinic authority riveted the attention of community leaders and their constituencies. At the same time, as the *régénérateur* movement came of age, greater success in the modification of religious ceremonies was achieved. These efforts rested on many of the same ideological and philosophical premises then prevalent in central Europe. Nevertheless, in contrast with neighboring Germany where reforms tended to be more radical and found extensive institutional expression, the demands of the *régénérateurs* remained relatively restrained. Among all but the most conservative sectors of the Franco-Jewish leadership there had nonetheless emerged a consensus concerning the necessity of ritual reform and the details of the reform agenda.

Appeals for religious reform generally focused on the aesthetics of synagogue worship, as an 1838 report by the Paris Comité de Secours et d'Encouragement reveals: "In order to fulfill their goal and in order not to be a vain comedy which profanes that which is most sacred, the forms of the *culte* must be in harmony with our mores and our education, and the Jew of our day should not need to turn away from the synagogue for fear of rediscovering there a semblance of the Middle Ages."[4] While the committee emphatically denied any reformist intent, claiming only that it wished to render order and dignity to the religious ceremonies, this was essentially a semantic distinction. Synagogue services were widely viewed as disorderly, unappealing, and ultimately incapable of satisfying the spiritual needs of contemporary Jews. Portions of the liturgy, including *piyyutim, yozrot,* and *selihot* were no longer intelligible to modern worshippers, appeared out of step with French mores, and only served to prolong the service and disrupt concentration. If the synagogue was to serve as a vehicle for the edification of the soul, argued reformers, it would be necessary to eliminate these prayers and to institute simple and solemn chanting of the liturgy by a cantor and choir, accompanied by an organ. They also urged the introduction of preaching each Sabbath morning and the elimination of the auctioning of synagogue honors. Paris reformers, as distinct from partisans of religious modernization elsewhere in France, also proposed the fusion of the Portuguese and German liturgies.[5] Other recommendations, including the introduction of the *initiation religieuse* (confirmation ceremony) for both boys and girls, the modernization of funeral ceremonies, the regulation of the circumcision rite, the elimination of *peri'ah* and *mezizah,* the introduction of new surgical procedures, and the licensing of *mohalim,* were strongly urged by proponents of *régénération.*[6] Finally, reformers argued that restrictions on social intercourse with non-Jews were incompatible with the demands of citizenship and its wider implications. From the 1840s, halakhic constraints on the consumption of gentile wine and the emulation of gentile customs (*hukkot ha-goi*) were cited as only the most egregious examples of the outmoded character of traditional Judaism.[7]

The main elements of religious reform as envisioned by liberal thinkers and the limitations they placed on the scope of their endeavors are evident in the first French attempt to introduce concrete liturgical and synagogue innovations. In 1841, before an assembly of twenty-six residents of Metz, Gerson Lévy proposed the formation of a society whose goal was to open a chapel (an *oratoire*) where worship could be conducted with "more fervor and contemplation." The initiative taken by the Metz group rested on the claim that during centuries of persecution Judaism had become obsessed with ritual details and lost sight of the essential principles of the religion. A pervasive lack of concern for synagogue music, solemnity, and majestic ceremonies was blamed for the indifference of many affluent Jews toward their religion. Accordingly, the remedy would require restoring Judaism's former dignity to the prayer service. All conversation would be prohibited, only the officiant and choir would be authorized to recite prayers aloud, and to enhance concentration the duration of the services would be shortened.[8] In defending this last innovation, the society accorded legitimacy only to ancient prayers composed by the Men of the Great Assembly and subsequently adopted by the Portuguese, German, and Polish rites. Although later additions, such as the *piyyutim,* were to be omitted, the society reserved the right to supplement the liturgy when deemed necessary. It also pledged to draw on the poetry of Solomon Ibn Gabirol, Moses Ibn Ezra, and Judah Halevi, and to set them to choral music, like the psalms for each holiday. The choice of these poets reveals a decided preference among reformers, both in France and Germany, for Spanish culture over the Ashkenazic tradition. The most innovative proposal concerned the establishment of two consecutive services, one exclusively in Hebrew, and the other in French. So as not to offend traditional sensibilities and for practical reasons as well, the sermon would be delivered only at the end of the French service.[9]

Although the foregoing reforms broke with accepted Ashkenazic norms and usages, there is ample evidence suggesting that the founders of the *oratoire* intended to remain within the general boundaries of Halakhah. Men and women were to sit separately, on either side of a middle aisle, and no organ was mentioned in the prospectus. The *aron ha-kodesh* (the holy ark) was placed in its traditional position at the east end of the sanctuary, facing Jerusalem. To defend the projected French language service, which was intended to attract the nonobservant, Gerson-Lévy cited rabbinic sources permitting the recitation of prayers such as the *Shema* and *Kaddish* in the vernacular, including the Mishnah (*Sotah* 7:1) and Tosafot (*Berakhot* 3a). What is most striking about the entire enterprise of religious reform in France, then, as compared with Germany, are the limits that guided the French activists in defining their objectives. Fearing that the formation of a *reform* society would sow dissension within families and communities, Gerson-Lévy and his Metz cohorts distinguished sharply between public and private aspects of Jewish ritual. The domestic ritual, portrayed as "full of gentleness and consolation," was beyond the purview of reform. Their exclusive focus was the enhancement of *la culte publique*.[10]

Despite the restrained character of these proposals, the Metz *oratoire* never opened. Its failure calls attention to the difficulties that faced the enterprise of religious reform throughout France. Radical reformers did not support the project because they regarded it as overly conciliatory to orthodox practice; in their estimation the plan failed to remove obstacles believed to impede the goal of *fusion sociale*. Conservative critics accused members of the society of seeking to destroy the Jewish religion by deviating from traditional norms.[11] Moreover, the Metz consistory's denunciation of this unofficial attempt at reform severely undermined its credibility in the community. Unable to attract the thirty heads of families initially required by the society's founders, the project suffered the same fate as other failed efforts throughout most of the nineteenth century to sustain a chapel where "reformed" or "enlightened" services were held. The single exception was the *oratoire* in the Metz elementary school, where a service embodying several of the same innovations later proposed by Gerson-Lévy was held on Sabbath mornings. The *Shema* was recited in both Hebrew and French, and the service included an invocation, a sermon, and a prayer for the king—all in French. The fact that these innovative services were held in a school precluded their being perceived by the religious establishment as a threat to the status quo, and it therefore encountered no opposition.[12]

Although ritual reform in France came under the unmistakable influence of liberal trends in Germany, it also developed positions of its own in contradistinction to tendencies it found unacceptable. French proponents of religious modernization regularly applauded the progress of the Reform movement in Germany,[13] but they did not, for the most part, accept the validity of thoroughgoing ritual reform. Though guided by many of the same principles, and despite numerous areas of agreement, the *régénérateurs* and the German reformers remained apart on several important ritual and liturgical issues. The differences in approach are evident in their respective positions on the doctrine of Jewish messianism and on the primacy of Hebrew in the liturgy. The traditional belief that a descendant of the house of David who will lead the dispersed Jewish people back to its ancient land and restore the Jerusalem Temple appeared to conflict with the political status—or aspirations—of western European Jewry. With its emphasis on the centrality of Eretz Israel and the national redemption of the Jewish people, the messianic doctrine was viewed as dangerously particularistic and political in an era when universalist ideals and the acceptance of the authority of the state were so prevalent.[14]

German efforts to reinterpret the traditional messianic idea focused first on liturgical reform. Increasingly, divine worship was viewed as the public expression of religious convictions that prevailed in the Jewish community. In the estimation of reformers, the synagogue service ought to reflect the social, cultural, and political changes of the nineteenth century. As patriotic devotion to the state intensified, as did the importance attached to defining Judaism in universal terms, reformers revised prayers related to the coming of the Messiah, the restoration of the sacrificial order, and the restoration of Zion. Instead of eliminating these prayers entirely, they argued that the prayers were essentially universal in character and implied no immediate political consequence. This permitted the retention of some, though not all, of the traditional references in the early Reform prayer books. At the Reform rabbinical conferences of the 1840s, which met during the period of intense struggle for full civil emancipation, reformers decided to delete all prayers that did not reflect the universal and spiritual interpretation of the messianic doctrine.[15]

In France, the reassessment of Jewish messianism followed an entirely different course. Proposals for liturgical reform were limited to relatively minor issues. Prayers for the coming of the Messiah and the restoration of the Temple presented a less urgent problem, in part because the Paris Sanhedrin had theoretically resolved the question of messianism. Still, at the height of the controversy in Germany, it was impossible to ignore the issue entirely. Joel Anspach, author of the first French translation of the prayer book according to the Ashkenazic rite (1820), addressed the question of what to do with the prayers for the Messiah and the Temple. Claiming that those who wished to delete the prayers had misunderstood Judaism's doctrine of the Messiah, he argued that the belief in the Messiah neither contradicted the contemporary spirit of universal benevolence nor impeded French Jewry's capacity to serve as patriotic citizens. Such prayers were directed at "the edification and the prosperity of the entire world" and aimed to unify peoples divided by religious opinions by promoting the eventual attachment of humankind to a single, true faith, united by peace. This characterization of the function and significance of prayers that had come under attack by radical reformers was an effort to represent the traditional liturgy in new terms. Like other *régénérateurs*, Anspach was genuinely convinced of the capacity of traditional rites to accommodate new meaning, an approach that may be discerned in school textbooks as well.[16]

The place of Hebrew in the liturgy also exemplified the deep differences separating German and French reformers. At the Frankfurt Rabbinical Conference it was decided that each congregation could determine for itself how much Hebrew to retain in the liturgy. In protest over this decision, Zacharias Frankel dramatically left the conference and formed the Positive-Historical movement. Sympathetic to Frankel's views, the *Archives israélites* reevaluated its previous position advocating the use of French in order to enhance synagogue worship for those ignorant of the Hebrew language. Taking a more conservative position, the *régénérateurs* insisted on the preservation of Hebrew in the public service, though they called for the recitation of certain prayers in Aramaic (*Kaddish, Kol Nidrei,* and *Aqdamut*). They had concluded, as had Frankel, that Hebrew was a universal language for Jews throughout the world, and its suppression would disrupt the unity of the Jewish people. Some even argued that the maintenance of the Hebrew language and the adoption of the Sephardic pronunciation would enhance the internal unity of French Jewry, insofar as Hebrew would be a definitive mark of identification for the Jews of France.[17] As a rule, the French were reluctant to abandon ritual ceremonies that they viewed as fundamental to traditional Jewish identity. For this reason, they adamantly rejected the demands by members of the Frankfurt Reformfreunde to abolish the practice of circumcision and were equally unwilling to consider radical proposals concerning intermarriage and dietary restrictions.[18]

Why were French Jews less receptive to ritual reform than their coreligionists in Germany? The moderate character of the French reform program was largely a product of political and legal conditions, institutional forces, and demographic factors that were peculiar to France. In Germany, where the political struggle for civic equality was frustrated by repeated setbacks, liberal Jewish thinkers concluded that a religion divested of its particularistic features would ultimately furnish government authorities with convincing proof that the Jews were worthy of citizenship. Most French Jews felt no such urgency to introduce religious reforms. From its inception, *régénération* was defined principally in socioeconomic terms, and the Paris Sanhedrin played a key role in leaving the question of religious reform off of French Jewry's political agenda. Accorded the status of law by the Napoleonic regime, the Sanhedrin's decisions were transformed into a powerful legacy whose impact could still be felt, or at least invoked, at mid-century. Government recognition implicitly confirmed the legitimacy of the Sanhedrin's relatively conservative character. For subsequent generations of *régénérateurs*, the Sanhedrin's decisions ultimately exerted a moderating influence on the process of regeneration. Most were in agreement that the fulfillment of civic duties did not require thoroughgoing religious reform and that the concrete implementation of the assembly's views was sufficient.[19] Moreover, by virtue of the recognition accorded to Judaism by the state, French Jews achieved virtual parity with their Catholic and Protestant neighbors, further reducing the urgency of reform. One result of state legitimization was the unprecedented emphasis on the manner in which Judaism represented itself in the public sphere; synagogue rituals of a less public character were relegated to a secondary status. By authorizing the consistory to modernize the religion as it saw fit, the state expressed limited interest in ritual affairs.[20]

The organization of French Jewry within the consistorial system precluded the emergence of a radical reform ideology. As the official representative of all regional, ethnic, and religious sectors of the Jewish population, the consistorial system discouraged measures that might fragment the unity, whether imagined or real, of French Jewry. In particular, it could ill afford to alienate the orthodox masses or the rabbinate. Though dominated by men who shared the *régénérateurs'* concern for reconciling religious practice with contemporary French mores, and therefore indisputably a supporter of reform, the consistory chose to mediate in the struggle between traditionalists and reformers. Despite considerable divisions, there emerged a de facto cooperative spirit. Together on various educational committees sat rabbis, communal leaders, and proponents of religious reform.[21] The faculty of the *école rabbinique* of Metz, for example, included traditionalist rabbis who adamantly rejected the idea of religious reform, and some whose position on the issue was virtually identical to that of Zacharias Frankel.[22] Owing to the premium placed on unity, there emerged a consensus on the necessity of moderation, at least at the level of formal relations in the community. The overall commitment to moderation, reflected in minor reforms introduced by the consistories, effectively undercut the prospects of a successful movement to reform the Jewish religion. Radical religious reform in Germany—as contrasted with more restrained religious modernization—fed on deep social and religious divisions within the Jewish community. In France, where the structure of the Jewish community imposed the notion of public discipline in religious matters and political affairs, it was extraordinarily difficult for a reform movement to emerge.[23] Nevertheless, the implementation of ritual reforms would ultimately depend on a host of factors, including the views of the local grand rabbi, his influence in his community, and local support for or resistance to innovations.

Several noted Jewish scholars exerted a profound impact within consistorial circles, especially in Paris, and generally, on the discourse of religious modernization. Owing to the unique structural dynamics of the Jewish community, the moderate views of scholars such as Salomon Munk and Adolphe Franck were given considerable weight in consistorial deliberations. Munk, who was actively engaged in every area of Jewish community affairs, articulated a broadly conceived religious ideology of emancipation that was embraced by all but the most traditionalist orthodox. Contemporary Jews, he maintained, made up a community that included individuals of various nationalities, interests, mores, and cultural origins. He rejected physical suffering as a legitimate expression of national identity and consciousness, insisting that faith alone was what unified Jews in different areas of the world.[24] Monotheism was the decisive and historic contribution that Jews made to civilization, and this entitled them to play an important role in the perfection of humanity. This, Munk insisted, ought to be the essence of Jewish identity. Considering trends earlier in the century to downplay the political dimension of Judaism and to interpret traditional messianism in universal terms, Munk might easily have eschewed the value of continued ritual observance. However, the messianic era, according to Munk, was only "the final victory of religious and moral ideas [and] . . . until that time we must keep intact the *dépôt* which has been entrusted to us." The *dépôt* to which Munk referred was the general corpus of Jewish ceremonial laws, excepting those "abuses" that could be legitimately abolished. Accordingly, adherence to ritual law was indispensable because it constituted the quintessence of the Jewish religion and was therefore essential for Jews to execute their historic mission. It is clear that although Munk and others spoke of the mission of the Jewish *religion*, the idea required a *people* to embody its ideals. Serving as symbols of unity and cohesion, the ceremonial law was thus understood to be crucial for the concretization of the monotheisitic idea and for the realization of the messianic promise.[25]

Although religious modernization was never specifically prescribed in the original legislation that established the Consistoire Israélite, it eventually came within the purview of consistorial responsibility and emerged as a subject of intense public debate. Searching for a mechanism to introduce reforms in *le culte publique*, the Central Consistory submitted a plan in 1839 for a thorough reorganization of its administrative constitution. Most controversial among the provisions contained in the so-called Crémieux Project, so named after the chairman of the consistorial commission, was the proposal to give lay members of the consistories ultimate authority in religious affairs. Article 24 would grant the consistory exclusive power to modify rituals and shorten the prayers as it saw fit and to determine which prayer books and textbooks would be used in synagogue and schools. Invited to comment on the draft proposal, the departmental consistories of the northeast objected strongly to the usurpation of rabbinic authority. The Metz, Strasbourg, Colmar, and Nancy consistories were apprehensive about the implications of lay domination of the rabbinate, centralization of power in the Central Consistory, and the creation of a rabbinic hierarchy. Remarkably, though, of all the consistories Bordeaux was the most critical of the plan to undermine rabbinic authority. It alone objected to limitations on rabbinic tenure (article 46), and opposed granting the Central Consistory the exclusive right to suspend grand rabbis (article 45). In fact, throughout the 1850s, Bordeaux continued to frustrate the Central Consistory's efforts at tighter control of the provinces and was the only consistory to join Metz in opposing the transfer of the *école rabbinique* to Paris.[26]

Rabbis and orthodox laymen fought the plan by submitting formal protests to the Ministry of Religions, by circulating public petitions, and by attempting to refute reformist claims. The grand rabbis recognized the threat that the 1839 project posed; virtually every major rabbinical figure in France and a host of communal rabbis voiced criticism of the plan.[27] In a remarkable display of solidarity with the rabbis, petitioners from 82 Bas-Rhin communities, totaling more than 2,300 heads of households, signed a petition opposed to religious reform.[28] In Metz a major public campaign aimed to persuade the Jews of the Moselle that the new bill posed a serious threat to the Jewish tradition; the organizers assembled proposals advanced by radical reformers in France and Germany in order to expose the "real" intentions of the Central Consistory leadership. In the city of Metz and in the outlying towns and villages "secret societies" formed to collect signatures and funds. The community's religious leader, Grand Rabbi Lion-Mayer Lambert, an outspoken critic of religious reform, spearheaded the resistance to the consistory project. First director of the *école rabbinique de Metz* and chief rabbi of the *département*, he refused to discuss any aspect of the plan, either in department consistory meetings or in a special committee of three rabbis and two laymen. Lambert's own public repudiation of the project and his energetic efforts in holding meetings to persuade community members to sign letters of protest to the Minister of Religions were impressive and effective.[29]

These efforts met with success, as evidenced by the modification of some of the more controversial provisions of the plan. When finally published in 1844, the ordinance included several provisions that balanced the potentially unchecked drive for reform. It included communal rabbis in the *notabilité*, thus giving them a voice in the selection of Central Consistory members; it required the approbation of the Central Consistory grand rabbi before any textbook could be used in Jewish schools; and it confirmed the authority of the grand rabbi in specifically religious matters. The consistory's proposed powers of censure, suspension, and dismissal of consistorial rabbis were also limited by the 1844 ordinance, stipulating that action in these areas could be taken only in accordance with the opinion of the local consistory and the grand rabbi. Although the ordinance did contain provisions for the increased participation of lay members in the

Central Consistory, the law fell short of its goal of investing the laity with unchecked powers to institute ritual reforms. The powerful trend toward lay domination, together with the cooperation of progressive rabbis, nevertheless enabled the consistories to introduce several reforms of a moderate nature: *initiation religieuse*; the abolition of the sale of religious honors in the synagogue; the modernization of funeral ceremonies; and the regulation of circumcision procedures. These reforms were related either to the improvement of the aesthetics of synagogue worship or to administrative centralization, but they do not reflect any doctrinal changes.[30]

Two central themes of the proposed legislation—lay domination of the rabbinate and the notion of a rabbinic hierarchy—each greatly alarmed traditionalists. The latter, especially, was of concern because its implications were very concrete. A hierarchical structure within the rabbinate would permit the consistory to achieve its goal of surveillance and censure at every level,[31] and new efforts to revise the 1844 *ordonnance* in accordance with the spirit of the 1848 revolution rekindled earlier debates concerning centralization and the lay domination of the rabbinate. In Paris, both in the departmental and central consistories, the lay leadership favored limiting suffrage to a small, elite group to whom decisions on the major issues of communal policy would be entrusted, while in the southern and northeastern provinces the preference was to adopt universal suffrage. Nevertheless, the 1853 decree determined that the election of communal rabbis and grand rabbis would remain under consistory control. Departmental grand rabbis were to be elected by the local consistory, voting together with twenty-five *notables* chosen by universal suffrage, and communal rabbis were to be appointed directly by the consistory. In other words, the revolution of 1848 left the election procedures followed by French Jewish communities virtually unchanged. By 1862 departmental grand rabbis were no longer chosen in their own districts but were selected from among three nominees submitted by each consistory to the central body.[32] Even more revealing of this trend is the fact that rabbis never elected their own leaders; rabbinic selection was lay imposed and lay dominated.[33]

Although the 1844 *ordonnance* contained provisions for the increased participation of lay members in the Central Consistory, the law failed to invest the laity with unchecked powers to institute ritual reforms. The most striking aspect of the *ordonnance* was its concession to the continued dominance of the rabbinic establishment in the areas of religion and education. Clearly, the public resistance of Alsatian Jewry and its leaders to the Crémieux Project was an important factor in shaping the final draft of the bill. As a result, the authority of the rabbinate was preserved, and the hands of would-be radical reformers were tied throughout the nineteenth century.

Traditionalists displayed their strength a second time when the Central Consistory attempted to control the election of a successor to Grand Rabbi

Emmanuel Deutz. Candidates were asked to state their position on nine reforms enumerated in the consistory's questionnaire: the fusion of the
Ashkenazic and Sephardic rites; the enhancement of the dignity of synagogue ceremonies; the suppression of *piyyutim* and several other prayers;
the introduction of the organ; the role of women in the synagogue; the regulation of circumcision; the adoption of the definition of a Jew as one born
of either a Jewish mother *or* father; improvements in the *école rabbinique*,
and the expansion of rabbinic duties to include pastoral activities.[34] It was
made clear that the enumerated reforms were important desiderata and
that the respondents would be judged by their readiness to implement
these reforms.[35] Following the appearance of the circular, Grand Rabbis
Lambert and Goudchaux, of Metz and Colmar respectively, issued a manifesto warning against the dangers of religious reform. They emphasized the
immutability of the Written and Oral Law, declared that no assembly of
rabbis had the authority to modify any aspect of Jewish law, and warned
that any attempt to introduce reforms was an act of rebellion that would ultimately have destructive consequences.[36] In Colmar, rabbis of both the
Bas- and Haut-Rhin assembled to refute each of the nine recommendations, and similar meetings were held in Strasbourg at the behest of Grand
Rabbi Aron.[37] Popular opposition to the circular was vigorous and well organized. Petitions to the Central Consistory from at least twenty-eight Haut-
Rhin communities attacked the legitimacy of ritual reform and claimed
that by making the nomination conditional upon adhesion to the nine
points, the consistory had violated the freedom of conscience of the rabbinical candidates.[38]

Comparing the struggle between reformers and traditionalists in France
and Germany, several important differences become apparent. First, the
battle over rabbinic authority and religious reform began more than two
decades later than in Germany. With the eruption of the Hamburg Temple
controversy in 1817–19, orthodox leaders began bitter attacks against synagogue reforms and the "lawless" deeds of reformers. A deep chasm was
created by the vehemence of orthodoxy's ideological war on reform, and it
was deepened by a virtual ban of non-contact that was articulated by Rabbi
Moses Sofer.[39] In France in this period, communities were preoccupied
with the work of building their institutions, and men of various ideological
perspectives shared these tasks. Moreover, the enhanced symbolic role of
religion in French public life boosted the prestige of the rabbinate. Once
the issues of religious reform were raised in earnest in France—in the
1840s—French Jews had already forged an ethos that viewed unity as a
cherished goal.

While the history of the consistory reveals an inexorable trend toward lay
domination in religious affairs, the narrow focus on consistorial legislation
runs the risk of overstating differences between lay and religious leaders as
polar opposites. When approached within a broader framework, however,

the study of nineteenth-century rabbinic leadership yields a host of crucial details concerning the various stages of its development and the varied strategies pursued by rabbinic camps of different stripes. As in the course of modernization generally, the full impact of the Revolution and the Napoleonic reforms on the leadership of French Jewry was not felt until the 1830s and 1840s. Compared to developments in Germany where cultural transformation was relatively swift, modernization in France appears to have been impeded, not accelerated, by the Revolution. A new Franco-Jewish consciousness did certainly emerge, but this occurred very deliberately: there was a lag of nearly a half-century between the dramatic progress achieved in the political arena and the rather lethargic process of cultural modernization.[40] For the majority of France's Jews, the encounter with the trauma of emancipation did not occur until several decades after the bestowal of civic equality. Moreover, with the emigration of numerous rabbis, *maskilim,* and intellectuals to Germany proper and to areas under French occupation during the latter Napoleonic years, no modernizing elite within the ranks of the Jewish community emerged until the 1820s and early 1830s. This was exacerbated by the disruptive effects of the post-revolutionary era—the closing of schools, synagogues, *yeshivot,* and Hebrew publishing, as well as the persecution of those who dared observe religious rites—which commanded the attention and diverted the energies of leaders who were obligated to rebuild communal institutions. By the time reformers were prepared to take up the issues that German Jewry had addressed decades before, the prospects for reform were already quite limited. The same was true of education. Modern schools and other institutions that might have become the training ground for more radical activity were established very late, *after* the rabbinate had emerged as a power in community affairs and had assumed a controlling interest in Jewish schooling.

An additional factor that had bearing on the functioning of religious leadership in France was the comprehensive, highly structured nature of the Jewish community. It imposed the façade of public discipline on religious and political debate, and by placing constraints on the dimensions of change, precluded either the emergence of a reform movement or the implementation of a radical religious reform program.[41] The structural impediments to reform are likewise evident in the educational sphere, where rabbis were full partners in the community leadership structure and tended to be strong supporters, not antagonists, of the movement for educational modernization.

Rabbinic participation was crucial for whatever success these ventures enjoyed, thanks to the central role of the rabbi and the synagogue in Jewish life. The involvement of rabbis in Jewish schooling points to a reconfiguration of community leadership in the nineteenth century, especially as reflected in the emergence of the rabbinate as a dynamic force in communal affairs alongside the lay elite. This was a conspicuous turnabout from the decline experienced by the rabbinate in the last decades before the Revolution.[42] Although the nineteenth-century rabbinate had been stripped of its judicial authority following the Revolution, its official status surpassed its standing in the *ancien régime*, when the lay leadership of the *kehillah* had been firmly in control. It is undeniable that the real power remained in the hands of the lay leadership in the nineteenth century as well, but the rabbis were now formally included in the decision-making process. They provided vital leadership in the establishment and direction of modern schools, in the central rabbinical facility, in Hebrew publishing, and in the organization of vocational societies and training. Moreover, rabbinic prestige clearly benefited from the enhanced symbolic role that religion had come to play in French public life by the 1840s and from the fact that Judaism had assumed a legitimate place alongside Catholicism and Protestantism. As a result, rabbis were normally preferred over lay consistory leaders to represent the community at public events. Finally, rabbis were uniquely entrusted with the important mission of teaching the ideals of patriotism in accordance with the Sanhedrin decisions.[43]

Leadership Changes in the 1840s

Some fifty years after the French Revolution, a new generation of leaders—both in the lay and rabbinic sectors—displayed an unprecedented responsiveness to the social and religious challenges of the nineteenth century. Within the consistory and among *maskilim* there emerged a cadre of reformers who approached the matter of religious modernization with increased urgency. Corresponding to the appearance of this reformist group were rabbis who had become receptive to the idea of moderate reform, while their more traditionalist rabbinic colleagues remained unyielding, even to modest changes. Despite their differences, each of the three groups was concerned with precisely how to balance the competing claims made by Jewish tradition on the one hand, and the intellectual, social, and political components of modern French culture on the other.

Although no bonafide religious reform movement was able to take root in France, challenges to the orthodox tradition and to the religious authority of the rabbinate were fierce and defining. The question which strategies might best be employed to counter reformist efforts was intensely debated within the ranks of the French rabbinate. While the two wings of the rabbinate each energetically defended the halakhic tradition against criticism and encroachments on its authority, there was considerable division on precisely how to respond. Here, it is important to distinguish between defensive measures aiming to stave off overt attacks on the religious authority of the rabbinate on the one hand, and more nuanced orthodox responses to the onslaught of modernity in the urban centers, where communities were threatened by the specter of increasing assimilation, poorly attended synagogues, a sharp decline in ritual observance, and the erosion of religious authority. No less than the reformers, the French rabbinate endeavored to come to terms with the grave problems facing the Jewish community at large.

Intrarabbinic discussions offer an important indication of how leaders understood these challenges, as well as the range of options available to them. From the perspective of the rabbinate, the key issue was authority, as is evident from the debate surrounding the convocation of a rabbinic synod. The idea had originated with proponents of reform who considered this the best way to address questions of religious accommodation to modernity. In an exchange of letters in 1843–45 with Seligmann Goudchaux, grand rabbi of the Upper Rhine Consistory, Salomon Ulmann (1806–1865) took exception to his elder colleague's categorical opposition to the idea. Born in Saverne, Ulmann was among the first graduates of the *école centrale rabbinique* in Metz; he began his rabbinic career in the Alsatian town of Lauterbourg, was subsequently appointed consistorial grand rabbi of Nancy in 1843, and ten years later was elected Central Consistory grand rabbi.[44] He supported the notion of a synod, on the condition that it comprise rabbis only, declaring that it was unthinkable that rabbis could sit with "men of no name, devoid of any wisdom." A synod, he argued, would permit a body of rabbis to consult with one another and to issue their collective view rather than a series of individual opinions. Ulmann also objected to Goudchaux's concern that the rabbis themselves might prove to be unreliable. A framework bringing them together would unify them against the consistory's manipulative efforts.[45] In his follow-up letter, Ulmann promised that even if all the rabbis of France were to agree to convene together with laymen, he would not join them under any circumstances, as this would only strengthen their hand. Painting a bleak picture of what the future held in store, Ulmann asserted that the survival of the Jewish people demanded a bold new expression of halakhic activism. Our "tender children and others who are weak-hearted" are in danger of being led "like sheep to slaughter until they . . . are ensnared in their trap. . . . [H]ow much longer shall we hide, how much longer shall we act like one who is besieged . . . [and] indifferent to the ruin of the house of Joseph?"[46]

Because cooperation with proponents of reform was not, in Ulmann's estimation, at all practical, he urged a rabbinic counterinitiative. He insisted that only by confronting the central claims advanced by the reformers would it be possible to avert the ominous threats to traditional observance. Foremost among their contentions was the assertion that the rabbis failed to differentiate between divine laws, which were widely accepted as immutable, and religious laws and customs that were the product of later times and were therefore less authoritative. Ulmann maintained that only pentateuchal prescriptions were unassailable; customs that were deemed to be incompatible with contemporary mores or were historically conditioned could be changed or eliminated by synodal assemblies, in accordance with established legal procedures. Support for a rabbinic synod was the distinguishing characteristic of progressive rabbis who believed that this would permit the rabbinate to control the pace of religious modernization.[47]

The gap separating traditionalists and reformers was most evident with respect to synagogue worship. Traditionalists approached the *siddur* as a sacred canon that could not be altered, while reformers sought to modify the Hebrew liturgy in accordance with their own ideological views.[48] Ulmann assured Goudchaux that his intention was not to introduce the slightest change in the liturgy transmitted by the Men of the Great Assembly and the Sages of the Talmud, but only to eliminate the medieval *piyyutim*.[49] Citing the ambivalence of those *poseqim* who questioned whether the *piyyutim* constituted an unwarranted interruption, he took the argument a step further: "In our generation, when the fear of God diminishes with each passing day, and faith is lost . . . we must, at the very least, elevate the divine service and enact reforms [*tikkunim*] according to the needs of the time, in order to salvage the little faith that still remains in the heart of the remnant of Israel."[50] In his judgment, the continued recitation of the *piyyutim* was counterproductive. Earlier generations, though unable to comprehend these texts, may have recited them piously, but today, he insisted, such piety is virtually unknown: "We need to weigh the needs of the generation and the condition of the nation, as our predecessors did—they wanted to enact many *gezerot*, but refrained from doing so because of impracticality, and because by instituting preventive measures by which the people might not be able to abide, it could be said that the rest of Torah law is not binding."[51]

Beyond the ideological debates contained in the Ulmann letters, concrete policy considerations and strategies emerged very clearly. With an eye to the future, Ulmann confronted the senior rabbi of Strasbourg about his decision to reduce the number of *kinot* recited in his own community. If this was justifiable at the local level, Ulmann inquired, could it not be implemented throughout France, thus serving as a precedent for the elimination of the *piyyutim* in other communities? To the end, this last point—the importance of instituting changes uniformly and centrally—would remain a central premise of Ulmann's ideology of halakhic reform. His efforts to convene a rabbinic synod were, clearly, an outgrowth of this thinking. When the first conference of French rabbis finally convened in 1856 at Ulmann's behest, its primary objective was to encourage the broad adoption of reforms that had already achieved success in isolated instances. Despite his assurance to Goudchaux, Ulmann proposed to a communal leader in Blâmont that, in addition to eliminating the *piyyutim*, he would reduce the weekly reading of the Torah by one-half. With the time saved, he asserted, it would be possible not only to add prayers in French, but also for the rabbi to explain the Torah portion and to deliver a sermon.[52]

Ulmann's public endorsement of the organ for use at Sabbath services offers further insight into his approach to halakhic decision making, which is crucial for understanding the dynamic relationship between his views and his leadership objectives. His position was based on the premise that there was no technical-halakhic objection to its use, provided that a non-Jew played it, and on the claim that it did not come under the prohibition of *hukkat ha-goi*.[53] Widely divergent rabbinic views on the question of whether the organ violated *hukkat ha-goi* and how extensively the principle ought to be applied in discrediting non-Jewish customs[54] permitted Ulmann to maintain considerable flexibility in developing his program for halakhic renewal:

> In my opinion, since only public worship remains, and the state of faith declines daily, and the Torah is being forgotten from the heart, the rabbinate has the obligation to think of methods to prevent further losses, and to seek in whatever manner to draw the House of Israel to the Lord, to elevate the house of God, and at the very least, to add greater dignity to the service, in order to close the mouths of those who speak with arrogance and disdain. . . . And in my opinion it is not proper what some rabbis are doing by saying that even for a shoestring one must give up one's life; for today the battle of the Lord should be waged not with poison and obstinacy, but rather with gentleness . . . not with the stringency of Shammai, but with the humility of Hillel. Our eyes are fixed on the present, let us say about a prohibition that it is prohibited, and about that which is permitted that it is permitted, according to the sight of our eyes and according to Torah tradition; we shall fear no man, to whichever side he inclines, we shall do our part, and we shall not heed those who say look, there is a new thing, nor to the cry of opponents who those say that the old ought to be cast off because of the novelty therein.[55]

This letter, like several others, reveals that Ulmann had concluded early in his career that certain innovations were halakhically justified and that his opponents were wrong to reject every innovation categorically, provided that no clear, explicit prohibition existed. Proudly, he declared that no opposition to the introduction of the organ was heard in his synagogue: "Not that I like music, nor do I see the organ as an index of progress; [but] I congratulate myself in seeing the gradual disappearance of the deplorable habit of rising up against the most innocent innovations." Accordingly, the tradition of interpreting the Halakhah liberally required sustained efforts against conservative opponents such as Rabbi Moses Sofer, to whom the foregoing excerpt clearly referred.[56]

Rabbis of several important communities in France shared Ulmann's approach to halakhic innovation; they were able to provide certain reforms with a religious stamp of approval, succeeding where reformers had failed. The most widely implemented innovation in France, the *initiation religieuse* (confirmation ceremony), illustrates the indispensability of the rabbinate to the success of reform. Endorsed by progressive rabbis, the ceremony was conducted for boys and girls who had passed examinations in Hebrew reading and mastery of the catechism. Usually held on two separate occasions each year and conducted in the presence of municipal leaders, members of the local public school committee, and special dignitaries, the *initiation religieuse* was an important and celebrated reform because it represented a public display of the new Franco-Jewish spirit. It included virtually all of the elements that proponents of religious reform had advocated but rarely achieved: a dignified service; equality for girls; a choir; an organ; and a sacred declaration of patriotic loyalty and love for the king and the royal family. While lay reformers and consistory activists were in the forefront of efforts to implement the *initiation religieuse*, progressive rabbis were centrally involved in designing the program and in officiating at the popular ceremony. By the mid-1840s the ceremony was routinely held in most communities and was finally adopted by the rabbis of Metz and Colmar, with certain modifications, in the early 1850s.[57]

Of course, other factors impinged on the implementation of such reforms, including an individual rabbi's own apprehensiveness or lack of authority, or the resistance encountered—or feared—within his local community. For example, R. Ennery of the Central Consistory subscribed to the theoretical permissibility of playing the organ, as is evident from his responses to the nine-point 1846 questionnaire for the position of Central Consistory grand rabbi. Proponents of reform were therefore disappointed by Ennery's frequent vacillations. Ennery chided the *commissaire surveillant* of Lille for introducing an organ into the synagogue without the authorization of the grand rabbi, but when his own daughter was married in the Paris temple in 1846, the organ was played. Only two years before he had opposed its use at the *initiation religieuse* ceremony. Despite these equivocations, the organ was introduced in numerous consistorial synagogues as musical accompaniment on national holidays, at confirmation ceremonies, at funeral rites, and, in a few instances, at regular Sabbath services. Even the consistorial synagogue of Colmar permitted the organ for limited purposes, such as the *initiation religieuse*.[58] In the case of circumcision, Ennery was more firmly supportive of reform. After consulting a medical commission in 1844, Ennery endorsed the suppression of *meziẓah*, an opinion that was not shared by all of his fellow grand rabbis and for which he encountered much criticism. Nevertheless, Ennery maintained that *meziẓah* was essentially a medical question and therefore did not warrant consideration by a rabbinical synod.[59]

The approach of Ulmann and like-minded progressive rabbis typified the mode of traditionalist thinking that had fallen out of step with nineteenth-century orthodox halakhists. Ulmann's halakhic method may be regarded as a reversion to premodern legal rulings that arose from an independent interpretation of the halakhic sources. His views were free of orthodox dogmatics, but his position on rabbinic authority was uncompromising. First, he was a strong advocate of rabbinic hierarchy, which, in his view, was essential for the rabbinate to police itself, and a vigilant defender of the rabbinate against consistorial incursions on its independence. His opposition to the participation of lay leaders in halakhic decision making was absolute and even vitriolic.[60] Second, he was thoroughly unwilling to acquiesce to approaches that deviated from traditional Halakhah. By mounting attacks against the authority of the Talmud and the Oral Law, the Reform rabbinical conferences in Germany had become, in his words, a modern form of "Karaism" and could not be resisted in silence. The time had come, he wrote to R. Arnaud Aron, grand rabbi of Strasbourg and successor to R. Goudchaux, for the French rabbinate to publicly declare its position on matters of faith; further, he concurred with Goudchaux's proposal to publish a manifesto affirming the authority of the Talmud, provided there were no recriminations against German rabbis nor any declaration invalidating what he regarded as sensible reforms. Accordingly, Ulmann rejected the appeal made by Hirsch Lehren of Amsterdam after the first Reform rabbinical conference in Brunswick (1844) to undertake an open battle with several leading German rabbis, and he refused to join the twelve French signators to R. Jacob Ettlinger's formal protest, which was published in the following year. A moderately toned declaration, he confided to Aron, would be less confrontational but equally effective by announcing to the Jews of France that French rabbis do not fear taking a public stand.[61] Undoubtedly to Ulmann's consternation, Rabbis Goudchaux and Lambert issued their strongly worded public warning that "every reformatory attempt to modify [any aspect of Jewish law] constitutes rebellion against the religion . . . and leads to the way of destruction."[62] Ulmann's own projected declaration, however, was never issued.

Ulmann's strategy for bolstering rabbinic authority was unambiguous. He affirmed the adoption of halakhically sanctioned changes, and this push, coupled with his vehement resistance to reform, distinguished him from moderate rabbinic colleagues elsewhere. By the end of 1846, however, Ulmann conceded to R. Samuel Dreyfus of Mulhouse that he was much less hopeful about the prospects for prompt, uniform changes. The Central Consistory could not be counted on to take a public stand, and the regional grand rabbis were unwilling to participate in a synod. In the absence of strong support and leadership, Ulmann even considered attending the proposed assembly in Dresden under the leadership of Rabbi Zacharias Frankel (founder of the Positive-Historical movement), but this never materialized. More important than the apparent convergence of Frankel's and Ulmann's views are the implications of his willingness to look beyond France for moral support. He had concluded that because the French rabbinate was composed of so many heterogeneous elements, its power had been neutralized and its influence virtually nullified. Moreover, he feared that if progressive rabbis were to take a public stand in France, the façade of unity would be destroyed and the rabbis themselves would be divided by schism, a scenario that would have dreadful consequences.[63] Ulmann believed that what little intercommunal unity existed within France, even if only imagined, was too fragile to be tampered with and, therefore, local reforms would need to suffice.

Having lost faith in the prospects of instituting additional moderate reforms, mainly because he judged his rabbinic colleagues unlikely to cooperate, Ulmann rejected a plea to head a new faction. He wrote to Samuel Dreyfus: "You give me too much honor in asking if you could count on me as leader of a new party that is forming. Although I agree with your views on the need to render greater dignity to the public service, and with the means to accomplish this, I do not think that we should separate from our colleagues by constituting a party."[64] At precisely the same time, Ulmann politely turned down an invitation issued by Cerfberr, president of the Central Consistory, to become a candidate for the position of chief rabbi.[65] Several years later, Ulmann reconsidered his previous stance and agreed to serve as chief rabbi, to which he was elected in 1853. Like his lay counterparts, he was disturbed by both the growing trend toward religious indifference and the lack of continuity and uniformity in the implementation of halakhically permissible religious reforms. In 1855 Ulmann issued a call for a conference of all the grand rabbis of France.[66]

With this decision to convene the Paris rabbinical conference, Ulmann proved himself to be the only rabbinic leader on the French scene who was willing to risk the unity that still prevailed, albeit precariously, within the traditionalist camp for the sake of broader social and religious goals. Even the Central Consistory was concerned about the expected reaction of conservative opponents of reform. In deference to their position, the consistory agreed to authorize a rabbinical conference, not a synod, to discuss the issues and to offer remedies for the problems facing French Jewry, though officially the goal of the conference was only to exchange views on "the most appropriate means of furthering the religious and moral progress" of French Jewry.[67] Prior to the opening of the conference, Ulmann already was aware that rabbinic support for his venture was waning. Shortly before the Paris meetings, Alsatian communal rabbis at the two preliminary rabbinical conferences held in Colmar and Strasbourg had voted decisively against synagogue reforms. Furthermore, R. Samuel Dreyfus, Ulmann's erstwhile ally, withdrew his support for aggressive action, arguing that if there were good reason to eliminate the *piyyutim*, "the fear of provoking divisions is a sufficient motive for maintaining even erroneous customs."[68] Among the various issues discussed in Paris—the religious initiation ceremony, sermons, religious instruction, standardization of marriage and burial ceremonies, transfer of the *école rabbinique* to Paris, and the adoption of clerical garb for rabbis and cantors—three innovations represented, in the opinion of conservatives, a departure from normative Halakhah: the reduction or elimination of *piyyutim*, the use of the organ on the Sabbath, and the adoption of a new ceremony for blessing newborn children.[69] Of the three, two reforms (*piyyutim* and organ) had already been introduced by Ulmann more than a decade before.

The leader of the traditionalist camp, R. Salomon Klein (1814–1867) of Colmar, asserted that the elimination or reduction of the *piyyutim*, the use of the organ, and the invention of a ceremony for newborns were unacceptable from the standpoint of Jewish law.[70] In order for a revision to warrant consideration, he insisted, it must be demonstrated that the proposed modification is demanded by a real need and that it will, in fact, remedy the problem. Thus, in the case of the *piyyutim*, he explained, reform was unwarranted and therefore unacceptable. He maintained further that no innovation was possible unless there were some historical or halakhic precedent. In rejecting the use of the organ, Klein asserted that there was no evidence of musical instruments ever having been played during the Temple sacrifices or prayers. Moreover, the use of the organ violated the spirit of Jewish prayer (that is, solemn concentration), and in a more technical-halakhic sense, the objection against employing a gentile to perform an act prohibited of Jews on the Sabbath was still valid. Interestingly, the argument of *ḥukkat ha-goi*, so prominent a decade earlier, was no longer utilized by traditionalists in 1856 in making their case against the organ, although it was used to discredit the ceremony for the newborn. Such a ceremony, Klein insisted, was foreign to Judaism and, in the particular case of boys, might be wrongly understood to take the place of circumcision. Finally, Klein asserted that any religious innovation is a violation of the status quo established by the Paris Sanhedrin (of 1807). In building his case against the 1856 conference, Klein masterfully invoked rhetoric normally associated with the era of the French Revolution. Ironically, liberty, democracy, and the Sanhedrin came to the defense of religious conservatism, as did the specter of communal and religious division in Germany. In order to avoid a similar catastrophe in France, Klein concluded that halakhic permissibility must not be interpreted as necessarily pointing to the advisability of ritual reform.[71]

Against the strenuous opposition mounted by Klein, Ulmann was able to enlist a majority of the consistorial grand rabbis in supporting the foregoing reforms. Ably using the press and the public *lettre pastorale* to circulate his views among the broader public, he seems to have succeeded in persuading his coreligionists that the adoption of the Sephardic pronunciation of Hebrew, the fusion of the Sephardic and Ashkenazic liturgies, the elimination of the Ashkenazic *piyyutim*, and the general receptivity to moderate religious change would promote the unity that French Jewry had desperately sought for itself. Ulmann's position rested on the assumption that developments within the Jewish religion ought to mirror the cultural and national forces that fashioned a unified polity under the civilization of France. This goal, he believed, would be served by the 1856 conference. The purpose of the initiative was not to break halakhically new ground, as most of the innovations discussed at the conference had been implemented earlier in various localities.[72] Rather, Ulmann's aim was to ratify halakhically acceptable reforms and thereby encourage their adoption throughout France. But as the absence of support within the traditionalist camp became increasingly apparent, Ulmann retreated slightly from his initial goal. The rabbinic conference decided that before any innovation could be adopted, the approval of departmental grand rabbis must first be sought.[73] In order to avert the ravages of schism, Ulmann and his colleagues had to come to terms with the powerful forces of religious conservatism and diversity. In contrast with the schism within German orthodoxy, the traditionalist camp in France had little choice but to cooperate and compromise on certain innovations, however minor.[74]

For French Jewry, the Revolution and the distinct character of emancipation fostered a set of values shared by moderates and traditionalists alike. Passionate patriotic devotion, an unequivocally positive attitude toward general culture, and a firm commitment to socioeconomic regeneration far outweighed the deep differences over ritual and liturgical issues, yielding a decided preference for pluralism over schism. By the 1860s bourgeois standards of decorum had penetrated into the Alsatian countryside. The auction of synagogue honors had largely disappeared, the religious initiation ceremony had been widely adopted, and quiet prayer had become, if only in theory, the desired mode of ritual conduct.[75]

Conclusion

Changes in the structural relationship between the Jews and the state deeply affected the role of religion in revolutionary France, and the role of religious leadership was radically altered as well. New developments within the French rabbinate also contributed significantly to the modernization of the Jewish religion. Although no sector of French Jewry, including the orthodox, remained unreconciled to emancipation, differences over religious issues split the rabbinic leadership into two main camps. The rift between progressive and conservative traditionalists revolved around the question of how to define the realm of religious authority. Progressive rabbis wanted to restrict the sphere of religious activity narrowly. In their view, not every question fell within the purview of Halakhah, and therefore fewer issues needed to be brought before halakhic authorities. For pragmatic reasons, they placed enormous faith in the authority of central institutions and preferred that reforms be sanctioned by a synod only, not by individual rabbis. The idea of hierarchy was crucial to this thinking, so that central decisions could be imposed on unreceptive outlying areas. Conservative traditionalists, on the other hand, preferred to widen the sphere of rabbinic authority to include issues not ordinarily under the rubric of religion, opposed the notion of hierarchy, and advocated a decentralized approach to decision making.[76] For lay reformers, progressive rabbis, and conservative traditionalists, emancipation continued to be an all-consuming project. Citizenship posed unremitting social, political, cultural, and religious challenges to French Jews of every stripe, as is evident in the range of conceptual and strategic views advanced by their leaders.

Chapter 9

Patrie et Religion: The Social and Religious Implications of Civic Equality

Even after nearly a half-century had elapsed since the Revolution of 1789, several fundamental questions concerning the compatibility of Judaism with citizenship remained unresolved. No longer was the issue whether ritual observance impeded the fulfillment of civic duties. Rather, an internal Jewish debate centered on how much of the legacy of traditional Judaism ought to be preserved in an age when social and cultural barriers were being dissolved. Certainly in northeastern France but elsewhere as well, Jewish life revolved around a distinct calendar, history, religious culture, and vision of messianic redemption. Could citizens, in good conscience, remain committed to the ethos of social separatism, cultural distinctiveness, and religious superiority that had characterized Judaism since its biblical beginnings? Would not the new status of citizenship demand significant changes in the way Jews related to the world around them, specifically to their non-Jewish neighbors? And should such changes be implemented, would the spiritual content and goals of Judaism still be recognizable? The issues were hardly new. As Voltaire had put it, the question was whether the Jews were willing to merge their identity in that of humanity. Or would the symbols of the Jewish past—*les symboles séparatistes*, in the words of Olry Terquem—continue to determine how Jews related to the world around them?

Political, legal, and social developments under the constitutional monarchy of Louis-Philippe in 1830 opened a new chapter in the history of France—one that was characterized by an intensification of the emancipation dynamic. During the 1830s when France became, in the words of Maurice Liber, "le foyer du libéralisme en Europe," extensive efforts to return to the ideals of 1789 were undertaken through a variety of government initiatives. In the case of the Jews, the new regime set in motion unprecedented opportunities for social integration and professional advancement that steadily became available in major urban centers. By mid-century, a secular, liberal philosophy had fostered an atmosphere of greater social acceptance enabling many to realize the promise that the Revolution had extended to them.[1]

The full legitimization of the Jewish religion was an important factor in the shaping of a new identity. Under the law of 8 February 1831, the last remaining example of inequity was remedied: members of the Jewish clergy were declared civil servants and thereby became eligible for state salaries. By funding clerical salaries and school budgets, the state assumed a share of the financial burden formerly borne by the Jewish community alone. The law gave the Jews of France a measure of confidence previously unknown. Community leaders forthrightly demanded equal support for Jewish educational establishments, basing their claims exclusively on the principle of *égalité*.[2] More important, perhaps, the law signaled a new stage in the full realization of the revolutionary ideal: the Jews and Judaism were recognized as an integral part of the socioreligious structure of France, having been placed on an equal footing alongside Catholicism and Protestantism.

In the estimation of contemporary observers, both Jewish and gentile, the law of 8 February 1831 signified the final step of emancipation. According to the 1843 report of the *préfet* of the Bas Rhin,

the real emancipation of the Jews does not date from the law that proclaimed their civil and political equality with Christians, but from that [law] by which the State recognized their religion and declared that its ministers would be salaried by the law . . . when the Jews saw their religion and its ministers placed under the protection of the State and treated equally with the Christian denominations, only then they began to believe in the extent of their civil and religious liberty. This belief lifted them in their own eyes, gave them self-assurance, and led them to divest themselves of this rampant humility, the result of their long oppression in their relations with their fellow citizens of other religions. Nor is the new law lacking in its effect on the Christian population, whom this legislative act taught to embrace a more positive equality, [with respect to those who] previously were the object of its contempt. Thus, a new era began for the Jews.[3]

The 1831 law was greeted with noticeable enthusiasm not only because it transformed the Jews' legal standing but because it appeared to contribute overwhelmingly to a positive self-image befitting their status as *citoyens*. Its legacy would outshine subsequent legal advances, such as the 1844 abrogation of the *more judaico*, which was viewed more as an embarrassment than a serious legal disability.[4] Out of gratitude to the new regime, Samuel Cahen dedicated his French translation of the Bible to the new king, Louis-Philippe, and Rabbi Lion-Mayer Lambert declared the law to be "the greatest act of justice in favor of the Jews since the destruction of the Second Temple."[5] Reactions to the Damascus Affair suggest, however, that the condition of French Jewry in the early 1840s was considerably more complex than the optimistic pronouncement of the *préfet*. The failure of the French government to act responsibly to quell the calamitous effects of the ritual murder accusation leveled against Damascus Jewry elicited among French Jews sentiments ranging from outrage and betrayal to political powerlessness. Overall, the French Jewish community was divided politically; its leadership was plagued by profound anxiety, uncertainty, and indecision.

The attainment of religious parity deepened the sense of loyalty that Jews felt toward the *patrie*. The legacy of the Revolution of 1789, enhanced during the 1830s, provided the theoretical underpinnings for the perception of French society as a single, unified family, and although this unity was never fully achieved, its mythic power captured the imagination of Jewish leaders. Their hope of joining in this undertaking was expressed by an allegiance to France that was to become the most central element—and ultimately the most irrepressible—in their new identity. Far more than simply a declaration of loyalty to the ruler and the state, devotion to the *patrie* was expressed by a growing identification with French society and culture, especially with the image of the Revolution that Jews inherited and transformed over the course of the century. As the ideals of 1789 were institutionalized and thus attained greater permanence, the myth of the Revolution grew stronger, constituting a critical element in French Jewry's ideology of emancipation.

Religious legitimization also strengthened their commitment to a wider range of societal and civic responsibilities than those normally subsumed under the revolutionary ideal of *fraternité*. In part, this was due to the rehabilitation of religion in French society and culture. Although the church was badly defeated by the Revolution, religion remained a vibrant societal force. Traditional Catholicism and Protestantism were strengthened by a religious revival in the nineteenth century, while the 1830s witnessed the birth of a liberal Catholicism. Inspired by the example of Lamennais, the latter sought to reconcile the church with modern liberty. Liberal Protestantism gained strength, as well, in the era of the July Monarchy, while Catholicism reasserted considerable influence in society over the next decades.[6]

Coinciding with advances in the political and legal standing of French Jewry was the coming of age of a new generation of Jewish intellectuals in the 1820s and 1830s. Virtually all had studied in traditional *hadarim* either in Alsace-Lorraine or in neighboring Germany and later attended French secondary schools and universities. Several were accomplished scholars whose professional achievements earned them entrée into the learned societies and intellectual circles of France. Once they turned their attention to the needs of the Jewish community, their efforts focused on improvements in Jewish education and rabbinic training and on making the case for moderate ritual reform. One vital concern was the socioeconomic transformation that the original bestowal of citizenship had presupposed. However, a second and ultimately more important objective concerned the growing indifference to traditional religious observance, as reflected in decreasing synagogue attendance, especially in urban centers. In light of the challenge posed by the almost limitless opportunities for social interaction and cultural exchange with non-Jews, they endeavored to develop expressions of Jewish identity that were faithful to the competing claims of revolution and tradition. The appearance of a new journal in Strasbourg, *La*

Régénération, in 1836–37, heralded the first sustained effort to probe the social and religious significance of emancipation. *Régénération*, and the corresponding *Wiedergeburt* (the German title of the bilingual journal), signified the rebirth—or restoration—of the original essence that Judaism had lost. As understood by contributors to the journal, *régénération* signified the forging of a traditional Jewish identity that did not shrink from the full implications of the revolutionary legacy. Ultimately, the goal was *fusion civile* as distinct from the more radical *fusion sociale* that Terquem had championed.[7] These were the origins of *le movement régénérateur*.[8]

The extreme nature of the proposals that Terquem published in his *Lettres Tsarphatiques* encouraged moderates to explore the meaning of emancipation and to articulate an alternative vision of its religious implications. First, the *régénérateurs* emphatically rejected Terquem's diagnosis of the problems facing French Jews, as well as his proposed solutions, as "dangerous and useless." According to Michel Berr, the *Lettres Tsarphartiques* generally sought to erase an "essential and radical demarcation that must exist between Judaism and Christianity."[9] Albert Cohn disputed Terquem's rationale for transferring the Sabbath to Sunday, arguing that Sunday was not the "national day of rest," as it had never been consecrated by the French nation and therefore enjoyed no national significance. By observing the Sabbath on Sunday, he cautioned, Jews would take a step closer to Christianity, not to the *patrie*, and would thereby deny the historic validity of Mosaism. Salomon Munk warned further that if implemented, the Sabbath proposal would be the ultimate death knell of the Jewish religion. Samuel Cahen attacked Terquem for ridiculing Jews and Judaism in public instead of bringing his proposals directly to the attention of the Jewish communal leadership.[10]

These differences emerged dramatically in an exchange between Terquem and Munk not long after news of the ritual murder accusation in Damascus had reached Paris, early in 1840.[11] Terquem had written that the *Shefokh Hamatkha* prayer intoned at the Passover Seder was a vengeful call for divine punishment against Christians. This, he insisted, typified a dark, anti-Christian tendency in Judaism, and he therefore urged that the text be removed from the Haggadah. In response, Munk established the historical origins of the prayer, defending it as an appeal for divine protection against the murderous Crusaders. But then he launched into a strongly worded invective, insisting that in light of the events of 1840, if France was not prepared to stand behind the Jews, "then we declare to the Christians: 'Take back what you have given us; you only repaid a sacred debt, but it was torn from you in a moment of revolutionary fever, and you have not yet reached that level of humanity that alone would enable you to view all men as brothers. Take it all back, but leave us our honor, and do not profane the dignity of our faith with your blasphemy and calumnies.'" Terquem countered by attacking Munk's readiness "to sell our *émancipation française* very cheaply." *Shefokh Ḥamatkha*, he argued, could not be viewed as "an inoffensive prayer." In nineteenth-century France, *all* such prayers were "abominations." In Terquem's view, Munk was urging the retention of symbols of separation (*symboles séparatistes*) that could never be reconciled with the status of citizenship.[12]

The *régénérateurs* vigorously rejected the social implications of Terquem's proposals. Their common assumption—that the religious distinctiveness of Judaism demanded the preservation of traditional rituals—rested in part on the realization that French society and culture were not religiously neutral but bore clear traces of Christian influence. Cohn, for one, therefore emphatically opposed the idea of substituting one form of nationalism (French) for another (Jewish). At the same time, sharp criticism of Terquem's radical ideas went hand in hand with the acknowledgment that moderate ritual changes were absolutely essential. They contrasted the dangerous implications in Terquem's system to the advantages of gradual, balanced change—a process that would lend strength to the foundations of religion and faith. They argued that ritual changes could be realized through cooperation with traditional Jewish institutions such as the Central Consistory and the rabbinate.[13] In the end, although they categorically rejected the social and ideological underpinnings of Terquem's program, moderate proponents of *régénération* nonetheless adopted several of Terquem's specific proposals for reform, including the regulation of circumcision, liturgical reform, alternatives to traditional worship, improvement of rabbinic training, and decentralization.[14]

This radical resolution of the Jews' cultural predicament *à la* Terquem and even the more moderate efforts of the *régénérateurs* collided with the traditionalism that persisted not only in the northeast provinces but even in urban areas where Jews lived in concentrated numbers. The continued commitment to traditional observance, even a half-century after the bestowal of citizenship, was a powerful force that could not be dismissed by proponents of religious modernization. Images of daily life that fill Daniel Stauben's *Scènes de la vie juive en Alsace* and Léon Cahun's *La vie juive* depict a traditional lifestyle that bore remarkable similarity to the religious steadfastness of the *ancien régime*. Members of the close-knit communities of the predominantly rural countryside continued to speak Alsatian Yiddish, attended synagogue regularly, called their children by their Jewish names, and structured their lives around the Jewish calendar. The observance of popular religious customs, especially relating to birth, marriage, and death, remained a vital part of the social and cultural fabric. As in the pre-revolutionary era, traditional confraternities (*ḥevrot*) were founded to visit the sick, bury the dead, offer loans, and assist poor brides. By serving crucial social and religious needs, they were the lynchpin of community cohesiveness and solidarity.[15] These religious commitments certainly did not remain untouched by the momentous transformations since 1789. Many,

especially in urban areas, became indifferent to Judaism, some because
they became preoccupied with professional advancement, others focused
on the material well-being of their families, and still others rejected Judaism as a philosophically outmoded religion. But there is no denying the
continuing role of the religious tradition as the keystone of group consciousness, especially as the process of religious modernization unfolded.
For all its weaknesses, the consistory system contributed organizationally
and symbolically to the sense of solidarity that persisted among French Jews
throughout the century.

Much as reformers began to rethink the role of Jewish tradition, it had
become quite obvious that the religious traditionalism of their coreligionists could hardly be ignored. For the vast majority of French Jews, the encounter with the trauma of emancipation occurred several decades *after* the
bestowal of civic equality. Samuel Cahen explained that the Revolution
caught French Jewry unprepared for the challenges it was about to face: "It
is recognized that liberty came as a surprise to our fathers who were not at
all prepared. . . . The epoch was hardly favorable for indispensable melio-
rations, for *émancipation intérieure*. . . . One was a Frenchman of the revolution and a Jew of the Middle Ages."[16] The timing of emancipation relative
to the state of socioeconomic and cultural modernization was, according to
Cahen, a determining factor in the way that French Jews responded. In the
case of Alsace-Lorraine, particularly the rural districts, the early bestowal of
citizenship may have ironically impeded the progress of cultural and religious regeneration.[17]

The important role of timing accounts for many of the crucial differences in the experiences of modern French and German Jewries. Owing to
the emigration of numerous *maskilim* and rabbis to Germany, including
French-occupied Mayence, during the latter Napoleonic years, no modernizing elite within the ranks of the Jewish community emerged until the
1820s and early 1830s. Furthermore, the disruptive effects of the post-
revolutionary era commanded the attention and energies of leaders upon
whom the work of creating urgently needed communal institutions was
thrust. By the time reformers were prepared to take up the issues that German Jewry had addressed decades before, the prospects for reform were already quite limited. In addition to the fact that there was so little
support—either popular or rabbinic—for ritual reforms, the comprehensive, highly structured nature of the Jewish community imposed constraints
on the dimensions of change, thus precluding the implementation of a
radical religious reform program. The same was true of education. Modern
schools and other institutions that might have become the training ground
for more radical activity were established very late, *after* the rabbinate had
emerged as a power in community affairs and assumed control of Jewish
education.

Rabbinic involvement in Jewish schooling points to a larger development, that is, a reconfiguration of community leadership in the nineteenth century. The reemergence of the rabbinate as a dynamic force in communal affairs alongside the lay elite was a conspicuous turnabout from its decline in the last decades before 1789. With the establishment of the consistorial system, the rabbinate attained an official status that surpassed its standing in the *ancien régime* when its authority was subordinated to that of the *kehillah* lay leadership. As an institution, the rabbinate was rehabilitated, and although rabbinic authority was no longer protected by community controls as before, rabbis emerged as the foremost leaders wherever Jewish life continued to be organized around the synagogue. Rabbis were now formally included in the decision-making process, and they provided vital leadership in the establishment and direction of modern schools, in the central rabbinical facility, in publishing, and in the organization of vocational societies and training.[18] Predictably, the traditionally observant rank and file—and, for the most part, even consistorial lay leaders—showed considerable respect for rabbinic authority. In Paris, by contrast, secularization, anticlericalism, and upward social mobility produced a growing indifference to religious observance and impassivity toward the religious leaders. Nevertheless, in the French capital and in other large cities, rabbinic prestige plainly benefited from the enhanced symbolic role of religion in French public life and from the religious parity that Judaism officially enjoyed with Catholicism and Protestantism. Rabbis were commonly preferred over lay consistory leaders to represent the community at public events and were uniquely entrusted with the important mission of teaching the ideals of patriotism in accordance with the Sanhedrin decisions.[19]

Three Perspectives on the Religious Implications of Emancipation

The chasm separating the moderate program of the *régénérateurs* from the radical vision articulated by Terquem underscores the defining issue dividing mainstream and nonmainstream French Judaism. Ultimately, the difference came down to the question whether the Jews would continue to live as a separate community with a distinct social and cultural identity. Within the Jewish community there were three distinct strategies on how to ensure the continued viability of Judaism in post-revolutionary France. These represented major differences of opinion on the religious implications of emancipation: (1) "separatist Judaism"; (2) "republican Judaism"; and (3) "spiritual-republican Judaism." These positions were developed clearly in three representative catechisms composed for Jewish schoolchildren in the span of twenty-five years.[20]

In the *Catéchisme du culte judaïque*, published in Metz in 1818 by Rabbi Lion-Mayer Lambert, Jewish ritual was portrayed as a haven from the onslaught of modernity and French culture. In his description of the signifi-

cance of Sabbath observance, for example, Lambert stressed the importance of spiritual reflection while sitting in one's home. The power of the
Sabbath rested in its creation of a private domain that was protected from
the harmful influences of the surrounding society. Lambert's attitude toward French society was distrustful, hardly typical of the enthusiasm expressed ten years earlier at the Paris Sanhedrin. In characterizing Judaism's
attitude toward non-Jews, Lambert also retreated from the Sanhedrin. His
admonitory instructions against mistreating non-Jews were based on the
Torah's proscription against desecrating the name of God (*ḥillul Hashem*),
not on its moral impropriety. Moreover, Lambert did not include a discussion of the duties that each person owed the state and its citizens in his text.
In fact, in the entire catechism there was no mention of France, the Revolution, citizenship, the Paris Sanhedrin, or the state, evidently because
these were outside the religious sphere. Lambert viewed separation from
French society and culture as a necessary condition for the continued viability of the Jewish community, especially in an era when many of the barriers separating the Jews from French society had begun to give way.[21]

Sharply at variance with the separatist perspective was a "republican Judaism" that identified closely with the state and the French nation. Its clear-
est exposition was Samuel Cahen's *Précis élémentaire d'instruction religieuse et
morale pour les jeunes français israélites*. Published in Paris in 1820, the Cahen
catechism underscored "the religious obligation to fulfill common duties
to the state: to serve and to defend France, to make all the necessary sacrifices, whether drawn from our possessions or from ourselves, in order to as-
sure the success of this land." As in the catechism authored in the same
year by Elie Halévy of Metz, *Instruction religieuse et morale à l'usage de la jeunesse israélite*, emphasis was placed both on privileging duties to the state
over personal interests and on the universalist interpretation of biblical
texts. The word *neighbor* (Lev. 19:18) was understood to refer unconditionally to all humans, and *brother* (Deut. 23:20) included "all men who recognize God." In these respects, the republican catechisms drew heavily on the
central doctrines of the Paris Sanhedrin. Accordingly, there was no distinction between Jew and non-Jew in the performance of ethical duties and
no difference with respect to lending money on interest, as the Halévy catechism stated: "Thus a Jew of today cannot, without both transgressing the
law of God and offending justice and humanity, allow himself to engage in
this illicit commerce with individuals whose religious opinions, it is true,
differ from his, but who are no less strict observers of these great principles,
foundations of all . . . civilized peoples."[22]

A variation on the republican model is exemplified by a catechism published in 1843 by R. Salomon Ulmann, then of Nancy, titled *Recueil d'instructions morales et religieuses à l'usage des jeunes israélites français*. In the
Ulmann text the universal dimension of Judaism emerged as the central
chord in the overall presentation, but in a manner distinct from the stan-

dard republican texts. Although the distinctive aspects of the Jewish religion and the particularity of Israel were assigned more limited attention than in the Lambert catechism, all of Ulmann's formulations were grounded in biblical and rabbinic sources. His discussion of the Israelite prophets stressed their universal message and function, while the Jewish messianic idea was viewed almost exclusively in terms of its universal-humanistic implications. The messianic era was described as the reign of truth and justice, as the triumph of the belief in the unity of God, and as the ultimate solution to the ravages of hatred and war upon humanity. The chosenness of Israel and its destiny were defined in accordance with its readiness to safeguard the knowledge of God, to embody it in their way of life, and to teach it to humanity. Ulmann's catechism, like most others—though the Lambert text did not—included the Decalogue as the premier example of universal law.[23]

Ulmann classified the duties pertaining to divine worship into two categories—internal and external ritual. This categorization was a clear departure from the usual distinction between duties to one's fellow and duties to God, and may well have been intended as an alternative to the disproportionate emphasis that liberals had placed on the ethical commandments. According to Ulmann's schema, the function of internal rituals was to direct the thoughts and emotions of man toward God, to believe in him, and to attain knowledge of divine perfection and of the Torah. These rituals, which naturally exuded "religious sentiments," were central in the hierarchy of religious values. The external ritual was made up of the more physical commandments—those pertaining to the body, to prayer, and to the observance of sacred festivals. In contrast to the clear tendency within republican Judaism to view the festivals as paradigms of the Revolution and of emancipation, Ulmann emphasized the simple meaning of these observances, that is, the straightforward details of ritual ceremonies and their ethical-moral dimension. Civic duties also figured prominently in the Ulmann system. Like the *régénérateurs*, he stressed the importance of integrating the fate of the Jews with the common destiny of France. However, despite obvious similarities with the republican catechisms, the Ulmann textbook placed greater emphasis on personal piety than on civic duties. Consequently, its reliance on the decisions of the Paris Sanhedrin was comparatively modest. But the most significant indication of divergence from the republican model was the effort to ground his universalist approach firmly in the religious realm, not in the political. Universalism, according to Ulmann, derived from an appreciation for the particularistic meaning of religious rites. The traditional observance of *mitzvot* was the central act of devotion in Judaism, but it was the universal perspective that informed the character of each and every *mitzvah*.[24]

Each of the foregoing perspectives was an archetypical interpretation of the significance of the Revolution and of emancipation. Rabbis Lambert and Ulmann were on opposite ends of the orthodox spectrum, as their attitudes toward religious reform amply revealed.[25] Relying exclusively on traditional sources, Lambert stressed the religious importance of detachment from French society, fearing that integration would lead to the attenuation of traditional Jewish loyalties. Ulmann's universalist vision was built on the Mendelssohnian avowal that Judaism was one of several legitimate religions. Nevertheless, his endorsement of social and cultural integration was largely theoretical, insofar as he feared the potentially harmful effects of excessive religious identification with the state, which could result in the political eclipse of the spiritual. The model of republican Judaism offered by Cahen and his fellow *régénérateurs* corresponded most closely to the image of the Revolution as a religiously transformative force. Over the course of the century, "republican Judaism" gained the enthusiastic endorsement of leading French rabbis, such as Zadoc Kahn and Lazare Wogue, and emerged as the dominant ethos of religious modernization.[26]

Religious Modernization

Efforts to adapt Jewish ritual to the changing status of nineteenth-century French Jewry assumed several discrete forms. The best-known—ritual reform—had emerged as a major issue, and clearly a divisive one, in the 1820s. It was linked, at the outset, to the long history of contempt and derision leveled at the role of ritual in promoting the social estrangement of the Jews. Beginning in the seventeenth century, theologians, ideologues, and intellectuals—critics and supporters alike—discussed, debated, and repeatedly disparaged the ritual character of Judaism. At issue was whether strict adherence to the Jewish ritual tradition precluded participation in public life, either because of its moral deficiencies or because it was fundamentally incompatible with the fulfillment of the duties of citizenship. Initially, the debate within the Jewish community related, inexorably, to the question of the compatibility of traditional Judaism with the fulfillment of broadly defined civic duties. In time, as the movement on behalf of religious reform matured, the debate focused more on developing strategies to forestall the growing attenuation of Jewish loyalties and, specifically, alienation from the synagogue.

Related to ritual reform was a second expression of religious modernization that entailed the creative reinterpretation of existing rituals and the formation of new ones. Corresponding to the dramatic changes in the social and political status of French Jewry, this innovative approach exuded a passionate identification with French society, a growing involvement in political life, and a positive self-image that had developed in the 1830s and 1840s. Self-confidently, rabbis and intellectuals succeeded in articulating an identity that was emphatically Jewish, one that ran parallel to the distinctively Jewish agenda formulated by modern scholars. Even so, beyond the usual signs of anxiety that many within the ranks of the Jewish communal leadership could sense, there was an acute awareness of the tensions related to the increasingly public profile of Judaism after 1830. Indications of sensitivity concerning the general court of public opinion, as well as signs of uneasiness about the pressures of cultural and religious transparency, would henceforth remain a part of the Jewish psyche in the modern era. Nevertheless, the dominant attitude was hopeful and optimistic.

On the theoretical plane, *régénération* qua religious revitalization placed special emphasis on the teleological role of ritual practices. The goal—to attain lofty spiritual ideals by appealing to the heart and other senses and to guard against the mechanical performance of religious rituals—was articulated in a wide range of writings, especially Jewish educational textbooks.[27] At the center of the ideology of *régénération* was the claim that during "centuries of darkness" and persecution Judaism had degenerated, acquiring foreign elements that obscured its "grand principles." Through "an invincible attachment to minutiae," wrote Gerson-Lévy, "we became enslaved to ritual practices that for us no longer make any sense. Of the ancient Egyptians it is said that to them everything was god except God Himself. One can say the same of our degenerated cult where everything is religion except religion itself."[28] While conceding that the "whole body had become gangrenous," Gerson-Lévy called for aggressive action to forestall the demoralization that threatened the religion that generations "had consecrated with precious blood."[29]

The remedy, the *régénérateurs* argued, required the reversal of the historical process responsible for the degeneration of the Jewish religion. Regenerative programs of various sorts aimed to restore a corrupted Judaism to its original state; however, *régénération* signified more than a restorative objective.[30] It also denoted the conviction that human history progresses steadily, forming a continuous movement toward a future far superior to the present or the past. Progress, in the words of Madame de Staël, was the undisputed law of history. It rested on Vico's vision of an ascending spiral, and it drew on the philosophical ideas of Condorcet, Kant, and Comte. Further, it strengthened the belief that human perfection was within reach and that it could be achieved through universal enlightenment and rational education.[31] For Jewish proponents of *régénération*, progress involved both a return to an idealized past and the accommodation of religious rituals to the demands of contemporary civilization. Such thinking not only strengthened efforts of reformers to eliminate rites that had developed in response to persecution.[32] It also provided a foundation for the innovative-interpretive perspective on ritual.

In a number of respects, the city was uniquely fertile ground for the development of this new approach. In the years of the July Monarchy, Jews were drawn in ever larger numbers to the urban centers of France, to such cities as Paris, Bordeaux, St. Esprit-Bayonne, Strasbourg, and Marseille. Individuals of various ethnic, religious, and social backgrounds and origins were attracted to the cultural, intellectual, economic, and political advantages of urban life, particularly to the public arena. In a most basic sense, this signified a dramatic departure from the social segregation that dominated the residential patterns of the *ancien régime* and early decades of the nineteenth century. Culturally, it presented new challenges as to how Jews would represent themselves to their non-Jewish neighbors with whom they shared the public space. This was not an unprecedented challenge, however, as is evident in the communal legislation of the pre-revolutionary era. The *takkanot* enacted by the Metz *kehillah* in the late seventeenth and eighteenth centuries aimed to regulate the Jews' public behavior precisely because of the new social opportunities created by economic prosperity. Communal legislation differentiated clearly between acceptable and unacceptable behavior in the public and private spheres. However, from the 1830s onward, religious and ethnic origins were no longer the foremost defining characteristic that would be noticed by others. Invariably, the erosion of traditional ritual observance often accompanied the move to the city, though the decision to leave the village was usually made in response to the waning of religious commitment.[33] The "public sphere" nonetheless implied that persons of diverse loyalties and interests could set aside their differences in order to affirm common goals and ideals.

The cultural significance of the public sphere can be discerned in ceremonies designed to meet the challenges of unprecedented social inclusiveness and religious legitimacy. One such ceremony, the *initiation religieuse*, was conducted for boys and girls who had passed examinations in Hebrew reading and mastery of the catechism. Performed in the presence of municipal leaders, members of the local public school committee, and special dignitaries, the *initiation religieuse* represented a public display of the new Franco-Jewish spirit. Two salient themes are recognizable in the initiation ceremony. First was the implicit need to offer continuing evidence of socioeconomic *régénération*. This was the thrust of a ceremony conducted in Thann (Haut-Rhin) in 1844, for example. Held in the local synagogue, it was attended by heads of the municipal administration, members of the local Comité d'Instruction Primaire, various "enlightened" persons, and strangers to the Jewish community. The local newspaper was impressed and pleased that in the Jewish schools there was no lack of effort to inspire students with love of the *patrie*.[34] A similar objective was evident in annual ceremonies marking the *distribution des prix* at Jewish elementary schools. There, too, the purpose was to impress the gathering, composed of representatives of the municipality, clergy, and local dignitaries, with the Jewish community's progress toward social and economic regeneration.

A second underlying objective was to exploit the *initiation religieuse* as a public showpiece in order to highlight the achievements of religious reform and the prospects for future innovation. The *Archives israélites* viewed the ceremony as a means, if only symbolic, to redress the deficiencies in traditional Jewish ritual and gender inequality. Describing the ceremony held at the Paris temple in 1844, the journal spoke of the "great effect" of the organ in a temple like that of Paris. It also emphasized the need for uniformity of customs in synagogues, a concern that R. Ulmann had voiced in the same years.[35] The *régénérateurs* viewed the *initiation religieuse* as a paradigm of ritual reform, as it included virtually all the reformist elements that proponents of reform had advocated but rarely achieved: a dignified service, equality for girls, choral singing to the accompaniment of an organ, and a sacred declaration of patriotic loyalty and love for the king and the royal family. Lay reformers and consistory activists were in the forefront of efforts to implement the *initiation religieuse*, but progressive rabbis were centrally involved in designing the program and in officiating at the popular ceremony. By the mid-1840s the ceremony was routinely conducted in most communities, and it was finally adopted by the rabbis of Metz and Colmar—the two outspoken opponents of religious reform—with certain modifications in the early 1850s.[36] The *Archives* emphasized that the ceremony was necessary because of disappointment with the traditional bar mitzvah ceremony and because of the need to train women to take an active part in the public rituals of the synagogue.

The new synagogue was the arena where the integration of *patrie et religion* was represented perhaps most effectively. Magnificent, large synagogues were built to accommodate the ever-increasing urban population and to establish a public presence, in some cases capable of seating thousands of worshippers. At the synagogue on Rue Victoire, which opened in 1875, the ushers wore hats with the tricolor emblem of the Revolution and rabbis wore clerical robes, similar to Protestant ministers and Catholic priests.[37] Like the ceremonies marking the *initiation religieuse* and the distribution of school prizes, the dedication of new synagogues offered opportunities for the Jewish community to celebrate important religious and civic occasions in the public sphere. At these carefully orchestrated public events, attended by Christian clergy, local town officials, and townspeople, Jewish leaders were able to enhance the image of Judaism. But such ceremonies also enabled Jews to define a broader urban community, and they located themselves at its center. The role of the rabbi in representing the community to the general public was crucial, as was the task of translating the particulars of Jewish religious culture into a universal idiom that was intelligible to varied sectors of the local population.

Critical to these efforts were communal leaders' repeated attempts to persuade rabbis to preach in French. Dating from the period of the Paris Sanhedrin, this demand was consistently ignored because of the popular preference for Yiddish. Consistorial leaders and proponents of *régénération* proposed a new argument, however: only the French-speaking rabbi would be able to represent Judaism appropriately to the larger, Christian society.

Many within the Jewish community looked to the rabbi to perform public religious functions and to fulfill, ceremonially, certain duties in his capacity as representative of Judaism vis-à-vis the non-Jewish community. Referring to the inauguration ceremony of the synagogue in Château-Salins in 1844, the local Nancy newspaper, the *Impartial*, reported on the sermon pronounced there by R. Salomon Ulmann: "This dignified priest spoke for an hour with such profound appropriateness, with such simplicity, modesty and distinction. . . . It is impossible to speak with greater nobility of the divine majesty, and with more charm of genuine *piété*, tolerance and especially of charity that . . . protects against selfish opulence."[38] The reaction of the newspaper implies the emergence of general agreement on moral issues, an accord that included Christians and Jews, and to which R. Ulmann succeeded in giving voice. From the standpoint of the Jewish community, it was extremely important that the rabbi interpret the meaning of Judaism for all citizens of the regime. Out of this emerged a broad consensus that the goal of social integration was to be realized not by ignoring religion but by approaching it as a corpus of values and ideals that were part of the national heritage.

That the *Impartial* took special pride in the role played by Catholics in these developments confirms, at least to a degree, the aforementioned view of the *préfet* of the Bas-Rhin concerning the positive effect of the 1831 law on the Christian population. The newspaper reported that "the Catholic population encouraged the free development of a religion that had suffered so much persecution, and which now flourishes alongside the Christian religions, under tolerance and liberty, which are the most precious conquests of the century." In its estimation, relations between Catholics and Jews had changed dramatically: "This ceremony ended by leaving vivid impressions and a positive sentiment in all hearts. The time has passed when Catholics go to the synagogue to laugh. Dignity has returned to the temple of Solomon with the civil emancipation of the Jews. They must comprehend all of the advances of French society on their behalf, and elevate their coreligionists of the inferior classes to the eminence of the title of *citoyen français*!"[39] But what might seem to be a very encouraging assessment of the Jewish condition appears considerably less enthusiastic on closer examination. First, the newspaper reminded its readers that not long ago, the synagogue had been an object of ridicule, but it did not state that such derision would be out of place, should conditions warrant it. Second, the report concluded with the patronizing caveat that the Jews ought to be cognizant of—and presumably grateful for—all that had been done for them, and that they must undertake the regeneration of those of a lower socioeconomic status so that they will be worthy of the "title" citizens. Though citizenship presumably derived from universal human rights, it belonged, in actuality, only to those who were deserving.

Of the main perspectives on emancipation, "republican Judaism" enjoyed the greatest popular appeal among French Jews. For the overwhelming majority, France's overall commitment to the ideals of the Revolution was the cornerstone of their newfound faith. Lay and rabbinic leaders viewed the Revolution as having heralded the messianic era, undoubtedly enabling them to play down periodic incidents of anti-Jewish hostility and to remain committed to the belief that the Revolution had laid the foundation for new relations between Jews and gentiles.[40] This perception was anchored in the view that the Revolution had opened a new era of promise with its bestowal of civic equality and was sustained by a firm faith in the reign of law. Typically, the Revolution was portrayed as having radically altered the destiny of French Jews by putting an end to persecution, discrimination, and intolerance. In the words of Samuel Cahen, it was the final rupture of a Jewish past comprised of "cette longue chaîne de persecutions, qui commence par la destruction du temple de Jerusalem et qui finit pour la France en '89."[41] Nevertheless, the numerous setbacks suffered during the Reign of Terror, throughout the 1790s and under Napoleon, are largely absent from the nineteenth-century Jewish collective memory. For Jews, as for most other Frenchmen, the inflated image of the Revolution went hand in hand with sentiments of profound patriotic loyalty that were, in turn, reinforced by the standardization of administration and law. Both as a framework for collective actions and consciousness and as a symbol of unity, the state, particularly through its educational system, played a pivotal role in the shaping of a collective identity for its citizens.[42] For many, France emerged as a latter-day Zion where the traditional messianic belief would be first realized.[43]

Foremost among lay and rabbinic efforts to reinterpret the rituals of Judaism was the tendency to retreat from the messianic meaning of traditional festivals. Holidays such as Passover, Hanukkah, and Tisha b'Av marked events that appeared out of step with the recent history of French Jews. However, instead of urging reform, the *régénérateurs* typically retained the traditional framework of the ritual, including the liturgical symbols, but modified their conceptual underpinnings. Samuel Cahen asserted that the declaration pronounced at the end of the Passover seder, "Next Year in Jerusalem," could no longer represent to emancipated French Jewry what it had once meant in times of oppression. "We are not speaking of an actual restoration," he explained. "It is a pipe dream of ailing minds; the times do not move backwards." He therefore interpreted the phrase in symbolic terms rather than as an indication of future aspirations.[44] Michel Berr construed prayers for the return to Zion in the broad sense of universalist strivings for human perfection. He recommended prayers for deliverance from evil, sin, and passion—as opposed to ritual remembering—as the principal mode of observance of Passover. It was only by dint of upright behavior that Jews could hope to merit deliverance from oppression and servitude and expect to see their coreligionists abroad come to enjoy the benefits of justice.[45] Ultimately, virtuous conduct itself was deemed to be re-demptive.

The biblical theme of freedom from servitude was integrated with the re-cent experiences of French Jewry and their less fortunate coreligionists elsewhere. However, it is important to note that the process worked in the other direction as well. Toward the end of the century, at the one hun-dredth anniversary of the Revolution, R. Zadoc Kahn of Nîmes could refer to the French Revolution as "our flight from Egypt . . . our modern Passover."[46] In this instance, the present (Revolution) was validated in bib-lical terms. Simon Bloch, in *La foi d'Israël*, similarly blurred the line sepa-rating past and present. He described the history of the Exodus in thorough detail, and then proceeded to enlist Passover as a historical par-adigm in order to shed light on the condition of Jews of his own day. What is most telling, however, is that when presenting his account of biblical his-tory, he employed the language of *liberté*, *émancipation*, and *la régénération spirituelle*, which resonated with the contemporary period.[47]

Both Tisha b'Av, the traditional day of mourning for the destruction of the Temple in Jerusalem, and Hanukkah, the festival marking the rededi-cation of the Temple in the second century B.C.E., also assumed a contem-porary focus. According to Michel Berr, the observance of Tisha b'Av ought to mirror "our obligations, our beliefs, and our present hopes." Its ultimate meaning could be grasped only by placing the day within a contemporary framework. This would require the subordination of the details of its his-tory to the transcendent issues of the present day. With respect to Hanukkah, R. Lazare Wogue shifted the emphasis from a festival of na-tional liberation to a holiday commemorating the restoration of the dignity of religious ritual. This is a clear example of the retreat from the messianic significance of the holidays, especially their restorative purpose. Although there are indications that Wogue subscribed to the universalization of the messianic idea, he did not go so far as to identify emancipation with the messianic era, which was the dividing line between rabbis and *régénérateurs*, but he did see it as a stage leading in that direction.[48] Rituals, generally, gave expression to the great changes that had taken place in recent history.

In contrast with the *ancien régime*, when rituals were formative elements of people's worldviews, from 1789, the Jewish self-image was powerfully transformed by the promise of full civic equality and the concomitant de-mand that Jews undergo transformation. Nineteenth-century ritual and the debates surrounding ritual reform signaled changes in the way that Jews re-lated to the state, French society, and French culture. Throughout the nineteenth century, ritual assumed more of a performative function that dramatized the epoch-making changes of the day.[49] Though undeniably expressive of how Jews defined their identity, especially in the public space of the French city, the newer rituals were mainly reflections of the life that was shaped so completely by the powerful forces of revolution.

The aggregate effect of these forces was the fashioning of an identity that was essentially autochthonous. The progressive break with a longstanding tradition linking the Jews of Alsace-Lorraine culturally, socially, and economically with territories to the east had already been set in motion by the Revolution and explains the tendency of French Jews to respond to challenges that were endemic to France, if not entirely unique. Their responses in the realm of religious ideology, intellectual pursuits, attitudes toward general culture, and their conception of Jewish responsibility set them apart from Jewish communities abroad. Pride in the political successes of France further enhanced their Jewish cultural distinctiveness, at least in the eyes of Jewish leaders who tended to measure the progress of their coreligionists against the condition of Jews elsewhere. Widespread experience as either émigrés or, in the case of Salomon Munk, as newcomers to France facilitated this comparison. Contrasting the ease with which he found work in France to the difficulties he had encountered in Germany, Munk reported to his brother-in-law that "in France, religion does not make the least difference"; to his mother Munk repeated his delight that religion played a minimal role outside of the church and synagogue.[50] Perhaps overzealous in their praise, Munk's remarks typify a tendency among the leadership of French Jewry to exaggerate the positive while understating the negative.

The fundamental relationship between civic equality and patriotic devotion had important cultural implications as well. More than simply a display of gratitude for the opportunities extended to the Jewish population, allegiance to the *patrie* was an expression of cultural affinity and aspiration. In the view of Jewish intellectuals, the fact that German Jewry was still denied the full rights of citizenship was an insurmountable obstacle to the creation of a genuine bond to the national culture. Culture and politics were, in the estimation of French Jews, inseparable.[51] Echoing the view of François Guizot and others, French Jews were united in their belief that France was the most spiritual and the most advanced of all civilizations.[52] This conviction, rooted in the mythology of the Revolution, enabled Jewish leaders of diverse orientations to embrace French society and culture without fear of publicly betraying their own Jewish values. For proponents of moderate ritual reform, France's intellectual and cultural advances validated their own liberal agenda. Conservatives were equally convinced that their position on religious issues rested firmly on the cultural legacy of the Revolution. Divisions were ultimately overshadowed by the formation of a broad consensus concerning the symbiosis of Judaism and French civilization: it was a sacred mission entrusted to the first Jewish population to have been molded by the ideals of 1789. Efforts to purify ritual observance, that is, to instill morality and virtue, were identified with the republican legacy and the *mission civilisatrice* that Jews shared with their fellow Frenchmen.[53]

French Jewry saw itself as a symbol of the liberal principles of the Revolution, both with respect to Jewish communities abroad and to general French society. The coherence of this orientation was sustained by the continued use of the term *régénération* throughout most of the nineteenth century, providing a semantic as well as thematic link to the Revolution. By mid-century the development of an attitude of superiority toward Jews in other countries was reflected in a rather striking reinterpretation of *régénération*.[54] Formerly viewed as a process through which the Jews of France were to be transformed into upstanding and productive citizens, *régénération* was now viewed as a program that French Jews would actively administer themselves. The reinterpretation of *régénération* reflected the changes in the way that French Jews viewed their role in the process of emancipation. In the minds of several mid-century rabbinic leaders, *régénération* was understood to be an expression of cultural and religious rebirth.[55] Furthermore, it signified the drive to forge bonds with Jewish communities beyond the borders of France. This trend was first evident during the July Monarchy, when French Jews felt sufficiently secure to protest the plight of Jews in Poland, Syria, and Switzerland.[56] More concretely, attention was subsequently directed at Algeria, the Near East, and the Ottoman Empire in the hope of bringing the blessings of the Revolution to their less fortunate coreligionists. Spearheaded by Baron James de Rothschild and his almoner, Albert Cohn, the general concern for these other communities was fully consistent with the sense of responsibility that French Jewry understood to be central to its ideology of emancipation. In articulating the goals of the Alliance Israélite Universelle, Adolphe Crémieux asserted that the *régénération* of the Jews was most urgently needed in far-flung areas amid populations "so distant from our present civilization, where Jews still live under the intolerable pressure of prejudice."[57] French Jews felt obliged to set an example for their coreligionists abroad, generally through their fulfillment of civic duties and specifically through their own successful *régénération*.[58] In short, *régénération* had become an international imperative.

But it was in their attitude toward French society that Jews across the religious and political spectrum displayed a truly revolutionary change in their thinking. This new direction had its roots in an interpretive tradition that identified the ideals of Judaism with those of the French Revolution. Revolutionary ideologues chose the "Tablets of the Law" to denote law and justice, and this symbol of Judaism was used to frame the Declaration of the Rights of Man and of the Citizen. The iconic representation of the Decalogue draped the revolutionary ideals in a "mantle of the sacred." During the Bourbon Restoration, Joseph Salvador argued that the Sinaitic revelation ought to serve as an example to modern France, claiming that Mosaic institutions were permeated with the principles of the Revolution. The Jewish nation, for its part, was destined to serve humanity as a model of justice, equity, and reason. By mid-century, French rabbis had also begun to endorse the parallel between the Revolution and Mount Sinai, and between the emancipation and the exodus from Egypt. Referring to the flag of the republic, Rabbi Arnauld Aron of Strasbourg declared that "the sacred banner that the Eternal One entrusted to Moses . . . is the symbol of the rights of humanity which our prophets courageously proclaimed," and before the end of the century others, such as James Darmsteter, would energetically argue that the Revolution was the fulfillment of the Judaic ideals of justice and progress.[59]

Even more remarkably, perhaps, the case was made for the centrality of Jewish ideals to modern France. Over the course of a half-century, the former objects of regenerative efforts came to view themselves as now bearing immense responsibility for the reformation of society at large. Thus, after discussing certain liturgical modifications that might be introduced in the synagogue on national festivals such as the first of May, Samuel Cahen issued the following warning to his Jewish readers: "We must [however] not merely imitate other religions by conducting an official service, but as their elders, we should serve as a model for the intervention of religion in the duties of citizenship." Simon Bloch went a step further. He insisted that Judaism must assume the duty of "penetrating more and more into the social fabric and to infuse its blood and soul into the veins of this generous land, through which Providence apparently wishes to redeem and to regenerate society."[60] The conjoining of *régénération* and *rédemption* was doubtless more than a turn of phrase; it aptly reveals the spiritual underpinnings of emancipation. Out of this emerged a distinctly Franco-Jewish approach to the notion of "mission," seeking to be free of emancipation apologetics while aspiring to considerably more than the appropriation of general culture. What was once regarded as an internal Jewish transformation was, by mid-century, envisioned, through the convergence of the ideals of Jewish and French civilizations, as a critical force in the regeneration of humanity. Judaism's ethical monotheism and universal messianic doctrine were set forth as models of universal teachings for humankind. Although this message may have been intended largely for those Jews who had long despaired of finding contemporary value in Jewish teachings, it also confirms the powerful impact of the legacy of the Revolution for those who equated the election of Israel with the destiny of France.[61]

Conclusion

Nowhere was the transition from ghetto to emancipation more dramatic, or more celebrated, than in France. Some two years after the storming of the Bastille, the National Assembly formally removed all disabilities pertaining to the Jews and declared them citizens of France. In response, French Jews identified enthusiastically with the fledging republic. In Paris about one hundred individuals—20 percent of the community—joined the National Guard even before they were admitted to citizenship, and others helped thwart royalist attacks in the early 1790s. From the start, the Jews of France viewed themselves as *enfants de la patrie*, to borrow Berr Isaac Berr's phrase. What was the cultural significance of this revolutionary break with a history most often remembered in lachrymose terms? What strategies did Jews employ to construct a new self-image as *citoyens* that could still be aligned with their historical identity?

These questions, as we have seen, demand a broad historical perspective. The central methodological claim of this book is that the range of Jewish responses to the complex challenges posed by emancipation cannot be appreciated without a clear understanding of the dominant social and cultural patterns that endured throughout the *ancien régime*. For the perspective gained from *la longue durée* alone permits the identification of ruptures and continuities in the cultural history of modern Jewry. What is perhaps less apparent are several significant paradigms that emerged in the late seventeenth and eighteenth centuries and left lasting impressions on the unfolding transformation of French Jewry in the century following 1789. These included the formation of a strong lay leadership and the tensions that ensued; the role of communal and religious controls; tensions between popular and elite religion; the strain between local and regional identities; and the sociocultural interaction between Jews and non-Jews. In each of these areas Metz and Alsace epitomize two distinct frameworks in which the encounter between tradition and modernity found expression. They also prefigured the two contrasting social contexts—urban and rural—that influenced how French Jews would interpret the diverse meanings and implications of emancipation.

Signs of transformation were very much in evidence during the century preceding the Revolution. In Metz, communal regulations dating from the late seventeenth century reflect the efforts of an increasingly powerful urban laity to assert its authority over a declining rabbinate. Sumptuary laws were used as a tool to freeze the existing hierarchy and to exclude from the communal power structure a younger generation whose wealth derived from new commercial opportunities. The goal of the Metz legislation was to maintain the internal equilibrium threatened by a steadily growing population, a widening gap between the generations, the erosion of sexual mores, and the blurring of class distinctions. In Alsace, communal ordinances ratified by the provincial assemblies established a quarter-century before the Revolution reveal a different set of concerns pertaining, in part, to the undesirable influence of village culture and the potentially harmful impact of modernity on moral and religious life; neither consumption nor class divisions were mentioned. The Metz legislation also suggests that the intermingling of Jews and gentiles had become fairly commonplace—certainly more than is normally assumed—a full century before the Revolution. There is no sign that this was as distressing to communal leaders as was the apparent decline in traditional observance. In Alsace, by contrast, rabbinic authority remained largely intact, while community members were overwhelmingly compliant with the dictates of the Jewish tradition. Comparisons between the urban and the rural areas suggest a clear correlation between economic condition and religious change.

Social and religious controls contain evidence of the unique challenges facing a minority that sought to preserve its cultural distinctiveness while also participating in the larger social and economic matrix. French Jews accomplished this goal by unconsciously incorporating elements of non-Jewish culture into the ritual system of Judaism. This strategy made it possible to share in a culture that might ordinarily have been viewed as a threat to Jewish survival. Efforts to regulate public and private behavior also call attention to the process by which central elements of a religious tradition undergo secularization. Driven by a general concern about the ordering of society, seventeenth-century Metz lay leaders assumed responsibility for defining moral and ethical norms of conduct.

Corresponding to wider trends in France, the Metz initiatives and those later undertaken in Alsace belong to the first stage of modernization. These quasi-governmental efforts to mold society and to establish public policy guidelines were rooted in the belief that tougher standards of order were necessary to counterbalance the potentially disintegrative trends associated with urbanization, population growth, and the increasing access to and affordability of luxury items. Such efforts were fully consistent with autonomy and, in fact, rested on its wide-ranging authority. New developments in Talmud study and rabbinic appointments in the mid-eighteenth century signify the emergence of an indigenous culture and consciousness in Alsace. This was consistent with expressions of loyalty to France that were becoming noticeable some years *before* 1789. These developments adumbrated French Jewry's sharp break with the cultural legacy of central and eastern Europe in the half-century following the Revolution and anticipated the emergence of a distinct Franco-Jewish identity in the nineteenth century.

The progressive dissolution of Jewish communal autonomy in the mideighteenth century marked a second stage of the modernization process. Launched by government intervention in community affairs, it corresponded to the intensification of efforts to level down corporations in central and western Europe. During this period, particularly in Metz, a dissatisfaction with traditional authority and mores became more conspicuous. Eroding standards of religious observance and a weakening of rabbinic authority signaled the breakdown of the *kehillah* well before the formal surrender of communal autonomy in 1791. Following the bestowal of citizenship, powerful forces unleashed by the Revolution intensively disrupted Jewish communal life for nearly two decades. Anti-Jewish hostility, deteriorating economic conditions, religious persecution, the emigration of an entire generation of *yeshivah* students and rabbis, and the closing of schools, synagogues, and the two Hebrew presses left their impact on most areas of Jewish culture, leadership, and the pace of modernization for much of the nineteenth century. Without a cohesive framework that could help them meet the new challenges they faced as French citizens, the Jews of France encountered a severe crisis for which they were not prepared. Contrary to expectation, modernization was sluggish and proceeded without direction.

The delay in the modernization of French Jewry precluded the emergence of a modernizing elite that otherwise might have assumed control over educational and religious reform efforts. In the early years of Jewish schooling, the rabbinate enjoyed full reign and was virtually unchallenged by lay leaders. With respect to religious reform, the main obstacle was structural. Jewish communities echoed the general French drive for political, social, and cultural unity through governmental centralization. Although in most instances unity would remain largely unattainable for much of the century, especially in the provinces, the drive for unity nonetheless occupied a prominent place in the national consciousness. It was enhanced by the burgeoning conception of the state as the broad framework for collective action and by the advancing process of *embourgeoisement*. With the influence of unifying concepts such as *la mission civilatrice*, the Jewish question was included in the more universal vision of *la question sociale*. All institutions under consistorial control tended to be pluralistic and therefore moderate in their religious and social outlook. Owing to the premium placed on communal unity, there emerged a consensus on the necessity of moderation among policymakers intent on avoiding internecine strife. This commitment to moderation also explains, to a large degree, the absence of a successful movement to reform the Jewish religion. In contrast to Germany, the structure of the Franco-Jewish community imposed public discipline in religious and political affairs, thus making it difficult for a potentially divisive movement to emerge. The unity theme inspired the invention of certain ritual ceremonies such as the *initiation religieuse*, the quest for a fusion of the Ashkenazic and Sephardic liturgies into a single rite, and the attempt in 1856 to ratify halakhically acceptable reforms for communities throughout France. Centralization made it possible not only to promote regenerative programs in the outlying provinces but also to foster the highly valued sense of unity. To the extent that unity was successfully realized, the achievement represented a significant departure from the mentality of the *ancien régime* where local and regional forces were paramount.[1]

Religious traditionalism continued to play an important role in the lives of French Jews throughout the nineteenth century. For the Jews of rural Alsace-Lorraine especially, traditional structures of meaning remained plausible long after the end of the *ancien régime*, as evidenced by the popularity of folk religion. The creation of the consistorial framework also contributed to the continued centrality of ritual to Jewish culture. Despite the sweeping changes that accompanied the Revolution of 1789, the nineteenth-century Jewish community evinced remarkable structural continuity with the traditional *kehillah*. Dominated by the same wealthy families as in the *ancien régime*, the consistorial leadership controlled the various community institutions, as before, and remained resistant to wider communal participation in the decision-making process. Although the consistory did not have the authority to control the religious behavior of community members as in the case of the *kehillah*, consistorial regulations appear to have blunted the effects of modernization, particularly in small communities where local pressures were more keenly felt. After 1831, when membership in the Jewish community became theoretically voluntary, failure to contribute financially to the synagogue resulted in loss of religious rights and privileges, including burial in the Jewish cemetery. In order to raise funds, communities imposed a voluntary taxation on those who participated in organized Jewish life. Individuals who failed to share the burden of these obligations were excluded from rights and honors in the synagogue and, in extreme instances, were subjected to what was, in effect, religious ostracism. Over the course of the century, communal controls became less effective, as they could be applied only to those who voluntarily bowed to communal authority.[2]

Throughout the nineteenth century, the course of Jewish emancipation remained interwoven with the revolutionary legacy of liberty, fraternity, and equality. The emergence of a modern Jewish ethos was guided by the progressive interpretation of this legacy, so profoundly influenced by political and social forces within and beyond the Jewish community. The dynamic interplay between gentile assessments of Jews on the one hand and Jewish self-assessment on the other played a crucial role in this process and accounted for many of the shifts in Jewish self-image. During the Napoleonic regime, the Bourbon Restoration, and the July Monarchy, aggressive efforts to reconstruct Jewish communal institutions proceeded under the watchful eye of governmental authorities. Building on the theme of *régénération*, leaders constructed a new identity that rested on the subordination of religion to the state, the depoliticization of Judaism, and the parity of Judaism with Catholicism and Protestantism. Each of these elements of the new consciousness found expression in the consistorial system.

Aside from the political and social difficulties that complicated the early phases of emancipation, the notion of citizenship posed unending cultural and religious challenges to French Jews, as is evident in the range of conceptual and strategic views advanced by their leaders. Debate centered on how much of the legacy of traditional Judaism, with all of its implications for continued separatism, ought to be preserved in an age when social and cultural barriers were viewed with increasing suspicion. Were Jews willing to break from their historical relationship to the world around them—especially to their non-Jewish neighbors and to gentile culture—and accept Voltaire's challenge to merge their identity in that of humanity? And what would become of the symbols of their separate culture?

There was wide agreement on the need to adapt Jewish ritual to the novel status of nineteenth-century French Jewry. In response to the claim that strict adherence to the Jewish ritual tradition precluded participation in public life, reformers went several steps further than the Paris Sanhedrin. The Napoleonic assembly had represented Judaism as a depoliticized religion, stressed several liberal interpretations of Jewish law, and emphasized the principle of *dina d'malkhuta dina* in order to absolve the Jewish religion of its purported moral failures and fundamental incompatibility with civic duties. Reformers further lobbied for the elimination of those aspects of the religious tradition, including ritual and liturgical elements that were unsuited to citizenship. They also insisted that greater attention to the aesthetic and spiritual dimensions of ritual would persuade the growing numbers of alienated Jews to return to the synagogue. Religious reform found justification for its agenda in the differentiation between the essential and nonessential in Judaism and in the interstices between custom and law.

Although their conclusions were in some instances unorthodox, the interpretive methods they employed were, on the whole, quite moderate. The most remarkable aspect of the French Jewish response to the profound challenges of their era was the refusal to discard the rituals and symbols of the Jewish tradition. In response to the decline in traditional observance, especially in urban centers, Jewish leaders of virtually every stripe developed strategies on how to ensure the continued viability of Judaism in post-revolutionary France. Despite significant differences, a clear consensus on the importance of preserving a distinct social and cultural identity had emerged. The result was a "republican Judaism" that sharply rejected both the separatism favored by certain sectors of the orthodox community, as well as the liberal demand for *fusion sociale*. Embodying the central doctrines of the Sanhedrin, it viewed service to state and society as a religious obligation and rejected any distinction between Jew and non-Jew in the performance of ethical duties. It understood the Jewish messianic idea almost exclusively in terms of its universal-humanistic implications: the reign of truth and justice, as the triumph of the belief in the unity of God, and peace. The mission of Israel was to protect the knowledge of God, to embody it in their way of life, and to teach it to humanity.

Defining the precise role of the ritual commandments in nineteenth-century French Judaism was a more divisive issue, however. Among proponents of *régénération* there was a clear tendency to interpret the rituals symbolically, as in the case of the festivals of the Jewish calendar, which they viewed as paradigms of the Revolution and of emancipation. This entailed the creative reinterpretation of existing rituals and the formation of new ones. R. Salomon Ulmann, by contrast, emphasized the straightforward details of ritual ceremonies and their ethical-moral dimension. Although he stressed the importance of integrating the fate of the Jews with the common destiny of France, he placed greater emphasis on personal piety than on civic duties. He argued for a symbiosis of the universal and the particular, insisting that every rite exuded universal significance. Concerned that excessive religious identification with the state could be harmful, Ulmann's was a voice of dissent against the more broadly accepted view of the Revolution as a religiously transformative force. In either case, there was clear acknowledgment that conditions demanded a new approach to traditional ritual practice.

It was in the realm of ritual that the contrast between the *ancien régime* and the post-revolutionary period was particularly striking. In the seventeenth and eighteenth centuries, rituals were formative elements of people's view of the world. Traditional communities developed ritual systems to explain the world and the individual's place within it. Rites of passage reflected the collective mentalities and served as a crucial repository of memories and values that were often specific to a community or region. They also represented a mode of continuity with past generations, which was of particular importance at a time of rampant social, cultural, and political transformation. Debates about the authenticity of such rituals also revolved, increasingly, around the question of the centrality of textual traditions. The rituals practiced by French Jews during the *ancien régime* reflected modes of thinking about their historical origins, their relationship to the surrounding culture and society, and their identification with certain Jewish cultural traditions. Ritual was a way of interpreting the world and reflected strategies enabling people to meet the demands and uncertainties of life within their own communities.

In the nineteenth century, ritual dramatized the experience of citizenship, nationalism, and religious pluralism. From 1789, the Jewish self-image was powerfully transformed by the promise of full civic equality and the concomitant demand that Jews undergo extensive social and cultural transformation. Nineteenth-century ritual and the debates surrounding ritual reform signaled changes in the way that Jews related to the state, French society, and French culture. Throughout the nineteenth century, ritual assumed more of a performative function that dramatized, especially for non-Jews, the epoch-making changes of the day. Though undeniably expressive of how Jews defined their identity, especially in the public space of the French city, the newer rituals were mainly reflections of the life that was shaped so completely by the powerful forces of the Revolution. For villagers, however, the older rituals remained central to the daily rhythms of life and culture long after the Revolution.[3]

Ritual reinterpretation was, ultimately, a conservative technique used to justify the retention of otherwise outmoded rites. This conservatism was consistent with a parallel trend among those engaged in the scientific study of Judaism to pursue a more emphatically Jewish agenda. Virtually every aspect of the methodological critique of Jewish tradition in the nineteenth century had its roots in the vast halakhic literature of the medieval and early modern periods. After the Revolution, a number of traditionalists took the lead in the development of critical approaches to classical texts. Nevertheless, both technically and conceptually, modern scholars in France remained remarkably conservative in their approach. And although modern scholarship reflected an abiding optimism in all that the Revolution implied, it became increasingly wary of the problematical nature of emancipation. In the face of growing challenges to the place of the Jews within French society and culture, *la science de judaïsme* emphasized the uniqueness of the Jewish tradition.

Despite many clear indications of continuity from the *ancien régime* to the post-revolutionary period, a close examination of the history of France's Jews suggests that their culture had become autochthonous within several decades of the Revolution. The progressive break with a longstanding religious and cultural tradition linking the Jews of Alsace-Lorraine culturally, socially, and economically with territories to the east began in the last stages of the *ancien régime* and gathered speed under the impact of the Revolution, the Terror, and the Napoleonic regime. More than their effusive patriotic devotion, French Jewry's identification with the successes and achievements of France contributed powerfully to the ethos of cultural distinctiveness. This was due, in no small measure, to the powerful role that religion continued to play in modern Jewish culture, even in its most secular form. Although the Jews of France underwent a radical transformation that redefined their relationship to the society around them, the terms and concepts of the Jewish religious tradition remained central to the discourse of modernization, no less than in the *ancien régime.* In fact, every reformist initiative of the nineteenth century, from the Paris Sanhedrin to the extensive synagogue reforms of R. Salomon Ulmann, and even in the realm of politics, drew heavily on the primary texts and paradigms of the Jewish tradition.

Equally significant was the dramatic role that religion played in helping French Jews interpret the meaning of emancipation. Their leaders articulated the belief that the Jews of France were entrusted with a sacred mission to model the ideals of 1789 to Jewish communities abroad and even within French society. By mid-century the term *régénération* had come to signify the mission of civilizing Jews in underdeveloped areas of the world. As for French society itself, the ideals of Judaism were identified with those of the French Revolution. Although admiration for the biblical covenant and the Mosaic legislation was a longstanding theme in the writings of several seventeenth- and eighteenth-century political philosophers, from Bodin to Rousseau, a number of Jewish writers went so far as to declare that Mosaic institutions were permeated with the principles of the Revolution and, conversely, that the Revolution was the fulfillment of the Judaic ideal of justice. From this it followed that the Jews were destined to complete the effort begun by the Revolution and would, ultimately, work toward the regeneration of society at large. This grandiose task, however it was imagined and defined, was an adaptation of an ancient aspiration to perfect the world. Belying the oft-heard claim that Judaism was morally and culturally bereft, it presumed the convergence of the particular and the universal commitments of Judaism. The process of joining French society as citizens was a complex undertaking that demanded not only difficult social and economic adjustment but also a sincere rethinking of the Jewish religious heritage. This ambitious project, drawing on the mythic power of both the Revolution and the Jewish tradition, was a crucial ingredient in the efforts of French Jews to negotiate their passage to modernity.

Abbreviations

AI	*Archives israélites de France*
Archives JTS	Jewish Theological Seminary of American Archives
Bordeaux *Registre*	Simon Schwarzfuchs, ed., *Le Registre des délibérations de la Nation Juive Portugaise de Bordeaux (1711–1787)* (Paris, 1981)
HUCA	*Hebrew Union College Annual*
JFR	Zosa Szajkowski, *The Jews and the French Revolutions of 1789, 1830, and 1848* (New York, 1970)
JQR	*Jewish Quarterly Review*
JSS	*Jewish Social Studies*
LBIYB	*Leo Baeck Institute Year Book*
Metz *Memorbuch*	Simon Schwarzfuchs, ed., *Le "Memorbuch" de Metz (vers 1575–1742)* (Metz, 1971)
MGWJ	*Monatsschrift für Geschichte und Wissenschaft des Judentums*
O.H.	*Orah Hayyim.* Part 1 of *Shulhan Arukh*
PAAJR	*American Academy of Religion, Proceedings*
R.	Rabbi
REJ	*Revue des études juives*
Resp.	Responsa
UI	*Univers israélite*
Y.D.	*Yoreh De'ah.* Part 2 of *Shulhan Arukh*

Notes

Introduction

1. For a fine example of the multipronged approach, see Birnbaum and Katznelson, *Paths of Emancipation*. Against the traditional partiality toward elites, a number of studies published in the last quarter-century have employed the methods of social history to study Jews living in rural areas. See Paula Hyman's treatment of socioeconomic and cultural adaptation, *Emancipation of the Jews of Alsace*, and her more recent book, *The Jews of Modern France*. Other studies devoted to similar concerns include Dubin, *The Port Jews of Habsburg Trieste*; Endelman, *The Jews of Georgian England*; and Marsha Rozenblitt, *The Jews of Vienna, 1867–1914: Assimilation and Identity* (Albany, 1983). Despite a growing appreciation for its manifold effects, the study of emancipation has focused overwhelming on relations between Jews and the state. See Magnus, *Jewish Emancipation in a German City*; Birnbaum, *Jewish Destinies*. Also see Hyman, *Gender and Assimilation in Modern Jewish History* and M. Kaplan, *The Making of the Jewish Middle Class*.

2. See Furet, "Ancien Régime," 604, and Gordon, *Citizens without Sovereignty*, 24–25.

3. For a valuable case study of the impact of the Revolution on perceptions of the past, see Fritzsche, "Chateaubriand's Ruins."

4. On the disdain for the history of the pre-revolutionary era, see Higonnet, *Goodness beyond Virtue*, 137–40.

5. Furet, *Interpreting the French Revolution*. The aversion to recalling the history of Jewish persecution is evident in M. Berr, *Appel à la justice nations et des rois*, 18. On efforts to endow the Revolution with a messianic ideology, see Talmon, *Political Messianism*. For Jewish views of the Revolution as a messianic and revelatory event, see the remarks of Adolphe Crémieux, quoted in Posener, *Adolphe Crémieux*, 2:149, 220; Reinach, *Histoire des israélites*, 325; Marrus, *The Politics of Assimilation*, 90–92, 106–07; and Chouraqui, "De l'émancipation des Juifs à l'émancipation du judaïsme." Among the historical works that stressed the centrality of emancipation, L. Halévy's *Résumé de l'histoire des Juifs modernes* was especially influential. On his role in the creation of a modern Franco-Jewish narrative, see Rodrigue, "Léon Halévy and Modern French Jewish Historiography." For others that emphasized the dramatic changes introduced by the Revolution, see Lambert, *Précis de l'histoire*, esp. 406–07; and Debré, "The Jews of France." On the impact of the Revolution on Jewish life, see Berkovitz, "The French Revolution and the Jews." On the state of the various community archives, see Szajkowski, *Franco-Judaica*, xxiii. The archives of the Avignon community were destroyed in the fire of 1827, and in 1885 the city archives of Bayonne, including those of the Jewish community, were also lost.

6. Typical of the trend to concentrate on individual communities are the valuable

studies by Moïse Ginsburger, appearing in *Revue des études juives* and as separate monographs.

7. Major studies devoted in part to an examination of communal life in the *ancien régime* include Blumenkranz, *Histoire des Juifs en France*; Hertzberg, *French Enlightenment*; Simon Schwarzfuchs, *Les Juifs de France* (Paris, 1975); and Schwarzfuchs, *Du Juif à l'israélite*.

8. Gennep, *Manuel de folklore français contemporain*. Also see Muchembled, *Popular Culture and Elite Culture in France*.

9. Muir, *Ritual in Early Modern Europe*, 1–9.

10. See, for example, Bonfil, *Jewish Life in Renaissance Italy*, and Stow, *Theatre of Acculturation*. For central and eastern Europe, cf. Sylvie-Anne Goldberg, *Crossing the Jabbok: Illness and Death in Ashkenazi Judaism in Sixteenth- through Nineteenth-Century Prague*, trans. from French by Carol Cosman (Berkeley, 1996), 60–65, and Fram, *Ideals Face Reality*, 29–32.

11. See *AI* 7 (1846): 602–08.

12. Cf. Lowenstein, "The Pace of Modernization."

13. On this general theme, see Noel Parker, *Portrayals of the Revolution: Images, Debates and Patterns of Thought on the French Revolution* (Carbondale, Ill., 1990).

14. See Geertz, *The Interpretation of Cultures*, 12, 89. By "culture" I refer to public, socially established structures of meaning that determine behavioral norms. Denoting any historically transmitted system of thought, belief, and values, culture is expressed in symbolic forms. "Identity," by contrast, lacks the dimension of continuity associated with culture. It is a consciousness that results from a confrontation with the realities of the day and is therefore given to more frequent shifts and mutations.

Chapter 1. Communal Authority and Leadership

1. See Yosef Yerushalmi, *From Spanish Court to Italian Ghetto: Isaac Cardoso, A Study in Seventeenth-Century Marranism and Jewish Apologetics* (New York, 1971); Ruderman, *Jewish Thought and Scientific Discovery in Early Modern Europe*; Katz, *Tradition and Crisis*; and M. Meyer, "Where Does the Modern Period in Jewish History Begin?"

2. See Bonfil, "Change in the Cultural Patterns of a Jewish Society in Crisis."

3. Katz, *Tradition and Crisis*, 183–236; Katz, *Out of the Ghetto*, 34–36.

4. For details, see Hertzberg, *French Enlightenment*, 78–112; Malino, *The Sephardic Jews of Bordeaux*, 1–22.

5. See G. Weill, "Recherches sur la démographie des juifs d'Alsace," 53–55, and Zosa Szajkowski, "Demographic Aspects of Jewish Emancipation in France during the French Revolution," *Historia Judaica* 21 (1959): 7–36.

6. Hertzberg, *French Enlightenment*, 19–28.

7. Basnage, *Histoire des Juifs*.

8. See Hertzberg, *French Enlightenment*, 45–48, 268–313; Berkovitz, *Shaping of Jewish Identity*, 34–36; Chisick, "Ethics and History in Voltaire's Attitude toward the Jews"; and Sutcliffe, "Can a Jew Be a *Philosophe*?" The Voltaire quote appears in *Essai sur les moeurs et l'esprit des nations*, ciii, II, 64.

9. See Hertzberg, *French Enlightenment*, 34, 249–54, and Behre, "Raphaël Lévy."

10. Szajkowski, "Jewish Status in Eighteenth-Century France"; Hertzberg, *French Enlightenment*, 54–63.

11. Hertzberg, *French Enlightenment*, 318–19; Miskimin, "Jews and Christians in the Marketplace."

12. Hertzberg, *French Enlightenment*, 41–42, 252–65.

13. The Portuguese Jewish Nation was divided into six communities: Bordeaux, Bayonne, Biarritz, Saint-Jean-de-Luz, Bidache, and Peyrehorade. According to the

census of 1784, there were 182 Alsatian communities where Jews lived. In Lorraine there were 52 such communities, according to the privileges of 1753, and in Metz and the Trois-Evêches there were about 50. In Lorraine there were 168 localities with a Jewish population under the First Empire; the province was divided into four *départements*: Boulay, Fénétrange-Luttelange, Lixheim, and Nancy. In the southeast there were four communities: Avignon, Carpentras, Cavaillon, and L'Isle-sur-Sorgue. See, generally, Szajkowski, "The Growth of the Jewish Population in France"; Szajkowski, "Demographic Aspects of Jewish Emancipation in France during the French Revolution"; Szajkowski, "Population Problems of Marranos and Sephardim in France." For the 1558 *takkanot* of Avignon, see de Maulde, "Les Juifs dans les Etats français du Pape au moyen âge." On the 1779 *takkanot*, see Loeb, "Statuts des Juifs D'Avignon," 233–34. For a full-length study of the Carpentras community, see Calmann, *The Carrière of Carpentras*.

14. See, for example, Baron, *The Jewish Community*, 2:50, 1:346.

15. On Jewish communal government in the Middle Ages, see also Yitzhak Baer, "The Origins of Jewish Communal Government in the Middle Ages," *Zion* 15 (1950): 1–41; Morell, "The Constitutional Limits of Communal Government in Rabbinic Law"; Avraham Grossman, "The Attitude of the Early Scholars of Ashkenaz towards the Authority of the 'Kahal'" [Hebrew], *Annual of the Institute for Research in Jewish Law* 2 (1975): 175–99; and Gerald Blidstein, "Medieval Public Law: Sources and Concepts" [Hebrew], *Diné Israel* 9 (1978–80): 127–64.

16. The main documents of Bayonne's history have disappeared. Thanks to the works of two Bayonne rabbis, however, it is possible to trace some of the main features of the community's history. See R. Meldola, *Mayyim Rabbim*, and D. Meldola, *Divrei David*. On the history of the Bayonne community, see Nahon, *Les "Nations" juives portugaises*, document LXIII–LXIV, pp. 172–211; and Nahon, "From New Christians to the Portuguese Jewish Nation in France," 2:348–52. On religious and communal life in Bayonne, see Schwarzfuchs, "Notes sur les juifs de Bayonne." On the Bordeaux *takkanot*, see Bordeaux *Registre*, no. 279 (25 December 1760), pp. 293–302, and Nahon, "Note sur les registres." Fragments of other registers exist. Regarding Saint-Esprit, see Nahon, "Une délibération"; and Nahon, *Communautés judéo-portugaises*, 2:199–201. On ritual observances in Peyrehorade, see Jacob Sasportas, *Resp. Ohel Ya'akov* (Amsterdam, 1737), no. xxx.

17. Each of the two traditions rested firmly on a shared talmudic legacy as interpreted by medieval halakhic authorities. See Katz, *Tradition and Crisis*, 66–67, 78–80, 295n. 12. For a dissenting view, see Kaplan, "The Portuguese *Kehillah* in Amsterdam."

18. While the early history of the communities in Bordeaux and Bayonne is obscure, evidence in the Bordeaux *pinkas* suggests that there already was an organized community in Bordeaux in the second half of the seventeenth century. In Bayonne (St. Esprit), the acquisition of a cemetery and the existence of a Jewish community ordinance enacted in 1666 suggest that the "new Christians" were already organized as a community by the mid-seventeenth century. This evidence is assembled by Hertzberg, *French Enlightenment*, 228–29.

19. See Loker, "From Converso Congregation to Holy Community," 56. On the persistence of certain practices, e.g., Jewish burials in the Christian cemetery (until 1724–25) and the performance of Jewish marriage ceremonies in the church before they were repeated by Jewish religious authorities (until 1753) that were characteristic of the earlier period when it was not possible to observe Judaism openly, see Cirot, *Recherches sur les Juifs espagnols et portugais à Bordeaux*, 112, 164.

20. Bordeaux *Registre*. This, the only surviving register of the Judeo-Portuguese communities of France, is at the Archives Départementales de la Gironde.

21. For the first recorded decision of the *beit din*, see Bordeaux *Registre*, no. 241

(14 August 1755). For examples of cases that came before the *beit din*, see Bordeaux *Registre*, no. 481, referring to the *beit din*'s decision to prohibit polygamy; no. 514 contains a judgment disallowing a clandestine marriage; no. 527 refers to a question about giving a writ of divorce. See Bordeaux *Registre*, no. 522. The *beit din* also functioned occasionally as a legislative body to which communal leaders would turn in order to clarify a law or to strengthen a policy.

22. This is based on the *mémoire* submitted by the Bordeaux delegation to the Malesherbes Commission in 1788. See Szajkowski, "Diaries," 40. The Bordeaux delegation insisted on preserving the community's right of arbitration in civil and criminal disputes and conceded that the disputes would be brought to the courts of the state only when the judges could not reach an agreement with the parties; divorce cases, according to the delegation's position, would remain under the authority of the Jewish courts.

23. Until World War II, the Metz community had preserved twenty-three *registres* (*pinkasim*), all listed in the Landman inventory at the Metz community archives. Only the first, however, covering the years 1595–1678, can be considered a genuine *registre* of the community. After the war they disappeared from the archive. On *pinkas* (ms. 8136 of the JTS library), which covers the years 1749–1789, see Bordeaux *Registre*, 55. As for Metz as a model for other communities, the Conseil Souverain confirmed R. Samuel Sanvil Weyl's authority in Haute-Alsace in 1719 by stating that the royal *lettres patentes* "conformed to the custom of Metz"; cited in Ginsburger, "Samuel Sanvil Weil," 61.

24. See A. Cahen, "Rabbinat," *REJ* 7 (1883): 103–07, 215–16; *REJ* 8 (1884): 257–58. Clément, *La condition des juifs de Metz*, 91–92; Kerner, "La vie," 224–34; and Hertzberg, *French Enlightenment*, 239–42. The 1595 text appeared in A. Cahen, "Rabbinat," *REJ* 7 (1883): 106–07.

25. For examples of challenges to the civil jurisdiction of the rabbis, see A. Cahen, "Rabbinat," *REJ* 8 (1884): 257–58, 262–66; Malino, "Competition and Confrontation," 327–32. In the face of the widespread use of non-Jewish courts, R. Jonathan Eibeschütz despaired that he "had no power to abolish it, because it has become ingrained"; see his *Urim ve-Tumim*, section 26.

26. *Lettres patentes*, 31 décembre 1715, microfilm no. 8347, Archives JTS.

27. This work was titled *Receuil des lois, coutumes et usages observés par les juifs de Metz*, m.s. 11 March 1743, in AN H 1641, Archives Nationales, Paris. According to Hertzberg, *French Enlightenment*, 240–41, the work was deposited with the Metz *parlement* in 1743. Prepared under the guidance of R. Jonathan Eibeschutz, it was eventually published in Metz in 1786.

28. The *lettres patentes concernant les Juifs d'Alsace*, issued at Versailles on 10 July 1784, article 13, cited in Loeb, "Les Juifs à Strasbourg," 166. On the rapid population increase in Alsace, see G. Weill, "Recherches sur la démographie des juifs d'Alsace."

29. G. Weill, "Rabbins et Parnassim," 97.

30. Hertzberg, *French Enlightenment*, 238.

31. Bordeaux *Registre*, 9–13. Cf. Y. Kaplan, "The Sephardim in North-Western Europe and the New World," 2:273–78.

32. Bordeaux *Registre*, pp. 13–14.

33. Bordeaux *Registre*, no. 279. Detailed notarial minutes of a meeting to protest against the leadership of the Nation, preserved in the departmental archives of Gironde, file 34, 24 June 1764, are published in Szajkowski, "Conflicts within the Eighteenth-Century Sephardic Communities of France." The king ordered that all disputes be referred to the authority of the Intendant. In December 1752 the Nation presented its statutes to the Intendant for his approval, which he subsequently granted. The fundamental issues were not resolved, however, and dissent continued

until the end of the *ancien régime*. The text has been reprinted in Nahon, *Les "Nations" juives portugaises*, 172–208; also see 219–28, 256–58.

34. On limitations imposed on rabbinic freedom, especially regarding officiation at weddings, see Bordeaux *Registre*, nos. 85, 121, 437. On the teaching duties of the rabbi, see Bordeaux *Registre*, no. 62. Cf. Nahon, *Les "Nations" juives portugaises*, doc. LXIII, art. 33, p. 196, and Hertzberg, *French Enlightenment*, 245. For Meldola's views, see *Resp. Mayyim Rabbim* (Amsterdam, 1737), pt. 2, nos. 62–65. Art. 33 of the 1753 *règlement* limited the rabbi's authority to Bayonne and prohibited him from taking part in the affairs of the Nation. See Nahon, *Les "Nations" juives portugaises*, 196.

35. For Alsace, see the extract from the "Protocol of the Medinah," 28 May 1777, arts. 2, 3, 14, published in *Blätter für jüdische Geschichte and Litteratur* 2 (1901): 18–22, 28–29, and paraphrased in French by Isidore Loeb, *Extrait du protocole de la nation de l'assemblée du 21 Iyyar 5537*, "Les Juifs à Strasbourg," 181–98. Of the sixty-eight *parnassim* mentioned in Metz *Memorbuch*, forty-one carried the title "rabbi" as well. For examples, see p. viii, and notice nos. 76, 57, 673, 839, 861.

36. See Fram, *Ideals Face Reality*, 40.

37. On Schwab's efforts to control the election of *parnassim* in 1724 and 1738, see Ginsburger, "Elie Schwab," *REJ* 44 (1902): 116.

38. See G. Weill, "Rabbins et Parnassim," 101–03.

39. See discussion of the contract of Rabbi Isaac Aaron of Phalsbourg in Schwarzfuchs, *Du Juif à l'israélite*, 45–46. A copy of the contract is in AN F^{19} 11023, Archives Nationales, Paris.

40. Cf. Reischer, *Resp. Shevut Yaakov*, pt. 1, no. 74, where the author defends the appointment of talmudic scholars to public office, despite their exemption from taxes and in spite of the opposition of some community members.

41. Hertzberg, *French Enlightenment*, 233; Pierre-André Meyer, *La communauté juive de Metz*, 69; Metz *Memorbuch*, viii. For examples of *parnassim* who served for long periods, see notice nos. 106, 177, 216, 261, 445, 528, 589, 624, 843.

42. From the seventeenth century, lay courts were regularly established in central European communities, mainly to handle commercial disputes. See Katz, *Tradition and Crisis*, 80–82, 297nn. 25–26, 298nn. 30–31. For examples of seventeenth-century rabbinic complaints against the abuse of lay authority in communal matters, see Jacob Sasportas, *Toledot Ya'akov* (Amsterdam, 1652), ii; and Sirkes, *Resp. Bayit Hadash*, no. 43. On additional complaints concerning the appointment of friends and relatives to positions as *dayyanim*, cf. J. L. Puhavitzer, *Divrei Ha-Yamim* (Hamburg, 1692), ch. 23. For the relevant text of the 1711 Reischer responsum, see *Resp. Shevut Ya'akov*, pt. 2, no. 143. For his position on the authority of lay judges, see pt. 1, no. 136, and the discussion in Quint and Hecht, *Jewish Jurisprudence*, 1:80–87, 163.

43. See Eibeschütz, *Ya'arot Devash*, vol. 2, sermon no. 3, p. 46 (Jerusalem ed.). Metz *pinkas*, fol. 8, art. 12; fol. 17, art. 13, cited in Kerner, "La vie," 39.

44. See the *arrêté* of the *tovim* (dated 20 Tevet 5406 = 5 January 1646), signed by the *av beit din* of Metz, cited in Kerner, "La vie," 111–12.

45. Metz *pinkas*, 17 Heshvan 5469 (1708), published in D. Kaufmann, "Extraits," 125.

46. Ibid., pp. 124–25. The *av beit din* could authorize others to speak in his stead only with the permission of the communal leadership. Neither he nor the *kahal* could ordain young men with the title *haver* until they were married for two years. If the *kahal* wanted to issue legislation to curb immorality or to prevent ritual infractions, the *av beit din* was required to lend his formal assent.

47. See Finkelstein, *Jewish Self-Government*, 228, 242–43; Israel Halperin, *Pinkas Va'ad Arba Arazot* (Jerusalem, 1945), 2; Koeber, "Documents," 46.

48. See art. 10 of the rabbinic contract issued to R. Nehemiah Reischer, published in Schwarzfuchs, "Three Documents," 12.

49. Generally more characteristic of self-government in Ashkenazic communities, the implications of democratization resonated in the halakhic literature. See, for example, the view of Bacharach, *Resp. Ḥavvot Ya'ir*, no. 81, where the authority of the *parnassim* was derived from their being "elected by a majority of the congregation," which gives the community the right to impose its will on the individual.

50. D. Kaufmann, "Extraits," 116. Originally, there had been a committee responsible for redacting the statutes, composed of twelve persons and an executive commission of nine members. See prologue to the Metz sumptuary regulations of 1690 (5450) in A. Cahen, "Règlements," 86, 97n. 2.

51. For these and additional details, see Hertzberg, *French Enlightenment*, 234–35.

52. See Loeb, "Les Juifs à Strasbourg," 163–67; Posener, "Social Life," 214–17, 226–28; Hertzberg, *French Enlightenment*, 238–39; and G. Weill, "Rabbins et Parnassim," 96–109. Also see the valuable archival sources published in Neher-Bernheim, *Documents inédits*, 1:108.

53. See A. Cahen, "Rabbinat" *REJ* 7 (1883): 103–16; *REJ* 8 (1884): 255–74; *REJ* 12 (1886): 283–97; *REJ* 13 (1886): 105–14; and Ginsburger, "Les Juifs de Metz."

54. See the rabbinic contract of R. Nehemiah Reischer, published in Schwarzfuchs, "Three Documents," 11–12.

55. On the earliest *takkanot* prohibiting the appointment of rabbis with kin in the local community, see Schepansky, *The Takkanot of Israel*, 4:408–09. On their spread to central and western Europe, see Shoḥat, *Im Ḥilufe Tekufot*, 93–94.

56. For interesting material on rabbinic succession and rabbinic duties in the Metz community, see A. Cahen, "Rabbinat," *REJ* 7 (1883): 219–20; D. Kaufmann, "R. Joseph Lévi Aschkenaz," 93–94. On the involvement of rabbis in the ranks of communal leadership, see Metz *Memorbuch*, viii, and notice nos. 76, 57, 673, 839, 861. On the separation of duties of judge and syndic, see Metz *pinkas*, fol. 8, art. 12; fol. 17, art. 13, cited in Kerner, "La vie," 39.

57. See Narol's description of King Louis XIV's visit to the Metz synagogue, published by Z. Frankel, "Eine historische Notiz." Also see Eidelberg, "Jews of Worms," 91–93.

58. See A. Cahen, "Rabbinat," *REJ* 7 (1883): 220–23, and Shulvass, *From East to West*, 42. Narol had studied with R. Solomon Luria; he was succeeded by Jonas Teoumim Fraenkel (1659–69), who also came to France to escape the Chmielnicki massacres. For details on the appointment of Eibeschütz, see his correspondence with the Metz communal leadership in Blum, "Trois lettres." Hilmann's contract was reprinted in *Blätter für jüdische Geschichte und Litteratur* 1 (1900): 39–40, and the Günzberg contract was published and annotated by Schwarzfuchs, "The Rabbinic Contract."

59. Metz *pinkas*, 39a–b, cited in Hertzberg, *French Enlightenment*, 169; also see Kerner, "La vie," 174–75, and Kerner, "Un registre messin," 43. On talmudic academies in early modern Europe, see Reiner, "Wealth, Social Standing, and the Study of Torah."

60. See Kerner, "Salaries et salaires," 34.

61. The Haguenau community first selected Tevele Scheuer, *dayyan* in Frankfurt am Main, to serve as its rabbi. Following Scheuer's refusal of the offer, R. Samuel Halberstadt, who had come to Alsace following the 1744 expulsion of the Prague Jewish community, was appointed to the position.

62. With the establishment of the Upper Rhine consistory in 1808, Katzenellenbogen (known as Lazare Hirsch) was named grand rabbi and consistory president, positions he held until his death in 1823. See Ginsburger, "Mémoriaux," *REJ* 41 (1900): 125–26.

63. The bishopric of Strasbourg was unique insofar as it was not an independent rabbinic precinct but was under the authority of the rabbi of one of the neighbor-

ing territories who added these duties to his regular responsibilities. At first the position was assigned to the rabbi of Hanau-Lichtenberg, Issachar Baer Wiener (1722–1731), then to the rabbi of Haute-Alsace, Samuel Sanvil Weyl (1731–1753), and finally to the rabbi of the territories of the Noblesse Immédiate, Joseph Steinhardt (1753–1763), who purchased the position. During these four decades, the rabbis who served the Mutzig community—headquarters of the bishopric of Strasbourg—apparently enjoyed authority in local affairs only. On the bestowal of positions of *parnas* from father to son, see G. Weill, "Rabbins et Parnassim," 98–99.

64. Natan Oury Cahen, a Metz native who had served as a rabbi in Pforzheim, was appointed as rabbi of Karlsruhe and of the Jews of the principalities in 1720; Joshua Heschel Lebub, a *dayyan* in Metz in the early eighteenth century, was subsequently named rabbi of Trèves and of Anspach. See Eliakim Carmoly, "Notice biographique," *Revue orientale* 2 (1842): 335–36.

65. On the community of Rosheim, see Freddy Raphaël and Robert Weyl, *Regards nouveaux sur les Juifs d'Alsace*, 100–101. In Avignon, Prague native Jacob Ispir (called Jacob Spire) served as rabbi from 1741 to 1775 and was succeeded by his son Elie Vitte (1755–1790). He subsequently served as rabbi of Nîmes in the 1770s. See *REJ* 101: 48–50, and S. Kahn, "Les Juifs à Nîmes," 232. Moses Jacob Polaque, from Poland, served as rabbi of Cavaillin, and in Isle the list of rabbis included Abraham Liptsis, from Poland (Mehier), in 1677 and Jesse Luria, from Germany (Bendic). The Carpentras community drew on rabbis from a wider area: Solomon Azubi, born in Sofia, served from 1617 to 1635; Abraham Shalom of Amsterdam served from 1650 to 1660; and Judah Aryeh Loeb b. Zevi of Krotoschin settled in Carpentras to assume the rabbinic post there after having first immigrated to Austria, Germany, and Holland. R. Samuel Hilman, another native of Krotoschin, succeeded Eibeschütz as *av beit din* of Metz in 1751 after serving in rabbinic positions in Moravia and Germany.

66. For documentation on rabbinic migration from Poland, see Zosa Szajkowski, *Yivo Bleter* 39 (1955): 83; Posener, "Social Life," 214, 222–24; Shulvass, *From East to West*, 28, 62–63, 100, 107. Shulvass cited the publication of the 1701 Amsterdam edition of Nathan Hanover's dictionary *Safah Berurah* (Prague, 1660), which included a French translation of its vocabulary, as one example of the interest in France as a possible point of destination. According to R. Jonathan Eibeschütz, superior conditions in the West account for the influx of Polish *yeshivah* students to Metz. See his sermon of Av 5509 (1749), *Ya'arot Devash*, 2:121. His remarks, as well as those of certain city councils, suggest that the number of Polish *yeshivah* students and immigrants was expanding over the course of the century.

67. In Upper Alsace, when the rabbinate was still based in Brisach, at least two of the appointees either served in or hailed from Metz. Eisik Werd (d. 1675) had previously served as rabbi in Metz; in 1681 he was followed by Aaron Worms, himself a native of Metz. However, once the seat of the rabbinate was moved to Ribeauvillé at the turn of the eighteenth century, the preference for native Alsatians grew stronger. In Rixheim as well, substitute or vice-rabbis were in nearly all instances from Alsace, with the sole exception of Joseph Steinhardt, a native of Bavaria.

68. In Grant, "The Government of Louis XIV," 5:27. For a comprehensive treatment of the subject, see Doyle, *Venality*. For parallels among the parochial clergy of Angers, see McManners, *French Ecclesiastical Society*, 134–36, and Ravitch, *The Sword and the Mitre*, 3–17.

69. Ginsburger, "Elie Schwab," *REJ* 44 (1902): 108–11.

70. For more examples, see P. Meyer, *La communauté juive de Metz*, 205–14.

71. See Carmoly, "Issachar Carmoly."

72. On precedents for the purchase of rabbinic positions, see Assaf, "On the History of the Rabbinate," 36–39. The Council of the Four Lands in Gramitz enacted

the first *takkanah* against the practice in 1587 (*Pinkas Va'ad Arba Aratzot*, p. 4, para. 8). Other communities in addition to Metz that followed this tradition included Ubin (Hungary), Fürth, Altona-Hamburg-Wandbeck, and Prussia; see Shoḥat, '*Im Ḥilufe Tekufot*, 93–94.

73. See Ginsburger, "Samuel Lévy," *REJ* 65 (1913): 275–76; Ginsburger, "Samuel Sanvil Weil," 54–57. Also see G. Weill, "Rabbins et Parnassim," 99.

74. Support for Weyl was undoubtedly related to the service he and his brother Meyer rendered to the prince. In 1700 they provided a loan of 3000 *écus* to the prince, in return for which they received special privileges. See the document published in Ginsburger, "Samuel Lévy," *REJ* 66 (1913): 130–31, cited in G. Weill, "Rabbins et Parnassim," 98.

75. G. Weill, "Rabbins et Parnassim," 99.

76. See Ginsburger, "Elie Schwab."

77. Ginsburger, "Samuel Sanvil Weil," 194, 58.

78. Ibid., 195, 59.

79. Ibid.

80. G. Weill, "Rabbins et Parnassim," 102–03.

81. Ibid., 63–64.

82. Ibid., 194–95, 58–59, 63–75.

83. G. Weill, "Rabbins et Parnassim," 102–03; Berkovitz, "Patterns of Rabbinic Succession in Modern France," 67. Despite his apparent neglect of rabbinic duties, Weyl was a respected halakhic authority. See Resicher, *Resp. Shevut Ya'akov*, pt. 3, no. 119.

84. G. Weill, "Rabbins et Parnassim," 98–99.

85. On the appointment of Enosch, see Ginsburger, "Une élection rabbinique," 625–28; the archival sources published by Neher-Bernheim, *Documents inédits*, 1:108–18; and Ginsburger, "Mémoriaux," 131.

86. Ginsburger, "Une élection rabbinique," 626.

87. Arch. dept. du Bas-Rhin C 335, "Mémoire pour Esther Philippe, veuve de Samuel Weyl, Rabbin de la hautte alsace, et Jacob Wolff Gugenheim son gendre (1753)," cited in Neher-Bernheim, *Documents inédits*, 1:108–13.

88. Arch. dept. du Bas-Rhin C 335, "Supplément du mémoire pour Jacob Gugenheim contre l'élection du nommé Suzel Hennès Juif de Creutznach, nommé Rabin des Juifs de Haute Alsace," cited in Neher-Bernheim, *Documents inédits*, 1:114–16.

89. See the list published in Carmoly, "Issachar Carmoly," 346–47.

90. On the founding of one of these academies, see Blum, "Le fondateur du grand Beth Hamidrash de Bouxwiller."

Chapter 2. Secularization, Consumption, and Communal Controls

1. R. Ya'ir Ḥayyim Bacharach, for one, was fully aware that this legislation was independent of the Halakhah. See *Resp. Ḥavvot Ya'ir*, nos. 57–59, and the discussion in Katz, "The Rule of Halakhah in Traditional Jewish Society," 179–81.

2. See Katz, *Tradition and Crisis*, 76–87, and Baron, *The Jewish Community*. The norms of internal discipline were established formally through the publication of regulations and contracts in the *pinkas*. See, for example, the Odratzheim *pinkas*, fols. 38b–39a, where the provisions of the cantor's contract stated his compensation and responsibilities, while affirming that he alone was authorized to serve as ritual slaughterer, even if others were certified by the community's *av beit din*, in Kerner, *La communauté juive*.

3. The Metz sumptuary laws of 1690–97 appeared in the Metz *pinkas*, 76a–84a,

and were published in a French translation in A. Cahen, "Règlements somptuaires"; for comparable laws issued in 1769, see Kerner, "Le règlement de la communauté juive de Metz." The decisions of the Alsatian provincial council of 28 May 1777 were published under the title "Protocol of the Medinah."

4. It can also be shown that the process of social and religious modernization was largely independent of emancipation. See Hyman, *Emancipation of the Jews of Alsace,* and Berkovitz, "The French Revolution and the Jews."

5. Rabbinic restrictions on physical pleasure and monetary expenditures were motivated by a general concern for the poor (see B.T. *Mo'ed Qatan* 27a–b) and by the need to engage in acts of repentance in the aftermath of a catastrophe. For examples of regulations limiting the indulgence in luxury and pleasure, see Maimonides, *Hilkhot Ta'aniyot* 5:12–15. For an example of a modern response, see Roth, "Sumptuary Laws."

6. Baron, *Jewish Community,* 2:301–07, 3:200–203nn. 13–19; Finkelstein, *Jewish Self-Government,* 228, 281–95, 373–75; Pollack, *Jewish Folkways in Germanic Lands,* 86–91.

7. Hunt, *Governance of the Consuming Passions,* esp. 4–11, 108–41.

8. See S. Simonsohn, *The History of the Jews in the Duchy of Mantua* (Jerusalem, 1977), 530–43, and Fram, "The Regulation of Luxury."

9. On the church's efforts to suppress superstition, see Delumeau, *Le Catholicisme entre Luther et Voltaire.* On opposition to the folk custom of *kapparot,* see R. Solomon ben Aderet, *Resp. Rashba* no. 395; Karo, *Shulḥan Arukh, O.H.* 605; and Isserles, *Darkhei Moshe, O.H.* 605:5. The voluminous Jewish moralistic literature includes *Sefer Ḥasidim;* Moshe Henoch Altshuler, *Brantspiegl* (Frankfort, 1676); Isaac ben Eliakim, *Lev Tov* (Amsterdam, 1723); Elhanan Kirchhan, *Simḥat Ha-Nefesh* (Sulzbach, 1798); and Horowitz, *Shenei Luḥot Ha-Berit.*

10. Burke, *Popular Culture and Elite Culture,* 208–41.

11. For an excellent discussion of the Burke thesis in relation to the history of Jewish ritual, see Horowitz, "The Eve of the Circumcision." For medieval evidence signaling the emergence of the community as a distinct body, separate from the *av beit din,* see the *takkanot* of thirteenth-century Mayence, para. 13, in Finkelstein, *Jewish Self-Government,* 228, 242–43; also see the 1575 *takkanah* prohibiting the rabbinic pronouncement of the *ḥerem* without the permission of the community, in Koeber, "Documents Selected from the Pinkas of Friedberg," 46. Cf. the efforts of Jewish communal authorities in sixteenth-century eastern Europe to regulate the choice of marriage partners, independent of rabbinic approval, in Blidstein, *Honor Thy Father and Mother,* 87–88.

12. See Mordechai Breuer, "The Status of the Rabbinate"; Zimmer, *Harmony and Discord,* 104–10; and Katz, "The Rule of Halakhah in Traditional Jewish Society," 171–90.

13. Raeff, "The Well-Ordered Police State." For a full elaboration of the idea of public law, first appearing in 1697, see Domat, *Le droit public.* On the evolution of the term *police,* see Gordon, *Citizens without Sovereignty,* 18–24.

14. See Bacharach, *Resp. Ḥavvot Ya'ir* no. 81. Under certain circumstances the public interest was understood to take priority even over Torah law. See Rashi, B.T. Bava Batra 8b, s.v. *lehassi'a al kizutan,* and Ritva, *Novellae.* Cf. R. Elijah ben Solomon Zalman, *Be'urei Ha-Gra, Y.D.* 228n. 93.

15. See Sirkes, *Resp. Bayit Ḥadash* no. 43.

16. D. Kaufmann, "Extraits," 124–25. From time to time, communal leaders turned to rabbis with technical questions on which public policy depended. See, for example, Reischer, *Resp. Shevut Ya'akov* pt. 3, nos. 10–12, on whether it is possible to burn holy writings that are torn, worn out, or too numerous to store. For a discussion of the appointment of talmudic scholars to public office, despite their exemp-

tion from paying taxes, see ibid. pt. 1, no. 74. On parallel developments in Poland, cf. Fram, *Ideals Face Reality*, 38–47.

17. ShoHat, *'Im Ḥilufe Tekufot*. For Katz's views, see *Tradition and Crisis*, esp. 183–236, and Katz, *Out of the Ghetto*, 34–36.

18. See, for example, Endelman, *The Jews of Georgian England*, and Dubin, *The Port Jews of Habsburg Trieste*.

19. See Owens, "Sumptuary Law and Social Relations in Renaissance Italy," and Catherine K. Killerby, "Practical Problems in the Enforcement of Italian Sumptuary Law, 1200–1500," in *Crime, Society and the Law in Renaissance Italy*, ed. T. Deana and K.J.P. Lowe (Cambridge, Mass., 1994), 99–120.

20. Léon, *Histoire des Juifs de Bayonne*, 387. According to Léon, R. Raphael Meldola of Bayonne made an unsuccessful attempt to enact sumptuary regulations.

21. On Sephardic acculturation, see Hertzberg, *French Enlightenment*, 161–65, 181, 212–13, and Malino, *The Sephardic Jews of Bordeaux*, 23–26.

22. On the Carpentras statutes of the seventeenth and eighteenth centuries, see Calmann, *Carrière of Carpentras*, 65–73.

23. See Roth, "Sumptuary Laws of the Community of Carpentras," and Calmann, *Carrière of Carpentras*, 67–69.

24. See Grant, "The Government of Louis XIV," 5:27; Meuvret, "The Condition of France."

25. The Metz law was issued on 1 Ellul 5450 (6 August 1690). See A. Cahen, "Règlements somptuaires," 79–80.

26. According to 1690 *règlement*, art. 20, wine goblets were not to exceed ten ounces.

27. Art. 1 refers to exemptions on the number of rings that can be worn by certain women celebrants, such as the woman who accompanies the bride to the synagogue on the morning of the wedding and on the first Sabbath after the wedding *until the exit from the synagogue* (emphasis mine). Art. 6 makes a similar stipulation; also see exemptions for brocades used for religious ceremonies in art. 14, and for exceptions, see art. 18. On the dress restrictions for those attending the ball, see art. 32. On restrictions at the Rhinport, see art. 7. On dispensations and restrictions for new mothers and brides, see art. 8. Concerning music restrictions, no musicians were permitted to play in the street following a wedding, and music was generally prohibited in the evening, unless it was on the morrow of the wedding; see art. 19.

28. Cf. the alleviation of luxury restrictions at Jewish weddings in sixteenth-century Italy in Sabar, "The Use and Meaning of Christian Motifs."

29. See Habermas, *Structural Transformation of the Public Sphere*, and Clark, "Commerce, Sociability, and the Public Sphere." On the possibility that sumptuary law aimed to reduce the tax liability of the community, see Fram, "The Regulation of Luxury."

30. 1691 *règlement*. Cf. Hughes, "Distinguishing Signs."

31. 1692 *règlement*.

32. See Jones, "Repackaging Rousseau." For contemporary comments on the moral dangers posed by women's fashion, see Hirsch Koydanover, *Kav Ha-Yashar* (Frankfurt am Main, 1705), ch. 82.

33. 1694 *règlement*, arts. 1, 6, 8. Compare the restrictive provisions in arts. 1, 6, 8–10, and 13 of the 1694 law with the more permissive arts. 7–8 of the 1697 law. The final series of *takkanot* was issued on 21 Heshvan 5458 (5 November 1697). For an earlier instance of regulating celebrations, see *takkanot* of Forlì, in Finkelstein, *Jewish Self-Government*, 286.

34. 1697 *règlement*, prologue. Concern about arousing the jealousy of neighboring gentiles had been a consistent theme in medieval sumptuary law. The 1418 Forlì restrictions aimed "to subdue our hearts and to walk modestly with our God so as

not to become conspicuous in the eyes of the gentiles" (Finkelstein, *Jewish Self-Government*, 281). The emphasis was on concealment, not on absolute prohibition. Cf. Bonfil, *Jewish Life in Renaissance Italy*, 108.

35. Hertzberg, *French Enlightenment*, 20–21. On conditions in Marseilles, see Cole, *Colbert*, 2:42. For evidence of Louis XIV's positive attitude toward the Jews, see Eidelberg, "The Jews of Worms," 73, 91, 93; and A. Cahen, "Les Juifs de la Martinique," 79. On local tensions, see Braudel, *The Identity of France*, 344–46.

36. Resistance to the legislation may be discerned from the text of the 1691 regulation. Noting the spread of "calumnies and slander" against members of the special commission charged with the enforcement of these laws, the commission of twelve issued a warning that the 1690 law must be obeyed. Stern warnings and threats of penalties and fines signaled the growing rift between the leadership and the masses on this issue.

37. Lowenthal, *Memoirs of Glückel of Hameln*, 222–77, esp. 266–67. See Davis, *Women on the Margins*, 5–62.

38. 1690 *règlement*, arts. 28, 32, repeated in 1697 *règlement*, art. 20. Based on the evidence in Italy, Bonfil has argued that sumptuary laws did not aim to prevent the intermingling of Jews and non-Jews but represent an attempt to dissuade Jews from adopting gentile fashion because these were defined as negative. See *Jewish Life in Renaissance Italy*, 104–11.

39. See Miskimin, "Jews and Christians in the Marketplace." French legislation requiring Jews to wear a yellow hat dated from earlier in the seventeenth century, but in 1657 it was modified to no longer apply to the *av beit din* and the seven syndics; for other community members the requirement would subsequently apply only in the city streets. Between 1708 and 1715 the community tried, unsuccessfully, to persuade the government to repeal this legislation; however, by mid-century the custom had disappeared entirely. See Cahen, "La région lorraine," 114.

40. See Roche, *France in the Enlightenment*, 144, 158–60; for an eighteenth-century defense of luxury, see 564ff.

41. See *Pinkas Ha-Kesherim shel Kehillat Pozna*, ed. Dov Avron (Jerusalem, 1967), para. 1798, p. 19, and Fram, "The Regulation of Luxury."

42. See the French translation of the 1690 *takkanot* in A. Cahen, "Enseignement obligatoire."

43. See Netter, "Les anciens cimetières israélites."

44. See A. Cahen, "Rabbinat," *REJ* 8 (1884): 257–58.

45. On the scope of Metz Jewry's economic activity, see G. Cahen, "La région lorraine," 110–13, and P. Meyer, *La communauté juive*, 32–33, 94–96.

46. Benedict, *Cities and Social Change in Early Modern France*, 29–32.

47. Hunt, *Governance of the Consuming Passions*, 4–11, 108–41. Cf. Roche, *The Culture of Clothing*, 38–39; also see p. 505, where the public sphere is identified with traditional norms, while the private realm is associated with personal choice. Cf. Roche, *France in the Enlightenment*, 423.

48. Roche, *France in the Enlightenment*, 110–11, and Roche, *The Culture of Clothing*, 27–29. On the relationship of clothing and social status, see 49–66.

49. The stipulation that communal leaders were to receive no reimbursement whatsoever for their efforts and travel expenses was agreed upon in 1699 and recorded in the Metz *pinkas* in 1702. This fragment was published in D. Kaufmann, "Extraits," 118.

50. 1690 *règlement*, art. 30. See the evolution of art. 25 in the 1690, 1694, and 1697 regulations. Cf. Roche, *Culture of Clothing*, 30–31. For a discussion of early seventeenth-century justifications of luxury in relation to commercial expansion, see Clark, "Commerce, the Virtues, and the Public Sphere."

51. The less expensive materials listed in the *takkanah* were *toile peinte* (painted

canvas), *perse* (chintz), or other fabrics not of silk, transparent fabric, or *en toile* (canvas). See the 1769 *règlement*, arts. 14–16, 5.

52. On the relaxation of restrictions on the elite, see the 1690 *règlement*, art. 30, and the 1697 *règlement*, art. 25. On synagogue honors, see the 1769 *règlement*, arts. 20, 25–26, and 29.

53. See Horowitz, "A Jewish Youth Confraternity." The Asti *takkanot*, for example, complained of "children escaping the study hall to wander in the streets and thoroughfares" (42). The introduction of Sabbath afternoon lessons was intended to keep the youth off the streets. For similar concerns, see Pollack, *Jewish Folkways*, 74–75; for additional sources, see Horowitz, "A Jewish Youth Confraternity," 43, and Horowitz, "Les mondes des jeunes juifs en Europe," 114–16.

54. See, especially, 1769 *règlement*, arts. 5–6, 20, 26, 29, 51, 80, 95. Cf. Kerner, "La vie," 89–90.

55. The Avignon *takkanot* dating from 1558 indicate that although education was not initially compulsory, taxpayers at all levels were required to pay six florins annually, aside from the *Capage* (the head tax exacted from each person fifteen years of age or older), to support the enterprise. According to the *takkanot* of 1779, however, education was compulsory until the age of fifteen. On the 1558 *takkanah*, see Maulde, "Les Juifs dans les Etats français," *REJ* 8 (1884): 99, art. 14. On the 1779 *takkanot*, see Loeb, "Statuts des Juifs d'Avignon," *Annuaire de la société des études juives* 1 (1881): 233–34.

56. For the French translation from the judéo-allemand, see A. Cahen, "Enseignement obligatoire." In Bordeaux, a *yeshivah* was functioning from the beginning of the 1720s, but it was not until 1760 that the community school came under the control of the Nation. The establishment of the *Thalmud Thora* aimed to prevent disturbances caused by children who were not in school because their fathers did not have the necessary resources to pay the teachers. See Bordeaux *Registre* no. 23 (28 April 1721) for the first reference to a *yeshivah* in Bordeaux, and nos. 273 and 280 for regulations. Cf. the regulations of the Talmud Torah of Bayonne, published in Nahon, *Les "Nations" juives portugaises*, document LXXV, pp. 240–44.

57. 1690 *règlement*, art. 22; 1694 règlement, prologue.

58. 1690 *règlement*, arts. 3, 9, 12, 13. On Saturday nights, on the night following a festival, on weeknights, and on Purim eve, women were free to remove their veils and *manteaux*.

59. 1769 *règlement*, art. 64. The *mantel* was part of the normal attire of Jewish men in Germanic lands. It had no sleeves and was thrown on the shoulders as a cape while worn over the coat. A separate *mantel* known as a *schülmantel*, also known in Hebrew as a *sarbal*, was reserved for the Sabbath. Generally, the prohibition against wearing the *schülmantel* was a penalty applied by the *conseil* for certain commercial violations. This penalty carried a measure of public humiliation. See Kerner, "La vie," 205–06. For details on the *mantel*, see Pollack, *Jewish Folkways*, 89–92, 263–64n. 50. This regulation was relaxed on Christian holidays, and exceptions were made for physicians, cattle and horse dealers, and men who had reached the age of seventy.

60. According to Pollack, *Jewish Folkways*, 258n. 19, the silence of the Metz ordinances was uncommon, but two of his references do not bear this out. See *Takkanot Moravia*, p. 99, no. 297, and Aryeh Leib Feinstein, "Nitei Ne'emanim," *Ha-Asif* 6 (1893): 171. According to Glückel, "[B]urghers and engaged couples among the non-Jews seldom or never wore jewels. Instead it was the fashion to wear gold chains." See Lowenthal, *Memoirs of Glückel of Hameln*, 33–34.

61. Eligibility requirements included, beyond the years of marriage, possession of the legal right to live in Metz; a net worth of at least 5,000 crowns (which would place one in the middle order—the highest order was 10,000+); and previous service as administrator of the charity for the poor. These property requirements were

subsequently raised to higher levels, thus ensuring that only the wealthier (and older) members of the community would assume positions of leadership despite the broadening of the electoral base. For these and additional details, see Hertzberg, *French Enlightenment*, 234–35.

62. See, for example, the 1769 *règlement*, arts. 5–6, outlining restrictions on the use of jewelry and clothing that depended on one's financial position.

63. 1769 *règlement*, arts. 20, 25–26, 29. The highest honors, which pertained to the completion and commencement of the annual Torah-reading cycle, included *Ḥatan Torah* and *Ḥatan Bereshit*; medium honors included being called as *maftir* on special Sabbaths. Cf. Hamburger, *The Minhagim of the Worms Community*, 1:123, where it is stated that the honors of *Ḥatan Torah* and *Ḥatan Bereshit* are to be sold to men who have been married recently (in the past year). It was also a well-established custom in Ashkenaz that in order to receive the title *morenu* (our teacher) or *ḥaver* one needed to be married. See Eibeschütz's explanation why he could not grant Mendelssohn the title *ḥaver* in *Kerem Ḥemed* 3, letter no. 21. For various *takkanot* stating that the title *morenu* would be offered to veteran students who had already been married five, ten, or twenty years, see *Takkanot Medinat Moravia*, cited in *Ha-Torah veha-Ḥayyim*, pt. 3, p. 227, and *Pinkas ha-Va'ad*, nos. 592–94.

64. 1769 *règlement*, arts. 46, 51.

65. For parallels, see Hundert, "Jewish Children and Childhood," 89; and Horowitz, "Les mondes des jeunes juifs," 1:113.

66. 1769 *règlement*, art. 80, and Kerner, "La vie," 89–90.

67. 1769 *règlement*, art. 95.

68. Ibid., art. 120.

69. See Horowitz, "A Jewish Youth Confraternity." The Asti Takkanot (para. 3), for example, contained complaints of "children who escaped the hall of study in order to wander in the streets and thoroughfares" (42). The establishment of new Sabbath afternoon lessons was therefore intended to keep the youth off the streets. See examples of similar concerns cited in Pollack, *Jewish Folkways*, 74–75, and Horowitz, "Les mondes des jeunes juifs," 114–16.

70. *Pinkas*, fº4, microfilm no. 8136, Archives JTS, published with translation in Kerner, "Acte de fondation d'un college hébraïque à Metz"; and Kerner, "La vie," 170–72. Both the date of the decision to establish this institution—February 1750—and the emphasis on assistance for poor students suggest that the establishment of the *beit midrash* (house of study) came in response to the urgings of R. Eibeschütz. See *Ya'arot Devash* vol. 1, p. 79.

71. See the 1769 *règlement*, art. 10. For a French translation of the 1769 regulations, see Kerner, "Le règlement de la communauté juive." On institutions for advanced study, including the creation of *batei midrash*, *yeshivot*, and a *kloiz*, see Kerner, "La vie," 174–75; *Pinkas*, fº 35, in Kerner, "Un registre messin"; and "Protocol of the Medinah," art. 12. On the founding of one Alsatian *yeshivah*, see Blum, "Le fondateur du grand Beth Hamidrash de Bouxwiller."

72. Menkis, "New Light on the Transformation of Jewish Education."

73. The 1690 *règlement*, art. 7, stated that even a betrothed girl who was permitted to wear a jewel-spangled headdress on the three Sabbaths immediately following her engagement was not permitted to go out in this attire on the Rhinport. Cf. Burke's discussion of bridges as culture centers in *Popular Culture*, 111–12.

74. The length of the robe was a marker of occupation and status. I have not yet determined its significance in this context, however. Cf. similar measures against the use of tobacco in the *takkanot* of Altona, Hamburg, and Wandsbeck (1715) and Fürth (1728).

75. *Règlement* of 1769, arts. 3, 5. The prohibition against groups of women walking together in the street, except to fulfill a religious obligation, was included in the

Forlì *takkanot* of 1418, in Finkelstein, *Jewish Self-Government*, 285–86. No more than three women, two maidens, or large groups of men were permitted to walk together through the streets. Cf. M. Y. Berdischevsky, "In Their Mothers' Womb," in *Kitvei Micha Yosef Bin-Gurion* (Tel Aviv, 1965), 1:102: "A generation went and a generation came and a new generation arose in Israel, a generation that began to walk on the Sabbath at the borders of the city."

76. 1769 *règlement*, art. 43. Although the practice of *fiançailles* was disappearing by the 1600s, premarital conceptions still accounted for 10 percent of the first births in the 1700s. See Briggs, *Early Modern France*, 190.

77. On the public announcement, see the 1769 *règlement*, art. 42. On domestic servants and sexual issues, see Horowitz, "Les mondes des jeunes juifs," 122–36. On the basis of the 1694 Metz laws restricting expenditures at servants' weddings, Israel Abrahams, *Jewish Life in the Middle Ages* (London, 1896; reprint, 1932), 175–76, concluded that servants were treated as virtual equals there. It would seem, however, that more evidence than this is needed to substantiate such a claim.

78. 1769 *règlement*, art. 62. Exceptions included women who lived in the home of the deceased, two women from the burial society, and two from the shrouds society.

79. See J. Marcus, "The Triesch *Ḥebra Kaddisha*," 180, and the Prague *takkanah* of 1692, art. 25 in *Jüdische Centralblatt* 8 (1889): 51–52. Cf. Noyrlinge, *Yosef Omeẓ* 327, on avoiding frivolity in the cemetery.

80. See Karo, *Beit Yosef, Y.D.* 359, where he cites the zoharic custom to prevent women from going to the cemetery "because if they were to go, they would cause terrible consequences." Also see Dinari, "The Profanation of the Holy," 35–36, where it is proposed that the prohibition derives from the Lurianic conception of impurity, based on Gombiner, *Magen Avraham, O.H.* 359, sub-para. 15. My thanks to Eric Zimmer for bringing the Dinari article to my attention. For an attempt to neutralize the halakhic significance of the zoharic passage, cf. Worms, *Od la-Mo'ed* 140a.

81. See Farr, *Authority and Sexuality*, 19–31. For Eibeschütz's concerns about men and women at the cemetery, see *Ya'arot Devash* vol. 1, p. 262. Eibeschütz regularly railed against sexual immodesty, excessive frivolity, and inappropriate physical contact. See *Ya'arot Devash* vol. 1, pp. 19, 37, 42, 61–62, 231, 240. Additional evidence of sexual immorality and claims of a breakdown in discipline are cited by Kerner, "La vie," 208–18. For Alsace, cf. "Protocol of the Medinah," arts. 23, 27–28. For similar concerns in Prague, see Landau, *Derushei Ha-Zelah*, fols. 4a, 25d, 52b. Nineteenth-century Metz halakhic authority R. Aaron Worms would later object to such efforts to limit women's cemetery visitations. See *Od la-Mo'ed* 141b.

82. For a fuller discussion, see Chapter 3.

83. See Blidstein, *Honor Thy Father and Mother*, 88–94; Philippe Aries, *Centuries of Childhood: A Social History of Family Life* (New York, 1962); David Hunt, *Parents and Children in History: The Psychology of Family Life in Early Modern France* (New York, 1970); and Gottlieb, "The Meaning of Clandestine Marriage." For additional sources, see Colon, *Resp. Maharik*, no. 166; Bacharach, *Resp. Ḥavvot Ya'ir* no. 126.

84. Published in D. Meldola, *Resp. Divrei David* nos. 73, 76. On the Avignon law, see Loeb, "Statuts des Juifs d'Avignon," 230. The discussion that follows draws heavily on Freimann, *Betrothal and Marriage Procedures*, 227–31.

85. Three technical points were adduced: (a) the fact that the *takkanah* disqualified the witnesses; (b) it was stated in advance that every case of *kiddushin* was being performed according to the will of the rabbinic court [*al da'at beit din*] and would otherwise be null; and (c) that the money that had been set aside for the *kiddushin* would be rendered ownerless. D. Meldola, *Resp. Divrei David* nos. 74–76.

86. *Lettres patentes*, 9 July 1718. See Szajkowski, *Autonomy and Communal Jewish Debts*.

87. See Schwarzfuchs, "Takkanot ha-Kahal."

88. See *takkanot* of 1769, arts. 69, 94. These regulations aimed to protect members of the Metz community from the commercial competition posed by residents of outlying towns. It also demanded that individuals seeking to settle in Metz, or anywhere in the province, first obtain the authorization of the *seigneur* and the council.

89. Szajkowski, "The Jewish Communities in France."

90. The protocols of two of the three meetings are apparently no longer extant. Referring to three *circulaires*, Loeb stated that they were addressed to the (local) *parnassim*. The first requested a list of the poor for the distribution of charity, and sought contributors for the *maḥazit ha-shekel* (half-shekel), an annual gift that was to be sent immediately to Jerusalem. The second pertained to temporary stay in Paris, again to the *maḥazit ha-shekel*, and to tax assessment. A third *circulaire*, published and translated by Loeb into German and French, is the protocol of a meeting that took place in Rosheim on either 20 Shevat 5534 or 5537 (the date is unclear). It dealt with marriages conducted by unauthorized persons, with the tax to be paid on dowries, and with the issue of men and women dancing together. Each of the three documents was signed by the general *parnassim*, Aron Meyer of Mutzig, Lehmann Netter of Rosheim, and Cerf-Berr, indicating that the decisions taken at these meetings were binding upon communities in the entire province. See Loeb, "Les Juifs à Strasbourg," 178–79 and 193–98. For a reference to a council of the Jewish communities of Alsace that met annually in Obernai, where its bylaws were adopted on 28 June 1763, see Szajkowski, "The Jewish Communities in France on the Eve of the French Revolution," 600.

91. G. Weill, "Rabbins et Parnassim," 102, 104. Also see the analysis of Hertzberg, *French Enlightenment*, 287–88, and R. Cohen, introduction to Grégoire, *Essai*, 14–15.

92. See G. Weill, "Rabbins et Parnassim," 103–04. R. Wolf Reichshofer was the head of a body composed of the *préposés* of all the communities of the county of Hanau. He played a central role as the convener of the *parnassim* for assemblies, which met at his home, and had the authority to take action against anyone who did not abide by the assembly's decisions. See Weil, "Contribution à l'histoire des communautés alsaciennes." On the provincial organizations of the northeast, see the "Extract from the Protocol of the Medinah," 28 May 1777, published in *Blätter fur jüdische Geschichte und Litteratur* 2 (1901): 18–22, 28–29, and summarized in detail in French by Isidore Loeb, *Extrait du protocole de la nation de l'assemblée du 21 Iyyar 5537*, "Les Juifs à Strasbourg," 181–98.

93. See "Protocol of the Medinah," art. 23. This restriction was binding even if the distance was within the Sabbath limits. Cf. Joseph Karo, *Resp. Avkat Rokhel* (Salonika, 1791) and *Sefer Ha-Ḥinukh*, introduction.

94. This may refer to "Viertel," a quarter measure of wine. See Zimmer, "Marriage Customs in Worms," 23, and *The Minhagim of Worms*, vol. 2, p. 3n. 14.

95. See "Protocol of the Medinah," art. 27. This custom appears to be a variation on the well-known *charivari* practiced in late medieval France and elsewhere. A ritual of disorder performed by young men, the *charivari* aimed to disrupt the first week of marriage of a couple, usually when it was a second marriage, and especially if there was a gross disparity in age between husband and wife. It could also be the placement of obstacles to a wedding ceremony or to the consummation of marriage that could be removed only if a payment of flowers, money, or a drink were made. For a general discussion, see Davis, "The Reasons of Misrule." For a specific example of the demand by the young that *vin donné* furnished by all newlyweds of the community as a tribute, see Muchembled, *Popular Culture and Elite Culture in France*, 96. For precedents in the *takkanot* literature forbidding or limiting the demands made of the groom, see the reference to the *takkanah* issued in Mayence in 1220, in Finkelstein, *Jewish Self-Government*, 225. For a discussion of similar marital customs

in Padua and elsewhere, see Horowitz, "Les mondes des jeunes juifs," 118–19. For a discussion of the paradoxical nature of *charivari*, see Burke, *Popular Culture*, 200–201. In the case of one *charivari* rite that remained part of Jewish life in rural Alsace in the nineteenth century, the Consistory of Wintzenheim abolished in 1823 "the established custom . . . whereby young men demanded or rather extorted certain sums or food and drink from the newlyweds." Archives JTS, box 18. Also see the description by Alexandre Weill, *Couronne* (Paris, 1857), 197, where he describes merry-making before the wedding: the bride-to-be would give sweets and liqueurs to all the young women of the village, and the groom, if he was from the same village, would give all the young men drink. The latter references are cited in Hyman, "The Social Contexts of Assimilation," 115.

96. See Epstein, *Sex Laws and Customs in Judaism*, 101.

97. See Ruel, "Les Chrétiens et la danse."

98. Steinhardt, *Resp. Zikhron Yosef* no. 17.

99. The Rosheim protocol was published and translated by Loeb into German and French in "Les Juifs à Strasbourg," 178–79, 193–98. Cf. the *arrêté* of the community council of Rosheim, art. 3, in *Annuaire de la Société des études juives* 2 (1883): 193–94. Shabbes Schenkwein was so called because of the custom of honoring the bridegroom on the Sabbath preceding his wedding with wine sent to his home. See *The Minhagim of Worms*, vol. 1, p. 40n. 27, 46n. 18; vol. 2, p. 46n. 1, 253.

100. See "Protocol of the Medinah," art. 28. In his note to art. 28, Loeb mistakenly concluded that this was the Sabbath that preceded the wedding.

101. The 1690 *takkanot* issued in Metz (art. 32), prohibited anyone invited to a ball in the city from wearing clothes other than those permitted by this *règlement*. Several years later, the 1697 *takkanah* (art. 20) forbade young men and women, including domestics, from attending a ball at night unless they were invited (this was the same as 1690, art. 28) and even stipulated that one may not go to a dance unless one is invited to the meal. The meaning of these provisions are not clear to me.

102. For a similar appraisal of the *takkanah* issued for Venice and Padua in 1507, see Bonfil, "Aspects of the Social and Spiritual Life of the Jews in the Venetian Territories," 84.

103. A fuller treatment of the historical significance of dancing and its relationship to popular culture would need to consider the role of *tanzhoyzn* (dance halls). These dance halls served as venues for weddings and theatrical productions, including Purim plays. Also see Friedhaber, "Religious Dancing in Marriages." For related sources, see *Pinkas* Runkel (Hesse-Cassel), on men and women dancing together and sleeping in the same room overnight, in Pollack, *Jewish Folkways*, 39; and *takkanot* of Karlesruhe, which permitted women to dance only with women and men with men, p. 221n. 103. See Ezekiel Landau's condemnation of mixed dancing at weddings in *Derushei Ha-Ẓelah*, no. 23, fol. 35b, no. 19; *Resp. Yosef Omeẓ* nos. 97, 103; *Resp. Binyan Zion* no. 139; and Reischer, *Resp. Shevut Yaakov* pt. 1, no. 103.

104. Cf. Jacob Katz's assessment that local *kehillot* had the means to enforce its rulings, while the provincial organization did not, in *Tradition and Crisis*, 107–08.

105. Arts. 21–23, 1784 *lettres patentes*, cited in Loeb, "Les Juifs à Strasbourg," 101–02.

106. "Protocol of the Medinah," art. 1. Cf. Resp. Rashi, ed. Elfenbein, no. 247.

107. "Protocol of the Medinah," arts. 3–4, 9, 13, 17.

108. Ibid., arts. 3, 12, 14, 15, 23, 27–29, 34. Half of the funding was to be provided by fines, two-ninths from the tithe on dowries, and the balance from contributions. The general *parnassim* were instructed to appoint two men to raise money, one from Upper Alsace and one from Lower Alsace; the two *yeshivot* were designated as beneficiaries of a tax of one-half of 1 percent on every inheritance, and on the occasion of marriage, at least *ma'aser* (10 percent) from each the dowry was to be paid to the

Ettendorf *yeshivah* if the groom was a native of Upper Alsace, or to the Sierentz *yeshivah* if he was from Lower Alsace. Those given special honors at a circumcision ceremony were required to make a contribution to the central *beit midrash*, assuming that they had at least 600 *zehuvim*. To ensure that these obligations were carried out, the *mohel* (circumciser) was instructed to provide the *gabbaim* with an *état* of the persons who performed these functions.

109. Bacharach, *Resp. Ḥavvot Ya'ir* no. 81. Cf. no. 57, where Bacharach upheld the authority of the *kahal* to act according to its own understanding without concern whether its policies accorded with the foundations of Jewish law. Elected leaders, he argued, could function as they saw fit, even if this involved action that ostensibly violated the Halakhah. On the question of halakhic *lacunae*, see Blidstein, "Halakhah and Democracy," 15. Significantly, the Bacharach responsum did not require the assent of a major rabbinic authority (*adam ḥashuv*) in order to provide halachic ratification of communal legislation. For a contrasting view, see Reischer, *Resp. Shevut Ya'akov* pt. 1, no. 11, where the approval of a major authority was considered absolutely necessary. On the challenges to religion posed by the new system of social morality, see Maza, "Luxury, Morality, and Social Change," 221. The Metz *takkanot* nonetheless diverged from the model she presents (p. 223), i.e., that the discourse of *moeurs* "ignores distinctions of social class." Bacharach's broad conception of communal legislation, accompanied by a more limited application of halakhic norms, was hardly representative of rabbinic thinking. For an example of the opposing position, see Jacob Sasportas, "The Letters of Rabbi Jacob Sasportas against the Lay Leaders of Livorno, 1681," ed. Isaiah Tishby, *Kobez al Yad* 4 (1946): 143–59.

Chapter 3. Ritual and Religious Culture in Alsace-Lorraine

1. See the derisive characterizations of Jewish ritual in Voltaire, *Essai sur les moeurs et l'esprit des nations*; Grégoire, *Essai*, ch. 25; and Anne-Louis Henri de la Fare, *Opinion de M. l'Evêque de Nancy, deputé de Loraine, sur l'admissibilité des Juifs à la plénitude de létat civil, et des droits de citoyens actifs* (Paris, 1790).

2. Gennep, *Manuel de folklore français contemporain*; Muchembled, *Popular Culture and Elite Culture in France*.

3. Muir, *Ritual in Early Modern Europe*, 1–9.

4. See the *maḥzor* (special prayerbook) for Rosh Hashanah, rite of Carpentras (1695), property of University College London. On rituals of Bayonne, see R. Meldola, *Resp. Mayyim Rabbim*, and D. Meldola, *Resp. Divrei David*. On the distinctive Hebrew pronunciation in Bordeaux and Bayonne, see Moshe Bar-Asher, "Les traditions de l'hébreu dans les communautés juives du sud-ouest de la France," *REJ* 160 (2001): 435–38.

5. The Prague community's inclination toward western traditions has been noted by Zimmer, "Reactions of German Jewry," 233. Virtually all of the rabbis who served Metz, and several in Alsace, had previously held positions in Prague or had studied in the Prague *yeshivah*. On westward migrations, see Shulvass, *From East to West*.

6. See A. Levy, *Die Memoiren des Ascher Levy*.

7. See A. Cahen, "Rabbinat," *REJ* 7 (1883): 220–23; Shulvass, *From East to West*, 42; and the valuable *Ma'aseh Tuviah* by Tuvia Cohen.

8. On the phenomenon in the medieval period, see Mordecai Breuer, "The Wandering Students and Scholars"; Ben-Sasson, "The Social Teaching of R. Yohanan Luria," 177; and Yuval, "A German-Jewish Autobiography of the Fourteenth Century."

9. See Heller, *Addendum to Megilat Eivah*. For evidence that Alsatians frequently looked eastward for their marriage partners, see Raphaël and Weyl, *Juifs en Alsace,*

133–34. In part, this was linked to patterns of *yeshivah* study; see, for example, Ginsburger, "La famille Schweich."

10. *Beit Yehonatan Ha-Sofer* 7b. In *Petaḥ Ha-Enayim* (Altona, 1750), 1b–2a, Emden listed Metz along with Frankfurt am Main, Altona, Hamburg, Wandsback, Nikolsburg, and Amsterdam as the seven most important European communities of his day, "and if I did not know their order, it would make no difference as they are all at the same level."

11. According to R. Jonathan Eibeschütz, superior conditions in the west accounted for the influx of Polish *yeshivah* students to Metz. See sermon of Av 5509 (1749), published in *Ya'arot Devash* 2:121. The linkage between economic prosperity and cultural prominence is discussed in Kerner, "La vie," 3. For indications that the Metz students were predominantly from poor families, both locally and from Poland, see Koblentz, *Resp. Kiryat Ḥannah*, introduction, and Eibeschütz, *Ya'arot Devash*, vol. 1, p. 93b; vol. 2, p. 40b. For the Günzberg contract, see Schwarzfuchs, "The Rabbinic Contract of the Sha'agat Aryeh in Metz."

12. For rare information on one of the several small Alsatian academies, see Blum, "Le fondateur du grand Beth Hamidrash de Bouxwiller." Also see Weil, "Contribution à l'histoire des communautés alsaciennes," 172–73.

13. Virtually all of Carmoly's writings have remained in manuscript, with the exception of *Yam Issachar* on Tosefta Beiẓa (Metz, 1768). See Carmoly, "Issachar Carmoly." Shlomo Lvov, another itinerant student originally from Mannheim, studied first in Alsace and then in Furth before coming to Metz. See *Ḥeshek Shlomo*, ms. (Dittwiller, 1784), intro., Institute of Hebrew Manuscripts, Jerusalem, no. 3394; Yedidiah (Tiah) Weil (1721–1805), whose father, Netanel (author of *Korban Netanel*), had studied in Metz under R. Abraham Broda, came to the Metz *yeshivah* himself in 1745 after the Prague expulsion.

14. See Israel, *European Jewry in the Age of Mercantilism*, 237.

15. See G. Weill, "Recherches sur la démographie des juifs d'Alsace," 53–55.

16. See Chapter 1. On changes in prayer rites introduced by newly arrived rabbis, see the examples of R. Süssel Moyse Enosch in Ribeauvillé and R. Petachiya in Worms in Kirchheim, "Birkhot Ha-Shaḥar," in *Minhagot Wormaiza*, gloss no. 8.

17. On rabbinic views of demons and magic, see Gafni, "Babylonia Rabbinic Culture," 238–53, and bibliography in nn. 113–14; the phrase "embedded in the rabbinic mind" is on p. 250.

18. See Brown, *The Cult of the Saints*, and Benin, "A Hen Crowing Like a Cock."

19. Lebrun, *La vie conjugale*, 139–42.

20. See Pollack, *Jewish Folkways*, 16–17; Raphaël, "Rites de naissance et medecine populaire."

21. See Margaliot, *Sefer Ha-Razim*, and Joseph Dan, *Torat Ha-Sod shel Ḥasidei Ashkenaz* (Jerusalem, 1968).

22. For the roots of this custom, see *Tze'enah u-Re'enah* on Genesis 3:6. On its cultural significance, see Fishman, "The Penitential System of Ḥasidei Ashkenaz."

23. See Hamburger, *The Minhagim of the Worms Community*, para. 288, pt. 2, pp. 158–64. Cf. Bacharach, *Mekor Ḥayyim* (Jerusalem, 1984), *O.H.* 88. On the custom in Metz, see Eibeschütz, *Kereti u-Feleti*, *Y.D.* 194:2, and Worms, *Kan Tahor* 135b. Also see Zimmer, *Society and Its Customs*, esp. 220–39. On the ritual itself, see Baumgarten, *Mothers and Children*, ch. 3, and Jay R. Berkovitz, "Minhag in the Halakhic System of R. Ya'ir Ḥayyim Bacharach" [Hebrew], in *Eric Zimmer Jubilee Volume*, ed. Gershon Bacon (Ramat Gan, Israel, in press). On childbirth rituals, see Sabar, "Childbirth and Magic."

24. See Hamburger, *Minhagim of the Worms Community*, pt. 2, para. 288, pp. 158–64, and notes of B. Hamburger. Also see Raphaël and Weyl, *Juifs en Alsace*, 231–86, and Pollack, *Jewish Folkways*, 27–29.

25. See Zeev Gries, *The Book as an Agent of Culture, 1700–1900* (Tel Aviv, 2002).

26. See the reference to Lurianic practice in *Tefilah ke-Minhag Ashkenaz u-Folin* 48b, and in "Seder Ha-Ma'amadot" 4b. In his "Ḥibbur ha-Siddur" (see n. 74), fol. 145, Worms referred to the practice, introduced by the rabbi of the Metz *beit midrash* at the turn of the eighteenth century, of reciting Psalms 86 and 124, as well as *seder ketoret ha-ma'amadot*, after *Aleinu*. This continued to be the community's custom in the nineteenth century.

27. *Seder Tefilah ke-Minhag Ashkenaz* pt. 2, pp. 1a–2a, 12b, 18a, 20b, 66b.

28. On *teḥinot* for pregnant women, see ibid., pt. 4, pp. 39b–40a; on *tashlikh* and *kapparot*, see ibid., pt. 2, p. 125b. The *tashlikh* ceremony was included in the *Maḥzor shel Rosh Hashanah ke-Minhag Ashkenaz* pt. 1, p. 125b, though there is no mention of the *kapparot* rite in the *Maḥzor shel Yom Kippur*. On Worms's criticism, see below.

29. Koblentz, *Resp. Kiryat Ḥannah* no. 2.

30. For other examples, see Hertzberg, *French Enlightenment*, 142, 176–77, 186, 201–04; Schechter, *Obstinate Hebrew*, 131–49.

31. The prayer, printed in Basel, does not include a date. The original text is in the National and University Library, Jerusalem, L 58. "TaNTA," an acronym for "teivot, nekudot, te'amim, ve-otiyot," refers to the words, vowels, notes, and letters of a Torah scroll. "Ha-ḥoḥim veha-koẓim" refer to husks of evil. I am indebted to Professor Paul Fenton for giving me a copy of the text and for his assistance. Copies of the text were distributed in honor of the marriage of his children, Mordecai and Saphia Weizman-Fenton, August 2003.

32. The seven volumes of *Me'orei Or* were published under the following titles: *Me'orei Or*, vols. 1–3; *Be'er Sheva; Od la-Mo'ed; Bin Nun;* and *Kan Tahor.* Worms's other works include a commentary to the Passover *Haggadah* (Metz, 1815) and several others in manuscript, including commentaries to Psalms and Job; a commentary to *Seder Eliah Rabbah* and *Seder Eliah Zuta*, titled *Ḥamishah Or;* halakhic addenda to *Me'orei Or*, titled *Shemonat Or;* and a commentary to the *siddur*, which included instructions for proper execution of *kavvanot*, based on the Zohar. On Worms's life and writings, see Nahum Brüll, "Ner la-Ma'or" [Hebrew], *Oẓar Ha-Sifrut* 1 (1887): 20–31; Moshe Catane, "R. Aaron Worms and His Student Eliakim Carmoly" [Hebrew,] *'Areshet* 2 (1960): 190–98; and Berkovitz, "Authority and Innovation at the Threshold of Modernity." Worms was a son of R. Abraham Aberlé Worms, author of *Pundaka d' Avraham*, an unpublished volume of responsa, and a great-grandson of R. Eliah Belin, *av beit din* of the community of Worms, and of the renowned R. Gershon Ashkenazi. Some additional details of his life are noted in *Bin Nun* 186a–b and *Kan Tahor* 146b.

33. *Be'er Sheva* 18a, 20a, 105b. Worms probably gained familiarity with the Lurianic Kabbalah from *Likkutei Ẓvi*, which was assembled by Zvi Hirsch of Williamsdorf; it included the *tikkunei haẓot* (mystical prayer vigils at midnight) from Hanover's *Sha'arei Zion*. Among the printings was Lunéville, 1798.

34. Aaron Worms, "Ḥibbur Ha-Siddur," is contained in *Ḥamishah Or* (ms. no. 288, Alliance israélite universelle), ca. 1819.

35. In the course of elucidating the ruling that the *tefillin* ought to be placed on one's head before completing the binding of the straps around the fingers, Worms explained the dissenting view of Luria as halakhically legitimate for those who recite a single benediction, in *Be'er Sheva* 18b. Cf. Worms's approval of the Lurianic custom, against *Magen Avraham*, to recite Ps. 130 between the morning benedictions *yishtabaḥ* and *yotzer*, claiming this was not an interruption in prayer, in *Me'orei Or* II 24a. Cf. Ezekiel Landau, *Dagul Me'Revavah*, *O.H.* 54:1 (based on Maimonides, *Hilkhot Tefillah* 7:11), and the view of R. Ḥayyim Ulma, as noted by Zimmer, "Reactions of German Jewry," 236–37. On the relationship between Halakhah and Kabbalah in the period between the discovery of the *Zohar* and the publication of the

Shulḥan Arukh, see Katz, "Post-Zoharic Relations between Halakhah and Kabbalah." On the period following the *Shulḥan Arukh*, see Moshe Ḥalamish, "Ma'amado shel ha-Ari ke-Poseq," *Meḥqerei Yerushalayim be-Maḥshevet Yisrael* 10 (1993): 259–85.

36. In *Be'er Sheva* 109a, Worms noted that the custom to recite Psalm 104 on Rosh Ḥodesh, as stated in *Arba'h Turim O.H.* 423, was confirmed by *Midrash Ne'elam (Va-Yera)*, though he offered a different explanation; in *Od la-Mo'ed* 31b, he observed that the Tosafist view requiring three *matzot* corresponded to the explicit demonstration in *Zohar* and *tikkunim.* Similarly, in *Shemonat Or* 10a (referring to *O.H.* 490:9), Worms cited the *Midrash Ne'elam* to explain that there is a kabbalistic reason for reading the book of Ruth on the festival of Shavuot.

37. See, for example, *Be'er Sheva* 1b, where Worms cited the *Zohar* in response to R. Samuel Eliezer Edel's question of why when Psalm 145 is recited at *minḥah* it is recited before the *Amidah*, not after.

38. On the views of Emden, see *Mitpaḥat Sefarim* (Lvov, 1871), 77–78, and of Eibeschütz, see his approbation to Zvi Horowitz, *'Aspaklariah ha-Me'irah* (Fürth, 1776), cited in Idel, "Perceptions of the Kabbalah." Also see Liebes, "Meshiḥiyuto shel R. Ya'akov Emden ve-Yaḥaso le-Shabeta'ut." On the views of Ezekiel Landau, see *Resp. Noda b'Yehudah*, vol. 1, *O.H.* no. 93; vol. 1, *Y.D.* no. 74. Steinhardt accused Hasidic leaders of teaching heresy. Their reckless behavior, he insisted, would only delay the long-awaited redemption. See *Resp. Zikhron Yosef*, introduction, and cf. Steinhardt's letter to R. Ezekiel Landau, discussed in Elior, "R. Nathan Adler and the Frankfurt Pietists," 42–49. Also see Nadler, *Faith of the Mithnagdim*, 29–43.

39. *Be'er Sheva* 18a. The quote from his *siddur* commentary was reproduced in *Kan Tahor* 164a. On the early seventeenth-century *ḥerem* against distributing Lurianic writings outside of the Land of Israel, see Benayahu, *Sefer Toldot Ha-Ari* 45, 65, and Elbaum, *Openness and Insularity*, 200–207.

40. *Od la-Mo'ed* 33a.

41. On Worms's opposition to swaying during prayer, see *Be'er Sheva* 20a. For kabbalistic sources on swaying, see *Zohar (Pinchas)* pt. 3, pp. 218b–219a; *Zava'at Ha-Rivash* (1793) 8b. For halakhic sources, see *Shulḥan Arukh O.H.* 48, and Spitzer, *Sefer Maharil*, "Laws of Prayer," 436. Also see Liebes, "R. Wolff ben Yonatan Eibeschütz's Work"; and Idel, "Perceptions of the Kabbalah," 98–99. For a detailed discussion of these and related issues, see Zimmer, "Poses and Postures during Prayer," esp. 116–27.

42. *Od la-Mo'ed* 33a; *Be'er Sheva* 28b (*O.H.* 108). Cf. Idel, *Hasidism*, ch. 1, on the opposition to Lurianism in eighteenth-century Europe.

43. *Be'er Sheva* 110a.

44. See *Be'er Sheva* 18a, for Worms's objection to the benediction over Rabbenu Tam *tefillin.*

45. See *Kan Tahor* 185b and *Be'er Sheva* 14b–15a.

46. See *Be'er Sheva* 31b.

47. Ibid., 105b–106a.

48. Worms also distinguished between the views of Luria himself and those attributed to him by his students and later generations. See, for example, *Be'er Sheva* 21a–21b, where he ascribed Luria's opposition to reciting the verse "ve'ata yigdal na ko'aḥ" (Num. 14:17) whenever it is forbidden to interrupt prayer to the fact that it does not appear in the *Tikkunei ha-Zohar* but in *Sefer ha-Kavvanot* 10b.

49. See Stefan Reif, *Shabbethai Sofer and His Prayer-book* (Cambridge, 1979); Reif, *Judaism and Hebrew Prayer*, 230–50; and Schacter, "R. Jacob Emden," ch. 4.

50. See *Od la-Mo'ed* 33a–b, 52b–55b, for corrections to festival liturgies, and *Shemonat Or* 10a for his notation of several other printing errors and his suggested corrections.

51. See, for example, *Od la-Mo'ed* 32a, where it is shown that the formula generally used to introduce the counting of the *omer* is incorrect, because, since the de-

struction of the Temple, the obligation to count the *omer* is only rabbinically ordained.

52. See *Be'er Sheva* 34b.

53. On faulty Hebrew pronunciation by Ashkenazim, see *Be'er Sheva* 32b, and M. Sofer, *Resp. Ḥatam Sofer* no. 275. For Worms's view of *Makhnisei Raḥamim*, see *Be'er Sheva* 53a. On the controversy surrounding the prayer, see Immanuel, "On the Recitation of *Makhnisei Raḥamim*," 5–11; and Malkiel, "Between Worldliness and Traditionalism." Worms issued biting criticism of the *kavvanot* and of petitions to angels to accept the sounds of the *shofar*, claming that "things of this sort that are not found in the Talmud and *midrashim* strengthen the hand of those who mock us," in *Be'er Sheva* 92b–93a. Cf. the similar objection of R. Elijah b. Solomon Zalman to the phrase *barekhuni le-shalom* in the *piyyut* "Shalom Aleikhem," reported in *Sefer Tosefet Ma'aseh Rav* (Jerusalem, 1986) no. 128, p. 18b; for Worms's apparent omission of the phrase; see *Be'er Sheva* 98a.

54. See *Me'orei Or* II, 23a; *Be'er Sheva* 19b–20a (on *O.H.* 46); and "Mahadurah Bet" (Second Ed.) in *Bin Nun*, summarized in *Shemonat Or* 4b. Cf. Kirchheim, *Minhagei Worms*, "Birkhot Ha-Shaḥar," gloss no. 8, and Hamburger, *Minhagim of Worms Community*, "Seder Birkhot Shaḥarit," para. 7, where it is stated that one should not say *she'asani Yisrael* but rather *shelo asani goi*. The form had been changed from *she'asani Yisrael* to *shelo asani goi* by R. Petachia b. Yosef following his appointment as *av beit din* in 1629, along with other changes in the community's *minhagim* (see I, p. ט, nn. 2–4). Cf. *Be'urei ha-Gra O.H.* 46, n. 8, where the preference for *she'asani Yisrael* is substantiated by a reference to *Menaḥot* 43b.

55. The view of R. Hai Gaon, quoted in Isserles, *Darkhei Moshe Y.D.* 116:4 and in *Od la-Mo'ed* 32b; and Ashkenazi, *Resp. Avodat Ha-Gershuni* no. 63, cited in *Be'er Sheva* 24b.

56. On *kapparot*, see *Od la-Mo'ed* 50b, following the Rashba, *Resp. Solomon ibn Aderet* no. 395; *Shulḥan Arukh O.H.* 605, and Isserles, *Darkhhei Moshe O.H.* 605:5. Concerning *tashlikh*, see *Od la-Mo'ed* 32b–33a, 50b. For Isserles's view, see *O.H.* 583:2. Worms's psychological explanation for the invention of these rituals is in *Od la-Mo'ed* 32b–33a. Cf. the similar view of Abraham Ibn Ezra, quoted in the *TaZ Y.D.* 116, n. 4. For the Maharil's view, see Spitzer, *Sefer Maharil*, "Hilkhot Rosh Hashanah." For the Lurianic sources, see Ḥayyim Zemah, *Nagid u-Meẓaveh* (Leghorn, 1785) 74b–75; Horowitz, *Shenei Luḥot Ha-Berit* II, Hilkhot Teshuvah (Josefow, 1878) 15; *Ḥemdat Ha-Yamim* (Leghorn, 1764), chs. 4, 7. Cf. Jacob Emden, *Siddur Yaveẓ* (Altona, 1739–60), "Seder Kapparot," para. 13. The major study of *tashlikh* remains Lauterbach, "Tashlik."

57. See *Be'er Sheva* 30b–31a, and his comments there on *Sefer Raziel*, which he regarded as having misrepresented itself by its citation of rabbinic sources.

58. *Bin Nun* 99a. On the use of the *ḥerem* in Alsace-Lorraine, see Posener, "Social Life," 215–17.

59. *Od la-Mo'ed* 26b.

60. Cf. *Be'urei Ha-Gra O.H.* 553n. 9, 558n. 1, 559n. 10.

61. *Od la-Mo'ed* 27b. Worms reported that in the early years of his career he was able to eliminate the practice of baking thick *matzot*, which had been popular in the countryside. The generic expression *mit'ḥasdim* to denote the excessively pious may have been read by contemporaries as a reference to followers of Hasidism. Worms also referred to a strange Metz practice to refrain from "mushroom flour," based on the analogy with *kitniyot*, "because it can be ground like flour" and thereby mistaken for wheat. This stringency persisted until Worms was able to annul it in 1794, when dire economic conditions justified leniency. See ibid., 28b. Also see *Od la-Mo'ed* 108a for his objection to the stringent view of the *Magen Avraham*, and *Be'er Sheva* 110a, where he warned of the dangers posed by unauthorized stringencies.

62. *Od la-Mo'ed* 26a.

63. See *Kan Tahor* 7b–8a, referring to B.T. Sanhedrin 46. Cf. ibid., 144a.

64. *Od la-Mo'ed* 30b. Cf. Noyrlingen, *Yosef Omeẓ*, where no mention is made of the cup of Elijah; in para. 788 he advised reciting "Shefokh Ḥamatkha" over the fourth cup of wine. For a similar, functional approach, see the view of *Knesset ha-Gedolah*, cited in M. Ḥagiz, *Resp. Shetei ha-Leḥem* (Wandsback, 1733) no. 46.

65. Cf. *Be'er Sheva* 92b–93a (n. 24 above). Similarly, he was critical of cantors who feigned crying during the week preceding Tisha b'Av. Sorrowful prayer, he insisted, was appropriate only in passages referring to the destruction of the Temple and Jerusalem, the hope for redemption, or on Tisha b'Av itself. See *Od la-Mo'ed* 109a (on *O.H.* 551).

66. Cf. *Be'er Sheva* 20a.

67. In one instance, in 1661–62, the rabbi of Bouxwiller turned to the Worms *av beit din* with a question. See *Resp. Ḥut Ha-Shani* nos. 51 and 52. On the conflict in Frankfurt, see Halperin, *East European Jewry*, 108–22, and on its resolution, see Ginsburger, "Familles Lehmann et Cerf Berr."

68. Ginsburger, "Mémoriaux," 138.

69. Steinhardt, *Resp. Zikhron Yosef* 52b. This collection of responsa spanned his career in Alsace and Bavaria. The expression *benei Rheinus* appeared innumerable times in volumes of *minhagim* assembled in the fourteenth century, including at least seventy references in *Sefer Maharil* alone.

70. On the history of specific Rhineland customs, see Zimmer, *Society and Its Customs*, esp. 198–203, 217–39, 256–61, 273–98.

71. Various orders of *seliḥot* point to the differences in the customs of the Upper Rhine and Metz. Compare, for example, *Seliḥot mi-kol ha-Shanah ke-Minhag Elsass* with *Seder Seliḥot ke-Minhag ha-Ashkenazim.*

72. See Metz *Memorbuch*, vi. Schwarzfuchs's observation concerning the orientation of Metz is based on his analysis of the places of origin of Metz residents. References to communities of Alsace and Lorraine are less common than to those of Worms, Trèves, Coblence, and Bingen, for example.

73. Attitudes toward the Isserles glosses ranged from strident criticism to effusive praise. For the harshest critique, see Ḥayyim ben Beẓalel Friedberg, *Viku'aḥ Mayyim Ḥayyim* (Amsterdam, 1712), introduction. Worms's disapproval of Isserles in the realm of *minhag* may have been a departure from his predecessors. Rabbis in the west frequently had only high praise for Isserles and the Polish sages. Reischer, *Resp. Shevut Ya'akov* pt. 3 no. 112, declared "we, the sages of Ashkenaz and Poland who accepted upon ourselves the opinion of the Rema [Isserles]," in Rosman, "The Image of Poland as a Center of Torah Learning," 440. R. Ẓevi Hirsch Ashkenazi found Isserles's selective approach to Maharil problematic. See, for example, *Resp. Ḥakham Ẓevi* (Amsterdam, 1712) no. 124. Cf. Emden's more critical view of Maharil, *Resp. She'elat Yaveẓ* I, no. 75. The last two references, as well as other attitudes toward Maharil in medieval and early modern writings, are in Hamburger, "The Historical Foundations of Minhag Ashkenaz," 101–05. The standard text of *minhagim* of Maharil is the collection assembled by Zalman of St. Goar, in Spitzer, *Sefer Maharil.* On the opposition of sixteenth-century German rabbis to the halakhic dominance of Poland, see Zimmer, *The History of the Rabbinate in Germany*, 17. For an example of the opposing trend, see Reischer, *Resp. Shevut Ya'akov* pt. 3, no. 121 (116). On Worms's preference for Maharil over Isserles, see *Be'er Sheva* 14b, 31b–32a; cf. *Od la-Mo'ed* 32b, 51a, 109a. Apparently at Worms's instruction, *Hadrat Qodesh*, a compendium of customs attributed to Maharil, was included in the *Maḥzor shel Yom Kippur* 9a–14b.

74. *Be'er Sheva* 31b–32a, referring to Isserles, *Darkhei Moshe O.H.* 127:3; *Od la-Mo'ed* 32a; *Be'er Sheva* 3b, 31b. Cf. the view of Emden that although "Oseh ha-shalom" was the proper Ashkenazic custom, one could not dismiss the opposition

of halakhic authorities and of Luria; he therefore recommended, in accordance with Sephardic custom, to recite "ha-mevarekh" year-round (*Siddur Yayez* 74a). Similarly, the Gaon of Vilna broke with *minhag Ashkenaz* on the two benedictions. See Sperber, *Minhagei Israel,* 2:178–81.

75. On lengthening Yom Kippur, see *Od la-Mo'ed* 53a and *Be'er Sheva* 21a–b. Isserles's ruling on the indispensability of a *minyan* for *selihot* is in *O.H.* 565:5; for Worms's comment, see *Od la-Mo'ed* 108a. On the proper time to recite *arvit* (evening prayer), see *Be'er Sheva* 33a. Also see Worms's recommendations regarding the order and language of the morning benedictions in *Me'orei Or* II, 13a, and cf. Kirchheim, *Minhagei Worms,* "Birkhot Ha-Shahar," 9b, and Hamburger, *Minhagim of Worms Community,* "Seder Birkhot Shaharit," p. ﬦ, nn. 3, 4. In the case of Metz, the locally produced *siddur* did not follow Worms's views.

76. See Daniel Goldschmidt, *Mahzor le-Yamim Nora'im* (Jerusalem, 1970), 1:xxxi–il; Jacques Dukan, "Un exégète de piyyutim en France au XIIIe siècle," *REJ* 144 (1986): 250–56.

77. See *Mahzor ke-Minhag Ashkenaz u-Folin* 7b–8a, 93b; Cf. Goldschmidt, *Mahzor le-Yamim Nora'im* 2:10–11, 14–16.

78. See the various *siddurim* and *mahzorim* published in Metz, beginning with *Seder Tefilah ke-Minhag Ashkenaz.*

79. Lough, *An Introduction to Eighteenth-Century France,* 70.

80. On the rite adopted in Ribeauvillé, see *AI* 5 (1844): 542–47, and on Enosch, see Chapter 2 (this volume). Concerning the Günzberg incident, see A. Cahen, "Rabbinat," *REJ* 12 (1886): 294–95. For a defense of the Metz custom, see Koblentz, *Resp. Kiryat Hannah* no. 7. Cf. Worms, *Od la-Mo'ed* 13a. On the general issue of rabbinic freedom to modify the local rite, cf. para. 13 of the rabbinic contract of R. Man Todros, recorded in Pinkas Friedberg, Elul 5335 (1575), where it was stipulated that the *av beit din* could not alter the liturgy of the community without the permission of the council. Published in Koeber, "Documents Selected from the Pinkas of Friedberg."

81. There may well be an additional indication of tension between Günzberg and the *kehillah* over local customs. In comments accompanying the *Kol Nidrei* prayer, published in *Mahzor shel Yom Kippur* of Metz, Aaron Worms referred to the fact that it had been customary "in our area" to recite the evening prayer before nightfall, "until the custom was changed about fifty years ago." Although there is no explicit reference to details, this would correspond to precisely the time when Günzberg assumed the chief rabbinical post in Metz.

82. *Selihot mi-kol ha-Shanah ke-Minhag Elsass.* The volume was republished in 1725 and numerous times thereafter, including an edition by Wolf Heidenheim (Roedelheim, 1838). On the 1691 edition, see S. Frankel, "Concerning Two Lost Books That Were Found," 141, and Hayyim Schmeltzer, note in *Kiryat Sefer* 59 (1984): 646.

83. The Metz *selihot* volume was titled *Seder Selihot ke-Minhag ha-Ashkenazim.*

84. For specific synagogue customs performed in Metz, see *Seder Tefilah ke-Minhag Ashkenaz;* concerning the order of *Tahanun,* see p. 35a–b; regarding the recitation of *Birkhat Kohanim* on a festival that falls on the Sabbath, see p. 48b. For Metz variants to the standard order of scriptural verses in the *Musaf* of Rosh Hashanah and Yom Kippur according to most Ashkenazic communities, see *Mahzor ke-Minhag Ashkenaz u-Folin* pt. 1, p. 28b; for other examples of similar variances, see pp. 14a, 42a, 43a.

85. *Mahzor* (1768) 5b–6a, 81a, 90a, 159b–160a, 169a, 174a.

86. *Mahzor* (1768) 65a–b; 93b; *Mahzor le-Pesach, Shavu'ot, ve-Sukkot* pt. 2, p. 49, 126b.

87. See Halamish, "Birkhat Magbiah Shefalim," 198.

88. *Mahzor le-Pesach, Shavu'ot, ve-Sukkot* pt. 2, p. 53b; for the opposing view, see is-

serles, *O.H.* 547:6, and cf. Gombiner, *Magen Avraham O.H.* 547:3. R. Aaron Worms noted that in his day many were not accustomed to rend their garments on *ḥol ha-mo'ed*, even for a parent. See *Od la-Mo'ed* 138a. On an unusual custom concerning *eruv ḥazerot* before the Passover holiday, see *Maḥzor le-Pesach, Shavu'ot, ve-Sukkot* pt. 2, p. 100a.

89. See, for example, *Od la-Mo'ed* 26b, 29a, and *Kan Tahor* 111a.

90. Narol's elegy for Polish Jewry, titled *Baqashah*, was first published in Amsterdam in 1699, and subsequently in Metz (1777) and Lunéville (1806). In these three instances, it was printed in a handbook that included the *piyyut* "Geroni Niḥar," which was recited in Metz on the "four fasts," and occasional prayers recited during the period between Rosh Hashanah and the end of Sukkot. For the point at which the *Baqashah* was recited, see *Seder Tefilah ke-Minhag Ashkenaz* 79b. For a listing of prayers composed in memory of the Chmielnicki martyrs, see Bernfeld, *Sefer Ha-Dema'ot*, 3:160–84, and Handel, *Gezerot Taḥ ve-Tat*, ch. 3. For Narol's account of his encounter with King Louis XIV in 1657, see Eidelberg, "The Jews of Worms," 91–93.

91. Behre, "Raphael Lévy."

92. "Yizkorbuch of Haguenau," HM 5010, Central Archives for the History of the Jewish People, Jerusalem (hereafter cited as CAHJP), cited in Hyman, *Emancipation of the Jews of Alsace*, 71–72. See also Simon Schwarzfuchs, "The Place of the Crusades in Jewish History," in *Culture and Society in Medieval Jewry: Studies Dedicated to the Memory of Haim Hillel Ben-Sasson*, ed. Menahem Ben-Sasson, Robert Bonfil, and Joseph Hacker (Jerusalem, 1989).

93. The Hilman contract was reprinted in *Blätter für Jüdische Geschichte und Litteratur* 1 (1900): 39–40, and the Günzberg contract was published and annotated in Schwarzfuchs, "The Rabbinic Contract."

94. Lvov, *Ḥeshek Shlomo* (see note 13 above). For examples of similar complaints voiced in the late seventeenth century and earlier in the eighteenth century, see Bacharach, *Resp. Ḥavvot Ya'ir* no. 125; Reischer, *Resp. Shevut Ya'akov* pt. 1, 4a; Eibeschütz, *Ya'arot Devash* sermon no. 5 (Metz, 5505 [1744]), pt. 1, p. 119; Eibeschütz, sermon no. 16 (Metz, 5507 [1747]) vol. 1, pp. 301–02, reprinted in 1983 Jerusalem edition; and Landau, *Derushei Ha-Ẓelah* 16a. Also see discussion in Shoḥat, *Im Ḥilufe Tekufot*, 110ff. It should be added that according to earlier sources, students at the Metz *yeshivah* were predominantly from poor families, both locally and from Poland, a condition that would undoubtedly affect their marriage prospects. See Eibeschütz, *Ya'arot Devash* vol. 1, p. 93b; vol. 2, p. 40b; and Koblentz, *Resp. Kiryat Ḥannah*, introduction.

95. On Metz's population decline, see Hertzberg, *French Enlightenment*, 129, and on Metz's economic troubles, see Labrousse, *Esquisse de mouvement des prix et des revenues*, 1:188, 304, 2:468, 598, 602; *Histoire économique et sociale de la France*, 2:399. Although population figures tend to be unreliable, it is clear that the number granted the right of domicile by the community was on the decline. In the years 1759–69, twenty-four foreigners were naturalized; the next two decades witnessed a total of thirteen. For a full description, see Kerner, "La vie," 75–78, and appendix, pp. XXII–XXXVI; on the 1782 decision of the *av beit din*, see p. 117; on the *yeshivah*, see p. 184. For further evidence of the material deterioration of the Metz community, see pp. 116–23.

96. Ford, *Strasbourg in Transition*, 142–57.

97. On the general economic decline in northeastern France, see Szajkowski, *Jews in the French Revolutions*, 204–05.

98. Information on the *yeshivot* of western and central Europe is scarce. According to local record books, the Frankfurt *yeshivah* counted 120–130 students in 1780; by 1793, the number declined to 60. On the *yeshivah*'s economic decline, see the description by the director, R. Zvi Hirsch Horwitz, in *Laḥmei Todah* (Offenbach, 1815). Figures for Fürth are only available for 1827, the year it closed, when there were 150

students. The *yeshivah* of Mainz had approximately 50 students in 1782, but declined after the death of its director, R. Hirtz Scheuer. For a brief history of these and other *yeshivot* in the region, see Eliav, *Jewish Education in Germany*, 149–53. On the sorry state of the Ettendorf *yeshivah*, see Cerf-Berr's comments to the director, R. Wolf Reichshofer, in a letter of 4 Iyar 5546 (May 1786), in Weil, "Contribution à l'histoire," 177–78. Although statistics for the Metz *yeshivah* are not extant, the rabbinic contract of R. Aryeh Loeb Günzberg allowed for the support of 25 students; the number of foreign students was at least 60 in 1780.

99. Katzenellenbogen returned to his native Haguenau in 1805 when he accepted the position of rabbi of that community. See *Revue orientale* 2 (1842): 339.

100. See the letter from Cerf-Berr to R. Wolf Reichshoffen, 4 Iyar 5546 (May 1786), published in Weil, "Contribution à l'histoire," 169–80.

101. Steinhardt, *Resp. Zikhron Yosef*, introduction.

102. "Protocol of the Medinah," art. 1.

103. The fact that no rabbis were appointed either to the Malesherbes commission (1788) or to the committee charged with drafting the *cahiers de doléances* for submission to the Etats Généraux (1789) only confirms that toward the end of the *ancien régime* the rabbis had little political power. The Jews of eastern France had been excluded from the assemblies that prepared the *cahiers de doléances* and from the election of delegates to the Etats Généraux. After complaints by Cerf-Berr, they were permitted to submit a report, though not a *cahier*, and R. David Sintzheim was included among the six delegates chosen to prepare the draft. On the preparation of the report, see Godechot, "Comment les juifs élurent leurs députés en 1789." On the efforts of Cerf-Berr, see Hertzberg, *French Enlightenment*, 314–18.

104. For his condemnation of excessive materialism, see Eibeschütz, *Ya'arot Devash* pt. 1, pp. 22–23; against gentile fashions and wigs, see pt. 1, p. 40; pt. 2, pp. 2–3, 22; on the preoccupation with luxury, see p. 127; on the preference for secular pursuits, see pt. 1, pp. 35–36.

105. See Hertzberg, *French Enlightenment*, 157–63, and Malino, *Sephardic Jews*, 23–26, 33, 56. It may be necessary to qualify the decline of tradition among the Sephardim, both because a number of the sources adduced by Hertzberg and Malino are given to exaggeration, and because the Sephardic community's history of acculturation ought to be considered more carefully when evaluating the erosion of its religious lifestyle.

106. 1769 *règlement*, art. 44, cited in Kerner, "La vie," 216.

107. Ibid., art. 43. On premarital cohabitation and conception, see Briggs, *Early Modern France*, 190. For Eibeschütz's remarks on the addition of a restrictive clause in the betrothal contract, see *Ya'arot Devash* 1:62.

108. See Eibeschütz, *Ya'arot Devash* 1:19, 37, 42, 61–62, 231, 240. Additional evidence of sexual immorality and claims of a breakdown in discipline are cited by Kerner, "La vie," 208–18. For Alsace, cf. "Protocol of the Medinah," arts. 23, 27–28. For similar concerns in Prague, see Landau, *Derushei Ha-Ẓelah* fols. 4a, 25d, 52b.

109. 1769 *règlement*, art. 62. On Eibeschütz's unease, see *Ya'arot Devash* 1:262.

110. On the social and religious importance attached to moral literature, see Eibeschütz, *Ya'arot Devash* sermon no. 5 (Metz, 5504 [1744]), pt. 1, p. 117, and on efforts to institute the study of *Shenei Luḥot Ha-Berit* on a regular basis, see sermon no. 12 (Metz, 5506 [1746]), vol. 1, pp. 225–26.

111. Eibeschütz, *Ya'arot Devash* 1:37, 62, 217, 231, 262.

112. For the first pronouncement, on 17 Kislev 5537 (23 November 1776), see Kerner, "La vie," 212; the second, on 13 Ḥeshvan 5542 (4 November 1781), is cited on p. 218.

113. For examples of rabbinic complaints about a decline in the respect for rabbinic authority and courts, see Reischer, *Resp. Shevut Ya'akov* pt. 3, nos. 121, 130.

114. On efforts to preserve the social and religious order, see, for example, art.

17 of the 1769 *règlement*, requiring the cantor and the *av beit din* to remind the congregants that those who violated the precepts of the Torah or who did not obey teachers would not be included in the special prayer recited on festivals on behalf of the entire community. On local challenges to rabbinic authority, see Malino, "Competition and Confrontation," and Malino, "Résistances et révoltes à Metz."

115. Cf. Reischer, *Resp. Shevut Ya'akov* pt. 1, no. 74, where the author defended the appointment of Torah scholars to public office, despite their exemption from taxes and in spite of the opposition of some community members. Also see Hertzberg, *French Enlightenment*, 233; P. Meyer, *La communauté juive de Metz*, 69.

116. Reischer, *Resp. Shevut Ya'akov* pt. 2, no. 143. Lay courts were regularly established by communities of central Europe, mainly to handle commercial disputes. See Katz, *Tradition and Crisis*, 80–82, 297nn. 25–26, 298nn. 30–31. For a seventeenth-century complaint against the abuse of lay authority in communal matters, see Sirkes, *Resp. Bayit Hadash* no. 43. On complaints of nepotism in the appointment of *dayyanim*, see J. L. Puhavitzer, *Divrei Ha-Yamim* (Hamburg, 1692), ch. 23.

117. Jonathan Eibeschütz, *Urim ve-Tumim* H.M. no. 26. Also see Eibeschütz, *Ya'arot Devash* vol. 1, 35a (Elul 5545), and pt. 2, 17a. Posener, "Social Life," 215–17.

118. See Malino, "Competition and Confrontation," and Hertzberg, *French Enlightenment*, 237–44. See the stern warning against bringing a fellow Jew before the general authorities or tribunals in the 1769 *règlement*, art. 68, in Kerner, "Le règlement de la communauté juive de Metz," 229–30. Also see art. 81 for the use of the religious sanctions issued by the *av beit din* and the *herem* as a deterrent in bankruptcy cases.

119. Schwarzfuchs, "The Rabbinic Contract"; Schwarzfuchs, *Du Juif à l'israélite*, 45–46.

120. 1769 *règlement*, arts. 108–11.

121. See Salo W. Baron, "New Approaches to Jewish Emancipation," *Diogenes* 29 (1960): 57–58, and Abramsky, "The Crisis of Authority within European Jewry in the Eighteenth Century."

122. See Dubin, *The Port Jews of Habsburg Trieste*, and Sorkin, "The Port Jew." On village-city differences, see Hyman, "The Social Contexts of Assimilation."

Chapter 4. The Ordeal of Citizenship, 1782–1799

1. In the *ancien régime* memories of persecution remained firmly within Jewish consciousness. See Kracauer, "Rabbi Joselmann de Rosheim," 85–86, 95–96, on the note on attacks on the Jews in 1475/76 recorded in an Alsace *siddur*. For assorted references to the Revolution in messianic-redemptive and revelatory terms, see Marrus, *The Politics of Assimilation*, 90–92, 106–07. On general efforts to endow the Revolution with a messianic ideology, see Talmon, *Political Messianism*. Among the works that emphasized the dramatic changes introduced by the Revolution, see Lambert, *Précis de l'histoire*, esp. 406–07; L. Kahn, *Les Juifs de Paris*, 356; and the triumphalist remarks of Debré, "The Jews of France." On the general tendency to use the Revolution for political purposes, see Hobsbawm, "Mass-Producing Traditions," 270–73. On the Revolution as myth, see Alice Gérard, *La Révolution: Myths et interprétations, 1789–1975* (Paris, 1976). On French Jewry's attenuated historical consciousness, see Birnbaum, "Grégoire, Dreyfus, Drancy, and the Rue Copernic."

2. See George Lefebvre, *The Coming of the French Revolution* (Paris, 1929); Maurice Agulhon, *La République au village* (Paris, 1970); Weber, *Peasants into Frenchmen*. For an excellent review of the literature on the role of the Revolution in the countryside, see Peter McPhee, "The French Revolution, Peasants, and Capitalism," *American Historical Review* 94 (1989): 1265–80. On developments in the pre-revolutionary era, see Alexis de Tocqueville, *L'ancien régime et la révolution* (Paris, 1856); Furet, *In-*

terpreting the French Revolution; and Schama, *Citizens*, esp. xv, 184–85. Also see Raeff, "The Well-Ordered Police State," 1222; Gordon, *Citizens without Sovereignty*, 18.

3. See Hyman, "L'impact de la Révolution sur l'identité et la culture contemporaine des Juifs d'Alsace," 29.

4. For a rich array of sources indicating a decline in religious observance in the early part of the eighteenth century, see Shoḥat, *Im Ḥilute Tekufot*. Cf. Barukh Mevorakh's review of Shoḥat in *Kiryat Sefer* 37 (1961/62): 150–55, and Katz, *Out of the Ghetto*, 34–36.

5. See M. Meyer, *Jewish Identity in the Modern World*, esp. 3–9. On trends in Germany, see Lowenstein, "The Pace of Modernization of German Jewry." Initially, the term *secularization* was used to describe the transfer of church property to state control. It has also been used to refer to the decline in religious observance and to the failure of religious rituals and symbols to answer questions about the meaning of life. Our use of the term will draw on its original meaning, i.e., expropriation—not with respect to property but in relation to domain or authority. Employing the tools of sociology, Peter Berger has made several important contributions to our understanding of secularization. See *The Sacred Canopy* and *The Heretical Imperative*.

6. See Berkovitz, "The French Revolution and the Jews."

7. Pierre Auberry, "Montesquieu et les Juifs," *Studies on Voltaire and the Eighteenth Century* 87 (1972): 87–99; Montesquieu, *L'esprit les lois*, ch. 12; Montesquieu, *Oeuvres complétes*, ed. M. André Masson (Paris, 1950), 2:746–49; J. Weil, Un texte de Montesquieu sur le Judaïsme," *REJ* 49 (1904): 117–19.

8. See, for example, Grégoire, *Motion*, 12.

9. See, for example, Dohm, *Concerning the Amelioration*, 18.

10. Ibid., 76, and Grégoire, *Motion*, 19. Victor Riqueti, marquis de Mirabeau, wrote that the Jews should be freed from the "dark phantoms of the Talmudists" in *Sur Moses Mendelsohn, sur la réforme politique des Juifs* (Paris, 1968), 28.

11. Grégoire, *Essai*, 176–77, 105. In an anonymous address to a member of the Société des Amis de la Constitution of Strasbourg, an advocate of Jewish emancipation wrote that it is the duty of the rabbis to purify their religion from "the infinite number of superstitions and ceremonies that are incompatible with citizenship." See *Observations sur la possibilité et l'utilité de l'admission des Juifs en Alsace aux droits de citoyens* (n.p., 1790).

12. According to Ruth Necheles, Grégoire considered ritual reform crucial to *régénération* and helped congregations locate liberal rabbis who would introduce innovations. See "The Abbé Grégoire and the Jews."

13. See Victor Tcherikover, *Hellenistic Civilization and the Jews* (Philadelphia, 1959), 320–27.

14. This line of reasoning was used by Poujol, *Quelques observations*, 126–29.

15. Dohn, *Concerning the Amelioration*, 1–16, 75–79.

16. Michaelis's position on the suitability of the Jews for citizenship was articulated in his review of Dohm's book, in *Orientalische und Exegetische Bibliothek* 19 (1782): 1–40.

17. Dohm, *Concerning the Amelioration*, 81; Grégoire, *Essai*, 70.

18. Dohm, *Concerning the Amelioration*, 80.

19. Grégoire, *Essai*, 105, 171, 176–77.

20. Katz, *Tradition and Crisis*, 246–47, 253–59; Katz, *Out of the Ghetto*, 20–21. On the early foundations of the Haskalah in Germany, see Feiner, *Haskalah and History*; on the Haskalah in France, see Szajkowski, "Conflicts between the Orthodox and Reformers in France."

21. Hertzberg, *French Enlightenment*, 141–58.

22. See Berkovitz, *Shaping of Jewish Identity*, 60–61. On the involvement of French *maskilim* in the Berlin Haskalah, see Helfand, "Symbiotic Relationship."

23. See Malino, "Attitudes toward Jewish Communal Autonomy."

24. For a more complete list of Bing's publications and biographical data, see "Notices Biographiques," *Revue Orientale* 2 (1842): 337–38; and Moshe Catane, "Isaiah Berr-Bing," *Encyclopedia Judaica* (Jerusalem, 1970).

25. Foissac [Jean Baptiste Annibal Aubert-Dubayet], *Le cri du citoyen contre les juifs de Metz, par un capitaine d'infanterie* (Lausanne, Metz, 1786), 19, 26, cited in Hertzberg, *French Enlightenment,* 289–90.

26. See Hertzberg, *French Enlightenment,* 289n. 52.

27. Bing, *Lettre,* 8–9.

28. Ibid., 18.

29. Shilo, "Moneylending."

30. Bing, *Lettre,* 19.

31. The Assembly of Jewish Notables insisted that the word *usure* was an incorrect translation of the Hebrew terms *neshekh* and *tarbit,* which signify interest of any kind. See Tama, *Transactions,* 197–98. On the history of Jewish attitudes toward lending on interest, see Rosenthal, "Interest from the Non-Jew."

32. Bing, *Lettre,* 12.

33. Tama, *Transactions,* 198.

34. Bing, *Lettre,* 19–29. Bing's conception of agriculture as a model profession bears similarity to the views of Fleury, *Les moeurs des Israélites et des Chrétiens.*

35. Bing, *Lettre,* 30, 32, 41, 54–55. Bing had an opportunity to develop his views further in his translation of Moses Ensheim's *La-Menaze'ah Shir,* which was sung in the synagogue of Metz at a celebration of the republican victory of Thionville: *Cantique composée par le citoyen Moyse Ensheim* (Metz, 1792). For an instructive analysis of Bing's translation and of Ensheim's composition, see Schechter, "Translating the Marseillaise."

36. Hourwitz, *Apologie.* See Malino, "Hourwitz," 82–83, and Malino, *A Jew in the French Revolution.*

37. Hourwitz, *Apologie,* 5, 34–38.

38. Ibid., 48–50; see also 17–18.

39. Ibid., 54–56, 60–62, 65.

40. Hourwitz, *Apologie,* 50–56. Compare the statement of one delegate to the Assembly of Jewish Notables on the question of intermarriage: "Great stress has been laid on the domestic inconveniences which would result from such marriages; but has a word been said of the great political advantages they would produce? If both should be put into the scale, could the superiority of the last be doubted? Certainly not." Tama, *Transactions,* 146.

41. Hourwitz, *Apologie,* 39–40. Hourwitz's demand for government controls on Jewish economic activities was a radical position generally espoused by gentile critics.

42. Hourwitz, *Apologie,* 38–39.

43. For the objections voiced in Ashkenazic and Sephardic circles, see Malino, "Hourwitz," 86–87. Cf. Hourwitz's letter to the government dated 8 May 1789 where he strongly condemned the self-interest of the Metz syndics and their resistance to modernity. Cited in Malino, "Résistances et révoltes," 125.

44. See L. Kahn, *Les Juifs de Paris.*

45. See Anne-Louis Henry de la Fare, *Opinion de M. L'Evêque de Nancy, député de Lorraine, sur l'admissibilité des Juifs à la plénitude de l'état civil et des droits de citoyens actifs* (Paris, 1790), 3–4.

46. See Berr's response, *Lettre du Sr. Berr-Isaac-Berr,* 18–19. Berr's idea had already been broached in the *mémoire* he drafted and submitted to the Malesherbes Commission in 1788. On this point, see Martine Lemalet, "L'émancipation des Juifs de Lorraine à travers l'ouevre de Berr Isaac Berr (1788–1806)," in *Juifs en France au XVIIIᵉ siècle,* ed. Blumenkranz, 159, and Moshe Catane, "Berr Isaac Berr de

Thurique," *Encyclopedia Judaica* (Jerusalem, 1970). A native of Nancy and owner of a tobacco factory, Berr followed his father, a wealthy banker, as syndic of Lorraine. He served as the spokesman for a six-member Jewish delegation sent to Paris from Alsace and Lorraine to argue the case for Jewish civic equality at the National Assembly. He returned to Paris as a leading delegate to the Assembly of Jewish Notables. A firm proponent of the Haskalah, Berr made an important contribution to its dissemination in France with the publication of *Instructions Salutaires adressées aux communautés juives de l'empire,* a French edition of *Divrei Shalom ve-Emet* by Naphtali Herz Wessely.

47. Hertzberg, *French Enlightenment,* 344, 347–48; Szajkowski, "Jewish Autonomy Debated," 37; and Szajkowski, "Conflicts between Orthodox and Reformers," 255–56. For the full Berr text, see J. Berr, *Lettre du Sieur Jacob Berr.* See "Adresse présentée à l'Assemblee Nationale le 21 Août 1789, par les députes réunis des Juifs, établis à Metz, dans les Trois Evêches, en Alsace et en Lorraine." Reprint, Paris, 1968.

48. Address of Bordeaux delegation to the National Assembly, 22 January 1790.

49. Clermont-Tonnerre, *Opinion relativement aux persecutions.*

50. B. Berr, *Lettre du Sr. Berr-Isaac-Berr,* 19–20.

51. After the Sephardic Jews were granted full citizenship in January 1790, the elders decided to dissolve the Nation and to remain organized as a philanthropic society only. See Szajkowski, "Diaries," 43n. 33. Still, the society took over most of the religious and social functions of the former Nation, and all taxpayers participated in meetings. See Szajkowski, *Autonomy and Communal Jewish Debts,* 132–34.

52. Even before the Revolution, many favored the elimination of Jewish communal autonomy, including Chrétien Guillaume Lamoignon de Malesherbes, Pierre Louis Roederer, Abbé Grégoire, and Zalkind Hourwitz. See A. Cahen, "L'Emancipation des juifs," 101; Grégoire, *Essai,* 151–61; Hourwitz, *Apologie,* 38–39. At the National Assembly, proponents and opponents of Jewish civic emancipation were largely in agreement that the Jews ought to renounce their separate communities. Cf. Szajkowski, "Jewish Autonomy Debated," and Malino, "Attitudes toward Jewish Communal Autonomy."

53. B. Berr, *Lettre d'un citoyen.*

54. Ibid., 12.

55. Ibid., 12–13. Berr's words resemble the *Lefikhakh* passage that precedes the recitation of Hallel in the Passover Haggadah. Note the similar use of religious imagery by Lévy, *Orgue et Pioutim,* 108: "Ce serait méconnaître les vues de la Providence, . . . de s'aveugler sur ce miracle, véritable doigt de Dieu, qui nous a fait passer, dans notre heureuse France de l'esclavage à la liberté, de la tristesse à la joie, du deuil à la fête, des ténèbres à la lumière."

56. B. Berr, *Lettre d'un citoyen,* 13.

57. Ibid.

58. B. Berr, *Lettre d'un citoyen,* 14–15.

59. Ibid., 15–17. Berr showed sensitivity to the prevailing gentile skepticism concerning the capacity of the Jews to become loyal citizens and to the likelihood that this skepticism would intensify if civil *régénération* were not immediately successful. Conceding that his coreligionists were not yet able to fulfill the full range of military and economically productive functions incumbent upon citizens, he offered to "do for the present what is within our power; let us take the civic oath of being faithful to the nation, to the law and to the king." In the absence of concrete contributions to the general good of society, he felt that the civic oath could guarantee their sincere intentions.

60. Ibid., 25–28.

61. Among Berr's recommendations for *régénération,* those that dealt with education figured most prominently. His program closely followed the guidelines set

down by Naphtali Herz Wessely in *Divrei Shalom ve-Emet*, a text that Berr himself had translated into French nearly a decade before. In accordance with the views of the Berlin *maskilim*, his primary emphasis was on the need to improve the teaching of the Bible. Cf. Alexander Altmann, *Moses Mendelssohn: A Biographical Study* (Philadelphia, 1973), 368–420, and Sandler, *Ha-Biur la-Torah shel Moshe Mendelssohn ve-Siato*. As a loyal disciple of Mendelssohn, Berr hoped to launch a similar program in France and therefore proposed the publication of a French translation of the Bible, modeled after Mendelssohn's German edition. On his education plan, see Berkovitz, *Shaping of Jewish Identity*, 75–76.

62. Moses Ensheim, *La-Menaze'ah Shir*. For a case study detailing how republican ideas penetrated Jewish consciousness, see Schechter, "Translating the Marseillaise." For literary echoes, see Verses, "The French Revolution as Reflected in Hebrew Literature," esp. 488–91. On Jacobin efforts to exploit religious symbols and rituals in order to sacralize revolutionary sentiment, see Higonnet, *Goodness beyond Virtue*, 238. On religious themes in the Revolution, see Lefort, "La Révolution comme religion nouvelle."

63. On Lacretelle's use of the term *régénération*, see R. Cohen, "The Rhetoric of Jewish Emancipation," 148–49, and on Grégoire, pp. 149–62. Grégoire's work originated as an essay submitted to the competition sponsored by the *Société royale des arts et sciences de Metz* in 1785 and was subsequently revised and published in Paris in 1789.

64. Grégoire, *Essai*, 132. Paul Gruenbaum-Ballin has argued persuasively that Grégoire's statements in his *Essai* and subsequent writings ought to be understood as having mystical significance only. See his "Grégoire convertisseur?" For an example of the reactionary-Christian position on this subject, compare the view of Louis de Bonald, *Mercure de France*, 8 February 1806, where the author argued that the *régénération* of the Jews would remain impossible until they first accepted Jesus. For a view of Grégoire that stresses his missionary intentions, see Gil Tzarfaty, "Une relecture de l'Essai de l'abbé Grégoire," in *Juifs en France au XVIIIe siècle*, ed. Blumenkranz, 213–21. For a balanced discussions of the question, see R. Cohen, introduction, 25–27. For a new attempt to defend Grégoire against the claim that he wanted to convert the Jews, see Hermon-Belot, *L'Abbé Grégoire*, esp. 259.

65. See Sepinwall, "Les Paradoxes," and François Manchuelle, "'The Regeneration of Africa': An Important and Ambiguous Concept in Eighteenth and Nineteenth Century French Thinking about Africa," *Cahiers d'études africaines* 144 (1996): 559–88.

66. Antoine Furetière, *Dictionnaire Universel* (Paris, 1690). The original reads: "La régénération se fait par le baptême, quand un payen se convertit."

67. For a useful discussion of the meaning of *régénération* in early Christianity, see Ladner, *The Idea of Reform*, 10–32, 50–51. Ladner notes that in the Gospel of John and in the Letter to Titus rebirth signified spiritual regeneration through baptism and that the individual "must die with Christ, be reborn in Him, and begin a new life following Him" (51).

68. On the term *régénération* in its revolutionary context, see R. Cohen, "The Rhetoric of Jewish Emancipation," 145–69, and Ozouf, "La Révolution française et l'idée de l'homme nouveau." We may infer from Ozouf (p. 218) that in the immediate aftermath of the Revolution the idea of *régénération* was still in transition between its religious and political meaning. For some, such as Lamourette, *régénération* was the meeting point between Christianity and the revolutionary ethos.

69. The full French text of the 1793 proclamation is cited in Rambaud, *Histoire de la civilisation contemporaine en France*, 136. For additional evidence of the secularization of *régénération*, see Kates, *The Cercle Social*, 99–120. Jews, too, would occasionally use the term *régénération* to refer to a universal-secular messianic vision.

See, for example, *Des réformes religieuses et du Judaïsme, par un habitat de Metz* (Metz, 1842), 8.

70. Sagnac, *La formation de la société française moderne*, 2:298.

71. Kates, *The Cercle Social*, 120. On the fear of degeneration, see Robert A. Nye, "Degeneration and the Medical Model of Cultural Crisis in the Belle Epoque," in *Political Symbolism in Modern Europe*, ed. S. Dreschler, D. Sabean, and A. Sharlin (New Brunswick, N.J., 1982), 19–41, and Nye, *Crisis, Madness and Politics in Modern France: The Medical Concept of National Decline* (Princeton, 1984), 132–70.

72. See Mona Ozouf, "Régénération," in *A Critical Dictionary of the French Revolution*, ed. François Furet and Mona Ozouf (Cambridge, Mass., 1989), 782.

73. Ibid., pp. 17, 206–10. On the preeminence of the religious over the secular in the definition of identity among French Jews, see Szajkowski, "Secular versus Religious Jewish Life in France," and Patrick Girard, *Les Juifs de France de 1789 à 1860* (Paris, 1976), 133–49.

74. On the modernization of the Jews in the Habsburg Empire, see Silber, "The Historical Experience of German Jewry." On modernization in Germany see Kober, "Emancipation's Impact," 160; on Jewish schools in Germany, see Eliav, *Jewish Education in Germany*, and Sorkin, *The Transformation of German Jewry*, 125ff.

75. The first societies for the encouragement of Jewish vocational training were founded in Metz and Paris in 1823, though Jewish apprenticeships had already been established through private initiative several years before. See Weissbach, "The Jewish Elite and the Children of the Poor"; Piette, *Les Juifs de Paris*, 43–44.

76. Posener, "Immediate Effects," 308–12.

77. See Marx, "La régénération économique des Juifs d'Alsace," and Hyman, *Emancipation of the Jews of Alsace*, 30–49.

78. The territorial marginality of Alsace-Lorraine in the period preceding the Revolution is evident in the customs restrictions that prevented the region from trading with the rest of France. On this point, see Lough, *Introduction to Eighteenth-Century France*, 70. The persistence of the view that the region was not an integral part of France accounts for the retrograde conditions well into the nineteenth century. See Weber, *Peasants into Frenchmen*.

79. On the general history of rural France in the nineteenth century, see Weber, *Peasants into Frenchmen*; on the slow pace of modernization of French Jewry, see Hyman, *Emancipation of the Jews of Alsace*, 64–85, and Job, *Les Juifs de Lunéville*, 145–60.

80. In his *Interpreting the French Revolution*, Furet argued that the Revolution was illiberal. For discussions of the Furet thesis, both sympathetic and critical, see the review by Lynn Hunt, in *History and Theory* 20/3 (1981): 313–23, and Isser Woloch, "On the Latent Illiberalism of the French Revolution," *American Historical Review* 95 (1990): 1452–70.

81. Loeb, "Les Juifs à Strasbourg," 142–53. For a full description of the legal disabilities imposed on Jews in the seigneurie of Oberbronn, see Peter, *Mertzwiller*, 140.

82. See Szajkowski, "Riots in Alsace," 88–91, and Jacob Toury, *Turmoil and Confusion in the Revolution of 1848: The Anti-Jewish Riots in the "Year of Freedom" and Their Influence on Modern Antisemitism* [Hebrew] (Tel Aviv, 1968). The right of refuge in Switzerland had been obtained in connection with trading permits. The 708 Alsatian Jews who fled to Basel in 1789 were granted only temporary asylum. See U. Kaufmann, "Swiss Jewry," and Feuerwerker, *L'émancipation des Juifs*, 288–92. Rürup, "The European Revolutions of 1848 and Jewish Emancipation," 33.

83. Reuss, "L'antisémitisme dans le bas-Rhin," 249.

84. Ibid., 247–50; *JFR*, 50–52.

85. Reuss, "Quelques documents nouveaux"; Reuss, "L'antisémitisme dans le bas-Rhin."

86. The election was for the canton of Oberhausbergen, and is noted in Gins-

burger, *Histoire de la communauté de Bischeim au Saum*, 54. Cf. Feuerwerker, *L'émancipation des Juifs*, 437–40, for a case where the town council of Bischeim au Saum prevented at least five prominent Jews from taking the civil oath by requiring them to cross themselves. Eventually in April 1792, the requirement was removed upon the order of the departmental directory.

87. Charles Mull, *Histoire économique et sociale de Haguenau* (Thèse pour le doctorat de 3ème cycle, Université de Strasbourg, 1974), 3:925–27.

88. Szajkowski, "Riots against the Jews in Metz in 1792."

89. For additional examples, see Ginsburger, *Histoire de la communauté israélite de Soultz*, 40.

90. See Ginsburger, "Arrêtés du Directoire," 47.

91. Reuss, "L'antisémitisme dans le bas-Rhin," 251, 253.

92. Ibid., 256.

93. Graetz, "Jewish Economic Activity between War and Peace." For the larger European context, see Jerome Blum, *The End of the Old Order in Rural Europe* (Princeton, 1978), esp. 95–304, 367–76.

94. Two-page broadside (Hebrew) issued by the Metz *kehillah*, 7 Ab 5552 (1792), beginning with words "El Azilei B'nei Israel."

95. Szajkowski, *Poverty and Social Welfare*, 7; Godechot, "Les Juifs de Nancy," 4–6.

96. See Szajkowski, "The Attitude of the French Jacobins toward Jewish Religion," 399–412; Szajkowski, "Jewish Religious Observance"; Ginsburger and Ginsburger, "Contributions à l'histoire des Juifs d'Alsace pendant la terreur"; Tribout de Morembert, "Les Juifs de Metz et de Lorraine"; Job, *Les Juifs de Lunéville*, 72–73; and Higonnet, *Goodness beyond Virtue*, 237.

97. Sintzheim, *Yad David*, introduction.

98. See Szajkowski, "Jewish Religious Observance."

99. The works that were set afire are referred to in *Me'orei Or* as *Sefer ha-Arukhim*, *Sefer ha-Derushim*, and *Sefer ha-Malbushim*; see Worms's confession in ms. 288 (fragment) of the library of the Alliance Israélite Universelle, Paris. On the halakhic question of the permissibility of burning such material in order to avoid its defilement, either from wear and tear or at the hands of gentiles, see Reischer, *Resp. Shevut Ya'akov* pt. 3, nos. 10–12.

100. U. Cahen, *Halakhah Berurah*, introduction.

101. See Berkovitz, "The French Revolution and the Jews."

102. On the travails of R. Simon Horchheim, see Scheuer, *Turei Zahav*, 175. Cf. Lunteschütz, *Kelilat Yofi*, introduction, where the author reported that "many Jews were forced to violate the Sabbath by working in the fields, cutting wheat, and bring it to the granary; it was dangerous to teach and respond to religious questions, even to pray, and recite the *Shema Israel*; to lay *tefillin* and wear *zizit* was dangerous and had to be done in secret."

103. On Gougenheim, see Ginsburger, "Mémoriaux," *REJ* 41 (1900): 127–28; Scheid, "Histoire des Juifs de Haguenau," 230.

104. For an example of a pamphlet that criticized the Jews for their alleged idleness, see *Les Juifs d'Alsace, doivent-ils être admis au droit de citoyens actifs?* (n.p., 1790). The Jacobin quotation is cited in Reuss, "Quelques documents nouveaux," 251–52.

105. See Bauer, "Les Juifs comtadins pendant la Révolution."

106. Information on the lives of French rabbis of this period is fragmentary. For Sarassin, see *UI* 16 (1860–61): 185–86, and *Souvenir et Science* (February 1934): 24–26. On Lunteschütz, see Kayserling, "Les rabbins de Suisse," and Eliakim Carmoly, "Galerie israélite française," *AI* 23 (1862): 157–59. Lunteschütz himself provided some autobiographical information in his collection of responsa titled *Kelilat Yofi*, preface and pp. 29a, 30a.

107. Grand Rabbis Arnauld Aron, Marchand Ennery, Lion-Mayer Lambert, and Emmanuel Deutz were all trained in Germany. The lone exception was Aaron

Worms (1754–1836), the only major rabbinic figure in the pre-1830 era who received his entire training in Alsace and Metz.

108. The letter is cited in Anchel, "Contribution levée en 1813–1814 sur les Juifs du Haut-Rhin."

109. Posener, "Immediate Effects," 285.

110. To Kassel alone nine Jewish families from Alsace immigrated in 1812. See Walter Roll, "The Kassel 'Ha-Meassef' of 1799," in *The Jewish Response to German Culture*, ed. Jehuda Reinharz and Walter Schatzberg (Hanover, N.H., 1985), 40. Szajkowski, "Riots in Alsace"; and Burns, "Emancipation and Reaction."

111. In some areas this situation persisted well into the 1800s. The training of rabbis in France at mid-century suffered from what Ismar Schorsch has called a "lack of determined government enforcement." See his "Emancipation and the Crisis of Religious Authority: The Emergence of the Modern Rabbinate," *Revolution and Evolution: 1848 in German-Jewish History*, 228.

112. See Anchel, *Napoléon et les juifs*, 14–45; Szajkowski, *Autonomy and Jewish Communal Debts*, 622–26.

Chapter 5. Religion, State, and Community

1. For an example of the use of the expression *émancipation intérieure*, see Olry Terquem's remarks, cited in M. Meyer, *Response to Modernity*, 166 and n. 74, and *AI* 4 (1843): 3. For examples of differentiation among the terms *émancipation industrielle, civile*, and *politique*, see the 1845 report of the *Société d'encouragement au travail en faveur d'Israélites du Bas-Rhin*, published in *AI* 7 (1846): 192.

2. Ellis, *Napoleon*, 59–65.

3. Publications honoring Napoleon include Jacob Meyer, *Mizmor le-Todah* (Paris, 1805); Menaham Mendel Kargeau and Jacob Meyer, *Shir u-Mizmor* (Paris, 1805); Netanel Wittersheim, *Mizmor Shir* (Paris, 1806; Moshe Milhaud, *Mizmor Shir [Cantique adressé à Napoléon le Grand]* (Paris, 1806); Abraham de Cologna, *Shir* (Paris, 1806); Jacob Meyer, Abraham de Cologna, and Abraham Chai, *Shirim Ivri'im* (Paris, 1806); Jacob Menaham Karkovia, *Shir Hadash* (Paris, 1807). For a most useful collection of Hebrew poems from this era, see Mevorakh, *Napoleon u-tekufato*. On Elie Halévy's effort to instill enthusiasm for the Napoleonic reform among schoolchildren, see his *Instruction religieuse et morale a l'usage de la jeunesse israélite* (Paris, 1820), and the discussion below. For the first—and still useful—effort to assemble this material, see Carmoly, "Napoléon et ses panégyristes hébreaux." See also the analysis of Schechter, *Obstinate Hebrew*, 194–235.

4. See Jeremiah 29:7: "Seek the welfare of the city to which I have exiled you and pray to God on its behalf, for in its prosperity you shall prosper." Also see *Avot* 3:2.

5. On "Elohim Hayyim," see Debré, "The Jews of France," 418–25.

6. Bonald's article appeared in *Mercure de France*, 8 February 1806; for the response, see Mayer [-Dalmbert], *Au rédacteur du journal de l'Empire*.

7. Berr, *Réflexions*.

8. Posener, "Immediate Effects"; Katz, *Out of the Ghetto*, 178–79.

9. Katz, *Out of the Ghetto*, 178–79.

10. See Ozouf, *Festivals and the French Revolution*.

11. Poujol, *Quelques observations*, iv–vi, 40–41, 71, 152, 154–56. For background, see Schwarzfuchs, *Napoleon, the Jews, and the Sanhedrin*, 34–37.

12. Poujol, *Quelques observations*, 93, 96–109, 119, 130–35, 154–55. Poujol's assessment of the Talmud was quite standard. Similarly, others, such as Bail, *Des Juifs au dix-neuvième siécle*, 47–48, emphasized the Talmud's preference for "subtleties and minutiae" over "the noble simplicity of the dogmas."

13. Overall, the most important vehicle for concretizing the revolutionary ideals

was the Code Napoléon. Promulgated in 1804, it endowed France with a uniform legal system, codifying the laws produced by the revolutionary assemblies. Equality before the law, freedom of conscience, freedom of trade and industry, and the registration of births, deaths, and marriages by municipal authorities were all reconfirmed by the new civil code. See Lough, *An Introduction to Eighteenth-Century France*, esp. 320–32, and the formulation of Kennedy, *A Cultural History of the French Revolution*: "Napoleon synthesized the egalitarianism of the Revolution with the authority and centralization of the old regime" (377).

14. Liber, "Napoléon."

15. Schwarzfuchs, *Napoleon, the Jews, and the Sanhedrin*, 49.

16. Ibid., 46–49. Also see Berkovitz, *Shaping of Jewish Identity*, 77–84.

17. Cited in Schwarzfuchs, *Napoleon, the Jews, and the Sanhedrin*, 55–56.

18. See, for example, Simon Dubnow, *History of the Jews*, trans. and ed. Moshe Spiegel (South Brunswick, Yoseloff, 1967–73), 4:552–55; Schwarzfuchs, *Napoleon, the Jews, and the Sanhedrin*. On the Reform movement's positive view of the Sanhedrin, see David Philipson, *The Reform Movement in Judaism* (New York, 1931), 149–63. For the view of an early Zionist thinker who condemned the Sanhedrin, see Peretz Smolenskin, "The Haskalah in Berlin," in *The Zionist Idea*, ed. Arthur Hertzberg (New York, 1959), 154–57.

19. Jean Baptiste Philibert Vaillant, ed., *Correspondance de Napoléon 1ᵉʳ* (Paris, 1858–70), 13:581–85, excerpts from the text of a letter to M. de Champagny, Minister of the Interior, 29 November 1806, cited in Maslin, "Napoleonic Jewry from the Sanhedrin to the Bourbon Restoration," 4–5.

20. Ibid.

21. See, for example, Moureau, *De l'incompatibilité entre le Judaïsme et l'exercise des droits de cité et des moyens de rendre les Juifs citoyens*, 37–60.

22. Maslin, "Selected Documents of Napoleonic Jewry."

23. From Vaillant, *Correspondance de Napoléon*, 12:700–711, no. 10537, cited in Schwarzfuchs, *Napoleon, the Jews, and the Sanhedrin*, 55.

24. Letter from Napoleon to M. Champagny, Ramboulliet, 23 August 1806, reprinted and translated in Maslin, "Selected Documents."

25. Vaillant, *Correspondance de Napoléon*, 13:101–02, 584.

26. Katz, *Exclusiveness and Tolerance*, 193.

27. This was certainly the case in Bordeaux. See Malino, *Sephardic Jews of Bordeaux*, 66.

28. See Freimann, *Betrothal and Marriage Procedures after the Talmudic Era*, 325–27.

29. Tama, *Transactions*, 152.

30. On the question whether the prohibition was limited to the seven Canaanite nations or extended to all non-Jews, compare Maimonides, *Mishneh Torah*, Hil. Issurei Bi'ah 12:1–2, where no distinction was made, and R. Jacob b. Asher, *Arba'ah Turim*, Even ha-Ezer 16:1.

31. Tama, *Transactions*, 154–56. For a brief discussion of the legal aspects of intermarriage and the citation of several striking precedents, see Frimer, "Israel, the Noahide Laws and Maimonides," 96–97. Frimer cited R. Joel Sirkes, *Bayit Ḥadash*, Even ha-Ezer 16, where it was assumed that Maimonides recognized the possibility of a marriage of a Jew to a gentile; and Reischer, *Resp. Shevut Ya'akov* pt. 1, no. 20, for a possible halakhic implication of this view as it relates to the disposition of leaven before Passover. Although Reischer conceded that the union of a Jew and non-Jew had no halakhic validity, "it appears that this is a *de facto* marriage in many respects." For Frimer's own explanation of Maimonides's position, see p. 97.

32. Mevorakh, *Napoleon u-tekufato*, 92–93.

33. "The Responses of R. Ishmael b. R. Avraham Yitzhak Ha-Kohen," in Judah Rosenthal, *Meḥkarim u-Mekorot* (Jerusalem, 1966), 2:513–32.

34. See Schwarzfuchs, *Napoleon, the Jews, and the Sanhedrin*, 115–16, and Gelber, "La police autrichienne et le Sanhédrin de Napoléon."

35. Elisheva Carlebach, "Early Modern Ashkenaz in the Writings of Jacob Katz," in *The Pride of Jacob: Essays on Jacob Katz and His Work*, ed. Jay Harris (Cambridge, Mass., 2002), 65–83.

36. Eisenmenger, *Entdecktes Judentums*.

37. Also see *Bava Qama* 111b.

38. Maimonides, *Mishneh Torah*, Hilkhot Gezelah va-Avedah 1:2.

39. In Hilkhot Gezelah va-Avedah 1:1, Maimonides used language that limited the prohibition of robbery to another Jew (*ḥavero*), whereas in 1:2 he ruled that the prohibition of robbery pertains to a gentile (idolater)'s money as well. For efforts to resolve the apparent inconsistency, see *Kesef Mishnah*; Landau, *Resp. Noda b'Yehudah*, vol. 1, *Y.D.* no. 81, and Frimer, "Israel, the Noahide Laws and Maimonides," 98. Maimonides's view of gentiles deserves a major monographic study, as it touches on complex halakhic and philosophic issues. See, generally, Menahem Kellner, *Maimonides on Judaism and the Jewish People* (Albany, 1991).

40. Maimonides, *Commentary on the Mishnah*, Kelim 12:7. Cf. Yosef Kapah's edition (Jerusalem, 1968), 6:126, where the word *goy* appears instead of *akum*. Also see Hilkhot De'ot 2:6 and Hilkhot Mekhirah 18:1.

41. For a parallel formulation concerning the prohibition against inflicting pain upon animals, see Maimonides, *Guide of the Perplexed*, pt. 3, ch. 17. On the perfection of man's moral character, see Isadore Twersky, *Introduction to the Code of Maimonides (Mishneh Torah)* (New Haven, 1980), 356–514.

42. For his general principle of tolerance, see Me'iri, *Beit ha-Beḥirah*, Avodah Zarah, 59, and specifically with regard to lost property, see *Beit ha-Beḥirah*, Bava Qama, 330. In the scholarly literature, see Katz, *Exclusiveness and Tolerance*, 114–28; Ephraim E. Urbach, "R. Menaḥem Me'iri's Principle of Tolerance: Its Origin and Limits" [Hebrew], in *Chapters in the History of Jewish Society in the Middle Ages and Modern Period, Presented to Professor Jacob Katz* (Jerusalem, 1980), 34–44, and Katz's reply in *Zion* 46 (1981): 243–46; Blidstein, "Me'iri's Attitude towards Gentiles"; and Halbertal, *Between Torah and Wisdom*, ch. 3.

43. In *Beit ha-Beḥirah*, Bava Qama, 219, Me'iri understood *amito* (Lev. 25:17) as referring to non-idolatrous gentiles. Cf. *Sefer Hasidim* no. 355, where it is stated in the name of R. Judah He-Hasid that a gentile who accepts the seven Noahide laws is to be treated as a brother with respect to the return of lost property. Cf. Landau, *Resp. Noda b'Yehudah*, preface. For a characterization of Me'iri's principle of tolerance as apologetic, see Broyde and Hecht, "The Gentile and Returning Lost Property According to Jewish Law." For an illustration of Me'iri's insistence that the distinction between Jew and gentile be firmly maintained in the ritual sphere, see Jacob Katz, *The Shabbes Goy: A Study in Halakhic Flexibility* (Philadelphia, 1989), 224–25.

44. See Me'iri, *Beit ha-Beḥirah*, Bava Qama 330, where the obligation to return an idolater's property is denied, but it is upheld in the case of one restricted by the ways of religion.

45. Benedict, *Cities and Social Change in Early Modern France*, 29–32.

46. Katz, *Exclusiveness and Tolerance*, 156–57.

47. Rivkes, *Be'er ha-Golah*, Ḥoshen Mishpat 348.

48. Ibid., 425:5, cited in Katz, *Exclusiveness and Tolerance*, 165. Note the striking similarity to the view of R. Judah Loew ben Beẓalel in his own *Be'er ha-Golah* (Prague, 1598), 143–46, ed. S. Honig (Jerusalem, 1971).

49. For his view that Christians are not idolaters, see Bacharach, *Resp. Ḥavvot Ya'ir* no. 1.

50. Bacharach, *Resp. Ḥavvot Ya'ir* no. 31. In the medieval period, Christians were

occasionally cited as exemplars of moral behavior and piety in family relationships and in prayer. See R. Shlomo Yitzḥaki, *Teshuvot Rashi*, ed. Israel S. Alfenbein (New York, 1943), no. 207, where Rashi chastised a man who wished to divorce his ill wife by citing the higher ethical behavior of men toward their wives in Christian society. Also see the criticism leveled against idle conversation and levity during prayer, as compared to Christians who pray quietly, in R. Isaac of Corbeil, *Sefer Mitzvot Katan* (Satmar, 1935), 18. Also see the comments of Eibeschütz, *Ya'arot Devash*, sermon dated 25 January 1745, recommending that Jews learn from the admirable behavior of nobles and dukes whose devotion to the king enables them to overcome their ordinary desires.

51. See Bacharach, *Resp. Ḥavvot Ya'ir* nos. 139, 146, and compare the similar conclusion drawn by R. Jacob Emden, *Resp. She'elat Yaveẓ* pt 2, no. 9. According to *Shulhan Arukh*, Ḥoshen Mishpat 388:9, it is prohibited to surrender a Jew or his property into the hands of non-Jews, even if he were an evil person or a criminal. However, one who harasses the community may be handed over to non-Jews in order to beat, imprison, or fine him, but this does not include one who harms an individual (sec. 12). Cf. Moses Isserles, Ḥoshen Mishpat 425:1. Against the plain meaning of *Tosefta Terumot* 7:20, R. David Ha-Levi ruled that an individual may be turned over to the government if he violated a law of the local authority and thereby endangered the community. See *Turei Zahav, Y.D.* 157:8. R. Joel Sirkes had gone a step further, stating that if an individual is accused of a crime against the general authorities, even though it is not known if indeed he was guilty, it is permissible to extradite him so that he may be tried by the general court. See Sirkes, *Resp. Bayit Ḥadash* nos. 43 and 44, and Elijah J. Schochet, *A Responsum of Surrender* (Los Angeles, 1973).

52. R. Cohen, *Jewish Icons*, 52ff.; Shoḥat, *Im Ḥilufe Tekufot*, 49–63.

53. In addition to the writings of Bing, Hourwitz, and Berr, treated above, see also a letter from the Abbé Grégoire to a Jew from Lunéville in which he sought clarification whether, in light of their distinctive laws concerning marriage customs, divorce, age of majority, inheritance, etc., "their customs are in opposition to ours"; published in *AI* 91 (1930): 182.

54. Szajkowski, "Diaries," 40. Also see Schwarzfuchs, *Du Juif à l'israélite*, 81–87.

55. See Tama, *Transactions*, 133–34. Berr Isaac Berr was one of the most influential members of the assembly; his son, Michel, secretary of the Sanhedrin, identified with the *régénérateur* movement and made several contributions in the realm of religious instruction. Zalkind Hourwitz, though not at the deliberations of the assembly, consulted regularly with members, and according to Anchel, *Napoléon et les Juifs*, 181, he even advised Champagny. On the continuity of the communal leadership in general, with particular reference to the Sanhedrin, see Graetz, *From Periphery to Center*, 25–26.

56. On *Me'orei Or*, see Chapters 3 and 7.

57. Worms's Sanhedrin address was reproduced in *Kan Tahor* (*Me'orei Or*, vol. 7) 10b–11b, *novellae* to B.T. Sanhedrin 58b; also see *Bin Nun* (*Me'orei Or*, vol. 6) 106a, 111a. Cf. the views of Emden, *Resp. She'elat Yaveẓ* no. 41, and the general discussion by Shoḥat, *Im Ḥilufe Tekufot*, 68–69, and nn. 152–67.

58. See *Kan Tahor* 11a, 16a. On the position of Me'iri, see Halbertal, *Between Torah and Wisdom*, 88–89.

59. *Kan Tahor* 11a, where citations include B.T. *Ḥullin* 94a and *Tanna Devei Eliyahu*, ch. 16. For a discussion of the broader meaning ascribed to *re'a*, see Worms's discussion of Sanhedrin 93a. For a comparable view of *gezel ha-goi*, see Landau, *Resp. Noda b' Yehudah*, vol. 1, *Y.D.* no. 81.

60. See *Kan Tahor* 10b–11b; *Bin Nun* 106a, 111a. Worms's position rested on Maimonides, *Mishneh Torah*, Hilkhot De'ot 2:6, and *Shulḥan Arukh*, Ḥoshen Mishpat 228, 231.

61. See Me'iri, *Beit ha-Beḥirah,* Bava Metzia 267. Also see Richard Emery, *The Jews of Perpignan in the Thirteenth Century* (New York, 1959), 28.

62. See *Od la-Mo'ed* 29a–b.

63. See *Be'er Sheva* 15b.

64. On Worms's refusal to permit the use of imported sugar on Passover unless there was a rabbinic statement attesting to its being absolutely free of any admixture of flour, see *Od la-Mo'ed* 28b–29a. Cf. Sofer, *Resp. Ḥatam Sofer,* no. 135, where a more lenient ruling was issued. Also see Worms's remarks in *Od la-Mo'ed* 27a, where he was highly critical of efforts to abolish the prohibition of legumes (*kitniyot*) on Passover, and his criticism of the contemporary failure to appreciate and observe the finer technical aspects of *heter isqa,* in *Od la-Mo'ed* 26b.

65. Katz, *Exclusiveness and Tolerance,* 24–36, 106–28.

66. Tama, *Transactions,* 76–80.

67. See Schwarzfuchs's note on the dissatisfaction of the commissioners with this answer in *Napoleon, the Jews, and the Sanhedrin,* 206n. 3.

68. Tama, *Transactions,* 194–96.

69. Katz, *Exclusiveness and Tolerance,* 182–93.

70. Tama, *Transactions,* 200.

71. Ibid., 199–200. Cf. Me'iri's similar formulation in his definition of "brother"; see *Beit ha-Beḥirah,* Bava Metzia, 329.

72. Cf. Halbertal, *Between Torah and Wisdom,* ch. 3, n. 25.

73. Prologue of Sanhedrin decisions, in Mevorakh, *Napoleon u-tekufato,* 89.

74. See Graetz, *From Periphery to Center,* 60.

75. Ibid., 56–59. For two popular textbooks that referred to the Sanhedrin's doctrines, see E. Halévy, *Instruction religieuse et morale,* 74–75, 83, 98–101, and Ulmann, *Recueil d'instructions morales et religieuses,* preface. For the views of Munk and Franck, see *AI* 2 (1841): 383–85; Munk, *Palestine,* 99; and Graetz, *From Periphery to Center,* 63–65. On the rabbinic embrace of depoliticization, see Wogue, *Guide du croyant israélite,* 77–79, 352–57, 386–95, 495–97; Charleville, *Réponse de M. le rabbin de Charleville,* 1–5.

76. For a discussion of Mendelssohn's views, see Alexander Altmann, *Moses Mendelssohn: A Biographical Study* (Tuscaloosa, 1973), 465–68.

77. See Chapter 9.

78. Maslin, "Selected Documents."

79. One example of reliance on the Sanhedrin's decisions by opponents of religious reform is a letter from Rabbi Salomon Klein to the Minister of Instruction Publique et les Cultes, in *AN* F[19] 11037, 31 December 1856, Archives Nationales, Paris. Klein argued that in recommending certain reforms, the 1856 Paris rabbinic conference had violated the religious status quo as set forth by the Sanhedrin and subsequently confirmed by the Napoleonic regime.

80. Graetz, *From Periphery to Center,* 31–34.

81. Berkovitz, *Shaping of Jewish Identity,* 76, 86–90.

82. On the Sanhedrin's moderating role in the struggle over religious reform, see Berkovitz, "The French Revolution and the Jews," 60–61.

83. Albert, *Modernization of French Jewry,* 50–61.

84. Ibid., 122–50.

85. See Neher-Bernheim, "Sephardim et Ashkenazim"; Berkovitz, *Shaping of Jewish Identity,* 148–49. For parallels in general society, see Zeldin, *France, 1848–1945,* 16, 20; Weber, *Peasants into Frenchmen,* 95–96.

86. Albert, *Modernization of French Jewry,* 197–204, 223–29, 232–33.

87. On efforts of the Strasbourg consistory to appoint its own delegates to sit on the board of the Société d' Encouragement au Travail en Faveur d'Israélites Indigents, see "Extrait des Registres des deliberations du Consistoire israélite du Bas-

Rhin," *AI* 4 (1843): 50–52; Albert, *Modernization of French Jewry*, 182–87; and Hyman, *Emancipation of the Jews of Alsace*, 77–78. The right to maintain private *minyanim* was protected by the new constitution. As in the case of the kosher meat monopoly, the French civil courts ruled that consistory authority was not enforceable. See Albert, *Modernization of French Jewry*, 218, 223–27.

88. Albert, *Modernization of French Jewry*, 178–80, and Hyman, *Emancipation of the Jews of Alsace*, 75–77. On criticism of the consistory, see Berkovitz, *Shaping of Jewish Identity*, 101.

89. Albert, *Modernization of French Jewry*, 151–69; Graetz, *From Periphery to Center*, 209–70; and Berkovitz, *Shaping of Jewish Identity*, 243–46.

90. Berkovitz, *Shaping of Jewish Identity*, 210–14; Albert, *Modernization of French Jewry*, 82–83, 280–81, 356–78.

91. See Berkovitz, *Shaping of Jewish Identity*, 203–28.

92. On rabbinic training, see Bauer, *L'ecole rabbinique de France*, Albert, *Modernization of French Jewry*, 245–55; and Berkovitz, *Shaping of Jewish Identity*, 192–202.

93. 1839 project, arts. 44–57, in Albert, *Modernization of French Jewry*, 364–66.

94. Ibid., 75–76, 82–95, 273–75.

95. See Albert, *Modernization of French Jewry*, 276. The *Archives israélites* strongly supported universal suffrage, as is indicated by its criticism of the Lyon rabbinic selection in 1850; see *AI* 12 (1851): 6.

Chapter 6. The "Jewish Question" during the Bourbon Restoration

1. Typical of the optimism in the first years of the new regime is Alphonse-Théodore Cerfberr's depiction of the 1814 *Charte*: "le vaste et magnifique édifice d'une législation nouvelle, temple sainte où sont gravées les libertés publiques, les sécurités nationales," in *Observations*, 9.

2. The vast literature on the Jewish question in Restoration France includes Bail, *Des Juifs*; Moureau, *De l'incompatibilité*; and a number of works generated by the 1824 essay contest sponsored by the Société des Sciences, Agriculture et Arts of Strasbourg on the Jewish question in Alsace. On the debate surrounding Bail's book, see Cologna, *Quelques observations*; De Sacy, "Lettre à M.***"; and Cologna, "*Réflexions*.

3. Betting de Lancastel, *Considérations*, 21; Bail, *Des Juifs*, 66–67.

4. Moureau, *De l'incompatibilité*, 37. On Grégoire's view of the Sanhedrin, see Necheles, "The Abbé Grégoire and the Jews," 139. For his support for the creation of modern Jewish schools and his criticism of rabbis who objected to sending Jewish children to Christian schools, see Grégoire, *Observations nouvelles*.

5. See Bail, *Des Juifs*, 2nd ed., esp. 52. Also note the addition of the phrase "Au fond" in the second edition (p. 62) to the passage "Les doctrines de leurs livres" appearing in the first edition (p. 22). Also see Cologna, *Quelques observations*, esp. 87–89.

6. Moureau, *De l'incompatibilité*, 26–27, 34, 37–60. Cf. Bail, *Des Juifs*, 112.

7. Katz, "A State within a State"; see also Katz, *Out of the Ghetto*, 99–103. See Moureau, *De l'incompatibilité*, 22–27 for examples; Grégoire, *Essai*, 110; and Bail, *Des Juifs*, 74.

8. See Febvre, "Civilization," 225, 231–33, 238, 241, 247; François Guizot, *La civilisation en Europe* (Paris, 1828), 12–15, 18. On the convergence of the processes of civilization and emancipation, see John Murray Cuddihy, *The Ordeal of Civility: Freud, Marx, Levi-Strauss and the Jewish Struggle with Modernity* (New York, 1974), 20–21.

9. "Programme," *Journal de la Société des Sciences, Agriculture et Arts, du département du Bas-Rhin* 1 (1824): 114–15. The Strasbourg Société's misgivings about the reli-

gious rituals of Judaism were shared by the Strasbourg Consistory, which considered several administrative, liturgical, and ritual reforms that it believed would advance the regeneration process. See Berkovitz, *Shaping of Jewish Identity*, 102–04.

10. "Programme," *Journal de la Société* 1 (1824): 114–15.

11. At least one French Jew, Michel Berr, criticized the Société for its phrasing of the second question. See *Lettre au rédacteur de l'Argus* (Paris, 1824), 4–5.

12. "Programme," *Journal de la Société* 1 (1824): 114–15.

13. Artur Beugnot, a lawyer, senator, and historian, was awarded first prize. Honorable mention was given to Prosper Wittersheim, a Jewish member of the Société and secretary of the Metz Société d'Encouragement des Arts et Métiers, and to Louis Blanchard. Wittersheim's essay was published as *Mémoire sur les moyens de hâter la régénération des Israélites de l'Alsace.* For the decision of the commission, see "Rapport de la commission chargée d'examiner les mémoires qui ont concouru pour le prix proposé en 1824, par la Société des sciences, agriculture et arts du département du Bas-Rhin," *Journal de la Société* 2 (1825): 299.

14. On the 1817 petition that was addressed to the two chambers of government by M. le marquis de Lattier, see M.D., "Sur la régénération civile, politique et morale des Israélites français, et sur la décret du 17 mars 1808," *L'Israélite français* 1 (1817): 358–69. For a vivid representation of the tone and substance of the arguments on behalf of exceptional legislation, expressing both punitive and rehabilitative motives, see Moureau, *De l'incompatibilité*, 73–74.

15. *Journal de la Société* 2 (1825): 312. Quotations are from the *mémoire* submitted by Arthur Beugnot. Although the essay was never published, a number of passages from the original text have been preserved in the commission's report, as well as an extensive summary of the arguments.

16. Ibid.

17. Moureau, *De l'incompatibilité*, 60–62, 81.

18. Betting de Lancastel, *Considérations*, 82; see also p. vi.

19. *Journal de la Société* 2 (1825): 309–12.

20. Tourette, *Discours*, 15–16. According to his plan, this institution would encourage Jews to save money and would enable Jews and non-Jews to borrow at the same rate of interest (5 percent). The profits, he suggested, could be devoted to various communal projects.

21. Betting de Lancastel, *Considérations*, 130.

22. Tourette, *Discours*, 17. Arthur Beugnot made a similar proposal for the creation of a government controlled credit institution; see *Journal de la Société* 2 (1825): 318–19.

23. Beugnot, *Les Juifs d'Occident*, 43–44.

24. Ibid., pt. 3, pp. 278–83. Cf. Betting de Lancastel, *Considérations*, 2, 12, 19, where the claim that the Karaites were morally superior to the rabbanites was adduced as proof that the Talmud was evil. The term *fatras* was also used by Grégoire in reference to rabbinic literature. See his *Mémoire*, 2:397.

25. *Journal de la Société* 2 (1825): 312–15.

26. Strasbourg had been proposed by the Bas-Rhin Consistory in 1816 as a possible site for the establishment of a central rabbinical seminary. See Alsace-Lorraine Collection, box 3, fols. 891–92, Leo Baeck Institute Archives, New York.

27. *Journal de la Société* 2 (1825): 311, 316–17.

28. Ibid., 317–18.

29. Tourette, *Discours*, 37; *Journal de la Société* 2 (1825): 317–18.

30. *Journal de la Société* 2 (1825): 305–06.

31. Grégoire, *Essai*, xx. On the notion of French society as a family, see Marc Shell, *The End of Kinship* (Stanford, 1988). The expression *la grande famille française*

appeared innumerable times in Jewish sources. See, for instance, Samuel Cahen's remarks in *AI* 1 (1840): 658. For an example of the claim that the refusal of Jews to marry gentiles impeded social integration, see Tourette, *Discours*, 37.

32. Bail, *Des Juifs*, 50, referred, ambitiously, to "la fusion morale, politique, et religieuse."

33. See Patrick Girard, "Les doctrines de l'assimilation en France au dix-neuvième siècle," in *Aspects du Sionisme* (Paris, 1982), 185.

34. Cologna, *Réflexions*, 9, 17. Later, Isidore Cahen expressed his opposition to the use of the term *fusion sociale*, see *AI* 21 (1860): 217–18. While it is true that even a staunch traditionalist as R. L.-M. Lambert (*Précis de l'histoire*) called for both civil and religious fusion with the French population, he clearly had a different meaning in mind. The term *fusion* was apparently used by some to signify emancipation and social integration. For a discussion of this issue, see Albert, "Israelite and Jew," 96–97.

35. The first nine *Lettres Tsarphatiques* appeared as follows: Tsarphati [Olry Terquem], *Première (-Neuvième) lettre d'un Israélite français à ses coreligionnaires* (Paris, 1821–37). The remaining eighteen letters appeared as letters to the editor of the *Courrier de la Moselle*, 1838–41, collected in Fondswiener, no. 16948. Although there is no full biography of Terquem, see Richard Menkis, "Les Frères Elie, Olry et Lazare Terquem," *Archives Juives* 15/3 (1979): 58–61.

36. Tsarphati, *Lettre* 20 (15 December 1839). For a fuller description, see Berkovitz, *Shaping of Jewish Identity*, 120.

37. Berkovitz, *Shaping of Jewish Identity*, 120–21.

38. Tsarphati, *Lettre* 15 (May 1839) and *Lettre* 16 (June 1839).

39. Tsarphati, *Première lettre*, 5–7.

40. Ibid., 5.

41. Ibid., 9–10.

42. Tsarphati, letter to the editor of *Courrier de la Moselle* dated February 1839.

43. Ibid., letter dated December 1838.

44. Ibid.

45. Terquem, letter to the editor of *Courrier de la Moselle* (18 July 1838), and *Lettre* 23 to *Courrier de la Moselle* (16 April 1840).

46. Terquem also insisted that ritual observance not interfere in the training of Jewish craftsmen. He attacked attempts by traditionalists to force the young apprentices of the Société d'Encouragement pour les Arts et Métiers of Paris to recite prayers, wear the *talit* and *tefilin*, and observe Sabbath and holiday laws. He attributed the demise of the Société in 1834 to the inability of the apprentices to balance the demands of labor with these religious restrictions (*Lettre* 18 to the editor of *Courrier de la Moselle*, 11 August 1839).

47. Tsarphati, *Première lettre*, 9–11.

48. Ibid., 11–13, and in the *Troisième Lettre* (Paris, 1822), 19.

49. צ [Tsarphati], "Réponse aux critiques de M. Salomon Munk," *AI* 2 (1841): 231–36. On Christian missionary activity, see Berkovitz, *Shaping of Jewish Identity*, 114–17, 232–38.

50. Terquem, letter to the editor of *Courrier de la Moselle* (December 1838).

51. צ [Tsarphati], "Sur l'ordonnance d'organisation du 25 mai 1844," *AI* 5 (1844): 453–57.

52. For excerpts of the *mémoire*, see *Journal de la Société* 3 (1826): 376–77. On the involvement of individuals in Jewish communal affairs before their conversion and on the related use of the term *régénération*, see *Philosophie du Christianisme: Correspondance religieuse de Louis Bautain* (Paris, 1835), 1:xliii–liii, lxxii, cvi, cviii. For links between radical religious reform, assimilation, and conversion, see Graetz, *From Periphery to Center*, ch. 4; Berkovitz, *Shaping of Jewish Identity*, 114–17; and the exchange in *Jewish History* 5 (1991): 47–71.

53. *L'Israélite français* (Paris, 1817–18). See *AN* C 2738, no. 72. Paris, 3 January 1816, and C 2741, no. 38, Paris, 1817. For a similar appraisal of the role played by the journal in the battle against the 1808 *règlement*, see Simon Dubnow, *History of the Jews*, trans. and ed. Moshe Spiegel (New York, 1967–71), 5:212.

54. While the journal did provide a forum for discussion of religious, philosophical, and literary subjects, political issues were accorded the highest priority, as is evident from the following excerpt appearing in the journals' introduction: "C'est pour arriver plus promptement à cette solution, et par conséquant à une amélioration desirée par les gens de bien et commandée par l'esprit du siècle, qu'on publie *l'Israélite français*. Le genre d'utilité qu'il présente, et le concours des savans qui se disposent à l'enrichir en font espérer le succès" (ii–iii).

55. See Abramsky, "The Crisis of Authority," and Sorkin, *Transformation*, 125–29.

56. On Jewish schools in France, see Szajkowski, *Jewish Education in France*, Albert, *Modernization of French Jewry*, 128–36; Berkovitz, *Shaping of Jewish Identity*, 150–91; and Hyman, *Emancipation of the Jews of Alsace*, 98–121.

57. See *AI* 9 (1848): 609–11.

58. The appeal for funds was published in Netter, *Vingt siècles d'histoire*, 312–17. The last part of the text reads: "Eicha, yashva badad kehilateinu, asher lifnim hay'ta zot be'yisrael mesos kol ha'aretz, bah hayu ba'alei trisin ba'alei qarnayim. Torah u-gedulah bekaneh eḥad oleh." Ben Yehudah lists some uses of *ba'alei quarnayim* in classical rabbinic literature as meaning "powerful people." Cf. the usage in *Bereshit Rabbah* 99:2.

59. On the restoration of the Metz *yeshivah* in 1820, see *AI* 5 (1844): 387–94. Netter, *Vingt siècles d'histoire*, 312–17.

60. Sharp criticism of the level of study and of the students was repeated frequently. See the report presented by the administrative council of the school on 20 January 1841, *AN* F^{19} 11052. For a listing of the first class at the *école centrale rabbinique*, see Bauer, "Ecole rabbinique," *REJ* 84 (1927): 53. For details on the geographical distribution of rabbinical students during the first thirty years of the institution, see Ulmann, *Lettre pastorale*. The dimensions of the Jewish marriage market contracted in similar fashion. See Hyman, *Emancipation of the Jews of Alsace*, 53.

61. Until recently, the most complete list of titles issued by the Metz press was published in Carmoly, "De la typographie hébraïque à Metz." Now see Yeshayahu Vinograd, *Thesaurus of the Hebrew Book* (Jerusalem, 1993), 458–61. On the disappearance of liturgical variants in the later prayer books, compare *Seder Tefilah ke-Minhag Ashkenaz* with *Maḥzor shel Rosh Ha-Shanah*; also note the detailed instructions concerning the recitation of *piyyutim* according to Metz custom, pp. 45b–47b.

62. *AI* 28 (1867): 154–16, and Berkovitz, *Shaping of Jewish Identity*, 141–46.

Chapter 7. Scholarship and Identity

1. De Sacy's letter, dated 7 October 1822, was published in L. Geiger, "Aus Leopold Zunz' Nachlag," *Zeitschrift für die Geschichte der Juden in Deutschland* 5 (1892): 259–60.

2. *Wissenschaftliche Zeitschrift für jüdische Theologie* 5 (1844): 449, cited in M. Meyer, *Response to Modernity*, 164–65. Cf. the harsh reaction of the *AI* 5 (1844): 862–64.

3. See Schorsch, "Emancipation and the Crisis of Authority," 243–44.

4. This is the conclusion of Simon-Nahum, *La cité investie*, esp. 48 ff. Simon-Nahum was not aware of the many Franco-Jewish studies devoted to Hebrew language, liturgy, and philosophical texts published in the first half of the nineteenth century, nor did she take note of the Bible translation project under the direction of Samuel Cahen.

5. M. Meyer, "Jewish Religious Reform and *Wissenschaft des Judentums*," 24–25.

6. See Schorsch, "The Emergence of Historical Consciousness in Modern Judaism," 419–20.

7. Ruderman, *Jewish Thought and Scientific Discovery*, 57–60. For the phrase "legacy of our fathers," see *Resp. Ha-Rema*, ed. Asher Siev (Jerusalem, 1971), no. 6. Also see Lawrence Kaplan, "R. Mordekhai Jaffe and the Evolution of Jewish Culture in Poland in the Sixteenth Century," in *Jewish Thought in the Sixteenth Century*, ed. Bernard D. Cooperman (Cambridge, Mass., 1983), 266–82; Elbaum, *Openness and Insularity*; Joseph Davis, "Philosophy and Law in the Writings of R. Yom Tov Lipman Heller," in *Studies in Medieval Jewish History and Literature III*, ed. Isadore Twersky and Jay Harris (Cambridge, Mass., 2000), 264–65; Mordechai Breuer, "The Early Modern Period," 1:234–39.

8. Mordecai Breuer, "The Documentary Hypothesis of the *Sha'agat Aryeh*."

9. In *Od la-Mo'ed* 50b, Worms followed R. Solomon b. Aderet, *Resp.* I, no. 395 and *Shulḥan Arukh, O.H.* 605; on *Makhnisei Raḥamim*, see *Od la-Mo'ed* 53a. On faulty Hebrew pronunciation by Ashkenazim, see *Be'er Sheva* 32.

10. See, for example, Worms's proposal to emend the text of Tosafot, *Berakhot* 11b to conform to general practice and to the text of the Tur (*O.H.* 48), in *Be'er Sheva* 3a, and his insistence that a difficult Maimonidean ruling was due to a copyist error, in *Bin Nun* 6b.

11. See, for example, the references to manuscript sources in *Be'er Sheva* 109b, 116b, 120b; *Od la-Mo'ed* 54b; and *Kan Tahor* 189a, 189b.

12. For doubts cast upon the reliability of the *Likkutei Maharil*, for example, because it had not been issued by Moellin himself but was compiled by his student R. Zalman, see *Od la-Mo'ed* 68a. Similar concerns had already been expressed by R. Solomon Luria, *Resp. Ha-Maharshal* no. 7; R. Samuel Bacharach, *Resp. Ḥut Ha-Shani* no. 31; and Ha-Levi, *Turei Zahav, Y.D.* 120:11 and *O.H.* 629:2. Cf. the contrasting views of Netanel Weil, *Netiv Ḥayyim* (Fürth, 1779), *O.H.* 629, and Moses Sofer, *Ḥiddushei Sugyot Ḥatam Sofer* (Jerusalem, 1991), p. 9, col. 1.

13. See, for example, Worms's analysis of *O.H.* 90 in *Be'er Sheva* 48a. Also see *Od la-Mo'ed* 50b where Worms resolved two contradictory views of Isserles by privileging the ruling in *Y.D.* 399 over the one in *O.H.* 548, because the *Yoreh De'ah* glosses were completed later.

14. *Od la-Mo'ed* 30b.

15. *Be'er Sheva* 46a. See the introductions to Yonah Landsofer, *Me'il Tzedakah* (Prague, 1757); Bacharach, *Resp. Ḥavvot Ya'ir*; and Ashkenazi, *Resp. Avodat Ha-Gershuni*, no. 48.

16. See *Be'er Sheva* 46a and *Kan Tahor* 131b. Cf. *Kan Tahor* 142a where the *Shulḥan Arukh* is referred to as *yated shelo timot*; in *Be'er Sheva* 18b, an Isserles formulation is termed *leshono ha-zahav*. Worms nonetheless reserved the right to point out occasional failings in the *Shulḥan Arukh*. For several examples, see *Be'er Sheva* 11b–12a.

17. See Menahem Elon, *Jewish Law*, Eng. ed. (Jerusalem, 1983), 1375–85.

18. The view of the Gaon of Vilna is summarized in his introduction to *Be'ur Ha-Gra* to the *Shulḥan Arukh*. For examples of his critical approach to the rulings of Karo and Isserles, see *Be'ur Ha-Gra, O.H.* 373, n. 10; *O.H.* 46, n. 17; and *O.H.* 25, n. 17. On his halakhic method, see Zvi Kaplan, "The Approach of R. Hayyim of Volozhin to Halakhah" [Hebrew], *Sinai* 69 (1971): 74–99.

19. See, for example *Od la-Mo'ed* 30b, where Worms objected to R. Judah Ashkenazi's *Ba'er Heitev* for its dismissive attitude toward the *Shulḥan Arukh*, such as in *O.H.* 477, n. 2. For a clear indication of the primacy of talmudic sources in *Me'orei Or*, see Worms's use of the expression *mekor ha-din* in *Kan Tahor* 165b (on *O.H.* 273),

which ought to be understood as the obverse of *hilkhita ke-batrai*. See the discussion in David Ellenson, *Between Tradition and Culture: The Dialectics of Modern Jewish Religion and Identity* (Atlanta, 1994), 106–07.

20. In the course of defending Isserles's lenient stance that the combing of wool when preparing *zizit* need not be performed with explicit religious intention, against the more stringent views of R. Meir Rothenberg (Maharam) and R. Judah Loeb ben Bezalel (Maharal) that it does, Worms argued that "the Maharam is not a *tanna* nor is the Maharal an *amora*." See *Be'er Sheva* 16b–17a and 110a for similar criticism of Lurianic stringencies.

21. R. Ezekiel Landau and R. Jacob Emden also privileged earlier authorities. See, for example, Daniel Sinclair, "Halakhic Methodology in the Post-Emancipation Period: Case Studies in the Responsa of R. Yechezkel Landau," *Le'ela* (April 1998): 16–22.

22. Etkes, "Immanent Factors and External Influences in the Development of the Haskalah Movement in Russia," 22–24; Harris, *How Do We Know This?* 137–41; David Fishman, "A Polish Rabbi Meets the Berlin Haskalah: The Case of R. Barukh Schick," *AJS Review* 12 (1987): 95–121; and Ruderman, *Jewish Thought and Scientific Discovery*, 332–43.

23. *Me'orei Or II*, 14a (on Berakhot 40a).

24. *Be'er Sheva* 42b; *Kan Tahor* 17b. Worms followed those who rejected philosophical study. Cf. the view of Elijah b. Solomon Zalman, *Be'ur Ha-Gra, Y.D.* 179, n. 13, where preference is shown for Kabbalah over philosophy. For Ashkenazic Jewry, the roots of the debate are in the controversy between R. Solomon Luria, who objected to philosophical study, and R. Moses Isserles, who favored it, referring to it as "a legacy of the fathers," in *Resp. Ha-Rema* no. 6. On Jewish attitudes toward philosophy in Poland, see Elbaum, *Openness and Insularity*, esp. 156–65.

25. See *Be'er Sheva* 112b (on *O.H.* 331).

26. For an earlier work devoted to a critical examination of the *Magen Avraham*, see Weil, *Netiv Hayyim* (n. 13 above); also see Bacharach, *Resp. Havvot Ya'ir* no. 9. Worms also focused, though to a lesser degree, on the *Ba'er Heitev* of R. Judah Ashkenazi Tiktin (Amsterdam, 1736–42). For examples of Worms's critical stance, see *Od la-Mo'ed* 29b (on *O.H.* 472, n. 16) and *Od la-Mo'ed* 30b (on *O.H.* 477, n. 2). For corresponding efforts to defend the *Shulhan Arukh* in the areas of civil and family law against the criticisms of *Siftei Kohen* and *Sefer Me'irat 'Einayim*, see *Kan Tahor* 25b–29a, 53b–59b, 113a–118b, 122b–124a, 138a–146b.

27. See *Magen Avraham* on *O.H.* 46:2 and response of Worms, *Me'orei Or II*, 23a.

28. See *Magen Avraham* on *O.H.* 46, n. 7, and Worms's criticism, *Me'orei Or II*, 24a.

29. See, for example, *Be'er Sheva* 46b, 146a, where it is noted that the *Magen Avraham* overlooked the *Ma'or* and a responsum of Maimonides.

30. See *Od la-Mo'ed* 25b where he criticizes the *Magen Avraham* on *O.H.* 441, following the *Eliah Rabbah* and the *Ba'er Heitev*, against the *Magen Avraham* (*O.H.* 450, n. 9).

31. See *TaZ* on *O.H.* 568, and *Be'er Sheva* 46b; also see *TaZ* on *O.H.* 90, and *Od la-Mo'ed* 111a.

32. See *Be'er Sheva* 47a, where Worms demonstrated that Isserles was referring to *hol ha-mo'ed*, not to *rosh hodesh*. Worms's reading of the Isserles gloss corresponded to the old custom in the Worms *kehillah*, which became the subject of dispute in the early eighteenth century, as noted in Kirchheim, first day *hol ha-mo'ed*, gloss 3; cf. Juspa, para. 60, n. 10.

33. See, for example, Jacob Emden, *Mor u-Keziah* (Altona, 1761), *O.H.* 4, 581, and Bacharach, *Resp. Havvot Ya'ir* no. 31. Also see Chaim Tchernowitz, *Toldot Ha-Poseqim* (New York, 1947), 3:110–12, for a summary of criticisms against Jaffe's *Levush*, including R. Joshua Falk's *Sefer Me'irat Eina'im*, introduction; and Benjamin

Selnick, *Resp. Mas'et Binyamin* (Cracow, 1633) nos. 8, 9. For Worms's formulation on the *Levush*, see *Be'er Sheva* 21a, 26b.

34. See *Be'er Sheva* 18a–18b.

35. See, for example, the effort to explain the difference between Isserles and Maimonides on the question of whether one ought to stand when reciting the *Shema*, in *Me'orei Or*, 2:25a.

36. On the dissemination of kabbalistic customs, see Gries, *Hanhagot Literature.*

37. Gershom Scholem, *Major Trends in Jewish Mysticism* (New York, 1961), 328. On the *herem* against the Brody *kloiz*, see Mordechai Wilensky, *Hasidim u-Mitnagdim: Le-Toldot ha-Pulmus Beineihem* (Jerusalem, 1970), 1:47–48; E. Reiner, "Wealth, Social Standing and Study of Torah"; and for the broader intellectual context, see Joseph Weiss, "The Kavvanot of Prayer in Early Hasidism," *Journal of Jewish Studies* 9 (1958): 163–92. On the mystical leanings of western and central European halakhists, see Shimon Dubnow, *Toldot Ha-Hasidut* (Tel Aviv, 1967), 434–41; Elior, "R. Nathan Adler and the Frankfurt Pietists"; Yosef Cohen, "Ha-Hatam Sofer veha-Hasidut," *Sinai* 69 (1971): 159–94; Jacob Katz, "Qavvim la-Biografiah shel ha-Hatam Sofer," *Mehqarim be-Kabbalah uve-Toldot ha-Datot Mugashim le-Gershom Scholem* (Jerusalem, 1968), 119–20; Alan Brill, "The Mystical Path of the Vilna Gaon," *Journal of Jewish Thought and Philosophy* 3 (1993): 131–51; Emmanuel Etkes, *Rabbi Yisrael Salanter ve-Reishit Tenuat ha-Musar* (Jerusalem, 1982), 37–40; and Nadler, *The Faith of the Mithnagdim*, 36–39. Other figures not normally known for their involvement with Kabbalah include R. Jacob Emden, R. Joseph Steinhardt, R. Pinhas Horowitz, R. Aryeh Loeb Günzberg, and R. Hirtz Scheuer (see his *Turei Zahav* [Mainz, 1875], grandson's introduction, p. 15). Even of R. Ezekiel Landau, generally viewed as an arch opponent of Kabbalah, R. Hayyim Sanzer of Brody reportedly said: 'Yehezkel envisioned *ma'aseh merqavah*."

38. See, for example, *Be'er Sheva* 3b, on switching from Ashkenazic to Sephardic pronunciation, and 17a–17b on women wearing *zizit*.

39. See Hayyim Yosef David Azulai, *Birkhei Yosef*, *O.H.* 421:1, cited in Moshe Halamish, "Ma'amado shel ha-Ari ke-Poseq," *Mehqerei Yerushalayim be-Mahshevet Yisrael* 10 (1993): 276.

40. See *Me'orei Or* I, 6b (on *Berakhot* 34b and 40a); II, 9b (on *Berakhot* 19), 10a (on *Berakhot* 26b), and 24b (*O.H.* 61).

41. Neither Jacob Joshua Falk (*Penei Yehoshua* [Frankfurt, 1752]) nor Ezekiel Landau (*Zelah*), for example, cited texts from the *Zohar* in the course of their talmudic and halakhic discussions, except for certain isolated efforts to explain difficult *aggadic* passages. In the latter regard, see *Penei Yehoshua*, Berakhot 10a. Cf. Jacob Emden, *Mor u-Keziah*, where the Zohar was cited regularly; also see *Resp. She'elat Yavez* no. 47.

42. *Be'er Sheva* 2a–2b. For example, he sought to harmonize the apparently conflicting traditions of the *Zohar* that prohibit eating anytime before sunrise and the talmudic proscription, which applies only from the time that the obligation of prayer can first be fulfilled. For details, see Berkovitz, "Authority and Innovation," 294–95.

43. *Be'er Sheva* 2a–2b. For Menahem Azariah de Fano's interpretation of *Zohar* (*Bemidbar*) 118b, see his *Resp. Ha-Rema* (Jerusalem, 1967), no. 3; and more generally, no. 128, for his approach to reconciling differences between the Talmud and *Zohar*. Also see *Iggeret Ha-Qodesh*, ed. Cohen (Rome, 1546), 77. Cf. H. Y. Bacharach, *Mekor Hayyim*, ed. E. Pines (Jerusalem, 1982), *O.H.* 3:6, where the author's attempt to reconcile the talmudic and zoharic passages resembles that of Worms, and Zvi Ashkenazi, *Resp. Hakham Zevi* no. 36, where the view of the *Zohar* was rejected when it ran contrary to the normative Halakhah. On the *Zohar* as an exegetical text, see Robert Bonfil, "Halakhah, Kabbalah and Society: Rabbi Menahem Azariah da

Fano's Inner World," in *Studies in Jewish Thought in the Sixteenth Century*, ed. I. Twersky and B. Septimus (Cambridge, Mass., 1987), 39–61, esp. 45. Cf. the view of R. Isaac Bardea, who denied the existence of a chasm separating the *Zohar* from normative Halakhah, cited in Ḥalamish, "Ari as *Poseq*," 275. Cf. Emden, *Resp. She'elat Yaveẓ* I, no. 47, where he argued that the *Zohar* ought to be viewed as an exegetical source that can, in most instances, clarify the meaning of the talmudic tradition.

44. See Worms's commentary to *Kol Nidrei* in *Maḥzor shel Yom Kippur* (Metz, 1816), and his additional comments in *Od la-Mo'ed* 52b–53a. On R. Tam's position, see *Sefer Ha-Yashar* (Vienna, 1811), 70. See Deshen, "The Riddle of *Kol Nidrei*"; Wieder, "Past and Future in *Kol Nidrei*."

45. See *Me'orei Or* I, 8a–8b, *Kan Tahor* 152b, especially Worms's use of the phrase *al pi ha-Torah asher yorukha* (Deut. 17:11) and *Raaya Mehemna*, Bemidbar 246a. For a full discussion of *mayyim aḥaronim*, including a different interpretation of the passage in *Raaya Mehemna*, Bemidbar 246a, see Israel Ta-Shma, *Ha-Nigle sheba-Nistar* (Tel Aviv, 1995), 59–66.

46. See *Resp. Rashba*, no. 191. According to Joel Sirkes, *Bayit Ḥadash, O.H.* 4, the fact that the source in the *Zohar* could not be found was the reason that the *Beit Yosef* failed to cite the *Tola'at Ya'akov*. For a more standard effort to resolve an inconsistency between the talmudic and zoharic traditions, cf. Reischer, *Resp. Shevut Ya'akov*, pt. 3, no. 1.

47. *Od la-Mo'ed* 33a; *Be'er Sheva* 28b [*O.H.* 108]. On the opposition to Lurianism in the eighteenth century, see Idel, *Hasidism*, ch. 1.

48. For a positive assessment of Worms, see Gerson Lévy, "Nécrologie de M. Aaron," *La Régénération* (1836): 226–31. Worms's positive image among *maskilim* may account for twentieth-century distortions of his biography. See, for example, Issachar Tamar, *Alei Tamar, Seder Mo'ed* (Alon Shevut, 1992), 311, where it is asserted that Worms had become, in his final days, a "Sadducee," i.e., a reformer. Tamar was misled by the entry in *Oẓar Israel* (London, 1924), itself an abridgment of Louis Ginzberg's entry in the *Jewish Encyclopedia* (New York, 1901).

49. On French involvement in the Berlin Haskalah, see Helfand, "The Symbiotic Relationship." On the cultural transfer from Germany to France, see Bourel, "La *Wissenschaft des Judentums* en France." On the early Haskalah, see Feiner, *The Jewish Enlightenment*.

50. The French translation of *Divrei Shalom ve-Emet* was published anonymously under the title *Instruction salutaire adressée aux communautés juives de l'empire* (Paris, 1782). Bing's Hebrew translation, *Phaedon hu sefer hash'arat ha-nefesh le-heḥakham ha-shalem rabbenu Moshe mi-Dessau ha-nikra Mendelssohn* (Berlin, 1787), was published with an introduction by N. H. Wessely. The translation of *Beḥinat Olam* appeared in Metz in 1794. Terquem published his translation of Rapoport, *Toldot Rabbenu Sa'-adia Gaon* in *AI* 3 (1842): 168–72, 518–21. On historical writing in this period, see L. Halévy, *Résumé*, esp. 318–26, along with the analysis of Marrus, *The Politics of Assimilation*, 88–93, 102–06; and Lambert, *Précis de l'histoire*. The work of Joseph-Cohen Moline was noted in Eliakim Carmoly, in *Revue orientale* 3 (1843–44): 315.

51. On these and related issues, see Etkes, "On the Question of the Forerunners of Haskalah in Eastern Europe."

52. In response to criticism of Azulai, Crémieux published *Kuntres Divrei Mordechai*. Also see Meir Benayahu, *Sefer Ḥida* (Jerusalem, 1959), 377–78.

53. See Roth, "The Liturgies of Avignon."

54. See Breuer, *The Limits of Enlightenment*, 59–62, and Uriel Simon, "Le-Darko Ha-Parshanit shel Ha-Ra'aba al pi Sheloshet Beiurav Le-Pasuk Eḥad," *Bar Ilan: Sefer ha-Shanah le-Mada'ei ha-Yahadut ve-ha-Ruaḥ shel Universitat Bar Ilan* 3 (1965): 100–111. For signs of dissatisfaction with conventional methods of Talmud study and analysis in central Europe, see Harris, *How Do We Know This?* 137–41.

55. On Sofer, see Stefan Reif, *Shabbethai Sofer and His Prayer-book* (Cambridge, 1979). On the genre itself, see Reif, *Judaism and Hebrew Prayer*, 230–50. Cf. Jacob Emden, *Luaḥ Eres* (Altona, 1769).

56. On Biding, see Berkovitz, "Jewish Scholarship and Identity in Nineteenth-Century France," 27n. 33. The laudatory description of Biding appeared in a letter of support from the Central Consistory to M. le Ministre Sécretarie d'Etat: "M. Biding est . . . *le premier hébraïsant de notre époque, ses vastes connaissances dans la langue de Moïse, et sons aptitude toute spéciale pour la correction des ouvrages hébraïques ont rendu son nom européen, et nos voisins de l'Allemagne rendent hommage, comme nos concitoyens français à sa profonde érudition.*" See letter of 7 August 1836, CAHJP FCC/81.

57. Intimations of tension within the Jewish community may be inferred by the use of the expression *benei aliyah*. See Biding, "Ma'amar Shekel Ha-Kodesh."

58. See Biding's analysis of the *piyyut* "Eleh Ezkerah" in an essay titled "Kaf Aḥat Asarah Zahav."

59. On the work of Elie Halévy, see Berkovitz, *Shaping of Jewish Identity*, 61, 184; for a summary of Halévy's ms. commentary to Ecclesiastes and Proverbs, see Cahen *Bible*, 16:xxxviii–xliii. On the contributions of several other leading *maskilim*, see Helfand, "The Symbiotic Relationship," 340–41.

60. On the history of *maḥzor* commentary, see Daniel Goldschmidt, *Maḥzor le-Yamim Nora'im* (Jerusalem, 1970), introduction.

61. On the debate concerning the retention or elimination of the *piyyutim*, see Chapter 8.

62. J. Sofer, *Even Yisrael*. The author, who pursued his talmudic training in Sierentz and Frankfurt am Main, apparently was introduced to the study of Hebrew grammar while in Berlin. For a brief description, see *AI* 3 (1842): 374–77.

63. See Hadas-Lebel, "Les études hébraïques."

64. Biding, *Em la-Mikrah*, introduction.

65. See, for example, the controversy that erupted over the portrayal of Moïse Ensheim by Olry Terquem in his *Lettres Tsarphatiques*, the critique by Moïse Biding, *Nikmat Yisrael: La Vengeance d'Israël* (Metz, 1840), and the response of Salomon Munk in *AI* 2 (1841): 325–32.

66. M. Meyer, "Jewish Religious Reform and *Wissenschaft des Judentums*," 19–41; Schorsch, "Breakthrough into the Past."

67. See M. Meyer, "Jewish Scholarship and Identity in Modern Germany," 186.

68. For the second half of the century, see Helfand, "French Jewry in the Second Republic."

69. Artz, *France under the Bourbon Restoration*, 158–63. Also see *AI* 28 (1867): 154–67. Opportunities for less conspicuous relations were limited to private study, as in the case of Salomon Munk (1803–1867), who studied Arabic with Sylvestre de Sacy, Sanskrit with Chezy, and Persian with Quatrième following his arrival in Paris in 1828.

70. See *AI* 28 (1867): 154–67, and Berkovitz, *Shaping of Jewish Identity*, 141–46. For the basic details of Munk's life and career, see Schwab, *Salomon Munk*. Trained in Vienna, Albert Cohn settled in Paris in 1836. See Isidore Loeb, *Biographie d'Albert Cohn* (Paris, 1878). Joseph Derenbourg received his degree from the Université rhénane Frédéric-Guillaume in 1832–34 and was naturalized as a citizen of France in 1845. He was elected to the Académie des Inscriptions in 1871 and was appointed to the chair of Hebraic and rabbinic languages in 1877.

71. Sylvestre de Sacy, "Une Extrait de Taḥkemoni," *Journal asiatique*, no. 70 (October 1833): 306–49. Earlier in the century, de Sacy wrote an extensive analysis of Yedayah Ha-Penini de Béziers's *Beḥinat Olam* in the *Magasin Encyclopédique* 3 (1808): 315–50. The fact that de Sacy's work appeared the same year that Michel Berr published a translation of the same text (Metz, 1808) raises the possibility of collabora-

tion. The Berr manuscript is reported to be in the municipal library of Nîmes, no. 13723.

72. See Eugène Boré, "Une séance du Tahkemoni," *Journal asiatique*, Troisième série, 3 (January 1837): 21–43; the Druse project appeared in *Temps*, 2 March 1838. On the assistance given to Renan, see Schwab, *Salomon Munk*, 44–120, and Graetz, *From Periphery to Center*, 225.

73. Auguste Pichard, "Le livre de la bonne doctrine (*Sefer Lekah Tov*)," *Journal asiatique* (October 1836): 305–37.

74. See, for example, Gerson-Lévy's report on Dukes's work, presented to the Académie de Metz and published in *AI* (February 1848). Gerson-Lévy was also a member of the Société Asiatique and the Académie de Stanislas, Nancy. For additional biographical data, see M. Thiel, "Notice sur la vie de Gerson-Lévy," *Extrait du mémoires de l'Académie de Metz* (Metz, 1864–65).

75. Franck, *La Kabbale*. Also see Schwab, *Salomon Munk*, 44–46, 68, 70, 131, and Fenton, "Qabbalah and Academia."

76. See Paul Robert, *Le Petit Robert*. 1: *Dictionnaire alphabetique et analogique de la langue française* (Paris, 1984).

77. Munk, *Palestine*, 2. Adolphe Franck's research on ancient philosophy and on the Kabbalah led him to the conclusion that the spiritual and political elements in Judaism were mutually exclusive, even antithetical. He viewed the history of Judaism as a process of progressive spiritualization and refinement that was accelerated by the Jewish people's loss of political independence. Franck saw in this development evidence of Judaism's universal character, a trait enabling the religion to adapt itself to varying circumstances. Accordingly, in a system where Judaism was viewed as ultimately free from the constraints of material and space, the role of the ceremonial law was minimized. See Baron, "The Revolution of 1848 and Jewish Scholarship," 14–18, and Graetz, *From Periphery to Center*, 63–65.

78. See, for example, David Eichhorn, *Einleitung in das alte Testament* (Gottingen, 1824); Heinrich Ewald, *Die Poetischen des alten Bundes* (Gottingen, 1837); Wilhelm De Wette, *Commentar uber die Psalmer* (Heidelberg, 1811); Friedrich Heinrich Wilhelm Gesenius, *Hebräische Grammatik* (Halle, 1813); F. Hitzig, *Die Zwoelf Kleinen Propheten* (Leipzig, 1830); and C. E. K. Rosenmüller, *Scholia in vetus Testamentum Salomonis regis et sapientis quoe perhibentur scripta* (Leipsig, 1819). The preference for German scholarship, particularly in the field of religion, mirrored a similar inclination among general French historians as noted by Rearick, *Beyond the Enlightenment*, 162. Cf. Clements, "The Study of the Old Testament." For examples in the Cahen *Bible*, see 13:x–xi, 15:xi–xvi; in the case of Munk's *Palestine*, the author critically engaged German scholarship, only rarely adopting their views, see pp. 116–28.

79. Peter Gay, *The Enlightenment: An Interpretation. The Rise of Modern Paganism* (New York, 1966), 31–126.

80. On the hostile attitude toward the Talmud, see Moshe Pelli, "The Attitude of the First Maskilim in Germany towards the Talmud," *LBIYB* 27 (1982): 243–60, and Feiner, *Haskalah and History*.

81. Schorsch, "The Emergence of Historical Consciousness."

82. See Salomon Munk, "Réflexions sur le culte des anciens Hébreaux dans ses rapports avec les autres cultes de l'antiquité," in Cahen *Bible*, 4:1–56.

83. Munk, *Palestine*, 108, 116; see "Lois de Manou," in Cahen *Bible*, 3:173, 9:97.

84. Cahen, *La Bible*.

85. See Wiener, "The Ideology of the Founders of Jewish Scientific Research." For an exception to the general pattern in Germany, see the efforts of Isaac Bernays, an orthodox rabbi and scholar, who defended the masoretic text against the criticisms of contemporaries such as Gesenius: [Bernays], *Bibel'sche Orient—Eine*

Zeitschrift in zwanglossen Heften, 2 vols. (1820–21), and Rivka Horowitz, "On Kabbala and Myth in Nineteenth-Century Germany: Isaac Bernays," *PAAJR* 59 (1993): 137–83. Also see Berkovitz, *Shaping of Jewish Identity,* 143–44.

86. Berkovitz, *Shaping of Jewish Identity,* 272n. 40.

87. Ibid., 142–44. Munk's views were articulated in his book *Palestine,* 99, 132–40. Cf. Mordecai Breuer, "The Documentary Hypothesis of the *Sha'agat Aryeh.*"

88. French-Jewish scholars regarded their approach as fully consistent with the talmudic and medieval exegetical traditions. See Salomon Munk, "Examen de plusieurs critiques du premier volume," in Cahen *Bible,* 2:xix–xxii; cf. E. Breuer, *The Limits of Enlightenment,* 26–27.

89. Cahen *Bible,* 9:vii–ix, vol. 11. Convinced of the indispensability of rabbinics for biblical research, Cahen had begun work on a volume of rabbinic vocabulary, *Secher le-Miriame,* but the projected work never came to fruition.

90. Cf. Harris, *How Do We Know This?* 141–47, where the treatment of the early Haskalah in Germany parallels our discussion of French Jewish scholars in the 1830s.

91. Cahen's interpretation of the word *Shiloh* (Gen. 49:10) was rejected by the *Archives'* editors, who preferred to explain the term as "Messiah." In Munk's view, the Christian claim was untenable from a historical perspective: the House of Judah had already disappeared six centuries before. Cahen refuted various christological references in the Hebrew Bible by citing Gesenius's interpretation of Isaiah 52:13–53:12 extensively. See Cahen *Bible,* 9:231–34.

92. According to Munk, "Examen," xxiv, the rabbis were disturbed by the note referring to the medical benefits of circumcision (p. 42). Cahen's error, Munk maintained, was in failing to emphasize that for Jews alone circumcision was a distinctive sign.

93. Salomon Klein, *Mippnei Koshet* (Frankfurt am Main, 1861), 14.

94. See Artz, *France under the Bourbon Restoration,* 158–63, 170–76.

95. See *AI* 4 (1843): 4–5. For the Cahen quote, see *La Bible,* vol. 9, preface; cf. *AI* 1 (1840): 66–67, and Cahen, *Bible,* 10:62, note.

96. Such conservatism was typical of early reform. See M. Meyer, "Jewish Religious Reform and *Wissenschaft des Judentums.*"

97. For a survey of the important contributions made by Jewish scholars in the field of Islamic studies, see Lewis, *Islam in History,* esp. 20–21, 123–37. Basing his translation of the *Guide of the Perplexed* on the Judeo-Arabic manuscripts at the Bibliothèque Royale and Oxford Library, Munk proceeded to publish the first installment of the translation (chs. 27 and 31) and notes in Cahen *Bible,* 4:80–89; it finally appeared in its entirety as *Le guide des égarés par Moïse ben Maimon,* 3 vols. (Paris, 1856–66). In vol. 9 (Paris, 1838), pp. 76–101, he published a biographical essay on Sa'adia, notes on Sa'adia's Arabic text of Isaiah (pp. 101–34), and notes on a Persian manuscript of Isaiah (pp. 134–59).

98. See Schorsch, "The Emergence of Historical Consciousness in Modern Judaism," 436, and I. Marcus, "Beyond the Sephardic Mystique," 35–36. Samuel Cahen wrote that "we hope for rapid progress in a branch of literature to which our possessions in Africa bestow even a political importance." For this quote, and for one of the earliest expressions of the desire to move the *école rabbinique* to Paris, see Cahen *Bible,* 9:xiv–xv. For a strong statement concerning the unparalleled value of the Sephardic literary and philosophical legacy, particularly in terms of its reconciliation of religion and science, see Cahen *Bible,* vol. 9, introduction to Abarbanel's commentary to Isaiah, p. 1.

99. See Cahen *Bible,* 9:xiv–xv.

100. See Cahen *Bible,* 14:ix.

101. For the Paulus letter (9 December 1832, to Cahen), see Cahen *Bible,* vol. 9,

introduction. Cf. the remarks of Wolf Fraenkel of Lemberg and of Solomon Judah Rapoport, reporting that the French Bible project was viewed very positively in the east and that the work of French scholars was viewed with the greatest respect (ibid.). Cf. Lowenstein, "The Readership of Mendelssohn's Bible Translation."

102. Cahen *Bible*, vol. 9, introduction.

Chapter 8. Rabbinic Authority and Ritual Reform

1. See M. Meyer, *Response to Modernity*, 53–61; Ellenson, "Traditional Reactions."

2. On attitudes of orthodox traditionalists toward religious reform in central Europe, see Katz, "The Changing Position and Outlook of Halakhists in Early Modernity"; Jacob Katz, *Ha-Halakhah be-Mezar* (Jerusalem, 1992); Mordechai Breuer, *Jüdische Orthodoxie im Deutschen Reich*; David Ellenson, *Rabbi Esriel Hildesheimer and the Creation of Modern Orthodoxy* (Tuscaloosa, 1990); Ellenson, *Between Tradition and Culture: The Dialectics of Modern Jewish Religion and Identity* (Atlanta, 1994); Ellenson, *Tradition in Transition: Orthodoxy, Halakhah, and the Boundaries of Modern Jewish Identity* (New York, 1989); Liberles, *Religious Conflict*; Silber, "The Emergence of Ultra-Orthodoxy"; and Judith Bleich, "Jacob Ettlinger, His Life and Works: The Emergence of Modern Orthodoxy in Germany" (Ph.D. diss., New York University, 1974).

3. "Consistoire de Strasbourg, 1831," French-Jewish Documents, box 18, pt. 2, Archives *JTS*.

4. Rapport présenté au Consistoire Israélite de Paris, par l'ancien comité de secours et d'encouragement de la même ville" (July 1838), in *AI* 2 (1841): 126.

5. Gerson Lévy, "Sur la necessité d'une régénération dans le Judaïsme," *La Régénération* 1 (1836): 273. Also see the report of the Comité de Secours et d'Encouragement, *AI* 2 (1841): 130.

6. See Albert, "Nonorthodox Attitudes in Nineteenth-Century French Judaism," and Albert, *Modernization of French Jewry*, 231–36.

7. See, for example, *AI* 8 (1847): 9. Also see Berkovitz, *Shaping of Jewish Identity*, ch. 10.

8. G. Lévy, *Culte israélite*, 5, 8–9.

9. Ibid.

10. Ibid., 7, 5; *AI* 5 (1844): 237–39.

11. Terquem, for one, criticized the project. See *Lettre* 27 (24 August 1841), in Fondsweiner, no. 16948; *AI* 5 (1844): 230–31.

12. G. Lévy, *Culte israélite*, 6; letter from thirty-one heads of households in Nancy to Metz consistory, reprinted in *AI* 2 (1841): 469; *AI* 5 (1844): 231, 234–35.

13. The *Archives israélites* reported regularly on developments in Germany. For an example of its concurrence with the general conception of messianism that emerged at the Frankfurt rabbinical conference in 1845, see *AI* 7 (1846): 538–39.

14. Baruch Mevorach, "The Belief in the Messiah in the Early Reform Polemics" [Hebrew], *Zion* 24 (1969): 189–218.

15. *Die Deutsche Synagoge oder Ordnung des Gottestdienstes fur die Sabbath-und Festtage des ganzen Jahre, zum Gebrauche der Gemeinden, die sich der deutschen Gebete bediene.* Hrsg, von Dr. E. Kley and Dr. E. S. Günsberg (Berlin, 1817). Also see Mevorach, "The Belief in the Messiah," 190–94.

16. Anspach, *Rituel des Prières journalieres*, vii–viii, and Anspach, *Paroles d'un croyant israélite*. For similar formulations of the messianic doctrine, see M. Berr, *Lettres*, 3–4; M. Berr, *Nouveau précis élémentaire*, 45–47; Charleville, *Réponse de M. le rabbin de Charleville*, 1–5; and Wogue, *Guide du croyant israélite*, 352–57. Cf. the translation of the Sephardic rite, Venture, *Prières journalières*.

17. *AI* 6 (1845): 859–63. On this point, see the comments of R. Lazare Isidor,

published in Schwarzfuchs, "La situation du Judaïsme français en 1883," *REJ* 146 (1987): 315.

18. *AI* 5 (1844): 602–08. Cf. the letter of R. Samuel Dreyfus, in *AI* 5 (1844): 589–91. For a discussion of the Reformfreunde's position on religious reform, see Liberles, *Religious Conflict*, 52–61.

19. One leading opponent of ritual reform, Rabbi Salomon Klein, argued that such changes were a violation of the religious status quo established by the Paris Sanhedrin. See his letter to the Minister of Public Instruction and Religions, 31 December 1856, in AN F^{19} 11037, Archives Nationales, Paris.

20. See Albert, *Modernization of French Jewry*, and Berkovitz, *Shaping of Jewish Identity*.

21. In 1841 the Metz primary school administrative committee, for example, was composed of the local chief rabbi, Lion-Mayer Lambert, and several *maskilim*. See *AI* 2 (1841): 538.

22. The *école rabbinique* of Metz exemplifies the pluralism that prevailed in French Jewish life. S. Krüger, a member of the Talmud faculty who had been affiliated with Frankel before assuming a position at the Metz school, issued a sharp attack against R. Samson Raphael Hirsch for having criticized the 1856 Paris rabbinical conference. In a pamphlet titled *De la compétence de M. S. R. Hirsch*, Krüger expressed the widely felt Franco-Jewish rejection of denominationalism that came to dominate Jewish life in Germany. Condemning religious extremism, Krüger warned Hirsch that his style of orthodoxy had no chance of success in France because French Jewry was protected from the abuse of rabbinic authority by the consistorial system.

23. Although the consistories were apparently overburdened by bureaucratic duties and therefore failed to provide effective leadership for the modernization of French Jewry, they nonetheless did play an absolutely decisive role by providing both a formal administrative structure and, no less important, a framework of symbolic unity. On the consistorial system, see Albert, *Modernization of French Jewry*. The absence of a religious reform movement is generally explained by the potent forces of cultural conservatism in the rural northeast and the resistance of the region's rabbinic leadership to ritual innovation. See Albert, *Modernization of French Jewry*, 263–65, 290–302, and Berkovitz, *Shaping of Jewish Identity*, 187–88, 210–14. My emphasis here on the structural impediments to religious reform stresses the Napoleonic foundations of this phenomenon.

24. *AI* 2 (1841): 383–85, and Munk, *Palestine*, 99. In defining this special role for religious ceremonies, Munk's position bore distinct traces of the Mendelssohnian legacy.

25. *AI* 1 (1840): 328–29. It may be noted that R. Salomon Ulmann viewed modern Jewish scholarship in extremely positive terms, arguing that rabbinical students had much to gain from the expertise and commitment of Jewish scholars, especially in the area of philosophy. For this reason, he strongly endorsed the transfer of the *école rabbinique* from Metz to Paris. See Ulmann Letters, letter to R. Marchand Ennery [1848].

26. "Consistoire Central, 1839," box 18, pt. 1, Archives JTS; Albert, *Modernization of French Jewry*, 74–75, 82–83, 280–81; "Sephardic Jews of France," 4/1 (1852–55), Hebrew Union College Archives, Cincinnati; D. Cohen, *La promotion des Juifs en France*, 2:130–31.

27. Albert, *Modernization of French Jewry*, 82–83.

28. Adhésions de 82 communes du Bas-Rhin à la petition de la communauté israélite de Strasbourg," AN F^{19} 11015, Archives Nationales, Paris.

29. Archives *JTS*, box 18, fols. 405–07. For information concerning the mass campaign, see the Metz consistory's letter of resignation to the Central Consistory in 1841, published in *AI* 2 (1841): 405–06.

30. See Berkovitz, *Shaping of Jewish Identity*, 203–28, and Albert, *Modernization of French Jewry*, 82–83, 280–81, 356–78. One of the principal areas targeted for reform by the consistories was the rabbinate. A continuing effort by lay leaders to exercise control over the rabbinate was motivated both by ideological and practical considerations. Rabbis were believed to be the major obstacle to the kinds of modifications that were judged to be crucial to the emerging Franco-Jewish ethos. Lay proponents of *régénération* argued that if rabbinic authority could be brought under control, ritual and synagogue reforms would be implemented more effectually. The recasting of the rabbinate into a modern force capable of leading the Jews of France forward would depend on establishing minimal rabbinic qualifications, modernizing rabbinic training, creating a rabbinic hierarchy, and revamping the process of rabbinic selection and dismissal. In each of these areas the cooperative efforts of the French government and the Central Consistory were evident from the beginning.

31. Despite strenuous efforts challenging the right of the Central Consistory grand rabbi to censure departmental rabbis, or of departmental rabbis to censure community rabbis, rabbinic hierarchy was retained in the 1844 *ordonnance* and would no longer be debated after this.

32. Albert, *Modernization of French Jewry*, 75–76, 82–95, 273–75.

33. Efforts by the Metz consistory to conduct elections for the rabbi of the Sarreguemines district (in 1850) were thwarted by the Central Consistory, and in 1853 the central body withdrew the communities' right to select their own rabbis and gave this authority to the departmental consistories. See Albert, *Modernization of French Jewry*, 276.

34. For the full text of the circular, see Albert, *Modernization of French Jewry*, 385–86.

35. Helfand, "The Election of the Grand Rabbi of France (1842–1846)," 2:142. The following responses to the 1846 questionnaire by candidates for the position of Central Consistory grand rabbi are extant: Samuel Dreyfus (Mulhouse) and Mahir Charleville (Dijon), in Archives *JTS*, box 18; Marchand Ennery (Paris), Leopold Lehmann (Belfort), Isaac Weil (Blotzheim), and Dittisheim (Wintzenheim), in Leo Baeck Institute Archives, New York.

36. For the text of the manifesto, see *AI* 7 (1846): 281–82, and *Allegemeine Zeitung des Judentums* 10 (1846): 290–91, cited in David Philipson, *The Reform Movement in Judaism* (New York, 1931), 460n. 63. See Albert, *Modernization of French Jewry*, 296–97, for Lambert's reply to the consistory's criticism of the manifesto. The Goudchaux-Lambert letter evoked stinging criticism of their position authored by Baruch Zeitlin, *Ḥazut Kashah* (Paris, 1846), and a defense of traditionalist orthodoxy, by Klein, *Ma'aneh Rakh*.

37. *UI* 2 (1846): 69–79. For a critical report on the Colmar meeting, see *AI* 7 (1846): 287–88.

38. Most of the petitions are in "Alsace Lorraine, 1808–1853," fols. 174–225, Alsace-Lorraine Collection, Archives of the Leo Baeck Institute, New York.

39. M. Sofer, *Resp. Ḥatam Sofer* 6:89, cited in Ellenson, "Traditional Reactions," 2:736.

40. See *AI* 7 (1846): 602–08.

41. On the decisive role of the consistories in providing both a formal administrative structure and, no less important, a framework of symbolic unity, see Albert, *Modernization of French Jewry*.

42. See Schwarzfuchs, *Napoleon, the Jews, and the Sanhedrin*, 183–84, and Albert, *Modernization of French Jewry*, 240–302. Schwarzfuchs and Albert view the nineteenth-century rabbinate as having been emasculated by the consistory. The stature of the rabbinate plummeted as consistory lay leaders endeavored to impose their author-

ity even in strictly religious affairs. Low prestige, decreasing representation in the consistory executive bodies, the pervasive view of the rabbis as opponents of *régénération*, and mounting secularization are typically adduced as prime elements in the argument. While these factors are largely incontestable, greater qualification is required.

43. On social mobility in Alsace, see Hyman, *Emancipation of the Jews of Alsace*, 122–37. For two examples of studies that argue for the decline of the rabbinate, see Albert, *Modernization of French Jewry*, 240–302, and Chouraqui, "De l'émancipation des Juifs à l'émancipation du Judaïsme."

44. Consisting of 250 letters, Ulmann's professional correspondence is available in manuscript at the Archives JTS (hereafter cited as Ulmann Letters). See Berkovitz, "On Rabbinic Authority."

45. Ulmann Letters, no. 5, January 1844.

46. Ulmann Letters, nos. 5–6, January 1844.

47. Ulmann Letters, no. 6; no. 32 (12 August 1845); see Ennery's letter to *AI* 6 (1845): 201.

48. Petuchowski, *Prayerbook Reform in Europe.*

49. See Ulmann Letters, nos. 14 and 19, to R. Seligmann Goudchaux.

50. Ulmann Letters, no. 5.

51. Ulmann Letters, no. 6.

52. Ulmann Letters, no. 32. On parallel developments elsewhere, cf. Petuchowski, *Prayerbook Reform in Europe*, 24–30, 128–60, and Robert Liberles, "The Rabbinical Conferences of the 1850s and the Quest for Liturgical Unity," *Modern Judaism* 3 (1983): 309–17. The 1856 conference sought to shorten the duration of the services by eliminating extra prayers, such as the Ashkenazic *misheberakh* and the Sephardic *hashkavah*. See Schwarzfuchs, "La situation du Judaïsme français en 1883: Le Rapport Isidor," 317–18. Isidor was critical of the pronounced inequality visible in the stark contrast between opulent and parsimonious weddings and funerals. For efforts to create more egalitarian wedding and funeral ceremonies, see ibid., 319–21.

53. *AI* 5 (1844): 377–79. In a letter to Central Consistory Grand Rabbi Marchand Ennery, Ulmann revealed the reasoning behind his decision. There, while hardly dismissive of *ḥukkat ha-goi*, as were the reformers, he argued that in this specific case it did not apply. Citing the opinion of Sirkes, *Resp. Bayit Ḥadash* no. 127, who held that the adoption of Christian melodies in the synagogue was permissible, Ulmann concluded that it was theoretically possible to borrow other customs from the church—such as the organ—as long as they were not peculiar to Christian ritual observance. See Ulmann Letters, no. 12, 8 Tammuz 5404 (1844).

54. Compare the view of R. Moses Sofer of Pressburg who argued that the organ had been an instrument of ancient idol worship and was therefore the only musical instrument prohibited in the Temple. See Ellenson, "A Disputed Precedent." For R. Salomon Klein of Colmar, the organ violated the spirit of Jewish prayer (i.e., solemn concentration) and, in a technical-halakhic sense, was objectionable because it required a gentile to perform an act clearly prohibited of Jews on the Sabbath. In Klein's criticisms of the 1856 rabbinic conference, the theme of *ḥukkat ha-goi*, so prominent a decade earlier, was absent from his argument in reference to the organ, although he employed it to discredit the ceremony for the newborn. See Berkovitz, *Shaping of Jewish Identity*, 226.

55. See Ulmann Letters, no. 12.

56. Ibid. On Sofer's oft-quoted statement, "all innovation is prohibited by the Torah," see Silber, "The Emergence of Ultra-Orthodoxy."

57. Berkovitz, *Shaping of Jewish Identity*, 216–17.

58. *AI* 7 (1846): 746–48.

59. See *AI* 6 (1845): 628; *AI* 7 (1846): 709; and *AI* 6 (1845): 200–201.

60. See Ulmann Letters, no. 8, to R. Arnaud Aron, 23 April 1844, and no. 6. In letter no. 13, to R. Goudchaux, July 1844, Ulmann argued for a united stand of consistorial rabbis against the Central Consistory.

61. Ulmann Letters, no. 20, to R. Aron (28 December 1844). Ettlinger succeeded in obtaining three hundred signatures. For a list of signators, see Jacob Ettlinger, *Shelomei Emunei Yisrael* (Karlesruhe, 1845). Also see Ellenson, "Traditional Reactions," 732–77.

62. For the text of the manifesto, see *AI* 7 (1846): 281–82. For additional expressions of vigorous opposition to the reform agenda sponsored by the consistory, see Berkovitz, *Shaping of Jewish Identity*, 214–15.

63. Ulmann Letters, letters of 8 May 1846 and 23 December 1846.

64. Ulmann Letters, 8 May 1846.

65. Ulmann Letters, letter to M. Cerfberr, 12 May 1846.

66. The text of the decisions of the conference was published in Uhry, *Recueil des lois.*

67. *AI* 17 (1856): 307.

68. *Le Lien d'Israël* 2 (July 1856).

69. Berkovitz, "On Rabbinic Authority," 218–19. For a description of the birth ritual for girls, see R. Lazare Isidor, "Rapport Isidor," 317–19. The ceremony was a recasting of the Sephardic ritual known as *zeved bat*, which consisted of a benediction pronounced over the head of the newborn at the afternoon service on the Sabbath. According to Isidor, this was less an innovation than a reasonable transformation of an ancient custom, i.e., the *Hollekreisch.*

70. On Klein, see Samson Raphael Hirsch, "Eulogy for R. Salomon Zev Klein," published in *Ha-Ma'ayan* 30 (1989): 30–37; Catane, "Rabbi Shlomo Zev Klein."

71. Klein, *Divrei Ha-Piyyutim ve-Za'akatam.* I am indebted to Dr. Shlomo Sprecher for sending me a copy of this rare work. Also see *Lettre Pastorale*, 7 October 1856; and his letter to the Minstre de l'Instruction Publique et des Cultes, 31 December 1856, in AN F[19] 11037, Archives Nationales, Paris. For another example of Klein's positive view of the Napoleonic Sanhedrin, see his *Judaïsme ou la vérité sur le Talmud*, 86.

72. On clerical garb worn by Rabbi Bigart at his installation as rabbi of Bergheim, see *Le Lien d'Israël* 2 (1856): 73. In Germany, Rabbis Isaac Bernays, Seligmann Baer Bamberger, and Samson Raphael Hirsch wore canonicals. See Leiman, "Rabbinic Openness to General Culture," 170n. 56.

73. One liberal critic of orthodoxy, Samuel Cahen, editor of the *Archives israélites*, called attention to this concession to conservatives who were able to retain a veto at the local level, despite clear directives from Paris indicating that the reforms were halakhically acceptable. See *AI* 17 (1856): 373.

74. See Hirsch's attack on the decisions of the 1856 Paris conference in *Jeschurun* (June 1856); also see the counterattack in *AI* 17 (1856): 429–36, and Ulmann's own defense of the decisions on pp. 491–92.

75. See the register of the Jewish community of Bouxwiller, 1828–1948, CAHJP, HM 1067, pp. 32–33, cited in Hyman, "The Social Contexts of Assimilation," 124.

76. Not surprisingly, the views of progressive rabbis bore some resemblance to the reformist distinction between essential and nonessential elements of Jewish tradition. In 1844, the Paris consistory objected to R. Ennery's rejection of the organ and a girls' choir on the grounds of *ḥukkat ha-goi* by arguing that these innovations were not matters that "essentially concern the religion." And in 1856, following the Paris rabbinic conference, Samuel Cahen asserted that "from the moment that the conference declared that the introduction of the organ was not contrary to Halakhah, the persona of the religious leader disappeared, replaced by the administration." Albert, *Modernization of French Jewry*, 290–91; *AI* 17 (1856): 373.

Chapter 9. Patrie et Religion

1. The Liber quote appeared in *UI* 77 (1922): 559. On acceptance into government positions, see Birnbaum, "L'entrée en République." For a detailed review of acculturation and social mobility in the Alsace region, see Hyman, *Emancipation of the Jews of Alsace*, 137. For specific data on individual communities see, for example, Job, *Les Juifs de Nancy*, 95–106, and Jean-Paul Aube, "Les Juifs de Toul (1789–1850)," *Archives juives* 27/2 (1994): 62–77.

2. On demands for state aid for schools, see Berkovitz, *Shaping of Jewish Identity*, 160.

3. Cited in D. Cohen, "L'image du Juif," 84–85.

4. Emphasizing the symbolism of the *more judaico*, Samuel Cahen referred to it as "ce dernier vestige de barbarie d'un autre age," in *AI* 6 (1845): 104. See Phyllis Cohen Albert, "The Jewish Oath in Nineteenth-Century France," *Spiegel Lectures in European Jewish History* (Tel Aviv University, 1982).

5. S. Cahen, *La Bible*, vol. 1, preface; Lambert, *Précis de l'histoire*, preface.

6. François Furet, *Revolutionary France, 1770–1880*, trans. Antonia Nevill (London, 1992), 365–66; Robert Tombs, *France, 1814–1914* (London, 1996), 133–35, 241–49.

7. See Simon Bloch, "Sur l'esprit et la tendance de ce recueil," *La Régénération* 1 (1836): 65–67, and the quote by Samuel Cahen, *AI* 3 (1842): 3.

8. The expression *le mouvement régénérateur* was used by Samuel Cahen, *AI* 7 (1847): 465; and G. Lévy, *Orgue et Pioutim*, 2. R. Salomon Ulmann used the expression as well; see, for example, Ulmann Letters, letter to Marchand Ennery (23 June 1846), and *Lettre pastorale* (11 December 1853).

9. Jacob Lazare, *Réponse à un écrit intitulé: Première lettre d'un Israélite français* (Paris, 1821); Calman de Metz, *Au pseudonyme Tzarphati malgré lui* (Paris, 1824); Godechaux Baruch-Weil, *Réflexions d'un jeune Israélite français* (Paris, 1821).

10. Albert Cohn, "Réflexions d'un Israélite allemand sur la huitième 'Lettre d'un Israélite français,'" *La Régénération* 1 (1836): 348. Salomon Munk, letter to editor, *La Régénération* 1 (1836): 330–31. For examples of how Terquem's views were an impetus for the development of moderate reformist thinking, see Munk's review of Moïse Biding, *La vengeance d'Israël* (Metz, 1840) in *AI* 1 (1840): 325–32, and Samuel Cahen, letter to the editor of *Courrier de la Moselle* (Paris, 1839): 5–7.

11. J. Frankel, *The Damascus Affair*, 236–49.

12. Tsarphati [Terquem], *Courrier de la Moselle*, 30 April 1840. Munk's critique appeared in *AI* 1 (1840): 325–32, esp. 332; Tsarphati's brief response followed in ibid., p. 399, and then more fully in *AI* 2 (1841): 231–36. See the discussion in J. Frankel, *Damascus Affair*, 247–49.

13. Cohn, "Réflexions," 347–48; Munk, letter to the editor, *La Régénération* 1 (1836): 331; Cahen, letter to the editor, *La Régénération* 1 (1836): 5–8, 12–13.

14. Albert, *Modernization of French Jewry*, 74–83; Berkovitz, *Shaping of Jewish Identity*, 210–14.

15. Stauben, *Scènes de la vie juive en Alsace*, and Cahun, *La vie juive*; Hyman, *Emancipation of the Jews of Alsace*, 64–77.

16. *AI* 4 (1843): 3–4. Cahen's son Isidore, who succeeded him as editor of the *Archives israélites*, commented on French Jewry's ill-preparedness with the following observation: "Nos coreligionnaires, appelés par la Révolution au bénéfice de la liberté civile et politique, n'avaient encore ni les moeurs ni même la conscience de leur nouvelle situation; il ne connaissaient guère que le trafic pour occupation, et leur foi était entachait d'abus et des superstitions; les chaines étaient tombées, mais les membres étaient engourdis; de nouveaux horizons s'ouvraient pour les Israélites, mais leur oeil n'était pas fait encore à les contempler." *AI* 28 (1867): 265.

17. See *AI* 7 (1846): 602–08.

18. See Berkovitz, *Shaping of Jewish Identity*, 155–56, 167–68, 171–72.

19. My position on the rehabilitation of the rabbinate is, admittedly, at odds with the prevailing view that the stature of the rabbinate plummeted in the nineteenth century. For examples of studies that argue for the decline of the rabbinate, see Albert, *Modernization of French Jewry*, 240–302; Schwarzfuchs, *Napoleon, the Jews, and the Sanhedrin*, 183–34; and Chouraqui, "De l'émancipation des Juifs à l'émancipation du Judaïsme." On social mobility in Alsace, see Hyman, *Emancipation of the Jews of Alsace*, 122–37.

20. On republican pedagogy and catechisms, see Kennedy, *A Cultural History of the French Revolution*, 152–59. On Jewish texts, see Petuchowski, "Manuals and Catechisms," and Berkovitz, *Shaping of Jewish Identity*, 185–90.

21. Lambert, *Catéchisme du culte judaïque*.

22. See S. Cahen, *Précis élémentaire*, and E. Halévy, *Instruction religieuse et morale*, 74–75, 83, 98–101.

23. Ulmann, *Recueil*. The 1860 edition was titled *Catéchisme ou elements d'instruction religieuse et morale à l'usage des jeunes israélites*.

24. Ulmann, *Recueil*, 51–118.

25. See Chapter 8.

26. See Chouraqui, "The Influence of Modernity."

27. Elie Halévy stated that the function of his work was to instill "in the young hearts the piety that is at the base of each precept" and that "the spirit of the religion [is] the morality and piety that flows from its totality, and that is its goal and principle"; see *Instruction religieuse et morale*, 7, 10–11. Also see Ulmann, *Catéchisme*, 52–53, and Simon Bloch, "Sur l'esprit et la tendance de ce recueil," *La Régénération* 1 (1836): 65–67.

28. Gerson Lévy, in *Revue orientale* 1 (Brussels, 1841): 460 ff., excerpted in *AI* 2 (1841): 531 ff., trans. W. Gunther Plaut, *The Rise of Reform Judaism* (New York, 1963), 104–05.

29. Ibid. Similarly, Alexandre Weill referred to religious reform as the act of "coupant un orteil malade d'une jambe gangrenée." See *Ma jeunesse*, 15.

30. See Paul Robert, *Le Petit Robert. 1: Dictionnaire alphabétique et analogique de la langue française* (Paris, 1984).

31. On the idea of progress, see Morris Ginsberg, "Progress in the Modern Era," *Dictionary of the History of Ideas* (New York, 1973), 3:633–50, and Harry Elmer Barnes, *A History of Historical Writing* (New York, 1963), 174–80.

32. See S. Cahen, *La Bible*, vol. 9, preface; *AI* 1 (1840): 66–67.

33. See Hyman, *Emancipation of the Jews of Alsace*, 93–97.

34. Cited in *AI* 5 (1844): 505.

35. See Ulmann Letters, no. 32, August 1845.

36. Berkovitz, *Shaping of Jewish Identity*, 216–17.

37. R. Cohen, "Urban Visibility and Biblical Visions," 747–48.

38. *AI* 5 (1844): 868.

39. Cited in ibid., 868–69.

40. Assimilationism may well have blinded many within France to the dangers of anti-Semitism, as Michael Marrus has argued, but it does not explain how those who rejected it were able to reconcile the occasional outbursts of anti-Jewish hostility with their abiding faith in the new order. One method was to marginalize Alsace, as the *Archives israélites* explained when anti-Jewish riots erupted in 1848: "l'Alsace . . . est, quant à la tolerance religieuse, une contrée à part," and that the hostilities should therefore not be regarded as a failure of the revolutionary legacy. See *AI* 9 (1848): 467, and *AI* 5 (1844): 868–69. Against this view, Reinhard Rürup viewed the riots as an indication of the limitations of the Revolution in transforming the pop-

ular image of the Jews. See Rürup, "European Revolutions of 1848," p. 33. For an example of an effort to explain away the harmful effects of the 1808 decree see L. Halévy, *Résumé de l'histoire des Juifs modernes*, 310. On the latter, see Rodrigue, "Léon Halévy and Modern French Jewish Historiography."

41. See, for example, the views of Simon Bloch and Rabbi Samuel Dreyfus, in *La Régénération* 1 (1836): 180, 340–41, cited in Hyman, "L'Impact de la Révolution," 30–31, and of Lambert, *Précis de l'histoire*, 406. The Cahen quote appeared in *AI* 4 (1843): 4. On the impact of the Revolution on perceptions of the past, see Fritzsche, "Chateaubriand's Ruins."

42. This last formulation in based on Hobsbawm, "Mass-Producing Traditions," 264. On the dissolution of Jewish memory in France, see Birnbaum, "Grégoire, Dreyfus, Drancy, and the Rue Copernic," 387–93. On Jews in high government posts, see Birnbaum, *The Jews of the Republic*.

43. Chouraqui, "The Influence of Modernity," 221.

44. *AI* 1 (1840): 235–37.

45. M. Berr, *Nouveau précis élémentaire*, 62; Berkovitz, *Shaping of Jewish Identity*, 188–89.

46. Mossé, *La Révolution français et le rabbinat français*, cited in Marrus, *The Politics of Assimilation*, 9.

47. Bloch, *La foi d'Israël*, 130–47.

48. M. Berr, *Nouveau précis élémentaire*, 62; Berkovitz, *Shaping of Jewish Identity*, 189–90; Graetz, *From Periphery to Center*, 58–59. Cf. Charleville, *Réponse de M. le rabbin de Charleville*, 1–5.

49. On the performative function of ritual, see Catherine Bell, *Ritual: Perspectives and Dimensions* (New York, 1997), 72–76, 160–61.

50. Schwab, *Salomon Munk*, 37, 56–58. Munk's statement should certainly not be construed as suggesting a lack of sensitivity to the tensions posed by religious elements within French society. Munk and others were critical of the Catholic resurgence and were concerned about the dangers of religious extremism. But this concern did not overshadow their optimism about the future, nor their conviction that conditions in France were still superior to those in Germany. Cf. the remarks of Olry Terquem, *AI* 4 (1843): 722–23.

51. See Samuel Cahen's assertion, in response to Ludwig Philippson, that "celui qui n'a pas de droit dans un pays, ne peut sincèrement soutenir que ce pays est sa patrie" in *AI* 5 (1844): 864.

52. See François Guizot, *La civilisation en Europe* (Paris, 1828), 12–18. For examples of admiration for French civilization and culture, see the remarks of Metz grand rabbin Lambert, *Précis de l'histoire*, 406–07, and those of Samuel Cahen in *AI* 2 (1841): 596.

53. See Nord, *The Republican Moment*, 81–82.

54. On parallel developments in French society at large, see Norman Hampson, "The Enlightenment in France," in *The Enlightenment in National Context*, ed. Roy Porter and Mikulas Teich (Cambridge, 1981), 53.

55. The term *régénération* was used in virtually all sectors of the community. Rabbi Samuel Dreyfus saw *régénération religieuse* as one of two objectives that were mandated by the Revolution, the other being political emancipation. Rabbi Salomon Lévy employed *régénération* to describe what R. Salomon Klein had accomplished at his combined *yeshivah* and *école de travail*. See *UI* 9 (1853): 211–13, 231. By mid-century the term had become part of the mainstream vocabulary. Central Consistory Grand Rabbi Isidor, like his predecessor R. Salomon Ulmann, referred in his 1867 inaugural discourse to *l'oeuvre de régénération* that had been pursued together during the preceding twenty years. See *AI* 28 (1867): 308.

56. Szajkowski, "French Jews."

57. Crémieux's remarks were made at the sixth annual general assembly of the Alliance Israélite Universelle, in *AI* 28 (1867): 14. See Michael Laskier, *The Alliance Israélite Universelle and the Jewish Communities of Morocco, 1862–1962* (Albany, 1983); Aron Rodrigue, *De l'instruction à l'émancipation* (Paris, 1989); Rodrigue, *French Jews, Turkish Jews*; Graetz, *From Periphery to Center*, ch. 3; and Albert, *Modernization of French Jewry*, 150–69.

58. According to Samuel Cahen, "notre liberté, nos droits publics, et la tolerance religieuse dont nous sommes l'objet, ne nous appartient pas à nous seuls; ils sont aussi le patrimoine de nos frères répandus sur la surface des deux hémisphères. Car la France est le phare qui éclaire le monde." And in more universal terms, "la régénération de toute l'Europe" dated from the era of liberty. *AI* 9 (1848): 209–10.

59. See Neher-Bernheim, "The Tables of the Law." Also see Salvador, *Loi du Moïse* and *Histoire des institutions de Moïse*; Hyman, "Joseph Salvador"; Graetz, *From Periphery to Center*, 154–85.

60. For the Cahen quote, see *AI* 1 (1840): 642. The festival of the first of May was originally a fertility festival that was transformed in the 1830s into a national holiday dedicated to King Louis Philippe. Many popular festivals went through a similar political transformation; see Weber, *Peasants into Frenchmen*, 377–98. The Bloch quote appeared in *UI* 17 (1861): 6.

61. See Z. Kahn, "Signification du nom d'Israël."

Conclusion

1. See Zeldin, *France*, 16, 20; Weber, *Peasants into Frenchmen*, 95–96; Berkovitz, *Shaping of Jewish Identity*, 148–49.

2. See Graetz, *From Periphery to Center*, ch. 1; Albert, *Modernization of French Jewry*, 310.

3. On the vitality of traditional ritual observance in Alsace well into the nineteenth century see Hyman, *Emancipation of the Jews of Alsace*, 72–79. For evidence of the prominent role that Lurianic Kabbalah enjoyed in Alsace in post-revolutionary culture, see the decorative "Lekha Dodi" prayer-sheet produced by a teacher in Muttersholtz, and the ornate Lurianic amulets for childbirth, in the Musée Alsacien, Strasbourg. These images have been reproduced frequently. See, for example, Geoffrey Wigoder, ed., *Jewish Art and Civilization* (Seacaucus, N.J., 1972), 76–77, and Esther Muchawsky-Schnapper, ed., *Les Juifs d'Alsace: Village, tradition, émancipation* (Jerusalem, 1991), 60.

Bibliography

Archival Sources

Archives of Jewish Theological Seminary of America, French-Jewish Documents, New York.
Archives Nationales, Paris.
Central Archives for the History of the Jewish People, Jerusalem.
Hebrew Union College Archives, Cincinnati.
Leo Baeck Institute Archives, Alsace-Lorraine Collection, New York.

Manuscript Collections

Alliance Israélite Universelle.
National and University Library. Institute of Hebrew Manuscripts. Jerusalem.

Printed Primary Sources

Journals

Allegemeine Zeitung des Judentums
Les Archives israélites de France
Le Courrier de la Moselle
L'Israélite français
Jeschurun
Journal asiatique
Journal de la Société des sciences, agriculture, et arts du département du Bas-Rhin
Kerem Ḥemed
Le Lien d'Israël
Mercure de France
La Régénération
Revue orientale
Univers israélite

Books and Pamphlets

Anspach, Joel. *Paroles d'un croyant israélite*. Metz, 1842.

———. *Rituel des Prières journalieres à l'usage des Israélites*. Metz, 1820.

Ashkenazi, Gershon. *Resp. Avodat Ha-Gershuni*. Frankfurt am Main, 1699.

Bacharach, Ya'ir Ḥayyim. *Resp. Ḥavvot Ya'ir*. Frankfurt am Main, 1699.

Bail, Charles-Joseph. *Des Juifs au dix-neuvième siècle*. Paris, 1816. 2nd ed.: Paris, 1817.

Basnage, Jaques. *Histoire des Juifs, depuis Jésus Christ jusqu'à present*. La Hague, 1716.

Bautain, Louis. *Philosophie du Christianisme: Correspondance religieuse de Louis Bautain*. 2 vols. Paris, 1835.

Berr, Berr Isaac. *Lettre du Sr. Berr-Isaac-Berr, négociant à Nancy. Juif naturalisé en vertu des lettres patentes dur Roi, à Monsieur l'Evêque de Nancy, Deputée à l'Assemblée National*. Paris, 1790.

———. *Lettre d'un citoyen, membre de la ci-devant communauté des Juifs de Lorraine, à ses confrères, à l'occasion du droit de citoyen actif rendu aux Juifs par le décrit du 28 Septembre 1791*. Nancy, 1791.

———. *Réflexions sur la régénération complète des Juifs en France*. Paris, 1806.

———, trans. *Instructions Salutaires adressées aux communautés juives de l'empire*. Paris, 1782.

Berr, Jacob. *Lettre du Sieur Jacob Berr, 25 avril 1790*. Nancy, 1790.

Berr, Michel. *Appel à la justice des nations et des rois*. Strasbourg, 1801.

———. *Lettres sur les israélites et le judaïsme*. Paris, 1825.

———. *Nouveau précis élémentaire d'instruction religieuse et morale, à l'usage de la jeunesse française israélite*. Nancy, 1839.

Betting de Lancastel. *Considérations sur l'état des Juifs dans la société chrétienne et particulièrement en Alsace*. Strasbourg, 1824.

Beugnot, Arthur. *Les Juifs d'Occident*. Paris, 1824.

Biding, Moïse. *Em la-Mikra*. Metz, 1816.

———. "Kaf Aḥat Asarah Zahav." In *Seliḥot Minhag Ashkenaz*. Metz, 1822.

———. "Ma'amar Shekel Ha-Kodesh." In *Maḥzor shel Pesaḥ, Shavuot, ve-Sukkot*, ed. M. Biding, 135–41. Metz, 1817.

Bing, Isaïe Berr. Lettre du Sr. I.B.B. Juif de Metz à l'auteur anonyme d'un écrit intitulé: "Le cri du citoyen contre les Juifs." Metz, 1787. Reprinted in *La Révolution française et l'émancipation des Juifs*, vol. 8, Paris, 1968.

Bloch, Simon. *La foi d'Israël*. Paris, 1859.

Cahen, Samuel. *Précis élémentaire d'instruction religieuse et morale pour les jeunes français israélites*. Paris, 1820.

———, ed. *La Bible, traduction nouvelle*. 18 vols. Paris, 1831–51.

Cahen, Uri Phoebus. *Halakhah Berurah*. Metz, 1793.

Cahun, Léon, *La vie juive*. Paris, 1886.

Cerfberr, Alphonse-Théodore. *Observations sur les voeux émis par les Conseils généraux des départements du Haut et Bas-Rhin, relativement aux mesures à prendre contre les Juifs, par suite de Décrit du 17 mars 1808*. Paris, 1817.

Charleville, Mahir. *Réponse de M. le rabbin de Charleville, aux questions de la commission consistoriale, publiée à la demande d'un grand nombre de notables*. Paris, 1847.

Clermont-Tonnerre, Comte Stanislas de. *Opinion relativement aux persecutions qui menacent les Juifs d'Alsace*. Versailles, 1789.

Cohen, Tuvia. *Ma'aseh Tuviah*. Venice, 1707.

Cologna, Abraham. *Quelques observations sur la deuxième édition de l'ouvrage intitulé des Juifs au XIXᵉ siècle de M. Bail*. Paris, 1817.

———. *Réflexions adressées à M. Le Baron S. de S.* Paris, 1817.

Colon, Joseph. *Resp. Maharik*. Cremona, 1557.

Crémieux, Moïse. *Ho'il Moshe Be'er*. Aix-en-Provence, 1829–36.

Crémieux, Mardochée. *Kuntres Divrei Mordechai.* Leghorn, 1787.

David ben Samuel Ha-Levi. *Turei Zahav.* Commentary on *Shulḥan Arukh,* Yoreh De'ah. Lublin, 1646.

De Sacy, Antoine Isaac Silvestre. "Lettre à M.***, Conseiller de S. M. Le Roi de Saxe, relativement à l'ouvragement intitulé: *Des Juifs au XIXe siècle.*" Paris, 1817.

Dohm, Christian Wilhelm von. *Concerning the Amelioration of the Civil Status of the Jews.* Trans. Helen Lederer. Hebrew Union College Series. Cincinnati, 1957.

Domat, Jean. *Le droit public, suite des lois civiles dans leur ordre naturel.* Vol. 3, *Oeuvres complètes, nouvelle edition revue corrigée.* ed. Joseph Remy. Paris, 1829.

Eibeschütz, Jonathan. *Kereti u-Feleti.* Altona, 1763.

———. *Ya'arot Devash.* Metz, 1789. Republished, Jerusalem, 1984. 2 vols.

Eisenmenger, Johann Andreas. *Entdecktes Judentums.* Frankfurt, 1699.

Elijah ben Solomon Zalman. *Be'urei Ha-Gra.* Commentary on *Shulḥan Arukh,* Oraḥ Hayyim. Shklov, 1803; *Yoreh De'ah.* Grodno, 1806.

Emden, Jacob. *Resp. She'elat Yaveẓ.* Altona, 1739–60.

———. *Siddur Yaveẓ.* Altona, 1745–48.

Ensheim, Moses. *La-Menaẓe'ah Shir.* Metz, 1792.

Fleury, Claude. *Les moeurs des Israélites et des Chrétiens.* Paris, 1681.

Franck, Adolphe. *La Kabbale ou la philosophie religieuse des hébreux.* Paris, 1843.

Geiger, Ludwig. "Aus Leopold Zunz' Nachlag." *Zeitschrift für die Geschichte der Juden in Deutschland* 5 (1892): 223–68.

Gombiner, Abraham. *Magen Avraham. Commentary on Shulḥan Arukh,* Oraḥ Hayyim. Dyhernfurth, 1692.

Grégoire, Henri. *Essai sur la régénération physique, morale et politique des Juifs.* Metz, 1789.

———. *Mémoire sur les moyens de recréer le peuple juif et partant de l'amener à la vertu et au bonheur, présenté à la Société philanthropique de Strasbourg.* In *Mémoires de Grégoire, precedés d'une notice historique sur l'auteur,* ed. H. Carnot. 2 vols. Paris, 1837.

———. *Motion en faveur des Juifs.* Paris, 1789.

———. *Observations nouvelles sur les Juifs et spécialement ceux d'Allemagne.* Paris, 1806.

Halévy, Elie. *Instruction religieuse et morale à l'usage de la jeunesse israélite.* Paris, 1820.

Halévy, Léon. *Résumé de l'histoire des Juifs modernes.* Paris, 1828.

Halperin, Israel. *Pinkas Va'ad Arba Araẓot.* Jerusalem, 1945.

Hamburger, Benjamin, ed. *The Minhagim of the Worms Community According to Juspe Shamash.* 2 vols. Jerusalem, 1988.

Ha-Me'iri, Menahem. *Beit ha-Beḥirah,* Avodah Zarah. Ed. Abraham Sofer. Jerusalem, 1965.

———. *Beit ha-Beḥirah,* Bava Metzia. Ed. Kalman Schlesinger. Jerusalem, 1963.

———. *Beit ha-Beḥirah,* Bava Metzia. Ed. Nissan Alpert. New York, 1959.

———. *Beit ha-Beḥirah,* Bava Qama. Ed. Kalman Schlesinger. Jerusalem, 1961.

Hanover, Nathan. *Safah Berurah.* Prague, 1660.

Heller, Yom Tov Lipmann. *Addendum to Megilat Eivah.* Ed. Y. L. Ha-Cohen Maimon. *Sinai* 35 (1954): 400–401.

Horowitz, Isaiah. *Shenei Luḥot Ha-Berit.* Amsterdam, 1698.

Hourwitz, Zalkind. *Apologie des Juifs.* Paris, 1789.

Isserles, Moses. *Darkhei Moshe.* Commentary on Jacob ben Asher, *Arba'ah Turim,* Oraḥ Hayyim. Fürth, 1759–60.

———. *Glosses to Shulḥan Arukh.* Cracow, 1569–71.

Kahn, Zadoc. "Signification du nom d'Israël." In *Sermons et allocutions,* 1st ser. Paris, 1875.

Karo, Joseph. *Beit Yosef. Commentary on Jacob ben Asher, Arba'ah Turim,* Yoreh De'ah. 1555.

―――. *Shulḥan Arukh*, Oraḥ Ḥayyim. Hoshen Mishpat. Venice, 1564–65.

Kaufmann, David, ed. "Extraits de l'ancien livre de la communauté de Metz." *Revue des études juives* 19 (1889): 115–30.

Kirchheim, Juda Löw. *Minhagot Wormaiza*. Ed. Israel Mordecai Peles. Jerusalem, 1987.

Klein, Salomon. *Divrei Ha-Piyyutim ve-Za'akatam*. Mulhouse, 1859.

―――. *Ha-Emet ve-Hashalom Ehavu*. Frankfurt am Main, 1861.

―――. *Le Judaïsme ou la verité sur le Talmud*. Mulhouse, 1859.

―――. *Ma'aneh Rakh*. Mulhouse, 1846.

―――. *Mippnei Koshet*. Frankfurt am Main, 1861.

Koblentz, Gershon. *Resp. Kiryat Ḥannah*. Metz, 1789.

Krüger, S. *De la compétence de M. S. R. Hirsch, rabbin de la confrérie religieuse à Francfort-sur-Mein*. Paris, 1856.

Lambert, Lion-Mayer. *Catéchisme du culte judaïque*. Metz, 1818.

―――. *Précis de l'histoire des hébreux depuis le patriarche Abraham jusqu'en 1840*. Metz, 1840.

Landau, Ezekiel. *Derushei Ha-Ẓelaḥ*. Warsaw, 1886. Reprint, Jerusalem 1966.

―――. *Resp. Noda b' Yehudah*. Prague, 1776.

Levy, A. *Die Memoiren des Ascher Levy (1598–1635)*. Ed. M. Ginsburger. Berlin, 1913.

Lévy, Gerson. *Culte israélite*. Metz, 1841.

Loeb, Isidore, ed. "Statuts des Juifs d'Avignon, 1779." *Annuaire de la société des études juives* 1 (1881): 165–275; 2 (1883): 165–275.

Loeb, Isidore. "Les Juifs à Strasbourg depuis 1349 jusqu'à la Révolution." *Annuaire de la société des études juives* 2 (1883): 137–98.

Lowenthal, Marvin, trans. *The Memoirs of Glückel of Hameln*. New York, 1932.

Lunteschütz, Abraham Isaac. *Kelilat Yofi*. Roedelheim, 1813.

Maḥzor ke-Minhag Ashkenaz u-Folin. Metz, 1768.

Maḥzor le-Pesach, Shavu'ot, ve-Sukkot. Metz, 1769.

Maḥzor shel Rosh Hashanah ke-Minhag Ashkenaz. Metz, 1817.

Maḥzor shel Yom Kippur ke-Minhag Ashkenaz u-Folin. Metz, 1817.

Maimonides, Moses. *Mishneh Torah*.

Maslin, Simeon. "Selected Documents of Napoleonic Jewry." Hebrew Union College, Cincinnati, 1957.

―――, ed. "Selected Documents." Hebrew Union College, Cincinnati, 1959.

Mayer [-Dalmbert], Simon. *Au Rédacteur du journal de l'Empire*. Paris, 1806.

Meldola, David. *Resp. Divrei David*. Amsterdam, 1753.

Meldola, Raphael. *Resp. Mayyim Rabbim*. Amsterdam, 1737.

Mevorakh, Barukh. *Napoleon u-tekufato*. Jerusalem, 1968.

Mossé, Benjamin. *La Révolution français et le rabbinat français*. Paris, 1890.

Moureau, Agricole. *De l'incompatibilité entre le Judaïsme et l'exercice des droits de cité et des moyens de rendre les Juifs citoyens*. Paris, 1819.

Munk, Salomon. *Mélanges de philosophie juive et arabe*. Paris, 1855.

―――. *Palestine: Description géographique, historique et archéologique*. Paris, 1845.

Nahon, Gérard, ed. *Les "Nations" juives portugaises du sud-ouest de la France (1684–1791): Documents*. Paris, 1981.

Narol, Moses. *Baqashah*. Amsterdam, 1699. Reprint, Metz, 1777; Lunéville, 1806.

Neher-Bernheim, Renée. *Documents inédits sur l'entrée des juifs dans la société française (1750–1850)*. 2 vols. Tel Aviv, 1977.

Noyrlingen, Joseph Juspa Hahn. *Yosef Omeẓ*. Frankfurt am Main, 1723.

Poujol, Louis. *Quelques observations concernant les Juifs en général et plus particulièrement ceux d'Alsace*. Paris, 1806.

"Protocol of the Medinah" [28 May 1777]. *Blätter fur jüdische Geschichte und Litteratur* 2 (1901): 18–22, 28–29. Paraphrased in French by Isidore Loeb, "Extrait du protocole de la nation de l'assemblée du 21 Iyyar 5537." *Annuaire de la société des études juives* 2 (1883): 181–91.

Reischer, Jacob. *Resp. Shevut Ya'akov.* Pt. 1: Halle, 1710. Pt. 2: Offenbach, 1719. Pt. 3: Metz, 1789.

Rivkes, Moses. *Be'er ha-Golah.* Amsterdam, 1660–66.

Rosenthal, Judah. "The Responses of R. Ishmael b. R. Avraham Yitzhak Ha-Kohen." In *Meḥkarim u-Mekorot*, by Judah Rosenthal, 2:513–32. Jerusalem, 1966.

Salvador, Joseph. *Histoire des institutions de Moïse et de peuple hébreu.* 3 vols. Paris, 1828.

———. *Loi du Moïse.* Paris, 1822.

Scheuer, Herz. *Turei Zahav.* Ed. Moshe Reis. Mainz, 1875.

Schwarzfuchs, Simon, ed. *Le "Memorbuch" de Metz (vers 1575–1742).* Metz, 1971.

———. *Le Registre des délibérations de la Nation Juive Portugaise de Bordeaux (1711–1787).* Paris, 1981.

Seder Seliḥot ke-Minhag ha-Ashkenazim. Metz, 1769.

Seder Tefilah ke-Minhag Ashkenaz. Metz, 1765.

Sefer Raziel. Amsterdam, 1701.

Seliḥot mi-kol ha-Shanah ke-Minhag Elsass. Frankfurt am Main, 1691.

Seliḥot Minhag Ashkenaz. Metz, 1822.

Sintzheim, David. *Yad David.* Offenbach, 1799. Jerusalem, 1969–2001.

Sirkes, Joel. *Bayit Ḥadash.* Commentary on Jacob ben Asher, *Arba'ah Turim,* Oraḥ Hayyim.

———. *Resp. Bayit Ḥadash (Additional).* Koretz, 1785.

Sofer, Jacob Joseph b. Meir. *Even Yisrael.* Metz, 1766.

Sofer, Moses. *Resp. Ḥatam Sofer.* Pressburg, 1855.

Spitzer, Shlomo, ed. *Sefer Maharil.* Jerusalem, 1989.

Stauben, Daniel. *Scènes de la vie juive en Alsace.* Paris, 1860.

Steinhardt, Joseph. *Resp. Zikhron Yosef.* Fürth, 1773.

Tama, Diogene, ed. *Transactions of the the Parisian Sanhedrin.* London, 1807.

Tefilah ke-Minhag Ashkenaz u-Folin. Metz, 1765.

Tourette, Amédée. *Discours sur les Juifs d'Alsace.* Strasbourg, 1825.

Tsarphati [Olry Terquem]. *Première (-Neuvième) lettre d'un Israélite français à ses coreligionnaires.* Paris, 1821–37.

Uhry, Isaac. *Recueil des lois, décrets, ordonnances, avis du conseil d'Etat, arrêtes et règlement concernant les israélites depuis 1850.* Bordeaux, 1878.

Ulmann, Salomon. *Catéchisme ou elements d'instruction religieuse et morale à l'usage des jeunes israélites.* Paris, 1860.

———. *Lettre pastorale.* 11 December 1853.

———. *Lettre pastorale.* 23 October 1860.

———. *Recueil d'instructions morales et religieuses à l'usage des jeunes israélites français.* Strasbourg, 1843.

Vaillant, Jean Baptiste Philibert, ed. *Correspondance de Napoléon 1er.* 32 vols. Paris, 1858–70.

Venture, Mardochée. *Prières journalières à l'usage des Juifs portugaises ou espagnols.* Nice, 1772–73.

Voltaire, François Marie Arouet de. *Essai sur les moeurs et l'esprit des nations.* Pomeau ed. Paris, 1990.

Weill, Alexandre. *Ma jeunesse.* Paris, 1870–88.

Wittersheim, Prosper. *Mémoire sur les moyens de hâter la régénération des Israélites de l'Alsace.* Metz, 1825.

Wogue, Lazare. *Guide du croyant israélite.* Paris, 1859.

Worms, Aaron. *Be'er Sheva.* Metz, 1819.

———. *Bin Nun.* Metz, 1827.

———. *Kan Tahor.* Metz, 1831.

————. *Od la-Mo'ed.* Metz, 1822.

————. *Me'orei Or.* 3 vols. Metz, 1790–93.

Secondary Sources

Abramsky, Chimen. "The Crisis of Authority within European Jewry in the Eighteenth Century." In *Studies in Jewish Intellectual and Religious History*, ed. Siegfried Stein and Raphael Loewe, 13–28. Tuscaloosa, 1979.

Albert, Phyllis Cohen. "Israelite and Jew: How Did Nineteenth-Century French Jews Understand Assimilation?" In *Assimilation and Community: The Jews of Nineteenth-Century Europe*, ed. Jonathan Frankel and Steven Zipperstein, 88–109. Cambridge, 1992.

————. *The Modernization of French Jewry: Consistory and Community in the Nineteenth Century.* Hanover, N.H., 1977.

————. "Nonorthodox Attitudes in Nineteenth-Century French Judaism." In *Essays in Modern Jewish History: A Tribute to Ben Halpern*, ed. Frances Malino and Phyllis Albert, 121–41. East Brunswick, N.J., 1982.

Anchel, Robert. "Contribution levée en 1813–1814 sur les Juifs du Haut-Rhin." *Revue des études juives* 82 (1926): 495–501.

————. *Napoléon et les juifs.* Paris, 1928.

Artz, Frederick. *France under the Bourbon Restoration, 1814–1830.* New York, 1963.

Assaf, Simha. "On the History of the Rabbinate" [Hebrew]. *Be'ohalei Ya'akov.* Jerusalem, 1943.

Baron, Salo W. *The Jewish Community: Its History and Structure to the American Revolution.* 3 vols. Philadelphia, 1942.

————. "The Revolution of 1848 and Jewish Scholarship." *Proceedings of the American Academy of Religion* 18 (1948–49): 1–66.

Bauer, Jules. *L'ecole rabbinique de France.* Paris, 1930.

————. "L'ecole rabbinique Metz." *Revue des études juives* 84 (1927): 51–65, 141–59.

————. "Les Juifs comtadins pendant la Révolution." *Revue des études juives* 54 (1907): 284.

Baumgarten, Elisheva. *Mothers and Children: Jewish Family Life in Medieval Europe.* Princeton, 2004.

Behre, Patricia. "Raphael Lévy—'A Criminal in the Mouths of the People.'" *Religion* 23 (1993): 19–44.

Benayahu, Meir. *Sefer Toldot Ha-Ari.* Jerusalem, 1967.

Benedict, Philip, ed. *Cities and Social Change in Early Modern France.* London, 1989.

Benin, Stephen. "A Hen Crowing Like a Cock: 'Popular Religion' and Jewish Law." *Journal of Jewish Thought and Philosophy* 8 (1999): 261–81.

Ben-Sasson, Haim Hillel. "The Social Teaching of R. Yohanan Luria" [Hebrew]. *Zion* 27 (1962): 166–98.

Berger, Peter. *The Heretical Imperative.* New York, 1979.

————. *The Sacred Canopy.* Garden City, N.Y., 1969.

Berkovitz, Jay R. "Authority and Innovation at the Threshold of Modernity: The *Me'orei Or* of Rabbi Aaron Worms of Metz." *Me'ah She'arim: Studies in Medieval Jewish Spiritual Life in Memory of Isadore Twersky*, 249–85. Jerusalem, 2001.

————. "The French Revolution and the Jews: Assessing the Cultural Impact." *Association for Jewish Studies Review* 20 (1995): 25–86.

————. "Jewish Scholarship and Identity in Nineteenth-Century France." *Modern Judaism* 18 (1998): 1–33.

————. "Patterns of Rabbinic Succession in Modern France." *Jewish History* 13 (1999): 59–82.

————. "On Rabbinic Authority and Religious Reform in the Nineteenth Century: The Correspondence of Rabbi Salomon Ulmann." *Proceedings of the Twelfth World Congress of Jewish Studies*, Division B, 209–19. Jerusalem, 2000.

————. *The Shaping of Jewish Identity in Nineteenth-Century France*. Detroit, 1989.

Bernfeld, Simon. *Sefer Ha-Dema'ot*. 3 vols. Berlin, 1926.

Birnbaum, Pierre. "L'entrée en République: Le personnel politique juif sous la Troisième République." In *Idéologies, partis politiques et groups sociaux*, ed. Y. Méry, 89–100. Paris, 1989.

————. "Grégoire, Dreyfus, Drancy, and the Rue Copernic: Jews at the Heart of French History." In *Realms of Memory: Rethinking the French Past*, ed. Pierre Nora, 1:379–423. Trans. Arthur Goldhammer. New York, 1996.

————. *Jewish Destinies: Citizenship, State and Community in Modern France*. Trans. Arthur Goldhammer. New York, 2000.

————. *The Jews of the Republic: A Political History of State Jews in France from Gambetta to Vichy*. Trans. Jane Marie Todd. Stanford, 1996.

Birnbaum, Pierre, and Ira Katznelson, eds. *Paths of Emancipation: Jews, States, and Citizenship*. Princeton, 1995.

Blidstein, Gerald. "Halakhah and Democracy." *Tradition* 32 (1997): 6–39.

————. *Honor Thy Father and Mother*. New York, 1975.

————. "Me'iri's Attitude towards Gentiles: Between Apologetics and Internalization" [Hebrew]. *Zion* 51 (1986): 153–66.

Blum, Raphael. "Le fondateur du grand Beth Hamidrash de Bouxwiller." *Univers israélite* 35 (1879): 85–88, 112–14.

————, ed. "Trois lettres autographes de feu Rabbi Jonathan Eibenschutz." *Univers israélite* 9 (1853): 27–32.

Blumenkranz, Bernhard, ed. *Histoire des Juifs en France*. Toulouse, 1972.

Bonfil, Reuven. "Aspects of the Social and Spiritual Life of the Jews in the Venetian Territories at the Beginning of the Sixteenth Century" [Hebrew]. *Zion* 41 (1976): 68–96.

———— [Robert]. "Change in the Cultural Patterns of a Jewish Society in Crisis: Italian Jewry at the Close of the Sixteenth Century." *Jewish History* 3 (1988): 11–30.

————. *Jewish Life in Renaissance Italy*. Trans. Anthony Oldcorn. Berkeley, 1994.

Bourel, Dominique. "La *Wissenschaft des Judentums* en France." *Revue de synthèse* 4 (April–June 1988): 265–80.

Braudel, Fernand. *The Identity of France*. 2 vols. London, 1988.

Breuer, Edward. *The Limits of Enlightenment: Jews, Germans, and the Eighteenth-Century Study of Scripture*. Cambridge, Mass., 1996.

Breuer, Mordecai. "The Documentary Hypothesis of the *Sha'agat Aryeh*" [Hebrew]. *Megadim* 2 (1986): 9–22.

Breuer, Mordechai. "The Early Modern Period." In *German-Jewish History in Modern Times*, ed. Michael A. Meyer, 1:79–255. New York, 1996.

————. *Jüdische Orthodoxie im Deutschen Reich, 1871–1918*. Frankfurt, 1986.

————. "The Status of the Rabbinate in the Leadership of Ashkenazic Communities in the Fifteenth Century" [Hebrew]. *Zion* 41 (1976): 47–67.

————. "The Wandering Students and Scholars—A Prolegomenon to a Chapter in the History of the Yeshivot" [Hebrew]. In *Culture and Society in Medieval Jewry: Studies Dedicated to the Memory of Ḥaim Hillel Ben-Sasson*, ed. Menahem Ben-Sasson, Robert Bonfil, and Joseph Hacker, 445–68. Jerusalem, 1989.

Briggs, Robin. *Early Modern France, 1560–1715*. Oxford, 1998.

Brown, Peter. *The Cult of the Saints*. Chicago, 1981.

Broyde, Michael J., and Michael Hecht. "The Gentile and Returning Lost Property According to Jewish Law: A Theory of Reciprocity." *Jewish Law Annual* 13 (2000): 31–45.

Burke, Peter. *Popular Culture and Elite Culture*. London, 1978.

Burns, Michael. "Emancipation and Reaction: The Rural Exodus of Alsatian Jewry, 1791–1848." In *Living with Antisemitism: Modern Jewish Responses*, ed. Jehuda Reinharz. London, 1987.

Cahen, Abraham. "L'emancipation des juifs devant la Société Royale des Sciences et Arts de Metz et M. Roederer." *Revue des études juives* 1 (1880): 108–11.

———. "Enseignement obligatoire édicté par la communauté israélite de Metz." *Revue des études juives* 2 (1881): 303–05.

———. "Les Juifs de la Martinique au XVIIe siècle." *Revue des études juives* 2 (1881): 93–122.

———. "Le rabbinat de Metz pendant la période française." *Revue des études juives* 7 (1883): 103–16, 204–26; 8 (1884): 255–74; 12 (1886): 283–97; 13 (1886): 105–26.

———. "Règlements somptuaires de la communauté juive de Metz à la fin du XVIIe siècle." *Annuaire de la Société des études juives* 1 (1881): 77–121.

Cahen, Gilbert. "La région lorraine." *Histoire des Juifs en France*, ed. Bernhard Blumenkraz, 77–136. Paris, 1972.

Calmann, Marianne. *The Carrière of Carpentras*. London, 1984.

Carmoly, Eliakim. "Issachar Carmoly." *Revue orientale* 2 (1842): 345–49; 3 (1843–44): 240–44.

———. "Napoléon et ses panégyristes hébreux." *Revue orientale* 2 (1842): 25–33.

———. "De la typographie hébraïque à Metz." *Revue orientale* 3 (1843–44): 209–15, 283–89.

Catane, Moshe. "Rabbi Shlomo Zev Klein (1814–1868): His Life and Writings." *Ha-Ma'ayan* 30 (1989): 7–29.

Chisick, Harvey. "Ethics and History in Voltaire's Attitude toward the Jews." *Eighteenth-Century Studies* 35 (2002): 577–600.

Chouraqui, Jean-Marc. "De l'émancipation des Juifs à l'émancipation du judaïsme: Le regard des rabbins français du XIXe siècle." In *Histoire politique des juifs de France entre universalisme et particularisme*, ed. Pierre Birnbaum, 39–57. Paris, 1990.

———. "The Influence of Modernity and the Ideology of Emancipation on the Discourse of the French Rabbis: Nineteenth to Early Twentieth Century." *Social Compass* 44 (1997): 217–25.

Cirot, Georges. *Recherches sur les Juifs espagnols et portugais à Bordeaux*. Bordeaux, 1908.

Clark, Henry C. "Commerce, Sociability, and the Public Sphere: Morellet vs. Pluquet on Luxury." *Eighteenth-Century Life* 22 (1998): 83–103.

———. "Commerce, the Virtues, and the Public Sphere in Early-Seventeenth-Century France." *French Historical Studies* 21 (1998): 428–29.

Clément, Roger. *La condition des juifs de Metz sous l'ancien régime*. Paris, 1903.

Clements, R. E. "The Study of the Old Testament." In *Nineteenth-Century Religious Thought in the West*, ed. Ninian Smart et al., 1:103–27. Cambridge, 1985.

Cohen, David. "L'Image du Juif dans la société française en 1843 d'après les rapports des préfets." *Revue d'histoire économique et sociale* 55 (1977): 70–91.

———. *La promotion des Juifs en France à l'époque du Second Empire (1852–1870)*. 2 vols. Aix-en-Provence, 1980.

Cohen, Richard I. Introduction to Hebrew edition of *Essai sur la régénération physique, morale et politique des Juifs*, by Henri Grégoire. Jerusalem, 1989.

———. *Jewish Icons: Art and Society in Modern Europe*. Berkeley, 1998.

———. "The Rhetoric of Jewish Emancipation and the Vision of the Future" [Hebrew]. In *The French Revolution and Its Impact*, ed. Richard I. Cohen. Jerusalem, 1991.

———. "Urban Visibility and Biblical Visions: Jewish Culture in Western and Central Europe in the Modern Age." In *Cultures of the Jews*, ed. David Biale, 731–96. New York, 2002.

Cole, C. W. *Colbert and the Century of French Mercantilism.* 2 vols. New York, 1939.

Davis, Natalie Zemon. "The Reasons of Misrule: Youth Groups and Charivaris in Sixteenth-Century France." *Past and Present* 50 (1971): 41–75.

———. *Women on the Margins: Three Seventeenth-Century Lives.* Cambridge, Mass., 1995.

Debré, Simon. "The Jews of France." *Jewish Quarterly Review* 3 (1891): 367–435.

Delumeau, Jean. *Le Catholicisme entre Luther et Voltaire.* Paris, 1971.

Deshen, Shlomo. "The Riddle of *Kol Nidrei*: Anthropological and Historical Clarification" [Hebrew]. In *Chapters in the History of Jewish Society in the Middle Ages and the Modern Era: Jacob Katz Jubilee Volume,* 136–53. Jerusalem, 1980.

Dinari, Yedidia. "The Profanation of the Holy by the Menstruant Woman and the 'Takanot of Ezra.'" *Te'uda* 3 (1983): 17–37.

Doyle, William. *Venality: The Sale of Offices in Eighteenth-Century France.* Oxford, 1996.

Dubin, Lois. *The Port Jews of Habsburg Trieste: Absolutist Politics and Enlightenment Culture.* Stanford, 1999.

Eidelberg, Shlomo. "The Jews of Worms during the French Conquest (1688–1697)." *Proceedings of the American Academy of Religion* 60 (1994): 71–100.

Elbaum, Jacob. *Openness and Insularity: Late Sixteenth-Century Jewish Literature in Poland and Ashkenaz* [Hebrew]. Jerusalem, 1990.

Eliav, Mordechai. *Jewish Education in Germany in the Period of the Enlightenment and Emancipation* [Hebrew]. Jerusalem, 1960.

Elior, Rachel. "R. Nathan Adler and the Frankfurt Pietists: Pietist Groups in Eastern and Central Europe during the Eighteenth Century." *Zion* 59 (1994): 31–64.

Ellenson, David. "A Disputed Precedent: The Prague Organ in Nineteenth-Century Central-European Legal Literature and Polemics." *Leo Baeck Institute Year Book* 40 (1995): 251–64.

———. "Traditional Reactions to Modern Jewish Reform: The Paradigm of German Orthodoxy." In *History of Jewish Philosophy,* ed. Daniel H. Franck and Oliver Leaman, 2:732–58. New York, 1997.

Ellis, Geoffrey. *Napoleon.* New York, 1997.

Endelman, Todd. *The Jews of Georgian England, 1714–1830: Tradition and Change in a Liberal Society.* Philadelphia, 1979.

Epstein, Louis M. *Sex Laws and Customs in Judaism.* New York, 1967.

Etkes, Immanuel. "Immanent Factors and External Influences in the Development of the Haskalah Movement in Russia." In *Toward Modernity,* ed. Jacob Katz, 13–22. New Brunswick, N.J., 1987.

———. "On the Question of the Forerunners of Haskalah in Eastern Europe" [Hebrew]. In *The East European Jewish Enlightenment,* ed. I. Etkes, 25–44. Jerusalem, 1993.

Febvre, Lucien. "Civilization: Evolution of a Word and a Group of Ideas." In *A New Kind of History: From the Writings of Febvre,* ed. Peter Burke. New York, 1973.

Farr, James R. *Authority and Sexuality in Early Modern Burgundy, 1550–1730.* New York, 1995.

Feiner, Shmuel. *Haskalah and History: The Emergence of a Jewish Awareness of the Past* [Hebrew]. Jerusalem, 1995.

———. *The Jewish Enlightenment.* Trans. Chaya Naor. Philadelphia, 2003.

Fenton, Paul. "Qabbalah and Academia: The Critical Study of Jewish Mysticism in France." *Shofar* 18 (2000): 45–54.

Feuerwerker, David. *L'émancipation des Juifs en France: De l'ancien régime à la fin du Second Empire.* Paris, 1976.

Finkelstein, Louis. *Jewish Self-Government in the Middle Ages.* New York, 1924.

Fishman, Talya. "The Penitential System of Hasidei Ashkenaz and the Problem of Cultural Boundaries." *Journal of Jewish Thought and Philosophy* 8 (1999): 223–26.

Ford, Franklin. *Strasbourg in Transition, 1648–1789.* Cambridge, Mass., 1958.

Fram, Edward. *Ideals Face Reality: Jewish Law and Life in Poland, 1550–1655.* Cincinnati, 1997.

———. "The Regulation of Luxury in the Jewish Community of Cracow at the Turn of the Seventeenth Century" [Hebrew]. *Galed* 18 (2002): 11–23.

Frankel, Jonathan. *The Damascus Affair: "Ritual Murder," Politics, and the Jews in 1840.* Cambridge, 1997.

Frankel, Sarah. "Concerning Two Lost Books That Were Found" [Hebrew]. *Alei Sefer* 10 (1982): 139–41.

Frankel, Zecharias. "Eine historische Notiz." *Monatsschrift für Geschichte und Wissenschaft des Judentums* 21 (1872): 44–47.

Freimann, Abraham. *Betrothal and Marriage Procedures after the Talmudic Era* [Hebrew]. Jerusalem, 1945.

Friedhaber, Zvi. "Religious Dancing in Marriages Conducted as Meritorious Deeds" [Hebrew]. In *Folklore Research Center Studies,* ed. Issachar Ben-Ami, 3:165–87. Jerusalem, 1972.

Frimer, Dov. "Israel, the Noahide Laws and Maimonides: Jewish-Gentile Legal Relations in Maimonidean Thought." *Jewish Law Association Studies* 2 (1986): 89–102.

Fritzsche, Peter. "Chateaubriand's Ruins: Loss and Memory after the French Revolution." *History and Memory* 10 (1998): 102–17.

Furet, François. "Ancien Régime." In *A Critical Dictionary of the French Revolution,* ed. François Furet and Mona Ozouf. Cambridge, Mass., 1989.

———. *Interpreting the French Revolution.* Trans. Elborg Forster. Cambridge, 1981.

Gafni, Isaiah. "Babylonia Rabbinic Culture." In *Cultures of the Jews: A New History,* ed. David Biale, 223–65. New York, 2002.

Geertz, Clifford. *The Interpretation of Cultures.* New York, 1973.

Gelber, N. M. "La police autrichienne et le Sanhédrin de Napoléon." *Revue des études juives* 83 (1927): 138–40.

Gennep, Arnold van. *Manuel de folklore français contemporain.* Paris, 1943.

Ginsburger, Moïse. "Arrêtés du Directoire du département du Haut-Rhin relatif aux Juifs (1790)." *Revue des études juives* 75 (1922): 44–73.

———. "Une élection rabbinique au XVIIIᵉ siècle." *Univers israélite* 58 (1903): 625–28.

———. "Elie Schwab, rabbin de Haguenau (1721–1747)." *Revue des études juives* 44 (1902): 104–21, 260–82; 45 (1902): 255–84.

———. "La famille Schweich." *Revue des études juives* 47 (1903): 128–31.

———. "Familles Lehmann et Cerf Berr." *Revue des études juives* 59 (1910): 106–30.

———. *Histoire de la communauté de Bischeim au Saum.* Strasbourg, 1937.

———. *Histoire de la communauté israélite de Soultz.* Strasbourg, 1939.

———. "Les Juifs de Metz sous l'ancien régime." *Revue des études juives* 50 (1905): 112–28.

———. "Les mémoriaux alsaciens." *Revue des études juives* 40 (1900): 231–47; 41 (1900): 118–43.

———. "Samuel Lévy: Rabbin et financier." *Revue des études juives* 65 (1913): 274–300; 66 (1913): 111–33; 68 (1914): 84–109.

———. "Samuel Sanvil Weil: Rabbin de la Haute et Basse-Alsace (1711–1753)." *Revue des études juives* 96 (1933): 54–75, 179–98.

Ginsburger, Moïse, and Ernest Ginsburger. "Contributions à l'histoire des Juifs d'Alsace pendant la terreur." *Revue des études juives* 47 (1903): 283–99.

Godechot, Jacques. "Comment les juifs élurent leurs députés en 1789." *Revue des études juives* 81 (1925): 48–54.

———. "Les Juifs de Nancy de 1789 à 1795." *Revue des études juives* 86 (1928): 1–35.

Gordon, Daniel. *Citizens without Sovereignty: Equality and Sociability in French Thought, 1670–1789.* Princeton, 1994.

Gottlieb, Beatrice. "The Meaning of Clandestine Marriage." In *Family and Sexuality in French History,* ed. Robert Wheaton and Tamara K. Hareven. Philadelphia, 1980.

Graetz, Michael. *From Periphery to Center: Chapters in the History of Nineteenth-Century French Jewry* [Hebrew]. Jerusalem, 1982.

———. "Jewish Economic Activity between War and Peace: The Rise and Fall of Jewish Army Suppliers" [Hebrew]. *Zion* 56 (1991): 255–73.

Grant, A. J. "The Government of Louis XIV." In *The Cambridge Modern History,* vol. 5, ed. A. W. Ward, G. W. Prothero, and Stanley Leathes. Cambridge, 1908.

Gries, Zeev. *Hanhagot Literature: Their History and Place in the Lives of the Hasidim of Irael Ba'al Shem Tov* [Hebrew]. Jerusalem, 1989.

Gruenbaum-Ballin, Paul. "Grégoire convertisseur? ou la croyance au 'Retour d'Israël.'" *Revue des études juives* 121 (1962): 383–98.

Habermas, Jürgen. *Structural Transformation of the Public Sphere: An Inquiry into a Category of Bourgeois Society.* Cambridge, Mass., 1989.

Hadas-Lebel, Mireille. "Les études hébraïques en France au XVIIIᵉ siècle et la création de la première chaire d'Ecriture sainte en Sorbonne." *Revue des études juives* 144 (1985): 93–126.

Ḥalamish, Moshe. "Birkhat Magbiah Shefalim." *Asufot* 2 (1988): 191–200.

———. "The Status of the Ari as *Poseq*" [Hebrew]. *Meḥqerei Yerushalayim be-Mahshevet Yisrael* 10 (1993): 259–85.

Halbertal, Moshe. *Between Torah and Wisdom: Rabbi Menaḥem Ha-Meiri and the Maimonidean Halakhists in Provence.* Jerusalem, 2001.

Halperin, Israel. *East European Jewry.* Jerusalem, 1968.

Hamburger, Benjamin S. "The Historical Foundations of Minhag Ashkenaz." In *Minhagim of Worms according to Juspe Shamash,* ed. Benjamin Hamburger. Jerusalem, 1988.

Handel, Michael. *Gezerot Taḥ ve-Tat.* Jerusalem, 1950.

Harris, Jay. *How Do We Know This? Midrash and the Fragmentation of Modern Judaism.* New York, 1995.

Helfand, Jonathan. "The Election of the Grand Rabbi of France (1842–1846)." *Proceedings of the Eighth World Congress of Jewish Studies.* 2 vols. Jerusalem, 1982.

———. "French Jewry in the Second Republic." Ph.D. diss., Yeshiva University, 1979.

———. "The Symbiotic Relationship between French and German Jewry in the Age of Emancipation," *Leo Baeck Institute Year Book* 29 (1984): 331–44.

Hermon-Belot, Rita. *L'Abbé Grégoire, la politique et la verité.* Paris, 2000.

Hertzberg, Arthur. *The French Enlightenment and the Jews.* New York, 1968.

Higonnet, Patrice. *Goodness beyond Virtue: Jacobins during the French Revolution.* Cambridge, Mass., 1998.

Hobsbawm, Eric. "Mass-Producing Traditions, 1870–1914." In *The Invention of Tradition,* ed. Eric Hobsbawm and Terrence Ranger. Cambridge, 1983.

Horowitz, Elliott. "The Eve of the Circumcision: A Chapter in the History of Jewish Nightlife." *Journal of Social History* 23 (1989): 45–69.

———. "A Jewish Youth Confraternity in Seventeenth-Century Italy." *Italia* 5 (1985): 36–97.

———. "Les mondes des jeunes juifs en Europe." In *Histoire des jeunes en Occident,* ed. G. Levi and J.-C. Schmitt. Paris, 1996.

Hughes, Diane Owens. "Distinguishing Signs: Ear-Rings, Jews and Franciscan Rhetoric in the Italian Renaissance City," *Past and Present* 112 (1986): 3–59.

Hundert, Gershon. "Jewish Children and Childhood in Early Modern East Central

Europe." In *The Jewish Family: Metaphor and Memory*, ed. David Kraemer. New York, 1989.

Hunt, Alan. *Governance of the Consuming Passions: A History of Sumptuary Law*. New York, 1996.

Hyman, Paula. *The Emancipation of the Jews of Alsace: Acculturation and Tradition in the Nineteenth Century*. New Haven, 1991.

———. *Gender and Assimilation in Modern Jewish History: The Roles and Representations of Women*. Seattle, 1995.

———. "L'impact de la Révolution sur l'identité et la culture contemporaine des Juifs d'Alsace." In *Histoire politique des Juifs de France: Entre universalisme et particularisme*, ed. Pierre Birnbaum. Paris, 1990.

———. *The Jews of Modern France*. Berkeley, 1998.

———. "Joseph Salvador." *Jewish Social Studies* 34 (1972): 1–22.

———. "The Social Contexts of Assimilation: Village Jews and City Jews in Alsace." In *Assimilation and Community: The Jews of Nineteenth Century Europe*, ed. Jonathan Frankel and Steven Zipperstein, 110–29. Cambridge, 1992.

Idel, Moshe. *Hasidism: Between Ectsasy and Magic*. New York, 1995.

———. "Perceptions of the Kabbalah in the Second Half of the Eighteenth Century." *Jewish Thought and Philosophy* 1 (1991): 55–114.

Immanuel, Simha. "On the Recitation of *Makhnisei Raḥamim*" [Hebrew]. *Ha-Ma'ayan* 38 (1997): 5–11.

Israel, Jonathan. *European Jewry in the Age of Mercantilism, 1550–1750*. London, 1985.

Job, Françoise. *Les Juifs de Lunéville aux XVIIIe et XIXe siècles*. Nancy, 1989.

———. *Les Juifs de Nancy du XIIe au XXe siècle*. Nancy, 1991.

Jones, Jennifer. "Repackaging Rousseau: Femininity and Fashion in Old Regime France." *French Historical Studies* 18 (1994): 939–67.

Kahn, Léon. *Les Juifs de Paris pendant la Révolution*. Paris, 1898.

Kahn, Salomon. "Les Juifs à Nîmes au XVIIe et au XVIIIe siècles." *Revue des études juives* 67 (1914): 225–61.

Kaplan, Marion. *The Making of the Jewish Middle Class: Women, Family, and Identity in Imperial Germany*. New York, 1993.

Kaplan, Yosef. "The Portuguese *Kehillah* in Amsterdam in the Seventeenth Century: between Tradition and Change." *Proceedings of the Israel Academy of Sciences* 7 (1988): 161–81.

———. "The Sephardim in North-Western Europe and the New World." *Moreshet Sepharad: The Sephardi Legacy*, ed. Haim Beinart. 2 vols. Jerusalem, 1992.

Kates, Gary. *The Cercle Social, the Girondins, and the French Revolution*. Princeton, 1985.

Katz, Jacob. "The Changing Position and Outlook of Halakhists in Early Modernity." In *Scholars and Scholarship: The Interaction between Judaism and Other Cultures*, ed. Leo Landman, 93–106. New York, 1990.

———. *Exclusiveness and Tolerance: Studies in Jewish-Gentile Relations in Medieval and Modern Times*. London, 1961.

———. *Halakhah in Straits: Obstacles to Orthodoxy at Its Inception*. Jerusalem, 1992.

———. *Out of the Ghetto: The Social Background of Jewish Emancipation, 1770–1870*. Cambridge, Mass., 1973.

———. "Post-Zoharic Relations between Halakhah and Kabbalah." In *Jewish Thought in the Sixteenth Century*, ed. Bernard Dov Cooperman, 283–307. Cambridge, Mass., 1983.

———. "The Rule of Halakhah in Traditional Jewish Society: Theory and Praxis." In *Divine Law in Human Hands: Cases Studies in Halakhic Flexibility*. Jerusalem, 1998.

———. "A State within a State: The History of an Anti-Semitic Slogan." *Israel Academy of Sciences and Humanities Proceedings* 4 (1971): 32–58.

————. *Tradition and Crisis: Jewish Society at the End of the Middle Ages* [Hebrew]. Jerusalem, 1958. English ed. trans. Bernard D. Cooperman. New York, 1993.

Kaufmann, David. "R. Joseph Lévi Aschkenaz, premier rabbin de Metz, après le rétablissement de la communauté." *Revue des études juives* 22 (1891): 93–103.

Kaufmann, Uri. "Swiss Jewry: From the 'Jewish Village' to the City, 1780–1930." *Leo Baeck Institute Yearbook* 30 (1985): 283–99.

Kayserling, M. "Les rabbins de Suisse." *Revue des études juives* 46 (1903): 269–75.

Kerner, Samuel. "Acte de fondation d'un college hébraïque à Metz, 1751." *Archives juives* 7 (1970–71): 45–50.

————. *La communauté juive d'Odratzheim au XVIII* et au XIX* siècles*. Paris, 1983.

————. "Salaries et salaires dans la communauté de Metz au XVIII* siècle, d'aprés un ancien registre messin." *Archives juives* 8 (1971–72): 11–17, 31–36.

————. "Un registre messin du XVIII* siècle." *Archives juives* 7 (1970–71): 26–28, 41–43.

————. "Le règlement de la communauté juive de Metz de 1769." *Annales de l'Est* 24 (1972): 210–53.

————. "La vie quotidienne de la communauté juive de Metz au dix-huitième siècle." Thèse de Doctorat de 3ème Cycle, Université de Paris, 1977–79.

Kennedy, Emmet. *A Cultural History of the French Revolution*. New Haven, 1989.

Kober, Adolf. "Emancipation's Impact on the Education and Vocational Training of German Jewry." *Jewish Social Studies* 16 (1954): 3–32, 151–76.

Koeber, Adolf. "Documents Selected from the Pinkas of Friedberg." *Proceedings of the American Academy of Religion* 17 (1947–48): 19–59.

Kracauer, J. "Rabbi Joselmann de Rosheim." *Revue des études juives* 16 (1888): 84–105.

Labrousse, C. E. *Esquisse de mouvement des prix et des revenues en France au XVIII* siècle*. 2 vols. Paris, 1933.

Ladner, Gerhart B. *The Idea of Reform: Its Impact on Christian Thought and Action in the Age of the Fathers*. Cambridge, Mass., 1959.

Lauterbach, Jacob Z. "Tashlik: A Study in Jewish Ceremonies." *Hebrew Union College Annual* 11 (1936): 207–340.

Lebrun, François. *La vie conjugale sous l'ancien régime*. Paris, 1975.

Lefort, Claude. "La Révolution comme religion nouvelle." In *The French Revolution and the Creation of Modern Political Culture*, ed. François Furet and Mona Ozouf, 3:391–99. New York, 1989.

Leiman, S. Z. "Rabbinic Openness to General Culture in the Early Modern Period in Western and Central Europe." In *Judaism's Encounter with Other Cultures: Rejection or Integration?* ed. Jacob J. Schacter, 143–216. Northvale, N.J., 1997.

Lemalet, Martine. "L'émancipation des Juifs de Lorraine à travers l'oeuvre de Berr Isaac Berr (1788–1806)." In *Juifs en France au XVIII* siècle*," ed. Bernhard Blumenkranz, 151–74. Paris, 1994.

Léon, Henri. *Histoire des Juifs de Bayonne*. Paris, 1893.

Lévy, Gerson. *Orgue et Pioutim*. Paris, 1859.

Lewis, Bernard. *Islam in History: Ideas, Men and Events in the Middle East*. New York, 1973.

Liber, Maurice. "Napoléon." *Revue des études juives* 72 (1921): 21.

Liberles, Robert. *Religious Conflict in Social Context: The Resurgence of Religious Orthodoxy in Frankfurt am Main*. Westport, Conn., 1985.

Liebes, Yehudah. "Meshihiyuto shel R. Ya'akov Emden ve-Yahaso le-Shabeta'ut." *Tarbiz* 49 (1979/80): 122–65.

————. "R. Wolff ben Yonatan Eibeschütz's Work Composed in the Language of the Zohar on his Group and the Secret of Redemption" [Hebrew]. *Kiryat Sefer* 57 (1982): 148–78.

Loker, Zvi. "From Converso Congregation to Holy Community: The Shaping of the Jewish Community of Bordeaux during the Eighteenth Century" [Hebrew]. *Zion* 42 (1977): 49–94.

Lough, John. *An Introduction to Eighteenth-Century France.* London, 1960.

Lowenstein, Steven. "The Pace of Modernization of German Jewry in the Nineteenth Century." *Leo Baeck Institute Yearbook* 21 (1976): 41–56.

———. "The Readership of Mendelssohn's Bible Translation." *Hebrew Union College Annual* 53 (1982): 179–213.

Magnus, Shulamit. *Jewish Emancipation in a German City: Cologne, 1798–1871.* Stanford, 1997.

Malino, Frances. "Attitudes toward Jewish Communal Autonomy in Prerevolutionary France." In *Essays in Modern Jewish History: A Tribute to Ben Halpern,* ed. F. Malino and Phyllis Albert. New York, 1982.

———. "Competition and Confrontation: The Jews and the *Parlement* of Metz." In *Les Juifs au regards de l'histoire: Mélanges en l'honneur de Bernhard Blumenkranz,* ed. Gilbert Dahan, 327–41. Paris, 1985.

———. *A Jew in the French Revolution: The Life of Zalkind Hourwitz.* Cambridge, Mass., 1996.

———. "Résistances et révoltes à Metz dans la première moitié du 18ᵉ siècle." In *Juifs en France au XVIIIᵉ siècle,* ed. B. Blumenkranz, 125–40. Paris, 1994.

———. *The Sephardic Jews of Bordeaux: Assimilation and Emancipation in Revolutionary and Napoleonic France.* Tuscaloosa, 1978.

———. "Zalkind Hourwitz, Juif Polonais." *Dix Huitième Siècle* 13 (1981): 79–89.

Malkiel, David. "Between Worldliness and Traditionalism: Eighteenth-Century Jews Debate Intercessory Prayer." *Jewish Studies, an Internet Journal* (Bar Ilan University) 2 (2003): 169–98.

Marcus, Ivan G. "Beyond the Sephardic Mystique." *Orim* 1 (1985): 35–53.

Marcus, Jacob R. "The Triesch Ḥebra Kaddisha, 1687–1828." *Hebrew Union College Annual* 19 (1945–46): 169–204.

Margaliot, Mordecai. *Sefer Ha-Razim.* Jerusalem, 1966.

Marrus, Michael. *The Politics of Assimilation: A Study of the French Jewish Community at the Time of the Dreyfus Affair.* Oxford, 1971.

Marx, Roland. "La régénération économique des Juifs d'Alsace à l'époque révolutionnaire et napoléonnaire." In *Les Juifs et la Révolution française,* ed. Bernhard Blumenkranz and Albert Soboul, 105–20. Paris, 1976.

Maslin, Simeon. "Napoleonic Jewry from the Sanhedrin to the Bourbon Restoration." Hebrew Union College, Cincinnati, 1957.

Maulde, R. de, ed. "Les Juifs dans les Etats français du Pape au moyen âge." *Revue des études juives* 7 (1883): 227–51; 8 (1884): 92–115; 10 (1885): 145–82.

Maza, Sarah. "Luxury, Morality, and Social Change: Why There Was No Middle-Class Consciousness in Prerevolutionary France." *Journal of Modern History* 69 (1997): 199–229.

McManners, John. *French Ecclesiastical Society under the Ancien Régime.* Manchester, 1960.

Menkis, Richard. "New Light on the Transformation of Jewish Education in Eighteenth-Century Bordeaux." *Proceedings of the Tenth World Congress of Jewish Studies,* 215–22. Jerusalem, 1990.

Meuvret, Jean. "The Condition of France, 1688–1715." In *The New Cambridge Modern History,* ed. J. S. Bromley, 6:316–25. Cambridge, 1970.

Meyer, Michael A. *Jewish Identity in the Modern World.* Seattle, 1990.

———. "Jewish Religious Reform and *Wissenschaft des Judentums*: The Positions of Zunz, Geiger, and Frankel." *Leo Baeck Institute Yearbook* (1971): 19–41.

———. "Jewish Scholarship and Identity in Modern Germany." *Studies in Contemporary Jewry* 8 (1992): 181–93.

———. *Response to Modernity: A History of the Reform Movement in Judaism.* New York, 1988.

———. "Where Does the Modern Period in Jewish History Begin?" *Judaism* 24 (1975): 329–38.

Meyer, Pierre-André. *La communauté juive de Metz au XVIIIᵉ siècle.* Nancy, 1993.

Miskimin, Patricia Behre. "Jews and Christians in the Marketplace: The Politics of Kosher Meat in Metz." *Journal of Economic History* 26 (1997): 147–55.

Morell, Samuel. "The Constitutional Limits of Communal Government in Rabbinic Law." *Jewish Social Studies* 33 (1971): 87–107.

Muchembled, Robert. *Popular Culture and Elite Culture in France, 1400–1750.* Flammarion, 1978. Trans. Lydia Cochrane. Baton Rouge, 1985.

Muir, Edward. *Ritual in Early Modern Europe.* Cambridge, 1997.

Nadler, Allan. *The Faith of the Mithnagdim: Rabbinic Responses to Hasidic Rapture.* Baltimore, 1997.

Nahon, Gérard. *Communautés judéo-portugaises du sud-ouest de la France (Bayonne et sa région), 1684–1791.* 2 vols. Paris, 1969.

———. "Une délibération de la 'Nation Portugaise de Saint-Esprit' relative aux synagogues (1776)." *REJ* 124 (1965): 423–27.

———. "From New Christians to the Portuguese Jewish Nation in France." In *Moreshet Sepharad: The Sephardi Legacy,* ed. Haim Beinart, 2:348–52. Jerusalem, 1992.

———. "Note sur les registres des délibérations de la nation juive portugaise de Bordeaux, 1710–1790." *REJ* 129 (1970): 239–43.

Necheles, Ruth. "The Abbé Grégoire and the Jews." *Jewish Social Studies* 33 (1971): 135–36, 139.

Neher-Bernheim, Renée. "Sephardim et Ashkenazim à Paris au milieu du XIXᵉ siècle: Un essai avorté de fusion des rites." In *Les Juifs au regard de l'histoire: Mélanges en 'honneur de Bernhard Blumenkranz,* ed. Gilbert Dahan, 369–82. Paris, 1985.

———. "The Tables of the Law: One of the Symbols of the French Revolution." *Jewish Art* 16–17 (1990–91): 82–91.

Netter, Nathan. "Les anciens cimetières israélites de Metz situés près de la porte chambière." *Revue des études juives* 51 (1906): 98–113.

———. *Vingt siècles d'histoire d'une communauté juive.* Paris, 1938.

Nord, Philip. *The Republican Moment: Struggles for Democracy in Nineteenth-Century France.* Cambridge, Mass., 1995.

Owens, Diane. "Sumptuary Law and Social Relations in Renaissance Italy." In *Disputes and Settlements: Laws and Human Relations in the West,* ed. John Bossy, 69–99. Cambridge, 1983.

Ozouf, Mona. *Festivals and the French Revolution.* Trans. Alan Sheridan. Cambridge, Mass., 1988.

———. "La Révolution française et l'idée de l'homme nouveau." In *The French Revolution and the Creation of Modern Political Culture,* ed. Colin Lucas, 2:213–32. Oxford, 1988.

Peter, Daniel. *Mertzwiller: Du village au bourg.* Mertzwiller, 1986.

Petuchowski, Jakob. "Manuals and Catechisms of the Jewish Religion in the Early Period of Emancipation." In *Studies in Nineteenth-Century Jewish Intellectual History,* ed. Alexander Altmann, 47–64. Cambridge, Mass., 1964.

———. *Prayerbook Reform in Europe.* New York, 1968.

Piette, Christine. *Les Juifs de Paris (1808–1840): La marche vers l'assimilation.* Quebec, 1983.

Pollack, Herman. *Jewish Folkways in Germanic Lands (1648–1806).* Cambridge, Mass., 1971.

Posener, Solomon V. *Adolphe Crémieux.* 2 vols. Paris, 1943.

———. "The Immediate Economic and Social Effects of the Emancipation of the Jews of France." *Jewish Social Studies* 1 (1939): 271–326.

————. "The Social Life of Jewish Communities in France in the Eighteenth Century." *Jewish Social Studies* 7 (1945): 195–232.

Quint, Emanuel, and Neil Hecht. *Jewish Jurisprudence: Its Sources and Modern Applications.* 2 vols. New York, 1980.

Raeff, Marc. "The Well-Ordered Police State and the Development of Modernity in Seventeenth- and Eighteenth-Century Europe: An Attempt at a Comparative Approach." *American Historical Review* 80 (1975): 1221–43.

Rambaud, Alfred. *Histoire de la civilisation contemporaine en France.* Paris, 1888.

Raphaël, Freddy, and Robert Weyl. "Rites de naissance et medecine populaire dans le judaïsme rural d'Alsace." *Revue de la société d'ethnographie française* 1 (1971): 83–94.

————. *Juifs en Alsace: Culture, société, histoire.* Toulouse, 1977.

————. *Regards nouveau sur les Juifs d'Alsace.* Strasbourg, 1980.

Ravitch, Norman. *The Sword and the Mitre: Government and Episcopate in France and England in the Age of Aristocracy.* The Hague, 1966.

Rearick, Charles. *Beyond the Enlightenment: Historians and Folklore in Nineteenth-Century France.* Bloomington, 1974.

Reif, Stefan. *Judaism and Hebrew Prayer: New Perspectives on Jewish Liturgical History.* Cambridge, 1993.

Reinach, Théodore. *Histoire des israélites depuis l'époque de leur dispersion jusqu'à nos jours.* Paris, 1885.

Reiner, Elḥanan. "Wealth, Social Standing, and the Study of Torah: The Status of the *Kloiz* in Eastern European Society in the Early Modern Period." *Zion* 58 (1993): 287–328.

Reuss, Rodolphe. "L'Antisémitisme dans le bas-Rhin pendant la Révolution (1790–1793): Nouveaux documents inédits." *Revue des études juives* 68 (1914): 246–63.

————. "Quelques documents nouveaux sur l'antisémitisme dans le Bas-Rhin, de 1794 à 1799," *Revue des études juives* 59 (1910): 248–76.

Roche, Daniel. *The Culture of Clothing: Dress and Fashion in the "Ancien Régime."* Trans. of *La culture des apparences: Une histoire du vêtement (XVII–XVIII siècle).* Paris, 1989. Trans. Jean Birrell. Cambridge, 1996.

————. *France in the Enlightenment.* Cambridge, Mass., 1998.

Rodrigue, Aron. *French Jews, Turkish Jews: The Alliance israélite universelle and the Politics of Jewish Schooling in Turkey, 1860–1925.* Bloomington, 1990.

————. "Léon Halévy and Modern French Jewish Historiography." In *Jewish History and Jewish Memory: Essays in Honor of Yosef Hayim Yerushalmi,* ed. Elisheva Carlebach, John M. Efron, and David N. Myers, 413–27. Hanover, N.H., 1998.

Rosenthal, Judah. "Interest from the Non-Jew" [Hebrew]. *Talpiot* 5 (1952): 475–92; 6 (1953): 130–52. Reprinted in *Meḥkarim u-Mekorot,* 2:253–323. Jerusalem, 1967.

Rosman, Moshe. "The Image of Poland as a Center of Torah Learning after the 1648 Persecutions." *Zion* 51 (1986): 435–48.

Roth, Cecil. "The Liturgies of Avignon and the Comtat Venaissin." *Journal of Jewish Bibliography* 1 (1939): 99–105.

————. "Sumptuary Laws of the Community of Carpentras." *Jewish Quarterly Review* 18 (1927–28): 357–83.

Ruderman, David. *Jewish Thought and Scientific Discovery in Early Modern Europe.* New Haven, 1995.

Ruel, Marianne. "Les Chrétiens et la danse dans l'Europe du nord-ouest, XVIᵉ–XVIIIᵉ siècles." *Historiens et Géographes* 84 (1984): 171, 180.

Rürup, Reinhard. "The European Revolutions of 1848 and Jewish Emancipation." In *Revolution and Evolution: 1848 in German-Jewish History,* ed. Werner Mosse, Arnold Paucker, and Reinhard Rürup, 1–54. Tubingen, 1981.

Sabar, Shalom. "Childbirth and Magic: Jewish Folklore and Material Culture." In *Cultures of the Jews: A New History,* ed. David Biale, 671–722. New York, 2002.

———. "The Use and Meaning of Christian Motifs in Illustrations of Jewish Marriage Contracts in Italy." *Jewish Art* 10 (1984): 62–63.

Sagnac, Philippe. *La formation de la société française moderne.* 2 vols. Paris, 1946.

Sandler, Peretz. *Ha-Biur la-Torah shel Moshe Mendelssohn ve-Siato.* Jerusalem, 1940.

Schacter, Jacob J. "R. Jacob Emden: Life and Major Works." Ph.D. diss., Harvard University, 1988.

Schama, Simon. *Citizens: A Chronicle of the French Revolution.* New York, 1989.

Schechter, Ronald. *Obstinate Hebrew: Representations of Jews in France, 1715–1815.* Berkeley, 2003.

———. "Translating the Marseillaise: Biblical Republicanism and the Emancipation of Jews in Revolutionary France." *Past and Present* 143 (1994): 108–35.

Scheid, Elie. "Histoire des Juifs de Haguenau pendant la période française." *Revue des études juives* 10 (1885): 204–31.

Schepansky, Israel. *The Takkanot of Israel.* 4 vols. Jerusalem, 1992.

Schorsch, Ismar. "Breakthrough into the Past: The Verein für Cultur und Wissenschaft der Juden." *Leo Baeck Institute Year Book* 33 (1988): 3–28.

———. "Emancipation and the Crisis of Authority: The Emergence of the Modern Rabbinate." In *Revolution and Evolution: 1848 in German-Jewish History,* ed. Werner Mosse, Arnold Paucker, and Reinhard Rürup, 205–48. Tubingen, 1981.

———. "The Emergence of Historical Consciousness in Modern Judaism." *Leo Baeck Institute Year Book* 28 (1983): 413–37.

Schwab, Moïse. *Salomon Munk: Sa vie et ses oeuvres.* Paris, 1899.

Schwarzfuchs, Simon. *Du Juif à l'israélite: Histoire d'une mutation, 1770–1870.* Paris, 1989.

———. *Napoleon, the Jews, and the Sanhedrin.* London, 1979.

———. "Notes sur les juifs de Bayonne au XVIIIᵉ siècle." *Revue des études juives* 125 (1966): 353–64.

———. "The Rabbinic Contract of the Sha'agat Aryeh in Metz." *Moriah* 15 (1986): 81–90.

———. "La situation du Judaïsme français en 1883: Le Rapport Isidor." *Revue des études juives* 146 (1987): 299–355; 147 (1988): 57–144.

———. "Takkanot ha-Kahal in the Village of Augny Near Metz in the Year 5516" [Hebrew]. *Asufot* 8 (1994): 387–96.

———. "Three Documents from the Lives of the Jewish Communities in Alsace-Lorraine" [Hebrew]. *Michael* 4 (1976): 9–31.

Sepinwall, Alyssa Goldstein. "Les paradoxes de la régénération révolutionnaire: Le cas de l'abbé Grégoire." *Annales historiques de la Révolution française,* no. 321 (2000): 69–90.

Shilo, Shmuel. "Moneylending." *Encyclopedia Judaica,* 12:244–56. Jerusalem, 1970.

Shoḥat, Azriel. *Im Ḥilufe Tekufot* (The Beginnings of the Haskalah in Germany). Jerusalem, 1961.

Shulvass, Moses. *From East to West.* Detroit, 1971.

Silber, Michael K. "The Emergence of Ultra-Orthodoxy: The Invention of Tradition." In *The Uses of Tradition: Jewish Continuity in the Modern Era,* ed. Jack Wertheimer, 23–84. New York, 1992.

———. "The Historical Experience of German Jewry and Its Impact on Haskalah and Reform in Hungary." In *Toward Modernity: The European Jewish Model,* ed. Jacob Katz, 107–57. New Brunswick, N.J., 1987.

Simon-Nahum, Perrine. *La cité investie: La "Science du Judaïsme" français et la République.* Paris, 1991.

Sorkin, David. "The Port Jew: Notes Toward a Social Type." *Journal of Jewish Studies* 50 (1999): 87–97.

———. *The Transformation of German Jewry, 1780–1840.* New York, 1987.

Sperber, Daniel. *Minhagei Israel.* 7 vols. Jerusalem, 1991–2002.

Stow, Kenneth. *Theatre of Acculturation: The Roman Ghetto in the Sixteenth Century.* Seattle, 2001.

Sutcliffe, Adam. "Can a Jew Be a *Philosophe?* Isaac de Pinto, Voltaire, and Jewish Participation in the European Enlightenment." *Jewish Social Studies* 6 (2000): 31–51.

Szajkowski, Zosa. "The Attitude of the French Jacobins toward Jewish Religion." *Historia Judaica* 18 (1956): 107–20.

———. *Autonomy and Communal Jewish Debts during the French Revolution of 1789.* New York, 1959.

———. "Conflicts between the Orthodox and Reformers in France" [Hebrew]. *Ḥoreb* 14–15 (1960): 253–92.

———. "Conflicts within the Eighteenth-Century Sephardic Communities of France." *Hebrew Union College Annual* 31 (1960): 167–80.

———. "The Diaries of the Delegates of the Bordeaux Jews to the Malesherbes Commission (1788) and the National Assembly" [Hebrew]. *Zion* 18 (1953): 31–79.

———. *Franco-Judaica: An Analytical Bibliography of Books, Pamphlets, Decrees, Briefs and Other Documents Pertaining to the Jews in France, 1500–1788.* New York, 1962.

———. "French Jews during the Revolution of 1830 and July Monarchy." In *The Jews and the French Revolutions of 1789, 1830, and 1848,* 1026–37. New York, 1970.

———. "The Growth of the Jewish Population in France." *Jewish Social Studies* 8 (1946): 179–92.

———. "Jewish Autonomy Debated and Attacked during the French Revolution." *Historia Judaica* 20 (1958): 31–46.

———. "The Jewish Communities in France on the Eve of the Revolution of 1789." In *Jews and the French Revolutions of 1789, 1830, and 1848.* New York, 1970.

———. *Jewish Education in France, 1789–1939.* New York, 1980.

———. "Jewish Religious Observance during the French Revolution in 1789." In *The Jews and the French Revolutions of 1789, 1830, and 1848,* 785–808. New York, 1970.

———. "The Jewish Status in Eighteenth-Century France and the '*Droit d'Aubaine.*'" *Historia Judaica* 19 (1957): 147–61.

———. *Jews in the French Revolutions of 1789, 1830, and 1848.* New York, 1970.

———. "Population Problems of Marranos and Sephardim in France, from the 16th to the 20th Centuries." *Proceedings of the American Academy of Religion* 27 (1958): 83–105.

———. *Poverty and Social Welfare among French Jews, 1800–1880.* New York, 1954.

———. "Riots against the Jews in Metz in 1792" [Hebrew]. *Zion* 22 (1957): 76.

———. "Riots in Alsace during the Revolutions of 1789, 1830, and 1848." *Zion* 20 (1955/56): 82–102.

———. "Secular versus Religious Jewish Life in France." in *The Role of Religion in Modern Jewish History,* ed. Jacob Katz, 107–27. Cambridge, Mass., 1975.

Talmon, Jacob. *Political Messianism: The Romantic Phase.* New York, 1960.

Thiel, M. "Notice sur la vie de Gerson-Lévy." *Extrait du mémoires de l'Académie de Metz.* Metz, 1864–65.

Tribout de Morembert, Henri. "Les Juifs de Metz et de Lorraine (1791–1795)." In *Les Juifs et la Révolution française,* ed. Bernhard Blumenkranz and Albert Soboul, 87–104. Paris, 1976.

Verses, Shmuel. "The French Revolution as Reflected in Hebrew Literature" [Hebrew]. *Tarbiz* 58 (1988–89): 483–521.

Weber, Eugen. *Peasants into Frenchmen: The Modernization of Rural France, 1870–1914.* Stanford, 1976.

Weil, J. "Contribution à l'histoire des communautés alsaciennes au 18ème siècle." *Revue des études juives* 81 (1925): 169–80.

Weill, Georges. "Rabbins et Parnassim dans l'Alsace du XVIIIe siècle." In *Les Juifs dans l'histoire de France*, ed. Myriam Yardeni, 96–109. Leiden, 1980.

———. "Recherches sur la démographie des juifs d'Alsace du XVIe au XVIIIe siècle." *Revue des études juives* 130 (1971): 51–89.

Weissbach, Lee Shai. "The Jewish Elite and the Children of the Poor: Jewish Apprenticeship Programs in Nineteenth-Century France." *AJSReview* 12 (1987): 123–42.

Wieder, Naftali. "Past and Future in *Kol Nidrei*." *Mikhtam le-David: David Ochs Memorial Volume*, 189–209. Ramat Gan, 1978.

Wiener, Max. "The Ideology of the Founders of Jewish Scientific Research." *YIVO Annual of Jewish Social Science* 5 (1950): 184–96.

Yuval, Israel J. "A German-Jewish Autobiography of the Fourteenth Century" [Hebrew]. *Tarbiz* 55 (1985–86): 550–54.

Zeldin, Theodore. *France, 1848–1945: Politics and Anger*. New York, 1982.

Zimmer, Eric. *Harmony and Discord: Analysis of the Decline of Jewish Self-Government in Fifteenth-Century Central Europe*. New York, 1970.

———. *The History of the Rabbinate in Germany in the Sixteenth Century* [Hebrew]. Jerusalem, 1984.

———. "Marriage Customs in Worms" [Hebrew]. *Sinai* 86 (1980): 14–54.

———. "Poses and Postures during Prayer" [Hebrew]. *Sidra* 5 (1989): 89–130.

———. "Reactions of German Jewry to Influences of the Center in Poland in the Early Seventeenth Century" [Hebrew]. *Sinai* 102 (1988): 226–40.

———. *Society and Its Customs: Studies in the History and Metamorphosis of Jewish Customs* [Hebrew]. Jerusalem, 1996.

Index

Abarbanel, Isaac, 185
Abulafia, 181
Académie française, 182
acculturation, 2, 7, 40, 55, 59, 80–81, 157.
  See also *ḥukkat ha-goi*
Adler, Nathan, 171
age, as index of social status, 46–49
Agulhon, Maurice, 90
Alsace: communal controls, 38, 53–58; contrast with Metz, 34, 79–81, 232–34; criticism of Jews in, 118–21, 146–50; disabilities of Jews in, 17; Haskalah in, 174–75; Jewish settlement in, 15–16; modernization in, 91–92, 107–13, 157–59, 218; modern scholarship in, 177; during Napoleonic regime, 121–23, 130, 136; rabbinic scholarship in, 167; religious observance in, 5, 59–85, 140–41, 235, 238; in revolutionary era, 89–114; self-government in, 18–34
Altona, 52, 61
Amsterdam, 22, 52, 65, 76, 85, 208
Anspach, Joel, 195, 196
anti-Jewish hostility and persecution, 16–18, 90–97, 108–12, 141, 145–47, 179, 184, 227, 234
antisemitism. *See* anti-Jewish hostility and persecution
Aqdamut, 76, 196
Archives de Christianisme, 186
Archives israélites, 182, 187, 196, 224
Aron, Arnaud, 201, 208, 231
Aron, Loeb, 29
Asher b. Yeḥiel, 172
Ashkenazi, Gershon, 19, 20, 28, 71, 79
Ashkenazic Jews: culture of, 7, 14, 60–63, 65, 73–77, 83–85, 160, 171; fusion of liturgy

with Sephardic, 139, 201, 210, 235; marriage laws, 51–53; ritual traditions, 68–78, 174, 194, 210; study of Talmud, 64; on surrender of communal autonomy, 101–3; system of self-government, 16–34; trends in scholarship, 167–76, 185
Assembly of Jewish Notables, 104, 113, 117, 121, 124–26, 130, 132, 138
assimilation of Jews in French society: as a goal of Napoleon, 123; as a goal of radical reformers, 151–56, 194, 216. *See also* social integration
Attias, Jacob Ḥayim, 23
Auerbach, Aviezri, 29
Augustine, Saint, 16
Avicebron, 188
Avignon, 18, 47, 52
Azulai, Ḥayyim Joseph David, 171

Bacharach, Ya'ir Ḥayyim, 58, 129, 167
Bail, Charles Joseph, 145
bar mitzvah ceremony, 48, 49, 63, 225
Barukh of Shklov, 170
Bas-Rhin, 29, 109, 113, 138, 157, 199
Bautain, Louis, 156
Bayle, Pierre, 16
Bayonne, 6, 15, 17, 18, 19, 22, 23, 26, 40, 52, 60, 85, 118, 223
Beaufleury, Louis Francia de, 96
Bedersi, Jedaiah, 175
beit din. See courts, rabbinic
Belin, Moyse, 29
Bergheim, 31, 32
Berlin, 7, 80, 95, 96, 101, 108, 117, 165, 175
Berr, Berr Isaac, 102–4, 117, 118, 165, 175, 232

Acknowledgments

The idea for this book first took root in a lecture I delivered in Jerusalem at a conference sponsored by the Zalman Shazar Center for the History of the Jewish People, at the bicentennial of the French Revolution. My interest in the impact of the Revolution on French Jewry has, since then, converged with a longstanding personal fascination with ritual. Opportunities to share my work at academic meetings have been an invaluable part of this intellectual journey; they included conferences, seminars, and symposia at the Association for Jewish studies, Bar Ilan University, Harvard University, the Institute for Advanced Studies of Jerusalem, the Society for French Historical Studies; the Jewish Theological Seminary of America; the World Congress of Jewish Studies, and the Orthodox Forum of Yeshiva University. In each instance, I have benefited from the constructive criticism offered by participants.

Thanks to my colleagues and students in the Department of Judaic and Near Eastern Studies and in the History Department at the University of Massachusetts at Amherst, I enjoy a stimulating intellectual environment. I am also grateful for the opportunity to share my work with faculty and students at the Boston Hebrew College and in the Me'ah Program, which is co-sponsored by the Combined Jewish Philanthropies of Boston.

Much of the research and writing of this book has been undertaken in Jerusalem. For the past several years, during summers and semester leaves, the Institute for Advanced Studies has graciously provided me with an office on the Hebrew University campus. I am deeply grateful to the director and staff of the institute for their amiable hospitality in a most supportive and congenial setting.

Over these last years, I have made extensive use of the rich collections at the National and University Library, Jerusalem, and at the Institute of Microfilmed Hebrew Manuscripts. I am enormously appreciative of the efforts of the entire library staff and, in particular, the staff of the Judaica Reading Room. Similarly, I am grateful for the opportunity to draw on the vast resources at the Jewish Theological Seminary of America, including the rare book division and the archives.

Numerous colleagues have offered generous assistance at various stages of this project. Shmuel Bolozky, a devoted colleague and friend, has unstintingly reviewed the Hebrew text of many academic papers I have presented in Israel these past eight years. Jean Baumgarten was kind enough to assist me with communal documents written in Alsatian Yiddish, and Menahem Kallus helped me decipher and decode a kabbalistic manuscript from Metz. Brett Berliner, Vicki Caron, and Ted Fram commented on an earlier version of Chapter 2, and David Ellenson offered help with issues concerning religious reform. Benjamin Braude, Elliott Horowitz, Ephraim Kanarfogel, David Malkiel, Stuart Miller, Michael Silber, Hagith Sivan, Kenneth Stow, Israel Ta-Shema, and Eric Zimmer have all been willing to discuss, as often as necessary, broader conceptual issues or specific queries. Richard I. Cohen has read and reread most of my work in the last decade and has consistently provided sound advice on numerous subjects. Daniel Gordon read various portions of the manuscript, generously offering valuable criticism and encouragement from the perspective of general French history. During the last stages of revision, Lois Dubin commented extensively on several chapters and prodded me to rethink some of the wider implications of this book.

Chapters 2 and 7 draw on the following journal articles that I previously published: "Social and Religious Controls in Pre-Revolutionary France: Rethinking the Beginnings of Modernity," *Jewish History* 15:1 (2001): 1–40; and "Jewish Scholarship and Identity in Nineteenth-Century France," *Modern Judaism* 18 (1998): 1–33. I wish to thank the editors for permission to reprint portions of these two articles. Portions of "The French Revolution and the Jews: Assessing the Cultural Impact," *AJS Review* 20 (1995): 25–86 are reprinted with the permission of the Association for Jewish Studies.

Finally, I wish to thank the Lucius N. Littauer Foundation for generously providing a grant that supported the publication of this book.

No book is independent of the author's personal life. This project has traveled between the United States and Israel many times, and more recently moved with us to Newton. I am deeply grateful for the wonderful friends who have enriched our lives, first when we lived in Springfield and now in Newton and Jerusalem. I wish to thank my mother, Lillian Berkovitz, for having made our transition to Boston so gratifying; my brother Joel for his constant helpfulness; and my mother-in-law, Goldie Levinson, for her support. Sadly, my father-in-law, Rabbi Joseph Levinson z"l, was not able to see the completion of this book, much as my late father, Melvin Berkovitz z"l, did not witness the publication of my first book. Their memories remain an unfailing inspiration.

This book is lovingly dedicated to my wife, Sharon. She has made it possible for me to devote myself to scholarship and teaching by assuming primary responsibility for our homes on both continents. With her exemplary commitment to communal welfare and to family, she is a wonderful role model for our daughter, Racheli, who reminds us both of the most important things in life.

CPSIA information can be obtained at www.ICGtesting.com
Printed in the USA
BVOW010429190112

280822BV00002B/46/A

9 780812 220087